THE COINAGE OF THE AYYŪBIDS

THE COINAGE OF THE AYYŪBIDS

BY

PAUL BALOG

ROYAL NUMISMATIC SOCIETY

SPECIAL PUBLICATION NO. 12

LONDON

1980

Printed in England by
Stephen Austin and Sons Ltd.,
Hertford

DEDICATION

With deeply felt gratitude

to

Mr. Samir Shamma of Jedda, Saudi Arabia,
and an unnamed friend,
whose outstanding generosity
made the publication of this
work possible.

I am also sincerely grateful

to

Prof. Jere L. Bacharach of Seattle, Washington,
who, with magnificent competence and
endless patience, gave this study
its final form and secured
its publication.

ACKNOWLEDGMENTS

It is my pleasant duty to express my gratitude to M. Raoul Curiel of the Bibliothèque Nationale in Paris, who was instrumental in starting me on this present work.

My warm appreciation goes to Mrs. Helen Mitchell-Brown of the Ashmolean Museum in Oxford, Nicholas M. Lowick of the British Museum, Dr. Michael L. Bates of the American Numismatic Society, İbrahim Artuk and Mrs. Cevriye Artuk of the Istanbul Archaeological Museum, and to İbrahim Tözen of the Yapı ve Kredi Bankası in Istanbul. They all went out of their way to make my task easy and sacrificed considerable time in assisting me. They all let me have innumerable plaster casts after allowing me to examine the coins in their care for great lengths of time.

Dr. Jarmila Stepková, Curator of Oriental Coins at the Prague National Museum, came to East Berlin especially in order to show me the large amount of Ayyūbid numismatic material in the Bode Museum then under her authority. My thanks are due as well to Dr. Lore Börner, at the time in charge of that museum's coin collections, for sending me many coin casts.

I must also thank Drs. H. Küthmann and B. Overbeck for their help at the Munich State Coin Collection, as well as Hofrat Bernhard Koch and Dr. G. Dembsky at the Vienna Kunsthistorisches Museum.

I am equally indebted to many collectors and specialists of Islamic coins for their ready assistance: to Dr. H. A. Awad of Cairo, Egypt; to Stephen Album of Santa Rosa, California; to M. R. Broome of Woodley, Reading, England; to M. G. Gautier in Paris, France; to M. Th. Horovitz in Geneva, Switzerland; to Lutz Ilisch of Billerbeck, Germany; to Dr. ing. E. Leuthold of Milan, Italy; and to C. M. Webdale of Bedford, England.

The names of more private collectors contributing information will be found among the coin references of this Catalogue; they are too numerous to be listed here individually. I am especially indebted to Dr. Kurt Munzel of Ismaning near Munich, Germany, for reading the manuscript; and to Mr. Samir Shamma of Jedda, Saudi Arabia, for sending me the handwritten catalogue of his Ayyūbid gold coins; also to Mr. John J. Slocum, for his friendly assistance.

Finally, I cannot express warmly enough my gratitude to Professor Jere L. Bacharach and his capable crew of Seattle, Washington, who kindly undertook the difficult and time-consuming task of editing the manuscript, a task that turned into a major enterprise of inestimable value. I wish to thank also my old friend Nicholas Lowick for correcting the proofs and guiding the work through the press.

Paul Balog

ACKNOWLEDGEMENTS

EDITOR'S ACKNOWLEDGMENTS

Without the active encouragement and support of Mr. Samir Shamma, this manuscript could never have been produced. Absolutely essential was the work of my former student and friend, Dr. Norman D. Nicol, who served as co-editor, Dr. Michael Bates and the American Numismatic Society's committee on Middle East and South Asian Coins played an important role in supporting the project in its early stages. Mr. Nicholas Lowick of the British Museum guided the manuscript through its final stages, edited the page proofs and supervised the Royal Numismatic Society's publication of this study. I am most grateful for the assistance of these two friends and that of the Royal Numismatic Society. Professor R. Stephen Humphreys made valuable comments on the historical outline. Mrs. Barb Shurin not only typed the original text but played a major role in designing it.

For all of us the key factor was our admiration of Dr. Balog and his many contributions to the field of Islamic numismatics. We are proud that we can associate ourselves in this small way with his work.

JERE L. BACHARACH

A WORD OF THANKS

Dr. Paul Balog has been a pioneer in the field of Islamic numismatics. In supporting this extremely important work, I wish to express my appreciation to him for the many contributions he has made in the past and my admiration for this study of Ayyūbid coinage. I am also proud that this work, published by the Royal Numismatic Society, is the result of international cooperation, including the active participation of Professor Jere L. Bacharach and Dr. Norman D. Nicol of the United States, Mr. Nicholas Lowick of the British Museum, Great Britain, and an anonymous Arab friend. I wish to thank all of them and the Royal Numismatic Society for aiding in the publication of this book.

SAMIR SHAMMA

TABLE OF CONTENTS

ARRANGEMENT OF CATALOGUE

Ayyūbid coins are quite common and are to be found in nearly every collection; and even quite large hoards are known to have been excavated, mainly in Syria. They are also mostly well known, and over 100 publications are listed in the Bibliography.

The other articles, catalogues and monographs, though many of them are valuable contributions, contain only information on parts of the coinage issued by the many rulers of a very complex empire. The Ayyūbid Empire was an often-changing structure based on the rule of vassal princes, all belonging to different clans of the same family. Their power was bestowed upon them by the recognized head of the dynasty, who was called 'Sultan', but who never asked for official investiture by the 'Abbāsid Caliph, who had no temporal ascendency on him. Only when Ayyūbid power was declining, did al-Ṣāliḥ Ayyūb ask for and receive investiture as Sultan of Egypt.

Saladin did not establish a 'constitutional' system of heredity; and as a result, there was a rapidly escalating struggle for power. His eldest son, al-Ẓāhir, to whom he bequeathed Aleppo, was strong enough to retain his important principality and to hand it down to his son and grandson. In Syria and the Jazīrah, Saladin's brother, al-'Ādil, very quickly gained the upper hand. Saladin's son, al-'Azīz 'Uthmān, Sultan of Egypt and overlord of the dynasty, still kept his position; but his son and successor, al-Manṣūr Muḥammad, was master only in name and was succeeded by al-'Ādil, who became the effective recognized head of the entire empire. The rulers of the provinces of Syria, Mesopotamia and the Yaman, the governors of districts and smaller possessions acknowledged him as their overlord; even the practically independent al-Ẓāhir of Aleppo was obliged to accept his suzerainty, at least nominally.

After al-'Ādil's death the struggle among his sons continued, with successes and setbacks for all the brothers involved. Every change of fortune sparked clashes among the smaller provincial lords, who endeavoured to profit from their own overlord's victory; or, when the latter lost out, sometimes changed allegiance with disconcerting ease.

The coinage almost always bears witness to the political situation with its changes, various alliances, and controversies; often members of different branches of the family controlled the same territory in rapid succession. It was therefore thought that a classification according to provinces would be better adapted to the requirements of the numismatic history of the Ayyūbids than the primarily genealogical ones used by earlier generations of numismatists. The coins of the Sultanate of Egypt are catalogued first, followed by those of the different principalities in Syria (Aleppo, Damascus, Ḥamāh), in Mesopotamia (the Jazīrah, Ḥiṣn Kayfā), and the Yemen. Within each section, the coins are listed by ruler and by metal: gold first, followed by silver and copper. In the case of the Sultanate of Egypt, the coins of each ruler are further subdivided according to their area of mintage: Egypt itself, Syria, Palestine, Mesopotamia and Arabia. The principal sections and their breakdown by ruler, area and metal are shown by means of running heads at the top of each page.

Several excellent modern works, though not numismatic studies, are of great assistance in clarifying the development of the Ayyūbid Empire and the intricacies of its further history. Both the development and the intricacies are reflected by the prodigious variety of the coinage. A. S. Ehrenkreutz's *Saladin* emphasizes that, after his tremendous achievement in creating his vast empire, Saladin failed to secure a stable succession to the throne, with disastrous consequences. The author also recognizes that the systematic drainage of Egypt's wealth, in order to promote his military campaigns in Syria and Mesopotamia, left the Nile Valley in an impoverished state. Another very valuable study is Hasanein Rabie's *The Financial System of Egypt*, written with great skill and authority, which is based on an abundance of medieval and modern literature. It deals with the monetary, financial and tributary problems of Egypt from Fāṭimid times well into the Mamlūk period.

H. L. Gottschalk's *Al-Malik al-Kāmil von Egypten und seine Zeit* depicts admirably the period leading up to al-Kāmil's reign, with al-Kāmil Muḥammad I's government itself as the main subject and, briefly, the subsequent decline. The entire work is profusely documented from medieval sources. R. S. Humphreys' *The Ayyūbids of Damascus* is another indispensable work for the study of Saladin's dynasty. In a really original manner this author analyses the many changes which occurred in the history of the Damascus province, the frequent changes of sovereignty over city and province—all with great competence—and the various and complicated links that connected it with the whole empire like a spider's web.

Although no chapter is included in this present work on minting techniques, three studies must be mentioned:

- Ehrenkreutz's *Extracts from the Technical Manual on the Ayyūbid Mint in Cairo*, in *BSOAS*, 1953 (English translation);
- Abdelrahman Fahmy Mohamed's *Kashf al-asrār* (the complete text of the original Arabic); both works deal with the eighteenth-century copy of Ibn Baʿrah's manual; and
- The exemplary edition of al-Hamdāni's *Kitâb al-ǧauharatain al-ʿatîqatain al-mâʾiʿatain al-ṣafrā wa lʾbaiḍā* (edited in the original Arabic, with German translation) by Christopher Toll.

HISTORICAL OUTLINE

Although many articles have been written on various aspects of Ayyūbid history, and there are books on Saladin and another on particular figures as well, a general history of this dynasty has hitherto been lacking. R. S. Humphreys' *From Saladin to the Mongols* partly fills the lacuna; in it Humphreys stresses 'constitutional' issues and places primary focus on Damascus. This survey emphasizes a different aspect: the political and military milieu in which coins were issued; here the primary focus will be on numismatic developments.

SALADIN

Saladin obtained his investiture as Lord of Egypt from the ʿAbbāsid Caliph al-Mustaḍī almost immediately after the last Fāṭimid Imām, al-ʿĀḍid li-Dīn Allāh died on the 10th Muḥarram 567 H. At the same time, however, he was the vassal of Nūr al-Dīn Maḥmūd, the powerful Zengid prince of Aleppo. Therefore, when he started to strike gold and silver in Cairo and Alexandria, he did so in the name of his liege lord, Maḥmūd b. Zengī; his own name was not included on these coins. Nevertheless, these issues must be regarded as the first Ayyūbid coins because Saladin controlled Egypt and her mints. Similarly, the last Ayyūbid issues from Egypt, irrespective of their inscriptions, date from 674 H, when al-Muʿaẓẓam Tūrānshāh was murdered and the Mamlūks commenced ruling in Egypt.

Saladin's first issue, as Nūr al-Dīn Maḥmūd's vassal, was struck in 567 H. Saladin was about 35 years old and, as demonstrated by Ehrenkreutz, had extensive administrative experience. He had been head of his clan and chief of the Syrian forces in Egypt since 564 H. When Nūr al-Dīn Maḥmūd died in 569 H, Saladin was entrenched in Egypt, secure of his military position, and prepared to issue coins in his own name.

The first autonomous coinage appeared in 570 H. It includes Saladin's protocol on one side and that of the ʿAbbāsid caliph al-Mustaḍī on the other. The name of Maḥmūd's son, al-Ṣāliḥ Ismāʿīl, whose purely nominal overlordship Saladin had not yet repudiated, is absent from this new issue. The ʿAbbāsid caliph died in late 575 H and the name of the new caliph, al-Nāṣir li-Dīn Allāh, appeared on the 576 H issues. There was also a change in the arrangement of the legends.

It is interesting to note how much the earliest Ayyūbid policy resembled the Fāṭimid one, although the latter was Shiʿite and the former Sunnī. The gold coins had similar styles, as had also the silver. In fact, the earliest Ayyūbid dirhems are a direct continuation of the Fāṭimid 'black dirhems'. Even the policy of issuing copper coins was the same; neither the Fāṭimid nor Saladin's Egypt produced them, but during both periods they were minted in Syria. Saladin, of course, invaded Syria only after Nūr al-Dīn's demise.

He did this in mid-570 H and easily took Damascus. He then approached the Zengid prince, al-Ṣāliḥ Ismāʿīl, who had been transferred to Aleppo from Damascus by his governing entourage earlier in the year, asking that he be allowed to occupy Aleppo with his troops, in order better to protect his interests. al-Ṣāliḥ and his counsellors and amīrs firmly refused the request and Saladin, for the time being, did not find it propitious to provoke Syrian public opinion by open hostility against al-Ṣāliḥ. On the contrary, he maintained the fiction of vassalage toward the young prince and struck copper in Damascus in 570 H with the name of al-Ṣāliḥ displayed on the reverse of the *fulūs*.

Saladin continued, nevertheless, to pursue his own goals against the Zengids, even if al-Ṣāliḥ Ismāʿīl did not capitulate. In addition to Damascus, Saladin was able, in 570 H, to gain control of Ḥamāh and Ḥimṣ; and, in 571 H, the silver dirhems of Damascus were inscribed with only Saladin's protocol. Propaganda and military campaigns failed, however, to dislodge al-Ṣāliḥ from Aleppo; and, in 577 H, the political picture became more complex.

al-Ṣāliḥ Ismāʿīl died that year and bequeathed his city to his kinsman, ʿĪzz al-Dīn Masʿūd I of Mawṣil. ʿĪzz al-Dīn hastened to incorporate Aleppo into his possessions. He was faced, however, with the competition of his brother, ʿImād al-Dīn Zengī, master of Sinjār, who threatened to surrender Sinjār to Saladin if ʿĪzz al-Dīn did not give him Aleppo in exchange for Sinjār. The transfer took place and ʿImād al-Dīn received Aleppo while ʿĪzz al-Dīn took over Sinjār.

These events confirmed Saladin's fear over developments in Aleppo and the Jazīrah, the northern part of Mesopotamia. This area was critical to Saladin in protecting his eastern flank. The Jazīrah was also an important reservoir for military and economic aid.

The rulers of the Jazīrah were well aware of Saladin's ambition to capture Upper Mesopotamia. These rulers included the Artuqids of Ḥiṣn-Kayfā and Mārdīn (the Mārdīn branch also controlled Mayāfāriqīn) and the Īnālids of Āmid.

The Artuqids entered into an alliance with the Zengid brothers. However, in an energetic campaign in 578 H, Saladin swept away their armies and, after a brief siege, stormed the powerful fortified city of Āmid. He also took Niṣibīn. Before these resounding successes the Artuqid/Zengid alliance melted away and the Artuqids subsequently became Saladin's allies and vassals. From Āmid the Ayyūbid forces moved to Aleppo; at Nūrīyah they overwhelmed the Zengid resistance. ʿImād al-Dīn decided to come to terms with Saladin and agreed to the exchange of Aleppo for his former domain in the Jazīrah Sinjār. He also received Niṣibīn. The now friendly relationship between these two princes lasted until Saladin's death.

These events are reflected in the coinage. After he had taken Niṣibīn in 578 H, Saladin had very large and heavy copper coins struck, which bore his full-face bust surmounted by a Sasanian crown. Once in possession of Aleppo, he introduced a new type of silver dirhem, characterized by an ornamented hexagram on both sides. This design became the standard for most of the Ayyūbid Aleppo dirhems. It was also adopted for certain issues in Ḥiṣn-Kayfā, and later by the Artuqids of Mārdīn. Even Hūlāgū issued such a stellated dirhem when he occupied Aleppo in 659 H.

In 581 H the conquest of the province of Diyār Bakr was concluded with the capture of Mayāfāriqīn. Abundant issues of copper currency followed, mostly inspired by the local Artuqid Turcoman coinage, which displayed busts, figures and groups derived from ancient Greek, Roman and Byzantine prototypes. These were astrological compositions; some of the coins show Saladin sitting on a low throne.

The Artuqids of Ḥiṣn-Kayfā received Āmid from Saladin in 579 H, and willingly placed the Ayyūbid overlord's name on their coinage. The Artuqids of Mārdīn had fought Saladin, but unsuccessfully; and, after 581 H, his name appeared on their coinage.

After having secured Upper Mesopotamia, Saladin turned to Northern 'Irāq and the Zengid prince of Mawṣil, 'Īzz al-Dīn Mas'ūd. 'Īzz al-Dīn submitted in 581 H and the coins of Mawṣil also show Saladin's name as their overlord. Mawṣil's antagonism toward the Ayyūbids did not cease but, for the moment, Saladin could devote all his attention to the invading Crusaders.

Saladin faced periods of success and defeat until, in 583 H, the main Crusader army was crushed and its leaders captured or massacred at the battle of the 'Horns' of Ḥaṭṭīn near Ṭabarīyah. This was a memorable event in the reign of Saladin and it is reflected in the coinage of Damascus. This victory was the occasion for the issuing of the only Ayyūbid gold coins struck in that city. On these coins Saladin assumed the title of *Sulṭān al-Islām wa-al-Muslimīn,* a pretentious but not quite official title. At the same time, a special copper series was also struck, on which Saladin's title was only *Sulṭān al-Muslimīn.* The copper issues were not limited to the year 583 H, but continued until Saladin's demise in 589 H.

When the threat from the Crusaders was significantly reduced, Saladin continued to consolidate his power in the East. Additional important cities were added to his growing empire. In 586 H he received Ḥarrān, al-Ruhā and Sumaysāt from the Bektekinid Gökbürī in exchange for recognizing Gökbürī's claim to Irbīl. In Ḥarrān, as in Mayāfāriqīn, Saladin struck copper coins with figure motifs. He adopted the style of the issues minted by Turcoman princes of that region.

Upon Saladin's demise, he left the leadership of his family to his eldest son, al-Afḍal 'Alī. al-Afḍal was already the ruler of Damascus and had been acknowledged by his kinsmen as the head of the family. al-Afḍal was not, however, a great leader and he quickly became involved in a struggle for power with members of his family, including his very ambitious and able uncle, Saladin's brother, al-'Ādil. In a matter of three years, al-'Ādil succeeded in attracting the support of the Syrian amīrs and princes and practically ousted al-Afḍal from his position as leader of the clan. A few silver coins, dated between 589 and 592 H and struck in Damascus, Ḥamāh and Ḥimṣ, testify to the ephemeral rule of al-Afḍal.

AL-'AZĪZ 'UTHMĀN

Saladin bequeathed Egypt to another of his sons, al-'Azīz 'Uthmān. His coinage, similar to his father's, consisted of gold and silver but no copper. He may also have issued glass jetons, but since those that survive have only the caliph's name, they cannot be attributed to his reign with absolute certainty. It is interesting that, contemporary with al-Afḍal, al-'Azīz issued dirhems in Damascus. Damascene coins could have been issued by another Ayyūbid, al-'Ādil, who, by 591 H, had become the most important member of the family and who controlled Central Syria, along with other areas. al-'Ādil maintained good relations with al-'Azīz, however, and did not issue coins in Syria with his name. When al-'Azīz died in early 595 H, his ten-year-old son, al-Manṣūr Muḥammad, succeeded him, but the youth was replaced shortly after by al-'Ādil, in 596 H.

AL-'ĀDIL I

Before al-'Ādil became head of the Ayyūbid Empire, he had held a number of areas, including Central Syria, parts of the Jazīrah, and Mayāfāriqīn. He had been striking coins in the latter area since 591 H. In 596 H al-Awḥad Najm al-Dīn Ayyūb was entrusted with the governorship of

Mayāfāriqīn and the large and important province that belonged to it. He struck copper in Mayāfāriqīn intermittently between 599 and 605 H. At the same time, his father, al-ʿĀdil, head of the empire, issued copper coins there. Therefore, we have a dual coinage series, struck intermittently by both father and son, over the same years.

al-ʿĀdil appointed a number of his sons to important positions. In 596 H he named his eldest son, al-Kāmil Muḥammad, Viceroy of Egypt and his heir. The governorship of Damascus was retained by his second son, al-Muʿaẓẓam ʿĪsā; a third son, al-Ashraf Mūsā, became ruler of al-Ruhā and Ḥarrān; while his fourth son, al-Awḥad Ayyūb, ruled over Mayāfāriqīn. Coinage in al-ʿĀdil's name was issued in all these areas, as well as at the fortress of Qalʿat Jaʿbar on the west bank of the Euphrates.

In 599 H, after lengthy, inconclusive operations against the Artuqids of Mārdīn, who had allied themselves with the Zengid prince of Mawṣil, al-ʿĀdil sent al-Ashraf Mūsā against the city. The Artuqids of Mārdīn became al-ʿĀdil's vassals. After his brother, al-Awḥad Najm al-Dīn Ayyūb, died in 607 H, al-Ashraf Mūsā received the governorship of the eastern province of Mayāfāriqīn and Sinjār. His copper coins, issued between 607 and 617 H, are well known.

The important province of Aleppo in northern Syria was now the only principality in the Ayyūbid Empire not under al-ʿĀdil's direct control. al-Ẓāhir Ghāzī, Saladin's fourth son, had received it in 582 H, and it was to remain in the possession of his direct successors until the Ilkhānid invasion. However, the government of Aleppo was understandably concerned at al-ʿĀdil's rapid ascension to the supreme power and by his obvious ambition. Consequently, the Council of Regency —al-Ẓāhir being still young—turned to their neighbour in the north, the Seljūq Sulṭān of Rūm (Asia Minor), to form a protective alliance. The Rūm-Seljūqs were not interested in a direct conflict with the Ayyūbids at this time, so Aleppo had to accept al-ʿĀdil's overlordship, even if this vassalage remained, most of the time, only nominal. From 596 H onward al-ʿĀdil's name was engraved on most of the Aleppo coinage. Unwelcome as it was for al-Ẓāhir Ghāzī and his regents, the acceptance of al-ʿĀdil's sovereignty ensured a period of tranquility that lasted until the death of al-ʿĀdil in 615 H.

In Egypt al-ʿĀdil's coinage included both the yearly issues of gold and the continued strikings of black dirhems; in addition, an attempt was made to improve the silver standard along the lines of Saladin's similar experiment in 585 and 586 H. al-ʿĀdil's normal flan dirhems have survived in relatively small numbers and are from the years 598, 600, 601 and 605 H. Whether the objective of issuing higher standard silver coinage was met is impossible to prove. We do know that the production of black dirhems continued on a large scale. There are no Egyptian copper coins for al-ʿĀdil's reign (cf. discussion of glass jetons).

Although al-ʿĀdil had established a commanding position within the Ayyūbid Empire, there was opposition. Under the leadership of Nūr al-Dīn Arslānshāh the Zengids of Mawṣil defied the Ayyūbids and became friendly only after 601 H, when a marriage was arranged between al-Ashraf Mūsā and a daughter of Arslānshāh. This entente, however, lasted only a short time. In 607 H, Nūr al-Dīn's son, al-Qāhir ʿĪzz al-Dīn Masʿūd, recognized al-ʿĀdil as his overlord, as will be demonstrated below. al-Qāhir ʿĪzz al-Dīn probably acted under the influence of his atabeg, Badr al-Dīn Lūʾlūʾ.

According to H. L. Gottschalk, *al-Malik al-Kāmil von Egypten und seine Zeit* (p. 41), neither Nūr al-Dīn Arslānshāh nor his son, ʿĪzz al-Dīn Masʿūd II, acknowledged al-ʿĀdil as overlord until 615 H. But some understanding must have been reached, at least in 607 and 610 H, between the Zengid, ʿĪzz al-Dīn Masʿūd, and al-ʿĀdil, because there are gold coins of Mawṣil for these two dates on which the name ʿal-Malik al-ʿĀdil Abū Bakr b. Ayyūbʾ is inscribed.

After 615 H the younger generation of the Zengids of Mawṣil, Arslānshāh II and his brother, Nāṣir al-Dīn Maḥmūd II; together with their tutor, the atabeg, Badr al-Dīn Lūʾlūʾ, who later succeeded them as Sulṭān of Mawṣil, changed their attitude, and submitted to Ayyūbid overlordship. However, in 638 H, when a coalition of the Syrian and Mesopotamian Ayyūbid princes joined with the Rūm Seljūq Sulṭān Kaykhusraw II against al-Ṣāliḥ Ayyūb, Badr al-Dīn Lūʾlūʾ changed sides and joined the alliance.

The Zengids of Sinjār remained faithful vassals, in spite of some temporary controversies, until their domain was absorbed by the Ayyūbids in 617 H. The loyalty of the Ḥiṣn-Kayfā Artuqids and problems with the Mārdīn Artuqids have been mentioned.

AL-KĀMIL MUḤAMMAD I

al-Kāmil Muḥammad started his reign from a position of weakness and had to scheme and fight during his entire reign. He fought Crusaders who threatened his possession of Egypt. He was also obliged to fight members of his own family, who made incessant attempts to dispute his supremacy and who tried to overthrow him.

At the beginning of 615 H the Crusaders received reinforcements from Europe and decided to attack the Ayyūbid Empire in Egypt. They sent a considerable armada with a large contingent of troops to Damietta, a strongly fortified city at the mouth of the eastern Nile branch. When the Crusaders disembarked near Damietta in Rabīʿ I 615 H, al-ʿĀdil, who was still head of the empire, was in poor health. He remained in his encampment near Damascus and was in no condition to decide on what action to take. After three months, during which the Egyptians received no help from their kinsmen in Syria, the Crusaders succeeded in capturing an important outpost of the Damietta fortifications. The news so upset al-ʿĀdil that he started for Egypt; however, he died *en route*.

While the Crusaders attacked Damietta, the Rūm-Seljūq leader, Sulṭān Kaykāwus, led his army against the Ayyūbid domains in the Jazīrah. He found allies among some of the Ayyūbid princes nursing grievances against al-ʿĀdil, including the exiled al-Afḍal ʿAlī b. Saladin, who hoped to regain his lost principality of Damascus.

In Aleppo, where al-Ẓāhir Ghāzī had died in 613 H, his young son, al-ʿAzīz Muḥammad, reigned, but the government was in the hands of a regency council. Naturally, there were notables whose interests did not coincide with those of the ruling council and who wanted the easily influenced al-Afḍal as head of the empire instead of al-Kāmil. They also wanted to eliminate al-Kāmil's brothers, al-Muʿaẓẓam ʿĪsā and al-Ashraf Mūsā, from Damascus and the Jazīrah. The Seljūq army captured several fortified towns in northern Jazīrah at the first onslaught, but later they met with a severe defeat between Aleppo and Manbīj. Kaykāwus became discouraged and withdrew to Anatolia.

After the defeat of the Rūm Seljūqs, the Ayyūbid princes agreed to recognize al-Kāmil as overlord, with the unofficial title of Sulṭān. al-Kāmil's name was inscribed on the Aleppo silver after 616 H, together with that of al-ʿAzīz Muḥammad.

In Egypt the war was not going well. After a long and tedious struggle, the Crusaders captured Damietta in Sha'bān, 616 H. Some of the Ayyūbid princes were greatly disturbed by the siege and feared other attacks by the Crusaders. In particular, al-Mu'aẓẓam ordered the dismantling of his fortresses in Palestine, including Jerusalem, which might be captured by the Crusaders.

The Crusaders' invasion of the Egyptian coast was still unresolved when a dangerous situation developed in al-Mawṣil after the demise of its prince, 'Īzz al-Dīn Mas'ūd II in 615 H, who had been a staunch ally of the Ayyūbids. The younger brother of the deceased Sulṭān, 'Imād al-Dīn Zengī, left out of the succession, started to conspire against the legal heir, Nūr al-Dīn Arslānshāh II, Mas'ūd's son. When 'Imād al-Dīn Zengī realized that he was not powerful enough, he involved the Begteginid prince of Irbīl, Muẓaffar al-Dīn Gökbürī in his intrigue. The family feud thus turned into an international conflict in which the Ayyūbids had to intervene. Three consecutive campaigns—known as the three al-Mawṣil wars—followed. In the first only al-Mawṣil forces of the atabeg Lū'lū' were engaged against the Begtekinid Gökbürī and the pretender, 'Imād al-Dīn Zengī. Later the Zengids of Sinjār, the Artuqids of Mārdīn, and the Ayyūbid forces participated. With the end of the wars in 617 H, Zengid rule in Sinjār ceased; the Artuqids of Mārdīn submitted to Ayyūbid rule; and Gökbürī withdrew to Irbīl.

The three brothers—al-Kāmil Muḥammad, al-Mu'aẓẓam 'Īsā, and al-Ashraf Mūsā—had cooperated and defended the empire against simultaneous threats from the Crusaders and their Muslim neighbours. However, personal considerations once again alienated the three brothers, as illustrated by events in Syria. The prince of Ḥamāh at the time was al-Manṣūr Muḥammad I. His eldest son and heir, al Muẓaffar Maḥmūd II, had been dispatched with his troops to assist al-Kāmil in Egypt in the Damietta campaign. During his absence the second son, al-Nāṣir Qilij Arslān, encouraged by al-Mu'aẓẓam 'Īsā, intrigued successfully with a group of notables against al-Muẓaffar Maḥmūd II. The entire affair served the interests of al-Mu'aẓẓam 'Īsā because Ḥamāh now became ever more dependent on Damascus and so escaped the influence of al-Ashraf Mūsā, whose pre-eminence in North Syria had been previously uncontested. The ruling prince of Ḥamāh, al-Manṣūr Muḥammad I, died in Ramaḍān 617 H.

After the Mawṣil wars al-Ashraf Mūsā returned to his residence in Sinjār. al-Mu'aẓẓam paid him a visit in Ḥarrān and persuaded him to aid al-Kāmil against the Crusaders in Damietta. al-Ashraf left the provinces of Mayāfāriqīn and southern Armenia in the hands of his brother, al-Muẓaffar Shihāb al-Dīn Ghāzī. A few copper coins struck in Khilāṭ, capital of southern Armenia, by al-Muẓaffar Ghāzī are our only numismatic evidence of this phase of Ayyūbid history. There is no evidence that, at this time, al-Ashraf considered a Mongol offensive a serious threat. On the contrary, he dismissed the entreaties of a Georgian delegation, who approached him with the request for a defensive alliance against the Mongols.

Other political changes were also taking place. The newly subjected Artuqid prince of Mārdīn, Nāṣir al-Dīn Artuq Arslān, entered into an alliance with al-Mu'aẓẓam while the new prince of Ḥamāh, until now a vassal of al-Mu'aẓẓam, became an ally of al-Ashraf. However, in the matter of helping al-Kāmil against the Crusaders, both brothers were in agreement and al-Ashraf arrived in Egypt at the head of his army in Jumādā II 618 H.

al-Kāmil now had more troops than the Crusaders. His superior knowledge of the terrain, of the seasonal changes of the water level, and of the effect of the annual flooding on the fields stood in sharp contrast with the total ignorance of these vital matters displayed by the Crusaders. The

'Franks' made tremendous efforts to beat the Muslims, but all their plans miscarried. They tried everything to extricate themselves from the treacherous terrain, from the impassable mud flats, and from the fields swamped by flood waters, but they failed. In the end the Crusaders were almost completely annihilated by the Ayyūbid forces. A few survivors were able to ransom themselves. The pitiful remains of the Frankish army rejoiced when they finally received permission to embark, in Rajab 618 H, with nothing to show for their heavy sacrifices.

After the victory in Egypt, a split of the Ayyūbid camp into two rival factions became more evident. On one side stood al-Muʿaẓẓam ʿĪsā with his only ally, the Artuqid prince of Mārdīn. On the other side were al-Kāmil, al-Ashraf Mūsā and his vassal, al-Nāṣir Qilij Arslān of Ḥamāh. al-Muʿaẓẓam was well aware of the danger that al-Kāmil and al-Ashraf's alliance meant to his position; therefore, he looked for allies outside the Ayyūbid Empire. One of these was to be, from 622 H, the Khwārizmshāh Jalāl al-Dīn Mingburni; others included the Begtekinid Gökbürī of Irbīl.

The first open clash among the three Ayyūbid brothers occurred over the issue of the Ḥamāh succession in 619 H, but ended without bloodshed. Later, in 626 H, al-Nāṣir Qilij Arslān, al-Ashraf's client, would be forced to hand Ḥamāh over to al-Muẓaffar Maḥmūd, his older brother and al-Kāmil's client. However, the antagonism between al-Kāmil, al-Muʿaẓẓam and al-Ashraf became evident before this event.

al-Ashraf stayed in Egypt with al-Kāmil for a lengthy political visit and left for Aleppo in Shawwāl 620 H in order to strengthen his recently concluded alliance with al-ʿAzīz Muḥammad, al-Ẓāhir Ghāzī's son and successor, against al-Muʿaẓẓam ʿĪsā. Both al-Kāmil and al-Ashraf confirmed al-ʿAzīz Muḥammad as prince of Aleppo and the new tripartite alliance was widely publicized.

It may be useful to recall now, that toward the end of 617 H, al-Ashraf Mūsā, the autonomous prince of the Jazīrah, Mayāfāriqīn, and the conquered part of Armenia, appointed his younger brother, al-Muẓaffar Shihāb al-Dīn Ghāzī, as his viceroy in Armenia with residence in Khilāṭ. The brutal assault of the Mongols on north-western Persia and the Caucasus in 619 H created confusion on the part of the Georgian cavalry, who fled into the Armenian territory controlled by al-Muẓaffar Ghāzī and were largely taken prisoner there. The king of Georgia, in order to liberate his captured soldiers, and knowing that al-Ashraf was the titular prince and al-Muẓaffar only his lieutenant, turned to the former with his request to free them. al-Ashraf granted this without consulting al-Muẓaffar Ghāzī. al-Muʿaẓẓam ʿĪsā, who had his own grievances against al-Ashraf, entered into a secret alliance with al-Muẓaffar Ghāzī, which in 621 H led to open warfare.

INTERNECINE WAR

The two sides began serious preparations for the conflict. The Begtekinid Gökbürī of Irbīl joined the al-Muʿaẓẓam ʿĪsā/al-Muẓaffar Ghāzī coalition. Gökbürī hoped to take al-Mawṣil from al-Ashraf's vassal, Badr al-Dīn Lūʾlū'. He met strong resistance, learned that the plans of al-Muʿaẓẓam ʿĪsā and al-Muẓaffar Ghāzī had failed, and retreated to Irbīl.

al-Ashraf, in order to do battle with al-Muẓaffar, had to march from Ḥarrān to Khilāṭ along a line which was within reach of Āmid and Mārdīn. Āmid belonged to Rukn al-Dīn Mawdūd, the Artuqid prince of Ḥiṣn-Kayfā, al-Ashraf's own vassal. However, Nāṣir al-Dīn Artuq Arslān of Mārdīn was an old antagonist. Thus, the line of communication between Ḥarrān and Khilāṭ was exposed, but al-Ashraf succeeded, with great diplomatic skill and personal charm, in winning the ruler of Mārdīn over to his cause. Instead of attacking him, Nāṣir al-Dīn Artuq Arslān promised to furnish him with an army contingent. With his supply lines secured, al-Ashraf was now able to march unmolested against Khilāṭ. al-Muẓaffar offered no resistance; Khilāṭ capitulated in Ramaḍān 621 H; and although al-Muẓaffar lost Armenia, he was allowed to keep Mayāfāriqīn, which he held until his death in 645 H.

The third member of the coalition, al-Mu'aẓẓam 'Īsā, accomplished even less. His plan was to attack al-Ashraf's capital Ḥarrān while al-Ashraf was leading his troops against al-Muẓaffar. As indicated above, al-Ashraf and al-Kāmil had been in close contact and al-Kāmil warned al-Mu'aẓẓam that if he marched north, al-Kāmil would attack Damascus. This threat was adequate to stop al-Mu'aẓẓam from marching to war. Thus, the year 621 H ended with little change in the political and military situation.

According to the historian al-Maqrīzī, the following year some major monetary developments took place in Egypt. The economic situation had worsened since the Damietta campaign and reached an open crisis in 622 H. al-Kāmil was obliged to introduce a currency reform to replace the black dirhems. According to al-Maqrīzī, not only were the worthless black dirhems abandoned in favour of a new 'round', globular, silver coin, but al-Kāmil was compelled to introduce a copper coinage. As mentioned above, neither the Fāṭimids nor the earlier Ayyūbids issued an Egyptian copper coinage. Instead, to my mind, the glass and glass/paste jetons that have been found in such large numbers were used as the fiduciary currency. In 622 H al-Kāmil, ceding to public demands, issued the copper coinage demanded by the public.

By 623 H developments in the other Ayyūbid lands became a growing concern for al-Kāmil. al-Mu'aẓẓam's coalition against al-Ashraf heralded a new military intervention. Gökbürī once more marched against al-Mawṣil and engaged Lū'lū' in skirmishes of varying success. al-Ashraf went to the rescue of Lū'lū', but had to turn away when news reached him that the Artuqid of Mārdīn, Nāṣir al-Dīn Artuq Arslān, had risen against him. To make matters worse, his own vassal in Āmid and Ḥiṣn Kayfā, Mas'ūd, also rebelled. Worried by so many enemies, al-Ashraf turned to the Rūm-Seljūq, Sulṭān Kayqubād, for assistance. The Seljūq came to his rescue and captured several strongholds so rapidly that Mas'ūd b. Mawdūd of Āmid, thoroughly frightened, surrendered to al-Ashraf. He was allowed to rule in Āmid, but the Seljūqs kept Mārdīn for themselves.

In the end the war was concluded with an uneasy reconciliation of the three brothers—al-Kāmil, al-Ashraf and al-Mu'aẓẓam—and by a truce that did not last long. Though newly arrived reinforcements of the Crusaders brought danger of a new confrontation, al-Mu'aẓẓam went on with his scheming and openly recognized the Khwārizmshāh Jalāl al-Dīn Mingburni as his overlord. During earlier hostilities al-Mu'aẓẓam had respected al-Kāmil's sovereignty and his right of *sikka*. He had never issued coins in his own name in Damascus. Now, according to Gottschalk, he proclaimed his intention to strike gold and silver independently and to put the Khwārizmshāh's name on them as his overlord. However, al-Mu'aẓẓam died suddenly in Dhū al-Ḥijjah 624 H without carrying out his threat.

al-Mu'aẓẓam bequeathed Damascus to his young son, al-Nāṣir Dā'ūd. As soon as he was sworn into office, al-Nāṣir Dā'ūd reversed his father's policy and offered his allegiance to al-Kāmil. A simple declaration of obedience did not, however, satisfy al-Kāmil, who demanded that his nephew relinquish to him the fortresses of Shawbak and al-Karak, both in controlling positions on the desert road between Egypt and Damascus. As the coastal roads were in the hands of the Crusaders, the desert road was vital for al-Kāmil; it was also a way for him to test al-Nāṣir Dā'ūd's allegiance.

al-Nāṣir Dā'ūd refused to comply with his uncle's demands and al-Kāmil, increasingly suspicious of al-Nāṣir Dā'ūd's loyalty, prepared for war against Damascus. al-Ṣāliḥ Najm al-Dīn Ayyūb, al-Kāmil's son, was named heir to the sultanate and governor of Egypt; and in Ramaḍān 625 H, al-Kāmil left Egypt at the head of his troops. When al-Nāṣir Dā'ūd learned about the armed expedition mounted against him by his uncle al-Kāmil and that some of his former allies had joined al-Kāmil, he turned to his other uncle, al-Ashraf Mūsā, for assistance.

al-Ashraf joined his nephew in Damascus, where he was in a position to outwit al-Nāṣir Dā'ūd and obtain Damascus for himself. He started secret negotiations with al-Kāmil over a new distribution of the various provinces and how best to encounter the still hovering menace represented by the Crusaders under Frederick II. Negotiations were already well advanced between al-Kāmil and Frederick when the ruler of Egypt encamped at Tall al-'Ajūl near Ghazzah (Gaza).

To revert to numismatic matters, al-Kāmil opened in 624 H a mint at Ghazzah that issued dirhems. Specimens for 625 and 634 H are also known. The Egyptian mint continued to issue dinars and dirhems in his name while Damascus, heedless of the growing political crisis involving al-Nāṣir Dā'ūd and al-Ashraf Mūsā, also minted dirhems in his name.

al-Ashraf arrived at Tall al-'Ajūl on 10 Dhū al-Ḥijjah 625 H, accompanied by Asad al-Dīn Shirkūh of Ḥimṣ and al-Muẓaffar Shihāb al-Dīn Ghāzī of Mayāfāriqīn, both former allies of al-Mu'aẓẓam. The negotiations with al-Kāmil proceeded smoothly; and toward the end of 625 H a treaty was drawn up, according to which the Syrian and Mesopotamian provinces were apportioned as follows:

1. al-Ashraf Mūsā received Damascus and Central Syria, which had been al-Nāṣir Dā'ūd's.
2. Palestine and southern Syria went to al-Kāmil, who also remained the head of the family.
3. al-Nāṣir Dā'ūd received al-Ashraf's dominions in the Jazīrah (Ḥarrān, Raqqah, al-Ruhā, Sarūj, etc.) as compensation for Damascus.
4. Ba'albak went to a son of al-'Ādil, al-'Azīz 'Uthmān.
5. Ḥamāh and its dependencies were taken away from the usurper, al-Nāṣir Qilij Arslān, and restored to the lawful heir, al-Muẓaffar Maḥmud II.
6. Salamīyah was restored to the province of Ḥimṣ, to which it had originally belonged.
7. al-Muẓaffar Shihāb al-Dīn Ghāzī retained Mayāfāriqīn.

In this major redistribution of the provinces al-Kāmil was the main beneficiary. He gained undisputed supremacy and fixed the newly distributed dominions within well-defined limits. Damascus lost its control of Ba'albak and Ḥamāh was drawn into al-Kāmil's orbit and away from the influence of Damascus. The prince of Ḥimṣ, formerly an ally of al-Ashraf, was now obligated to al-Kāmil for his new possession of Salamīyah. al-Jazīrah was weakened politically by the division of its territories among al-Ashraf, al-Nāṣir Dā'ūd and al-Muẓaffar Ghāzī.

The Treaty of Tall al-'Ajūl was drawn up and signed, but al-Nāṣir Dā'ūd was not prepared to relinquish his inheritance of Damascus. al-Ashraf tried to persuade him to accept the lands allotted to him in the Jazīrah, but failed. al-Nāṣir Dā'ūd broke off contact with al-Ashraf and prepared to resist any siege of Damascus. al-Ashraf began to invest the city in Rabī' II 626 H, but he soon realized that his forces were insufficient to seal it off. He therefore requested al-Kāmil's assistance, who sent some troops and forced al-Ashraf to agree to surrender to him his Jazīrah possessions, which the treaty had promised to al-Nāṣir Dā'ūd. Thus, as punishment, al-Nāṣir Dā'ūd was to be stripped of all his possessions, except a few places in Palestine that al-Kāmil deigned to turn over to him. When al-Ashraf agreed, al-Kāmil sent his full force against Damascus.

The siege of Damascus began in earnest in Jumādā II 626 H; it lasted, with bitter fighting, until Rajab, when al-Nāṣir Dā'ūd, realizing how hopeless the situation was, capitulated. Magnanimity displayed by al-Kāmil led to a quick reconciliation and al-Nāṣir Dā'ūd received lands in Palestine and Transjordan. In Sha'bān al-Ashraf took possession of Damascus.

With the new arrangement the situation in the Jazīrah became more complicated:

- Ḥarrān, Raqqah, Sarūj, and a few other places went to al-Kāmil;
- al-Ashraf retained Niṣibīn, Sinjār, al-Khabūr and Khilāṭ in Armenia; and
- al-Muẓaffar Ghāzī held Mayāfāriqīn as viceroy for al-Ashraf—though, in truth, he was practically independent.

At the same time the Artuqids held the principalities of Mārdīn and Āmid with its dependency, Ḥiṣn-Kayfā.

Although al-Kāmil held the most important position, there was still opposition to his leadership in the Ayyūbid Empire. One problem arose in Syria: al-Nāṣir Qilij Arslān had not reconciled himself to the loss of his principality of Ḥamāh and started preparations for its defence. On the other hand, the princes of Buṣrā, Banyās, and also the lawful heir to Ḥamāh, Qilij Arslān's elder brother, al-Muẓaffar Maḥmud II, proclaimed their loyalty to al-Kāmil.

Ḥamāh was a strongly built fortress, manned by good troops, and the inhabitants were well disposed toward Qilij Arslān; with some skill, courage and determination, he could have gained important concessions from al-Kāmil. Somehow, however, his courage suddenly deserted him and he unexpectedly capitulated unconditionally on 17 Ramaḍān 626 H. When the leading families supporting Qilij Arslān were reassured about their future, al-Muẓaffar Maḥmud was able to take over Ḥamāh without further trouble. Some dispute arose around the possession of Ba'albak, but after more negotiations, this city and its territories were simply incorporated into the principality of Damascus.

About this time the Khwārizmshāh Jalāl al-Dīn Mingburni succeeded in organizing a new army and settled in the freshly conquered Adharbaijān, which was still out of the reach of the Mongols. From here his troops harassed Georgia and Armenia with continuous savage raids, devastating the countryside, and laying siege to the cities, even to Khilāṭ. In Jumādā I 626 H his siege of Khilāṭ culminated in its capture and destruction. Jalāl al-Dīn was now a very serious threat to the Ayyūbids.

Reluctantly, al-Kāmil concurred with al-Ashraf that the Khwārizmian troops were now a major problem and had to be dealt with by force. The bulk of the Ayyūbid force was raised by al-Ashraf, who was able to effect an alliance with the Rūm Seljūqids. The decisive battle took place at Yasi Chimen, 27 Ramaḍān 627 H, where Jalāl al-Dīn was defeated. Before he could reorganize, a new Mongol force attacked. Jalāl al-Dīn Mingburni fled the Mongols in 628 H, but was killed in an obscure village by a Kurdish peasant.

A joint expedition by al-Kāmil and al-Ashraf was undertaken in 629 H against the ruler of Āmid and Ḥiṣn-Kayfā, al-Mas'ūd Mawḍūd. By early 630 H the Ayyūbid forces had taken the cities, which were assigned to al-Ṣāliḥ Najm al-Dīn Ayyūb. Ayyūbid control over Ḥiṣn-Kayfā continued after the disappearance of the rest of the empire and, with the apparent consent of the Ilkhānids, the Ayyūbids continued to mint their own dirhems.

al-Ashraf seems to have lost interest in Armenia and al-Kāmil was too far off to protect it. His lieutenant in Āmid, Ḥiṣn-Kayfā and Mayāfāriqīn, al-Ṣāliḥ Najm al-Dīn Ayyūb, did not have enough power to keep out foreign invaders, and the Rūm Seljūq Sulṭān captured it without encountering much resistance. But he found the province so badly ruined that he was compelled to bring in livestock, grain seed and other basic necessities.

When all the Ayyūbid princes returned to their provinces after the campaign against the Khwārizmshāh, al-Kāmil found his country in a depressed and unstable economic state. The globular dirhem—in the chronicles the rather ambiguous term 'round dirhem' is used—of the 622 H reform was so unpopular that a decision to withdraw it from circulation was made. However, it continued to circulate; and the silver coinage was not improved, because of a lack of bullion. At the same time, the black dirhems circulated in great numbers. According to a source cited by Gottschalk (p. 210), the rate of exchange between the globular dirhem and the normal flan *nuqrah*—which, to my mind, was the normal-size flan Syrian silver dirhem of high silver content—was fixed at 7 to 1.

News of the Rūm Seljūq conquest of Armenia reached Cairo around the end of 630 H. In spite of the fact that neither al-Kāmil nor al-Ashraf had the means to restore Armenia after the Mongol devastation, they felt that Kayqubād had to be removed from the area, and so they decided to conduct a punitive expedition against him. It is possible that al-Kāmil dreamed of a huge Ayyūbid Empire incorporating Asia Minor too. al-Kāmil started the campaign into Asia Minor, leading his troops in person; he left Egypt under the governorship of his second son, al-ʿĀdil II, whom he also appointed heir to the throne.

When the Ayyūbid troops started to advance, all the 16 reigning Ayyūbid princes were in al-Kāmil's camp. This great army marched through the province of Aleppo, past Manbij to Tall Bāshir, but found the commanding mountain passes leading north well fortified and heavily manned. The Ayyūbid forces were not equipped to attack such formidable strongholds. There were also difficulties in the high command, and the unusual unity displayed by the princes at the beginning of the campaign came to an end. Morale was low and after a few unfavourable skirmishes, al-Kāmil decided on a new plan. At the invitation of the ruler of Kharput, al-Kāmil sent a strong detachment to join him. This force was thoroughly beaten by the Rūm Seljūqids and Kharput fell to Kayqubād's troops. This event brought al-Kāmil's expedition to an end.

The Jazīrah was now devoid of Ayyūbid military forces and the Rūm Seljūq armies marched against al-Ruhā, Ḥarrān and Raqqah. al-Ruhā tried to resist, but was stormed and sacked with great cruelty. After this incident the two other cities immediately capitulated. Āmid, which was also invested, resisted successfully, but Suwaydāʾ fell into the hands of the invaders. When, at the end of 632 H, al-Kāmil received the news of the Rūm Seljūq advance through the Jazīrah, he hurried through Syria, crossed the Euphrates, fell on the Seljūqs, and recaptured all the lost territories. Then he invested his son, al-Ṣāliḥ Najm al-Dīn Ayyūb, with the whole of the Jazīrah.

We have seen that, at the beginning of the campaign against the Rūm Seljūqids, all the Ayyūbid princes had rallied under al-Kāmil's leadership. The failure of the military operations was serious, but its consequences were rapidly repaired. The breach between the princes, which caused the campaign to collapse, was not really serious and did not mean lasting alienation. Even the relationship between al-Kāmil and al-Ashraf became quite cordial, although the Egyptian sultan's prolonged visit in Damascus with his troops and numerous retinue weighed heavily on al-Ashraf's budget. However, when at a later date al-Ashraf tried to obtain compensation for the large loss of revenue caused by the transfer of his dominions in the Jazīrah to al-Ṣāliḥ Ayyūb, and when he also requested reimbursement for expenses incurred during the stay of al-Kāmil's army in Damascus, al-Kāmil bluntly refused to pay. al-Ashraf was deeply offended and the events that followed quickened their mutual alienation.

The prince of Aleppo, al-ʿAzīz Muḥammad, suddenly died in Rabīʿ I 634 H and left the throne to his seven-year-old son, al-Nāṣir Yūsuf II. The newly instituted Regency Council requested that al-Kāmil confirm al-Nāṣir Yūsuf. The request was granted under the condition that al-Kāmil could choose the commander of the Aleppo army, who at the same time should be the prince's tutor or *atabek.* This would have terminated the regency and drawn Aleppo under the direct tutelage of al-Kāmil. Neither the Regency Council nor al-Kāmil gave way and finally the council decided to break with al-Kāmil. al-Kāmil's manoeuvre angered the other Ayyūbid princes, who felt their own independence threatened, and an anti-al-Kāmil league was formed. Its members were al-Ashraf, al-Mujāhid Shirkūh of Ḥimṣ, and al-Muẓaffar Maḥmūd of Ḥamāh, who joined it reluctantly and under great pressure. Some time during the development of this general discontent al-Ashraf approached the Rūm Seljūqid, Sulṭān Kayqubād; and, although the latter died during the negotiations, his son, Kaykhusraw II, agreed to help the allies with all his available resources.

The only Ayyūbid prince who hesitated to join one or the other of the two factions was al-Nāṣir Dā'ūd of Karak; but as al-Kāmil promised him Damascus and as al-Ashraf had deserted him earlier, he took al-Kāmil's side. The news of al-Nāṣir Dā'ūd's alliance with the Egyptian camp caused al-Ashraf to strengthen his pact with Kaykhusraw and Aleppo. In an exchange of messages al-Kāmil and al-Ashraf challenged each other to respect their respective rights and privileges. However, when al-Kāmil's envoys reached Damascus, al-Ashraf was already gravely ill; he died on 4 Muḥarram 635 H. [The date of al-Ashraf's death was mistakenly advanced by Zambaur to 634 H, based on the erroneous reading of the date on a dirhem (BMC, IX, No. 437e).]

As al-Ashraf Mūsā had no male heir, he had appointed his brother, al-Ṣāliḥ Ismāʿīl of Buṣrā, to succeed him on the throne of Damascus. al-Ṣāliḥ Ismāʿīl had no trouble in establishing himself in Damascus and took immediate steps to strengthen his position as leader of the Syrian faction of the Ayyūbid clan. al-Mujāhid Shirkūh of Ḥimṣ and the regent princess of Aleppo recognized his leadership, but al-Muẓaffar Maḥmūd of Ḥamāh preferred to acknowledge al-Kāmil as his sovereign.

When the news of al-Ashraf's death reached him, al-Kāmil lost no time mustering his troops and, in early 635 H, left Cairo at the head of his army for Damascus. He was accompanied by his nephew, al-Nāṣir Dā'ūd, and was joined *en route* by two sons of al-ʿĀdil I who had deserted the Syrian alliance. On the other hand, Ḥimṣ and Aleppo sent reinforcements to Damascus. The city was duly besieged, and with a cold winter and food and fuel running out, al-Ṣāliḥ Ismāʿīl surrendered. He gave up his newly acquired principality and received Buṣrā, Baʿalbak and the Biqā'. al-Kāmil entered Damascus on 19 Jumādā I 635 H.

Ḥimṣ, an ally of al-Ṣāliḥ Ismāʿīl's, surrendered as soon as it felt the threat of al-Kāmil's armies, but Aleppo decided to resist with the help of the Rūm Seljūqs. Dirhems of 635 and 636 H, on which

Kaykhusraw is named as overlord, attest this alliance. The unexpected demise of al-Kāmil on 21 Rajab 635 H prevented further hostilities.

al-Kāmil was the recognized lord of Damascus only during his last days, but throughout his sultanate the mint of that city struck silver and copper in his name. The right of *sikka* belonged, by tradition, to the head of the family. In Syria only the great northern principality of Aleppo retained its own right of *sikka*, but it also had al-Kāmil's name engraved on its coins, as well as that of the local lord. Only during the period of alliance with the Rūm Seljūqid sultan was the latter's name displayed as the overlord.

In the Jazīrah al-Kāmil issued silver in Ḥarrān, al-Ruhā and Mayāfāriqīn, but only a few dirhems have survived. Copper coins were struck in his name in Qal'at Ja'bar over a longer period, in Niṣibīn beginning with 631 H, and in Ḥarrān. There are silver coins of al-Ashraf from Ḥarrān, from 617 and 618 H, before al-Kāmil seized the city from his brother. al-Muẓaffar Ghāzī began using the mint of Mayāfāriqīn when he became governor, but took care to include the names of al-Kāmil, the head of the empire, and al-Ashraf, his immediate overlord, on the copper coins. The rare surviving dirhems of Khilāṭ bear the name of al-Ashraf, but the copper *fulūs* of 618 H show the protocol of the new local governor, al-Muẓaffar Shihāb al-Dīn Ghāzī.

Immediately after al-Kāmil's death his son, al-'Ādil Sayf al-Dīn II, became Sulṭān of Egypt and the nominal overlord of the empire. In Damascus, however, the Council of Regency, constituted by the local notables, elected al-Jawād Yūnus, al-Kāmil's nephew, as governor of the city, after much haggling and prolonged and complicated negotiations. Jawād Yūnus proved himself incapable, rapacious and cruel; and he rapidly became unpopular. When he tried to detach Damascus from the central power and make himself independent, al-'Ādil II decided to remove him from his post. In order to escape al-'Ādil's wrath, Jawād hurriedly exchanged Damascus for Sinjār and other territories in the Jazīrah held by al-Ṣāliḥ Ayyūb. In Rajab 636 H al-Ṣāliḥ Ayyūb entered Damascus. For the first time in Ayyūbid history silver coins were struck by the ruler of Damascus without mentioning his overlord—in this case, al-'Ādil II.

al-Ṣāliḥ Ayyūb soon became involved in a power struggle for the sultanate with his younger brother, al-'Ādil II, ruler of Egypt. His initial successes ended in failure. While he marched toward Cairo with a large but non-integrated military force, his uncle, al-Ṣāliḥ Ismā'īl, seized the largely undefended city of Damascus and annexed it to his domains in Central Syria. al-Ṣāliḥ Ismā'īl followed the precedent of al-Ṣāliḥ Ayyūb and issued dirhems in his own name only. Specimens exist for the years 637, 638, 639, 640 and 641 H. In the meantime, contingents of al-Ṣāliḥ Ayyūb's army, hearing of the capture of Damascus, began to desert, leaving him relatively isolated. He sought refuge with al-Nāṣir Dā'ūd of Karak, who, however, imprisoned him.

After seven months of captivity al-Ṣāliḥ Ayyūb reached a mutual understanding with al-Nāṣir Dā'ūd and, at the head of a small army, they set out for Egypt, hoping to surprise al-'Ādil II. However, in Ghazzah they suddenly found themselves trapped between al-'Ādil's Egyptian forces and his Syrian allies arriving at their rear. Even worse, each one of al-'Ādil's armies was much larger than the entire army of al-Karak. The two princes escaped and fled to al-Karak. When al-Ṣāliḥ Ayyūb reached Nablus, he received the astonishing news that al-'Ādil's own armies had rebelled, dethroned him, and invited al-Ṣāliḥ Ayyūb to occupy the throne of Egypt. In Dhū al-Hijjah 637 H al-Ṣāliḥ Ayyūb entered Cairo.

In 640 H it became evident to al-Ṣāliḥ Ismā'īl that his nephew in Egypt was determined to take Damascus. Worried, he tried to revive the Syrian alliance against Egypt; when he met with little success, he started negotiations with the Crusaders in Acre. His dirhems of 640 and 641 H show that he also had dealings with Kaykhusraw of Asia Minor, as they have Kaykhusraw's name engraved on them.

When al-Ṣāliḥ Ismā'īl's efforts to constitute an efficient defence pact were fruitless, he accepted al-Ṣāliḥ Ayyūb's sovereignty. One Damascus dirhem for 641 H shows al-Ṣāliḥ Ayyūb's protocol only; several others display al-Ṣāliḥ Ayyūb's full protocol in the place of honour and al-Ṣāliḥ Ismā'īl's name after the caliphal protocol on the reverse. This understanding lasted only two months, however; then uncle and nephew quarrelled again and there was no more reconciliation. al-Ṣāliḥ Ayyūb's name was dropped from the Damascus coin during the remainder of 641 and through 642 and 643 H.

al-Ṣāliḥ Ayyūb was now finally determined to put an end to his uncle's scheming and intriguing. The Egyptian army set out to invest Damascus and the city fell after a short siege in Jumādā II 643 H. Dirhems and copper *fulūs* of an entirely new design were then issued in Damascus by al-Ṣāliḥ Ayyūb, who then emphasized the new political arrangement. Under al-Ṣāliḥ Ayyūb, Damascus lost its independence and became, a few years before the fall of the empire, an integral part of a unified, centralized administration.

The new sultan imposed his authority on nearly all the still-ruling princes during the following years and annexed Transjordan to his direct administration so that practically only Aleppo remained independent. In 645 H al-Nāṣir Yūsuf, apprehensive that al-Ṣāliḥ had designs on Aleppo too, annexed Ḥimṣ as a preventive move. Although the Egyptian sultan protested, Aleppo was allowed to retain Ḥimṣ. al-Ṣāliḥ Ayyūb faced a more direct threat to his throne from the Crusaders.

When news of the invasion of Egypt by St. Louis and his Crusaders reached him, al-Ṣāliḥ Ayyūb was already very ill. He travelled to the Nile Delta in order to direct the military operations in person, but died in his camp on 15 Sha'bān 647 H. During the next several days his death was kept secret until the Crusaders were routed by his troops. Then his son, al-Mu'aẓẓam Tūrānshāh, was hastily summoned from his residence at Ḥiṣn-Kayfā. He arrived in Damascus late in Ramaḍān and was proclaimed Sulṭān the next day. He remained there three weeks, was persuaded to proceed on to Egypt, and finally arrived in Manṣūra after another month. He was, however, present when the Frankish army, totally crushed, surrendered and the French King Louis IX was taken captive. Tūrānshāh speedily alienated the Egyptian Mamlūk amīrs by his rudeness and by favouring his own courtiers, which was part of his plan to establish his own authority. When he began to threaten the Egyptian nobles personally, rebellion broke out and he was murdered at the end of Muḥarram 648 H. With his assassination Ayyūbid rule of Egypt ceased; many authorities date the end of the Ayyūbid Empire from this time.

The year of 647 H saw an important numismatic event: on the Damascus silver of that year al-Ṣāliḥ Ayyūb used the title of *al-Sulṭān al-Malik*. His son, al-Mu'aẓẓam Tūrānshāh, also adopted this new exalted protocol on his own silver struck in Damascus. Interestingly, both father and son refrained from using the title of 'Sulṭān' on their Ḥamāh coinage.

After al-Mu'aẓẓam Tūrānshāh's untimely death the Egyptian amīrs elected al-Ṣāliḥ Ayyūb's widow, Shajār al-Durr, to the throne and Egypt thus became a Mamlūk kingdom. The throne of Syria, on the other hand, remained vacant; and in order to save the remaining portion of the Ayyūbid Empire, the Kurdish nobles in Damascus invited the only possible candidate, al-Nāṣir

Yūsuf of Aleppo, to assume the leadership. The delighted prince of Aleppo hastened to accept the invitation that made him the sovereign of the whole of Syria. al-Manṣūr Muḥammad II of Ḥamāh became his vassal and al-Mughīth ʿUmar of al-Karak also recognized his sovereignty. When al-Nāṣir Yūsuf began to strike currency in Damascus in 648 H, it was on the traditional lines of the Syrian silver coinage.

In that same year two Mamlūk regiments, who had deserted Egypt, made their submission to al-Nāṣir Yūsuf. He now felt strong enough to challenge the Egyptians, but lacked the skill to act resolutely. This most opportune period, when the Mamlūks were not yet in a strong position, passed and the succeeding years were spent in half-hearted political and military experiments that failed to subdue Egypt. In 652 H al-Nāṣir Yūsuf married a Rūm Seljūqid princess, but his new ally, the Rūm Seljūq sultan, was now too weak to be of any significant use. The shadow of the roving Ilkhānid Mongols, who by now had occupied Persia and were already foraying through Armenia and the Jazīrah to Asia Minor, loomed large in the minds of the Muslim princes west of Persia.

In 656 H the Mongols conquered Baghdad, assassinated the caliph and his male relatives, and established themselves firmly in ʿIrāq. They began the siege of Mayāfāriqīn in 656 H, but with a relatively small force. After one and a half years its prince, al-Kāmil Muḥammad II, was killed with the garrison and the Ilkhānid army overran the entire Jazīrah and Syria. Aleppo had already fallen to the main Mongol army under Hūlāgū. The city resisted for a short time only and then surrendered. For having resisted, however, it was made to suffer a terrible blood bath, in accordance with Mongol custom. The citadel surrendered soon afterward.

al-Nāṣir Yūsuf fled to Egypt in sheer terror and the Mamlūk Sulṭān Quṭuz agreed to combat the Mongols. However, the clash with the Ilkhānid invaders was postponed. The Khāqān Mangū had died and Hūlāgū, learning this and that his two brothers were quarrelling over the inheritance, suddenly left for Mongolia to see that his own interests did not suffer from the family disagreement. al-Nāṣir Yūsuf, not trusting the Mamlūks, decided to leave Egypt.

In the meantime, the Mongol armies, left behind under the command of a general, captured nearly all of Syria, except al-Karak whose lord, al-Mughīth ʿUmar, voluntarily submitted to them. al-Nāṣir Yūsuf arrived as a fugitive with all his family and his retinue near al-Karak, where al-Mughīth persuaded him to submit to Hūlāgū. He then went to Tabriz, where he was well received by the Ilkhānid chief. However, when the news of the disastrous defeat suffered by the Mongols at ʿAin Jālūt, at the hands of Quṭuz and his general Baybars, reached Hūlāgū and the Mamlūks in Tabriz, al-Mughīth accused al-Nāṣir Yūsuf of treachery and spying and had him and his entire retinue massacred (Shawwāl 658 H).

As already mentioned, the last prince of Mayāfāriqīn, al-Kāmil Muḥammad II, committed the mistake—unpardonable in Mongol eyes—of resisting. There was a terrible devastation throughout the entire province of the Jazīrah. The prince of the least significant branch of the once-powerful Ayyūbid dynasty, al-Muwaḥḥid ʿAbdullāh, was the only Ayyūbid to understand the immensity of the disaster brought upon them by the Mongols. He acted swiftly and diplomatically. There is no record of how he managed to have his submission accepted by the Mongols, but the fact is that he and his direct successors were allowed to keep their small principality of Ḥiṣn-Kayfā, which consisted of the castle, some lands around it with a number of villages, and the small town of Hīzān, a short distance to the north-east. al-Muwaḥḥid ʿAbdullāh's reign, successful in spite of the

Mongol invasion, is attested by a handful of silver dirhems on which his own name and that of his Mongol overlord are mentioned. The principality of Ḥiṣn-Kayfā survived for 200 years, finally surrendering to the Ottomans in 866 H (AD 1461).

Last but not least, a remote province, administered by a branch of the Ayyūbids, should be mentioned. The Yemen had been conquered by one of Saladin's brothers (Tūrānshāh), administered by another, and passed on to his successors. Later the Ayyūbid ruler, al-Kāmil, concerned himself with it. The last prince, Mas'ūd Yūsuf, left the government in the hands of his able major-domo, who made himself independent and founded the dynasty of the Rasūlids.

GENEALOGICAL TABLES

I. THE HEIRS OF SHĀDHĪ IBN MARWĀN

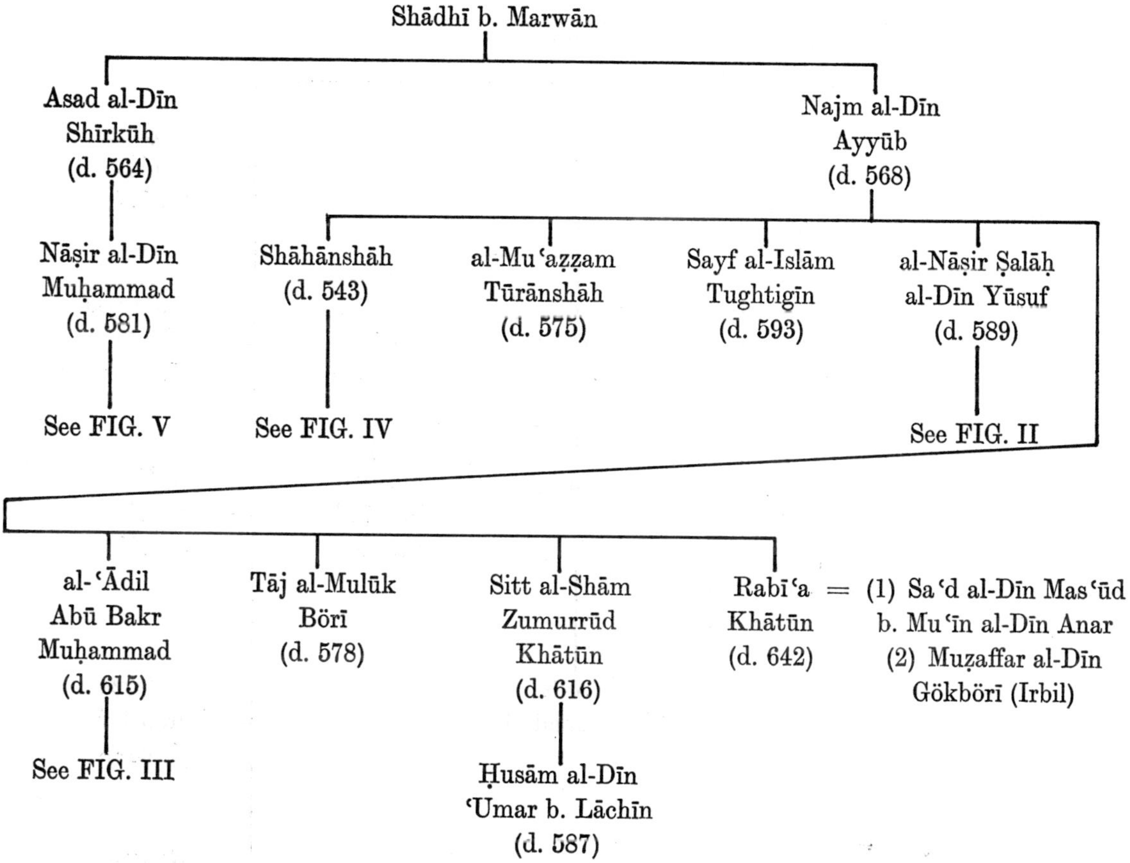

II. THE HOUSE OF SALADIN

- Shādhī b. Marwān
  - Najm al-Dīn Ayyūb (d. 568)
    - al-Nāṣir Ṣalāḥ al-Dīn Yūsuf (d. 589)
      - al-Afḍal ʿAlī (d. 622)
      - al-ʿAzīz Uthmān (d. 595)
        - al-Manṣūr Muḥammad (dep. 596)
      - al-Ẓāhir Ghāzī (d. 613)
        - al-ʿAzīz Muḥammad (d. 634)
          - Ghāzīya Khātūn = Kaykhusraw II (Rum Seljukids)
          - al-Nāṣir Yūsuf (d. 658)
            - al-ʿAzīz Muḥammad II
          - al-Ẓāhir Ghāzī II (d. 658)
        - al-Ṣāliḥ Aḥmad (d. 650)
      - al-Ẓāfir Khiḍr (d. 627)
      - al-Mu'ayyad Masʿūd (d. 606)
      - al-Ẓāhir Dāwūd (d. 632)
      - al-Muʿaẓẓam Tūrānshāh (d. 658)
      - Nuṣrat al-Dīn

III. THE HOUSE OF AL-'ĀDIL

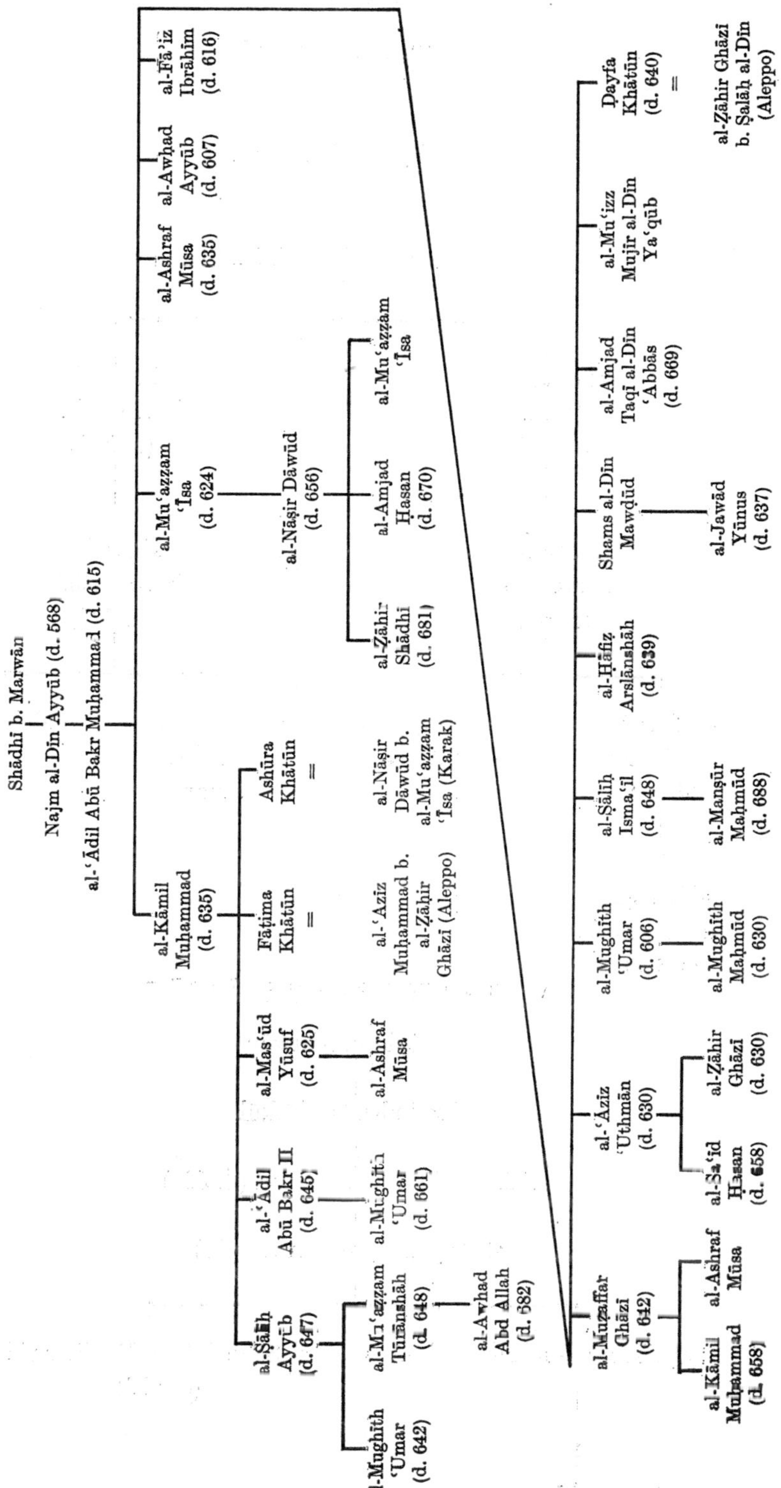

IV. THE HOUSE OF SHĀHĀNSHĀH

- Shādhī b. Marwān
  - Najm al-Dīn Ayyūb
    - Shāhānshāh (d. 543)
      - Taqī al-Dīn ʿUmar (d. 587)
        - al-Manṣūr Muḥammad (d. 617)
          - al-Muẓaffar Maḥmūd (d. 642)
            - al-Manṣūr Muḥammad II (d. 683)
          - al-Nāṣir Kiliç-Arslān
      - ʿIzz al-Dīn Farrukhshāh (d. 578)
        - al-Amjad Bahrāmshāh (d. 627)
          - al-Muẓaffar Taqī al-Dīn ʿUmar
          - al-Saʿid

V. THE HOUSE OF SHĪRKŪH

- Shādhī b. Marwān
  - Asad al-Dīn Shīrkūh
    - Nāṣir al-Dīn Muḥammad (d. 581)
      - al-Mujāhid Shīrkūh (d. 637)
        - al-Manṣūr Ibrāhīm (d. 644)
          - al-Ashraf Mūsa (d. 662)
        - al-Ṣāliḥ Nūr al-Dīn Ismaʿīl (d. 658)

POST-647 H EGYPTIAN COINAGE

The assassination of al-Mu'aẓẓam Tūrānshāh, in Muḥarram 648 H, brought to an end effective Ayyūbid rule in Egypt. The conspirators had acted for their own personal ends and political power was now in the hands of the Mamlūks. However, some semblance of Ayyūbid rule persisted and is apparent in certain post-647 H Egyptian issues. The issues of Shajār al-Durr, al-Ṣāliḥ Ayyūb's widow, and those of Aybak, her subsequent husband, are clearly Mamlūk, although references to the Ayyūbid, al-Ṣāliḥ Ayyūb are to be found on their coinage.

A more complex situation obtained with the coins minted in the name of al-Ashraf Mūsā II, the son of al-Mas'ūd Yūsuf, the last Ayyūbid ruler of Yemen. al-Ashraf Mūsā, six years old at the time, was placed on the Egyptian throne in mid-648 H by Aybak to placate popular feeling and in response to Syrian pressure for an Ayyūbid sovereign. Aybak held power, but some Egyptian coins were struck with inscriptions exclusively in al-Ashraf Mūsā's name (649 and 650 H). At the end of 651 H, Aybak deposed the young prince and sent him into exile. Then in 652 H, Aybak issued coins inscribed in the name of the deceased Ayyūbid, al-Ṣāliḥ Ayyūb. Later that year Aybak started minting gold and silver issues in his own name, although he refrained from removing al-Ṣāliḥ Ayyūb's protocol from the coins.

The Egyptian issues of 649, 650 and 652 H that have Ayyūbid inscriptions have been excluded from this Catalogue. They are Mamlūk issues, regardless of their specific inscriptions.

THE RIGHT OF COINAGE OR *SIKKA*

The right to issue coinage was exercised on two different levels in the Ayyūbid Empire. The overlord, sultan or head of the family was entitled to strike coins in his hereditary principality and also in many important cities of his relatives' domains. This right is what I have called the imperial *sikka*. In addition, some important princes had the right to issue coins in their own names. Various degrees of authority existed regarding the extent of this privilege. One prince was permanently entitled to strike silver and copper in the capital of his province (Aleppo); another was allowed to produce silver and copper, or copper only in his domains in al-Jazīrah, although he was officially endowed with Damascus too. Thus the principality of Damascus (Central Syria) belonged to Prince al-Mu'aẓẓam 'Īsā, but its right of *sikka* fell to al-'Ādil I.

Immediately after the first partition of the empire following Saladin's death, al-Afḍal was recognized as head of the clan, but his personal fief was restricted to Damascus and Central Syria, where he issued silver dirhems. As mentioned already, Damascus even at that early stage probably enjoyed a special status because, since in 590 H, al-'Azīz 'Uthmān, as Sulṭān of Egypt, and already head of the empire, struck dirhems in Damascus concurrently with those of al-Afḍal. Some of the mints, such as Mayāfāriqīn in eastern Jazīrah, Ḥarrān, al-Ruhā, Āmid in the Jazīrah, and Akhlāt in Armenia, produced silver. Manbij, Qal'at Ja'bar and the local mint of the princes of Ḥamāh produced only copper.

The minting of gold was the prerogative of the sultans of Egypt who, at the same time, were overlords of the empire. They struck gold first in both Cairo and Alexandria and, after al-Kāmil Muḥammad I, only in Cairo. Saladin, however, did issue a pale gold coin in Damascus in 583 H, probably to celebrate his brilliant victory over the Crusaders at Hattīn near Tiberias. A few brittle, pale gold coins were issued in the Yemen, freshly conquered by Saladin's brother, Tūrānshāh, and administered by him in Saladin's name. The first coin which has survived is dated 569 H and bears the name of the governor, Tūrānshāh, but not that of Saladin. It took only a short time for the evidence of this unauthorized practice to reach Saladin. The disappearance of Tūrānshāh's name from the following year's issues, replaced by Saladin's protocol, suggests that the latter must have reprimanded his brother for this show of independence.

The coinages of the semi-independent or vassal princes in most cases bear the name of the overlord, the recognized head of the family, on one side or the other. The suzerain's name may be of the same size as that of his vassal or smaller and is even omitted occasionally from the coin. This omission seems to have been ignored, except in troubled times when tributary princes thought their overlord pursued an aggressive, expansive policy that threatened their frontiers, their power, or even their existence. Then they did not shrink from a defensive alliance, not only among themselves, but also with a foreign power such as the Rūm Seljūqid sultan of Asia Minor. The visible effect of such an alliance was the engraving of the foreign sovereign's name as overlord on the dirhems instead of that of the Ayyūbid sultan.

Some of the great princes of the main branch, who were lords of large provinces in the Jazīrah, struck coinage (mainly copper) in the capital of their domain. They sometimes changed their personal residence at a later stage and left a relative at the old capital as their representative. The great prince may have started silver coinage at his new capital while his lieutenant continued the striking of copper in his own name, but with his immediate overlord's and the supreme lord's names added (al-Ashraf Mūsā and al-Muẓaffar Ghāzī). Members of the family who owned less important territories or small fiefs—Ḥimṣ, Buṣrā, Ba'albak, Banyās, al-Karak, etc.—never received the right to issue their own coins.

The Yemen owed its special standing to the fact that it was too far away for effective political interference by the Egyptian sultans. Apart from the already-mentioned ephemeral gold issue, it produced a steady, abundant, good quality silver coinage of a characteristic design, which varied only at the beginning.

Ḥiṣn-Kayfā, on the other hand, remained under Artuqid rule until 629 H, when it became an Ayyūbid stronghold. However, its mint did not operate again until 658 H when, during the Mongol invasion, its Ayyūbid prince struck dirhems as a vassal of Hūlāgū. After the Ilkhānids retired from the Jazīrah, this tiny principality developed a multifarious and prolific coinage that lasted a long time.

'OBVERSE' AND 'REVERSE'

Jere L. Bacharach and Henry A. Awad, in their very commendable article on 'The Problem of the Obverse and the Reverse in Islamic Numismatics', discuss the literary and numismatic evidence, with emphasis on the few published surviving coin dies, in order to decide whether there are any constant elements to indicate the obverse and the reverse. These authors observe that neither medieval historians nor modern numismatists provide a consistent definition. It is widely accepted, however, by modern scholars that the side with the date and mint was struck from the upper or trussel die; whereas, the lower, pile or anvil die served for the side with the Kalima. The name of the caliph, or that of the local ruler, is not necessarily linked with the Kalima, but may appear on either of the two sides—a rather confusing fact. The authors conclude that, for practical purposes, 'The only solution is for the scholars to define obverse and reverse in terms of the priorities they consider most important . . .'.

I had already anticipated this advice in *The Coinage of the Mamlūk Sultans of Egypt and Syria* (1964), in which I regarded the obverse as the side on which the name of the ruler was placed. On the anonymous copper my guideline was to seek out the side on which the legend started.

I believe that the same rule should apply to the coinage of the Ayyūbids. The Kalima may have been a matter of foremost importance to the die cutter, a 'true believer', but to the modern numismatist the identification of the dynasty and the individual ruler comes first, then the mint name and the date and, in third place only, the religious legends with the sectarian formulas or special Koranic verses preferred by one dynasty or another. The placing of the caliph's name on all issues of local dynasties is also of subsidiary importance as, in the case of the Ayyūbids, the mention of the pontiff's name became a mere gesture of politeness.

Therefore, regardless of which side of the coins was struck by the trussel and which by the anvil die, for the Ayyūbid issues the side with the ruler's name will be designated as the obverse. On coins struck by local princes the obverse is regarded as the side on which their own name is written, even when an overlord is mentioned. To this rule there is only one exception: when al-Ṣāliḥ Ismā'īl of Damascus submitted to al-Ṣāliḥ Ayyūb in 641 H he struck silver with his overlord's full protocol in the place of honour in the obverse area, and that of the caliph on the reverse. He omitted his own name altogether. For the next issue he added his name, but only very discreetly, inscribing it on the reverse at the end of the caliphal protocol. On certain copper coins the name of the prince (obverse) and that of a caliph (reverse) are inscribed; on some others only that of the prince, in which case, the name starts on the obverse and ends on the reverse.

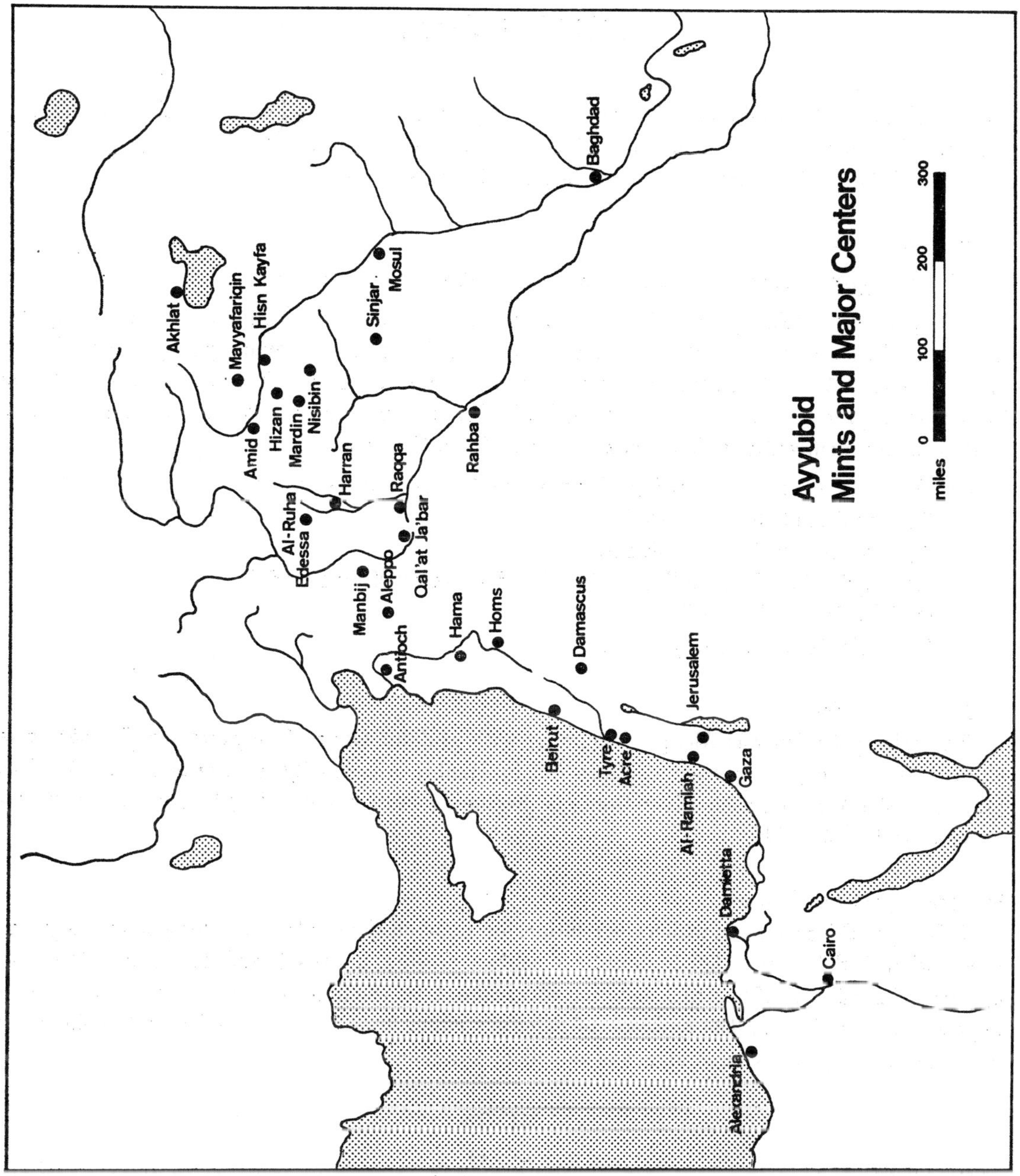
Ayyubid
Mints and Major Centers
0
100
200
300
miles
Akhlat
Mayyafariqin
Hisn Kayfa
Amid
Hizan
Mardin
Nisibin
Sinjar
Mosul
Baghdad
Harran
Al-Ruha
Edessa
Raqqa
Qal'at Ja'bar
Rahba
Manbij
Aleppo
Antioch
Hama
Homs
Damascus
Beirut
Tyre
Acre
Jerusalem
Al-Ramlah
Gaza
Damietta
Cairo
Alexandria

MINT NOTES

Twenty-eight Ayyūbid mints are known: two in Egypt, five in Syria, three in Palestine, eight in the Jazīrah, one in Lesser Armenia, one (fictive) in Arabia, two in the district of Ḥiṣn-Kayfā, and six in the Yemen. These mints belong in the following categories:

1. *Imperial Mints*

(*a*) *The Egyptian Mints*: Alexandria and Cairo; also Old Cairo (Miṣr).

(*b*) *Syrian Mints*: Aleppo, Ḥamāh, Ḥimṣ, Damascus. The Aleppo mint functioned as an imperial mint under Saladin and after 648 H, when Syria became part of the remaining Ayyūbid territories under al-Nāṣir Yūsuf. Damascus remained an imperial mint after Saladin's death, when it started to issue coinage in the name of the sultan, beginning in 590 H. In addition, Afḍal struck silver in Damascus concurrently with the new Sulṭān al-ʻAzīz ʻUthmān.

(*c*) *Certain Mints in the Jazīrah* (under the direct control of the sultan):

(1) Ḥarrān in 586 H for Saladin;
(2) Niṣibīn in 578 H for Saladin;
(3) Mayāfāriqīn for Saladin, al-ʻĀdil I and al-Kāmil Muḥammad I;
(4) Ḥarrān for al-ʻĀdil I;
(5) Āmid for al-Ṣāliḥ Ayyūb, etc.

2. *Provincial Mints*

The principal mint was Aleppo, beginning with al-Ẓāhir Ghāzī. The princes of Ḥamāh were allowed to issue copper in their capitals and in Manbij occasionally, and once in Ḥarrān. The branch in the Yemen struck silver from the beginning until the last Ayyūbid governor left his province to the Rasūlids.

3. *Independent Local Issues*

Coinage of this nature, in which the relationship between the local ruler issuing the coinage and the overlord is deliberately left in doubt for political reasons, is exceptional. It occurs only on the dirhems of al-Ṣāliḥ Ismāʻīl struck between 635 and 641 H, when he was in open opposition to his nephew, al-Ṣāliḥ Ayyūb. The omission of Saladin's name from Tūrānshāh's first gold coin of the Yemen is not to be considered an act of rebellion, however.

MINTS

Egypt

ALEXANDRIA

Alexandria issued gold under Saladin, al-ʻĀdil I, al-Kāmil I, al-ʻĀdil II, and al-Ṣāliḥ Ayyūb. It struck irregular-shaped 'black' dirhems under Saladin and al-ʻĀdil I.

CAIRO

Cairo's main issue was in gold, of which there was a steady flow from the beginning of the dynasty until the death of al-Ṣāliḥ Ayyūb. Silver was in the form of black dirhems under Saladin as well as al-ʿĀdil I, although both sultans tried to improve the silver currency by introducing Syrian type, normal flan, round (*nuqrah*) dirhems, with a higher silver content. These sporadic attempts failed, probably because of the chronic shortage of silver bullion in Egypt. The black dirhems continued to be issued and circulated even under al-Kāmil Muḥammad I.

According to the historian al-Maqrīzī, al-Kāmil introduced a monetary reform in 622 H. This consisted of the production of the so-called 'round' dirhems, which were globular, irregular in diameter and weight, and sometimes even in shape. It was a fraudulent reform. My repeated chemical analysis of these globular dirhems has revealed that they were just as poor in silver content as the black dirhems. The Egyptian shortage of silver bullion was not resolved and globular dirhems continued to be minted up to the reign of al-Muʿaẓẓam Tūrānshāh, and even under the first Mamlūk, Shajār al-Durr. Earlier al-Ṣāliḥ Ayyūb made an attempt at the introduction of normal flan dirhems, but that too failed.

An important feature of the Egyptian coinage is the absence of copper from the Cairo (and Alexandria) mints. The only exception is a unique *fals* of the *black dirhem* type. However, several medieval Arab chronicles state that copper was used: they probably refer to much earlier issues that were still circulating. They also mention that al Kāmil ordered copper *fulūs* struck in Cairo in 622 H. There are no Kāmilī copper coins with the Cairo mint name, but there do exist *fulūs*, mintless and undated, which could be the copper coins mentioned by the chronicles.

On the other hand, we have a fairly large number of glass/paste jetons with the names of the ʿAbbāsid caliphs, al-Mustaḍī and al-Nāṣir. Some of them have the name of al-Kāmil, but not that of the caliph. The role of the glass/paste jetons, which I consider to be the direct continuation of the Fāṭimid glass or glass/paste jetons, is still debated. I believe that they served as a fiduciary currency.

MIṢR

The old mint of Miṣr (or Old Cairo) was revived by Saladin in 573 H and was also used by al-Kāmil I in 623 and 624 H for striking gold coins.

Greater Syria

ALEPPO

After Saladin's death in 589 H the province of Aleppo became a near-independent principality, with the right to issue silver and copper coins in the name of its ruling prince. Aleppo was assigned by Saladin to his son, al-Ẓāhir Ghāzī, and he and his direct descendants ruled over it until the empire was destroyed by the Ilkhānid Mongols in 658 H.

Many Aleppo dirhems display the name of the head of the dynasty, as well as that of the local prince. However, on other silver coins the sultan is not mentioned and on the half dirhems his name never appears. The last case may be due to the fact that there is not enough space on the small flan. The copper may or may not contain the overlord's protocol, but as it served only the needs of the local circulation, the political implications of the inscriptions are less important. The Aleppo dirhem was among the best quality silver coins at that time.

al-Ẓāhir Ghāzī's demise in 613 H was followed by a curious *posthumous* coinage. There were the regular issues of al-Ẓāhir's son, al-ʿAzīz Muḥammad, and then after 634 H the issues of his son, al-Nāṣir Yūsuf. However, from 614 H and concurrently with the normally inscribed coinage, silver dirhems were struck in the names of al-Ẓāhir Ghāzī and Caliph al-Nāṣir. Even the caliph's name was not changed after he died in 622 H.

The al-Ẓāhir *posthumous* dirhems could not have been struck at the official mint in Aleppo. The only explanation is that they were contemporary counterfeit money, probably manufactured at some Crusader mint. It is even possible that such forgeries were being made during al-Ẓāhir Ghāzī's lifetime. Dr. Michael Bates of the American Numismatic Society is of this opinion and has produced a very fine discussion of the problem (Bates, Miles Festschrift).

ḤAMĀH

Ḥamāh was usually ruled by a separate branch of Ayyūbid princes, but tended to be drawn into the political orbit of Aleppo. The numismatic evidence suggests that it was entitled to issue only locally valid copper coinage. However, it was also an imperial mint, in the sense that dirhems were issued there by several overlords of the empire.

ḤIMṢ

Ḥimṣ was an imperial mint. The local princes had no legal right to strike coins, however, not even copper ones.

DAMASCUS

Damascus was the capital of Central Syria and a mint of great importance. From the reign of Saladin until the death of al-Kāmil Muḥammad I, only the sultan of the Ayyūbid Empire was entitled to issue coins. Only silver and copper were struck in abundance, although gold was minted in Damascus in 583 H. Such was respect for the sultan's right of *sikka* that, although al-Muʿaẓẓam ʿĪsā and al-Ashraf Mūsā after him were the lords of Damascus and actually had the city in their possession, they never put their own names on the coins, but continued with the protocol of al-Kāmil Muḥammad.

Only after al-Kāmil's death did the nature of the inscriptions at the Damascus mint change. al-Ṣāliḥ Ismāʿīl, being ill disposed toward his nephews, al-ʿĀdil II and al-Ṣāliḥ Ayyūb, struck coins there in his own name. He did not even mention his overlord on the dirhems. The coin legends reflect the kaleidoscopic changes in the political situation. For example, in 641 H, when threatened by al-Ṣāliḥ Ayyūb, al-Ṣāliḥ Ismāʿīl solicited the alliance and protection of the Rūm Seljūqid, Kaykhusraw II, whose name appeared on the Damascus dirhems of that year. The alliance did not work because later, in 641 H, al-Ṣāliḥ Ismāʿīl was obliged to capitulate to al-Ṣāliḥ Ayyūb, whose protocol appeared on the obverse of the dirhems while that of al-Ṣāliḥ Ismāʿīl and the caliph was relegated to the reverse. In 644 H, when al-Ṣāliḥ Ismāʿīl lost Damascus to al-Ṣāliḥ Ayyūb's domain definitively, Damascus became an imperial mint once more.

In 648 H the prince of Aleppo, al-Nāṣir Yūsuf, accepted the invitation of the Damascus leaders and united northern Syria with the central province. He became the first and only Ayyūbid ruler to reign over Aleppo and Damascus at the same time. This reduced empire held out until al-Nāṣir Yūsuf was captured by the Ilkhānids in 658 H.

MANBIJ

The town of Manbij is situated in the province of Aleppo west of the Euphrates. East of it, on the west bank of the river, is the fortress of Jiṣr Manbij, which is, however, a mint in its own right, called Qal'at Najm (Gottschalk, p. 32). Manbij, among other places, was given to al-Muẓaffar Taqī al-Dīn 'Umar. His son, al-Manṣūr Muḥammad I, inherited the lands and struck copper coins in Manbij, some dated 595 H.

AL-RAMLAH

al-Ramlah, on the road from the Mediterranean to Jerusalem, was an important mint under the Umayyads and the 'Abbāsids when its name was synonymous with Filasṭīn. Afterwards the town lost its importance, the mint ceased to function, and it is not clear for what reason Saladin revived the mint for a unique copper issue. The gold dinar of 592 H, inscribed *Filasṭīn* (see below), may have been minted in al-Ramlah.

FILASṬĪN

A unique gold dinar of al-'Azīz 'Uthmān, struck in 592 H, has the mint name Filasṭīn, probably meaning al-Ramlah. The mint name on this coin is written in the same style as that of the latest Fāṭimid dinar struck in Filasṭīn, dated 459 H (cf. George C. Miles, *Fāṭimid Coins*, ANS-NNM (1951), p. 121).

GHAZZAH

Ghazzah (Gaza), near the Mediterranean coast, is the southernmost large city of Palestine. It had a long mint history in classical times and produced Umayyad copper coins, but later was inactive.

In 625 H a general redistribution of their possessions was negotiated by the Ayyūbid princes under the leadership of al-Kāmil Muḥammad I. During and after the protracted negotiations that took place in Tall al-'Ajūl near Ghazzah, al-Kāmil had a new mint opened in Ghazzah, probably to underline the importance of current political events. The issues started in 624 H and continued until 625 H. After a lapse of ten years there was an issue in 635 H.

JAZĪRAH

ĀMID

Āmid, a suburb of which was called Diyār-Bakr and which is today known only by the name of Diyarbekir, was the chief town of the district of the same name. al-Ṣāliḥ Ayyūb, as governor from 629 until 636 H, struck copper coins there in 636 and 637 H. In 637 H he became governor of Damascus and left Āmid in the care of his son, Ghiyāth al-Dīn al-Mu'aẓẓam Tūrānshāh. Accordingly, the coinage of Āmid was engraved with al-Ṣāliḥ Ayyūb's protocol in 637 H also and Tūrānshāh was not even mentioned. Āmid's coinage consisted of copper, the last issue of which bore the name of al-Kāmil Muḥammad II ibn al-Muẓaffar Ghāzī (see Ḥiṣn-Kayfā).

ḤARRĀN

Ḥarrān belonged to the Begtekinid prince, Muẓaffar al-Dīn Gökbürī, Saladin's friend and ally, who in 586 H ceded it to Saladin. The Ayyūbid leader issued a copper *fals* in Ḥarrān—probably during the same year—but then gave the city to his favourite nephew, al-Muẓaffar Taqī al-Dīn ʿUmar I of Ḥamāh. ʿUmar died shortly afterward and his son, who inherited Ḥarrān with all his other possessions, continued to strike copper similar to those first issued by Saladin. After 589 H, al-ʿĀdil I chose Ḥarrān as his residence and issued coins there, first as governor of the Jazīrah and later as Lord of the Empire. After ʿĀdil's death his son, al-Ashraf Mūsā I, inherited the Jazīrah and struck coins in Ḥarrān, which once again became a provincial mint. When al-Kāmil started to strike silver and copper there, it was toward the end of his reign in his capacity as overlord of the Ayyūbid Empire. After his death the output of the mint declined and only occasional copper coins were minted; e.g. in 636 and 637 H by al-Ṣāliḥ Ayyūb when he was governor.

ḤĪZĀN

The small town of Ḥīzān, according to Yāqūt, stood near Saʿirt (the modern Isʿirt), north of Tall Fāfān, which is about 50 miles east of Ḥiṣn-Kayfā, of which it was a dependency. The two extant coins from the reign of al-ʿĀdil Sulaymān are in Istanbul.

ḤIṢN-KAYFĀ

Ḥiṣn-Kayfā was a strong fortress with a small town or large village at its foot and a few scattered stretches of land on the right or western bank of the Euphrates, between Mayāfāriqīn in the north and Niṣibīn in the south.

After the Mongol conquest and the destruction of the Ayyūbid Empire, Ḥiṣn-Kayfā became a prolific mint. Unfortunately, while numerous silver coins have been preserved, very few show a date and there are many blanks in the local history.

AL-RUHĀ

al-Ruhā, Edessa, was another well known and important centre in the Jazīrah, but only al-ʿĀdil I and al-Kāmil Muḥammad I used it as a mint for silver and copper.

SINJĀR

Though an important mint under the Sinjār branch of the Zengids, under the Ayyūbids it issued copper only during the reign of al-Ashraf Mūsā I.

QALʿAT JAʿBAR

This was a fortress situated on the west bank of the Euphrates, south-east of Aleppo and north-east of Ḥamāh. It was also called Jiṣr-Manbij. al-ʿĀdil I struck copper here in 601 H, as did al-Kāmil between 631 and 634 H.

MĀRDĪN

Mārdīn never belonged to the Ayyūbids. It was the seat of the Mārdīn branch of the Artuqids. However, after Saladin's resounding victory in 581 H, when he conquered practically all of the Jazīrah, the Artuqids of Mārdīn, in a state of panic, issued a purely Ayyūbid-style copper coin in Saladin's name. They discontinued the coinage the next year, however.

MAYĀFĀRIQĪN

Mayāfāriqīn was the administrative capital of the Jazīrah and its principal mint. The city fell to Saladin's armies in 581 H and he made its annexation official by a copper issue in the same year. Only one other copper *fals* of his is known and that is from the year 587 H. His brother, al-ʿĀdil, struck copper in Mayāfāriqīn as Lord of the Jazīrah from 591 until 595 H, and then again as sultan in certain subsequent years. At the same time he allowed his son, al-Awḥad Najm al-Dīn Ayyūb, whom he invested with the Jazīrah after he himself became sultan, to strike copper coins concurrently with his son. al-Awḥad did so from 599 until 605 H. After his demise his brother and successor in the Jazīrah, al-Ashraf Mūsā, continued to issue copper and examples are known for 608 and 612 H.

al-Muẓaffar Ghāzī, another son of al-ʿĀdil I, and then his own son, al-Kāmil Muḥammad II, continued the copper coinage in Mayāfāriqīn. Between 642 and 644 H al-Kāmil II was obliged to seek a protective alliance with Kaykhusraw II, the Rūm Seljūqid sultan, whose name was placed on the Mayāfāriqīn coins as overlord.

NIṢIBĪN

Niṣibīn, about halfway between Āmid in the north and Sinjār in the south, was conquered by Saladin as early as 577 H. A few months later he gave it to ʿImād al-Dīn Zengī II in exchange for Sinjār. Saladin struck very large copper coins engraved with his crowned bust in 578 H in Niṣibīn. Previous to Saladin's first issue, the Zengid, ʿImād al-Dīn, struck copper in Niṣibīn. After the 578 H Saladin issue, the coinage continued in ʿImād al-Dīn Zengī's name, and he did not even mention Saladin on the *fulūs*, in spite of the vassal/overlord relationship that existed between them.

Later Niṣibīn became, with most of the Jazīrah, the domain of al-Ashraf Mūsā. Neither he nor his successor, al-Ṣāliḥ Ismāʿīl, struck coins in this city; only al-Kāmil I, in 631 H, issued coinage there.

Armenia

KHILĀṬ OR AKHLĀṬ

The prolonged struggle for southern Armenia ended with the final capture of Khilāṭ by al-Awḥad Najm al-Dīn Ayyūb in 604 H. He issued silver in Khilāṭ between 604 and 607 H, when he died. His brother, al-Ashraf Mūsā, inherited not only the Jazīrah, but also the Province of Armenia, its capital Khilāṭ, and all the trouble which seemed to accompany its possession. Nevertheless, he managed to retain it until 617 H, when it was lost definitively. A few silver dirhems remain from this agitated corner of the Ayyubid Empire.

Arabia

MECCA

Fourteen gold dinars with the mint name Makkah (Mecca), struck in 594 H by al ʿAzīz ʿUthmān, are known to me. There is no historical *raison d'être* for these extraordinary coins, all of which have come from some dealer or occasional sources in Saʿūdi Arabia. The best explanation seems to be that they were issued by the Cairo mint as an offering to the holy shrine in Arabia and were probably conveyed there by one of the pilgrim caravans.

Yemen

TA'IZZ

A detailed description of this town, its location and other particulars, are given in George C. Miles' *The Ayyūbid Dynasty of the Yaman* (pp. 83–4). Silver coins of Tughtegīn, Ismā'īl ibn Tughtegīn, al-Nāṣir Ayyūb, and of Mas'ūd Yūsuf are known.

AL-DUMLŪWAH

A very rare silver coin struck at this mint has been described by Şerafettin Erel in *Nadir Birkaç Sikke*, I (1963), pp. 2–3. Another specimen is in the Archaeological Museum in Istanbul. This place is described by Yāqūt as a fortified castle in the Jabal Ṣulw or Jabal Mu'allas, built by the Zuray'ids. As the Zuray'ids were the lords of 'Adan, the castle cannot have been very far away.

RAYDAḤ

According to George Miles, the mint name Raydaḥ is clearly legible. He could not find such a town in the literature, the nearest one in spelling being Raydah [ريده], about 40 miles north and slightly west of Ṣan'ā'. The various aspects of this problem are discussed by Miles.

ZABĪD

The town of Zabīd still exists on the plain of the Tihāmah, about 25 kilometres from the coast. It was one of the prolific Yemeni mints issuing silver (28 existing) and some copper, of which one specimen is known.

ṢAN'Ā'

Notwithstanding its importance under the 'Abbāsids, and again as the capital of modern Yemen, Ṣan'ā' issued only a few silver coins under the Ayyūbids.

'ADAN

'Adan is, of course, the best-known city in the Yemen. Under the conquerors, Shams al-Dīn Tūrānshāh and his brother, Tughtegīn, it was also the only Yemeni Ayyūbid mint to issue gold, albeit of poor quality. Tughtegīn's son, Ismā'īl, reverted to the striking of silver and duly acknowledged his sovereign on the coinage.

METROLOGY

THE COINAGE: ITS WEIGHT AND FINENESS

GOLD

Gold currency under the Ayyūbids was struck almost exclusively in Egypt. The only exceptions were the 583 H dinar struck in Damascus by Saladin and the low-alloy gold issued in the Yemen by Saladin's brother, Tūrānshāh I, and soon discontinued. There is also a dinar of al-ʿAzīz ʿUthmān, ostensibly struck in Mecca in 594 H. No trace of a political event can be found to justify the actual setting up of an Ayyūbid mint in Mecca at this time, and it seems probable that the dinar was struck at the Cairo mint and shipped to the holy city with the yearly pilgrimage as a royal offering.

At the time Saladin overthrew the Fāṭimid caliphate, he became master of Egypt as the vassal and lieutenant of Maḥmūd ibn Zengī, the lord of Aleppo. From 567 until 569 H, Saladin issued gold on which only Maḥmūd ibn Zengī's name was inscribed. In arrangement and design these dinars were similar to the Fāṭimid dinars on which the legends were arranged in three concentric rows. After his overlord's death, Saladin made himself independent, and in 570 H he issued his first sovereign coinage. These dinars were similar to the first issue, except that Maḥmūd's name was replaced by that of Saladin.

After the death of the ʿAbbāsid caliph, al-Mustaḍī, in 575 H, a new series of dinars appeared. The name of the new caliph, al-Nāṣir, was engraved in the centre of the reverse, but instead of three, there were only two circular legends. This dinar became the prototype for the issues of Saladin's successors until his brother, al-ʿĀdil, introduced a new type with only one marginal legend and five to six horizontal lines in the obverse field, and four in the reverse. The inscriptions on all these coins were in *Kūfic* script. Only in 623 H was the style of writing changed to *Naskhi* script.

With the declining economy of the later Fāṭimids, the stocks of gold in Egypt began to diminish and Saladin inherited a serious shortage of bullion. Although there were still insufficient quantities of gold to enable Saladin to strike dinars every year, his policies contributed to the dwindling of the existing reserves. He was obliged repeatedly to send very large presents of gold treasure and many thousands of minted dinars as tribute to his liege-lord, Maḥmūd ibn Zengī. Later, when he was an independent sovereign, had started on the conquest of Syria and the Jazīrah and had initiated the wars against the Crusaders, Saladin replenished his coffers from the taxes levied in Egypt and so systematically drained that country of its wealth. Naturally, his army spent the sums drawn from Egypt for the purchase of food, fodder, arms and war machinery in Syria or in Mesopotamia.

As gold became scarcer, the weights of the individual gold coins began to vary, even more than in earlier periods. Many specimens were underweight, even under four grams, though coins of five or more grams were not exceptional. Consequently, the gold coins, although they continued to bear the denomination dinar, could not be traded by tale, but only by weight.

According to Ehrenkreutz, the gold crisis must have affected the economy during the initial period of Ayyūbid rule even more seriously than under the later Fāṭimids, as Saladin's dinars contain a lower percentage of fine gold than those of al-Musta'lī up to al-'Āḍid (see table below):

Distribution of the Examined Specimens
According to their Standard of Fineness

Degree of Purity	Fāṭimids (al-Musta'lī to al-'Āḍid)	Saladin	Ayyūbids (al-'Azīz to al-Kāmil)
%	%	%	%
100	79	—	11
99	10	5	7
98	11	2	5
97	3	5	2
96	8	6	4
95	2	6	4
94	3	2	1
93	2	—	2
92	—	1	—
91	3	3	—
90	1	1	—
Under 90	12	13	—

From A. S. Ehrenkreutz, 'The Crisis of the Dīnār in the Egypt of Saladin', *JAOS* 76 (1956), p. 181.

SILVER

Practically all the silver circulating in Egypt at the later stages of the Fāṭimid period consisted of those called *black dirhems* (*dirham aswad*), also called *dirhem waraq*. These were rough, uneven, small rectangles or squares of low silver content, the weight of which depended on the haphazard way the cold chisel of the flan cutter fell. This was the kind of silver coinage that Saladin inherited and which he continued to strike, as did his successors. Even al-Kāmil Muḥammad issued it, at least until the famous monetary reform of 622 H. According to Ibn Sa'īd al-Andalusī, a contemporary of al-Ṣāliḥ Ayyūb, the black dirhems were still circulating under this ruler, but their quality was poor (Hassanein Rabie, *The Financial System of Egypt* (Oxford, 1972), p. 184).

In Syria there was no shortage of silver and, in fact, the first dirhem struck by Saladin in Damascus dates from 571 H. It contains a high percentage of silver and has a pleasing design arranged on a normal-sized round flan. The weight of the Syrian dirhem, which was produced in great quantities each year, was based on that of the legal dirhem of 2·97 grams. A visible effort was made to conform to the weight of the theoretical dirhem. In Syria, where the basic currency was already the dirhem, the exchange rate between gold and silver was regulated without difficulty; and where gold was no longer minted, but only imported, there seems to have been no need for a monetary reform.

Gold, having become too scarce for general use in Egypt and Syria, lost its status as the currency standard and became only a commercial commodity. The silver dirhem standard of 2·97 grams took its place and was introduced in Egypt a few years after Saladin's accession. I accept Professor Rabie's view that the reform was carried out some time in 583 H, based upon his reference to a letter of that year sent by al-Fāḍil to Saladin, in which the success of the new silver coinage was praised.

To this literary document I can now add some numismatic evidence. In order to boost the value of the much-depreciated Egyptian silver, Saladin tried to introduce the normal-flan Syrian dirhem. The earliest preserved Cairo coin of this experiment is dated 585 H. For lack of the necessary bullion, the attempt to improve the Egyptian silver currency seems to have been abandoned; only one dirhem of 585 H and six of 586 H are known to have survived. I know of no further Cairo issues of the round-flan dirhem of normal size struck by Saladin. Unfortunately, no tests on the fineness of these coins have been undertaken.

All the normal-size, round-flan dirhems are called 'Nāṣirī' by Maqrīzī, including those which were issued after Saladin's death. But the designation 'Nāṣirī' should apply only to Saladin's dirhems and not to those struck by al-ʿĀdil, or even by al-Ṣāliḥ Ayyūb. To my mind the designation 'normal-size or round-flan dirhem' would be much more to the point. In addition, Maqrīzī's general term 'Nāṣirī' could be applied to the silver coins issued in Damascus or elsewhere.

To summarize: Saladin succeeded in shifting the monetary standard from the 4·25-gram gold dinar to the theoretically pure silver dirhem of 2·97 grams. In practice, the public still had to struggle with the problem of converting the value of the low silver content, oddly shaped *black dirhems* of uncertain weight to that of the high silver content *round-flan dirhem* of normal size and canonical weight.

The situation does not seem to have changed under Saladin's successors in Egypt. We find *black dirhems* struck by al-ʿAzīz ʿUthmān, al-Manṣūr Muḥammad, al-ʿĀdil I and al-Kāmil Muḥammad I. By 622 H the monetary situation had become so desperate that al-Kāmil had to yield to public pressure and introduce a currency reform. He called in the *black dirhems* and issued a new type of silver coin. These new dirhems were minted by a special procedure, so that the flans took on irregular shapes, roughly round or oval, occasionally with protuberances. Their thickness was variable, but always out of proportion to the diameter of the coin.

According to al-Maqrīzī, the new dirhems—called by me *globular dirhems*—consisted of two-thirds silver and one-third copper. However, Maqrīzī's statement is not accurate, as a series of chemical tests I conducted proved that the globular dirhem was as low in silver content as the black dirhem. Also, the globular dirhem's weight was just as irregular as that of the *dirham waraq*. The only new feature of the reformed coinage was that, instead of being an irregular square or a rectangle, it was round, oval, or with one or two protuberances at the edge. The globular dirhem must have held, however, some attraction because similar coins were struck by al-Ṣāliḥ Ayyūb, and even by his son, Tūrānshāh. Nevertheless, the black dirhems already in existence continued to circulate until the end of Ayyūbid rule in Egypt.

To return to the history of the normal-size, round-flan dirhem in Egypt, al-ʿĀdil repeated Saladin's experiment by reintroducing this coin into the Egyptian circulation, apparently with more success. A goodly number of his round-flan dirhems have been preserved. After him only al-Ṣāliḥ Ayyūb seems to have struck normal-size dirhems and half dirhems in Cairo. Few specimens have survived, however, and their silver content dropped to 75%.

In Syria the monetary situation for silver coinage was good. Trade must have been flourishing, as there was an abundance of silver. The *round-flan*, normal-size dirhem, with its characteristic 'square-in-circle' design introduced by Saladin in Syria, became the sole currency standard of the Ayyūbids. Examination of a great number of these coins shows that their weight is as near the theoretical dirhem weight (2·97 grams) as practically possible. There are many which are a little deficient in weight, but this is often due to wear. The quality of the round-flan Ayyūbid dirhem is also very high, the silver content of most Syrian and Mesopotamian dirhems being at least 90%. During the last period of Ayyūbid rule in Syria economic difficulties, coupled with a worsening political situation, were the probable causes of an increasing debasement of these coins.

The degree of fineness of the relatively few Ayyūbid dirhems that have been tested for their silver content are summarized in the following tables. The data derives from my article, 'History of the Dirhem . . .' and from Messrs. Bacharach and Gordus:

EGYPT

Black Dirhems

Ruler	No. Coins in Sample	Weight Range	Silver %
Saladin:			
As Vassal of Maḥmūd b. Zengī	5	0·69–1·33	33
With Caliph al-Mustaḍī	13	0·36–1·30	33
With Caliph al-Nāṣir	48	0·53–2·15	33
al-'Azīz 'Uthmān:	21	0·75–1·74	26–28
al-Manṣūr Muḥammad:	6	0·81–1·52	28
al-'Ādil I:	4	0·76–1·82	28
al-Kāmil Muḥammad I:	7	0·75–1·81	20–29

Globular Dirhems

Ruler	No. Coins in Sample	Weight Range	Silver %
al-Kāmil Muḥammad I:			
With Caliph al-Nāṣir	22	0·44–2·54	23–30 (for all three)
With Caliph al-Ẓāhir	4	0·93–1·79	
With Caliph al-Mustanṣir	12	0·55–2·00	
al-Ṣāliḥ Ayyūb:	12	0·76–2·00	26–28·5
al-Mu'aẓẓam Tūrānshāh:	5	0·73–2·73	—

Normal-Size, Round-Flan Dirhems

Ruler	No. Coins in Sample	Weight Range	Silver %
Saladin:			
Cairo, 585H	1	2·34	—
Cairo, 586 H	5	2·83–2·95	—
al-Ādil I:			
Cairo, 598 H	3	2·71–2·93	—
Cairo, 600 H	3	2·55	—
Cairo, 601 H	2	2·78–2·96	—
Cairo, 605 H	1	2·93	—
al-Ṣāliḥ Ayyūb:			
Cairo, 645 H	2	2·36–2·89	75
Cairo, 645 H (½ dirhem)	3	1·43–1·62	—
Cairo, 646 H	2	2·73–2·75	75

SYRIA AND MESOPOTAMIA
Dirhems

Ruler	No. Coins in Sample	Weight Range	Average Weight	Silver %
Saladin:				
Damascus, 571–575 H	7	2·60–2·96	2·91	92–94
Damascus, 571–575 H (½ dirhem)	6	1·18–1·47	1·40	—
Damascus, 575–589 H	73	2·45–3·00	2·92	—
Damascus, 575–589 H (½ dirhem)	14	1·40–1·50	1·45	—
Ḥamāh	19	2·19–3·01	2·90	—
Ḥamāh (½ dirhem)	5	1·25–1·49	1·40	—
Ḥimṣ	1	—	2·88	—
Ḥimṣ (½ dirhem)	1	—	1·46	—
Aleppo	65	2·62–3·05	2·90	94
Aleppo (½ dirhem)	3	—	1·40	—
al-ʿAzīz ʿUthmān:				
Damascus	15	2·32–2·92	2·90	—
Ḥamāh	2	2·93–2·96	2·95	—
Ḥimṣ	1	—	2·78	—
al-ʿĀdil I:				
Damascus	50	—	2·90–2·98	94
Damascus (½ dirhem)	16	—	1·40	—
Ḥamāh, 597 H	2	—	2·83–2·94	—
Ḥimṣ, 599 H	1	—	2·63	—
al-Ruhā, 605 H	1	—	2·72	—
al-Kāmil Muḥammad I:				
Damascus	64	2·43–3·20	2·90–2·97	80–91
Damascus (½ dirhem)	16	1·35–1·60	1·40–1·50	—
Ghazzah	9	—	2·90	—
Ḥarrān	2	—	2·75	—
al-Ruhā	3	—	2·70–2·88	—
Mayāfāriqīn (½ dirhem)	1	—	1·13	—
al-ʿĀdil II:				
Damascus	17	—	2·84	86
al-Ṣāliḥ Ayyūb: 1st Reign:				
Damascus, 636 H (Group 1)	7	2·20–3·00	2·80	70
(Group 2)	—	—	—	80
Damascus, 636 H (½ dirhem)	2	—	1·42–1·45	—
Ḥarrān, 634 H	1	—	2·75	—
al-Ṣāliḥ Ayyūb: 2nd Reign:				
Damascus, 645–647 H	43	—	2·90	69
Ḥamāh, 645–646 H	19	—	2·80–2·90	—
al-Muʿaẓẓam Tūrānshāh:				
Damascus, 648 H	19	2·70–2·95	2·80–2·90	80
Ḥamāh, 647 H	—	2·70–2·95	2·80–2·90	76
al-Ẓāhir Ghāzī:				
Aleppo, 589–613 H	128	2·70–3·00	2·80–2·95	—
Aleppo, 589–613 H (½ dirhem)	18	—	1·40–1·50	—
[Posthumous], 614–638 H	49	2·55–2·97	2·80–2·90	—
Ḥamāh, 595 H	1	—	2·80	—
Ḥamāh, 600 H	1	—	2·76	—
al-ʿAzīz Muḥammad:				
Aleppo	22	2·75–3·00	2·90	—
Aleppo (½ dirhem)	2	—	1·40–1·50	—
Aleppo (¼ dirhem)	1	—	0·60	—
al-Nāṣir Yūsuf:				
Aleppo, 634–658 H	64	2·75–3·00	2·90	60–79
Aleppo, 634–658 H (½ dirhem)	8		1·40–1·50	—
Damascus, 648–658 H	10	2·85–2·98	2·90	60–79
Damascus, 648–658 H (½ dirhem)	4	1·12–1·47	1·35	—
Damascus, 648–658 H (¼ dirhem)	1	—	0·60	—
Ḥamāh	10	2·75–2·85	2·80	—

PRINCIPALITY OF DAMASCUS

Ruler	No. Coins in Sample	Weight Range	Average Weight	Silver %
al-Afḍal ʿAlī:				
Damascus	12	2·65–3·00	2·85–2·90	—
Ḥimṣ	3	2·75–2·86	—	—
al-Ṣāliḥ Ismāʿīl: 1st Reign:				
Damascus	4	2·98–3·00	2·99	70
al-Ṣāliḥ Ismāʿīl: 2nd Reign:				
Damascus	57	—	2·90	80
Damascus (½ dirhem)	11	—	1·40–1·50	—

PROVINCE OF ARMENIA

Ruler	No. Coins in Sample	Weight Range	Silver %
Najm al-Dīn Awḥad:			
Akhlāṭ	2	2·62–2·75	—
al-Ashraf Mūsā:			
Ḥarrān	4	1·13, 2·95, 3·02	—
Akhlāṭ	3	2·62, 2·76, 2·97	—

PRINCIPALITY OF ḤIṢN-KAYFĀ

Ruler	No. Coins in Sample	Weight Range	Silver %
al-Muwaḥḥid ʿAbd Allāh:			
Ḥiṣn-Kayfā	3	2·02–2·45	—
Ḥiṣn-Kayfā (½ dirhem)	6	1·50–1·70	—
*Following Princes Issued New 4·20–4·25 Gram Weight Coins**			
Sulaymān ibn al-Ghāzī:	29	4·20–4·25	—
Aḥmad ibn Sulaymān:	8	4·20–4·25	—
Khalīl ibn Aḥmad:			
Large Flan	6	4·20–4·25	—
Small Flan	7	4·20–4·25	—
Aḥmad ibn Khalīl:	3	4·20–4·25	—

* This Ḥiṣn-Kayfā silver is in many ways similar to that of the Ilkhānids.

*YEMEN**

Ruler	No. Coins in Sample	Weight Range	Silver %
Struck by all Governors:	101	*ca.* 1·90–2·20	—

* The Yemeni Ayyūbid silver has not only a lighter weight—well under that of the dirhem—but it has also different designs, which are discussed in greater detail by Miles.

COPPER AND GLASS-PASTE JETONS

EGYPT

A solitary copper coin, produced by the same technique as the black dirhems, is the only proof that Saladin tried to introduce copper coinage into Egypt. However, as the Ayyūbids inherited not only Fāṭimid institutions and traditions, but also their economic situation, Saladin was obliged to abandon the attempt to restore copper coinage, for the simple reason that there were no adequate stocks of copper in the country. Therefore, Saladin continued to issue glass-paste jetons, and so did his successors. However, neither he nor his successors put their names on the jetons, but only that of the ruling ʿAbbāsid caliph. Thus, those jetons bearing the name of Caliph al-Mustaḍī can all be attributed to Saladin. Those naming al-Nāṣir could have been issued by Saladin, by al-ʿAzīz ʿUthmān, by al-Manṣūr Muḥammad, by al-ʿĀdil I, or even by al-Kāmil Muḥammad before al-Nāṣir's demise in 622 H. The only ruler who had his own name inscribed on the jetons, without mention of the caliph, is al-Kāmil Muḥammad I. As the writing is in *Naskhi* script, the date of issue of these jetons may be a little before, or at the beginning of 622 H. This is the year in which he introduced *Naskhi* on the coinage. A more detailed discussion of the use of glass jetons is presented in the Catalogue.

There is literary and numismatic evidence that, in 622 H, al-Kāmil Muḥammad I struck copper coins in Egypt. After Saladin's abortive experiment with copper, these are the first Ayyūbid copper *fulūs* issued in Cairo. One kind shows the name of Caliph al-Ẓāhir, so that this variety must have been struck in 622 to 623 H; the others have the name of al-Mustanṣir. They are in *Naskhi* and have no mint nor date, so that it is not possible to establish how long they circulated.

SYRIA AND MESOPOTAMIA

Saladin

Damascus

Saladin's first copper coins date from 570 and 571 H, when he was still a nominal vassal of the prince of Aleppo, al-Ṣāliḥ Ismāʿīl, the young son of Maḥmūd ibn Zengī. The few existing coins weigh between 4·00 and 5·70 grams. Saladin's copper coinage in Damascus seems to have started in 583 H only. The initial date of 583 H and his title on the coins indicate that this series was meant to celebrate his capture of Jerusalem from the Crusaders. Issues continued to be struck without interruption until his death in 589 H. It is also the only copper series on which Saladin used the title *Sulṭān al-Muslimīn*. Other copper coins, with various arrangements of the legends on which the mint is missing, are also clearly Damascene products, recognizable from the style of writing.

The weight of the various Damascus issues ranges from 4·27 to 0·80 grams, or in terms of the *kharrūbah* (1/36th of a *fals*, or 0·19 gram): 14/36ths of a *fals* to 35/36ths of a *fals*. There is a broad but flat peak between 24/36ths and 30/36ths of a *fals*. The coins from Ḥamāh are rare. One weighs 4·27 and the other 1·75 grams. The Aleppo mint produced two main types, struck between 585 and 589 H. They both weigh between 10/36ths and 27/36ths of the *fals*, *ca.* 2·00 to 5·26 grams.

Mayāfāriqīn

Two types of copper were struck in Mayāfāriqīn by Saladin. One had legends only; the other represents the sultan sitting on a low throne. The Mayāfāriqīn coins are especially heavy. Nearly all the specimens weigh a *fals* or more. The heaviest is a double *fals* of *ca.* 14 grams (72/36ths), and even the lightest weighs *ca.* 6 grams (3/36ths). There is no peak and nearly all the coins are different fractions: 61/36ths, 53/36ths, 49/36ths, 46/36ths, 41/36ths, 36/36ths (i.e. 1 *fals*), 31/36ths and 30/36ths.

Niṣibīn

The rare Niṣibīn *fulūs* of Saladin show his facing portrait wearing a Sasanian crown. Furthermore, they are unusual because of their weight, which is even heavier than that of Mayāfāriqīn coins. Only seven coins are known at present, so that it may be useful to enumerate their individual weights here as well as in the Catalogue:

21·70 grams	=	108/36ths	=	3 *fals*		
17·92	,,	= 92/36ths	=	2	,,	+ 20/36ths
16·96	,,	= 87/36ths	=	2	,,	+ 15/36ths
16·95	,,	= 87/36ths	=	2	,,	+ 15/36ths
16·06	,,	= 83/36ths	=	2	,,	+ 15/36ths
15·80	,,	= 81/36ths	=	2	,,	+ 9/36ths
13·34	,,	= 69/36ths	=	1	,,	+ 33/36ths

No mint [but without doubt al-Jazīrah]

Type A depicts the constellation Leo in the shape of a seated lion on the reverse. All these coins weigh well over the *fals* of 7 grams. The largest weighs *ca.* 14 grams (= 2 *fals*), while the lightest is a little less than 1½ *fals* (*ca.* 10 to 11 grams).

Type B has the sultan sitting on a throne on the reverse. This series is also a heavy coinage. The largest is about 13 grams, and even the lightest piece weighs over 9·50 grams.

al-ʻAzīz ʻUthmān

About 30 copper coins are extant from the Damascus mint struck by Saladin's son, al-ʻAzīz ʻUthmān. They weigh from 4·70 grams (24/36ths) to 1 *fals* of *ca.* 7 grams.

al-ʻĀdil I

al-ʻĀdil I started to issue copper coins in Damascus only when he was already the overlord of the empire, but in the Jazīrah he began to mint as soon as he was appointed governor by Saladin. The existing *fulūs* of Damascus are rather scarce, and those which are known weigh from a full *fals* to 22/36ths or 23/36ths of the *fals*. Only one coin from the Ḥamāh mint exists with its weight noted, a 22/36ths fraction of the *fals*.

For the Jazīrah we have two coins of Mayāfāriqīn, each weighing a little over 9 grams, struck by al-ʻĀdil when he was still governor. Another two were issued when he was sultan and weigh about 14 grams each, thus corresponding to the double *fals*. The few coins from Qalʻat Jaʻbar weigh between one-third of a *fals* (12/36ths) and almost one-half (16/36ths), and are dated 601 H. Those of al-Ruhā, dated 602 H, weigh between 20/36ths and 33/36ths of the *fals* (*ca.* 3·90 and 6·40 grams). Finally, Ḥarrān: the issues, when he was governor, weigh between 12/36ths and 18/36ths; and when sultan, between 23/36ths and 33/36ths.

al-Kāmil Muḥammad I

Very few copper coins from Damascus seem to have survived and their weight is well under that of the *fals*. They weigh between 4·20 grams (22/36ths) and 2·74 grams (14/36ths). The coins from Ḥarrān are somewhat heavier, similar to the Mesopotamian *fulūs* of Saladin, although not quite as heavy. In a series of 19 coins, the heaviest was 1 *fals* (7 grams), and the lightest was 20 *kharrūbahs* (or 3·85 grams). Among the *fulūs* from the mint of Qal'at Ja'bar the small coins (2·08 grams = 11/36ths) are more numerous than the large ones (4·90 grams = 25/36ths).

al-Ṣāliḥ Ayyūb

From the Damascus mint only two copper coins with weights noted are known to me. One weighs 3·88 grams (*ca.* ½ *fals*); the other 1·51 grams (¼ *fals*). A few coins struck at Ḥamāh are also preserved: three are one-fourth and two are one-third of a *fals*. Ḥarrān is represented by one weighing one-third of a *fals*; and, finally, 11 copper coins have been preserved with the mint Āmid, all between two-thirds of a *fals* and one-fourth of a *fals*.

PRINCIPALITY OF ALEPPO

al-Ẓāhir Ghāzī

Aleppo's first ruler issued a steady flow of copper currency, which lasted from the first year of his reign until his death in 613 H. There were two consecutive types of coins, but the two series show the same weight pattern. Between a maximal weight of 6·38 grams (33/36ths) and a minimal weight of 2·97 grams (13/36ths), the various fractions are evenly distributed among the individual coins. As with the other Syrian copper issues, the upper limit is the *fals* of 7 grams, and the smallest fraction is 9 *kharrūbah*.

al-'Azīz Muḥammad

al-Ẓāhir Ghāzī's son and successor struck smaller copper coins than his father. None weighs near the whole *fals*; the heaviest is 4·10 grams (20/36ths) and the lightest is 2·29 grams (⅓ *fals*). There is a broad peak between 3·30 and 2·95 grams (17/36ths and 15/36ths), so that the bulk of the coins consists of ½ *fals* pieces.

al-Nāṣir Yūsuf

al-Nāṣir Yūsuf continued the copper coinage along the same lines as his father, al-'Azīz Muḥammad. His heaviest coin weighs 3·96 grams (Miles' 'high' 20 *kharrūbah*) and the lightest only 1 gram (5/36ths). His *fulūs* show no mint, so that they cannot be arranged in chronological order. Neither is it possible to say whether they are from Aleppo or Damascus, both of which belonged to al-Nāṣir Yūsuf after 648 H.

PRINCIPALITY OF ḤAMĀH

al-Manṣūr Muḥammad I

The princes of Ḥamāh, more vassals than allies—first of al-'Azīz 'Uthmān of Egypt, then of al-Ẓāhir Ghāzī of Aleppo, and lastly of the rulers of Damascus—apparently were allowed to issue only copper coinage. The few *fulūs* of the Ḥamāh mint, which bear the name of al-'Azīz 'Uthmān as overlord, belong to the first period. They weigh between 3·24 and 2·40 grams and are, therefore, less than the ½ *fals*. The second type, with al-Ẓāhir Ghāzī as overlord, also does not exceed 4·59 grams. No *fulūs* with the prince of Damascus as overlord (al-'Ādil) are known.

al-Manṣūr Muḥammad I struck copper coins in Ḥarrān also. As soon as he inherited the town from his father, he issued heavy copper, identical in design with the *fulūs* struck by Saladin the year before. The two issues, on which Saladin's seated figure appears holding a large crescent, differ from each other only in that al-Manṣūr Muḥammad has his name inscribed around Saladin's figure. These coins weigh between 8·85 and 4·74 grams; i.e. 45 *kharrūbah* and 24 *kharrūbah*, respectively.

al-Manṣūr Muḥammad II

The two coins known show al-Nāṣir Yūsuf as overlord. Although there is no date, the coins must have been issued after al-Nāṣir Yūsuf occupied Damascus in 648 H. The coins appear light but, unfortunately, the weight is not noted.

PRINCIPALITY OF MAYĀFĀRIQĪN AND SINJĀR

al-Awḥad Najm al-Dīn Ayyūb

The copper struck in both towns by this ruler consist of heavy, large-size coins, similar to the other pieces struck in the Jazīrah. The largest weighs more than the double *fals* of 14 grams, the smallest is only 4·73 grams. Most of the coins are heavy.

al-Ashraf Mūsā I

His copper coins of Mayāfāriqīn are rather common and about 85% weigh between 13 and 11 grams. A few exceed the double *fals*. The coins of Sinjār are slightly lighter, although they still weigh between 11 and 9 grams.

al-Muẓaffar Ghāzī

He minted only in Mayāfāriqīn. A first series, of the square-in-circle type, weighs between 14 and 6 grams. A second type, with a six-pointed star and hexalobe design, is lighter and weighs between 5 and 3 grams. There is also a third type, with the square-in-circle design, but on which Ghāzī is titled *al-Sulṭān al-Malik*. This last type weighs between 3·55 and 1·86 grams only.

al-Kāmil Muḥammad II

Only seven coins of this ruler are known with their weight noted, and they range from 6·00 to 2·08 grams.

PRINCIPALITY OF ḤIṢN–KAYFĀ

al-Kāmil ibn Aḥmad

Only two copper coins of this branch of the Ayyūbids are known. They are of Sulṭān al-Kāmil ibn Aḥmad (836 to 856 H) and weigh 2·00 and 1·50 grams.

THE YEMEN

The Catalogue contains only three Yemeni copper coins. Two belong to Ismāʿīl ibn Tughtegīn and weigh 9·87 and 7·92 grams. The third has only the name of the overlord, al-Kāmil Muḥammad I, without that of the local Ayyūbid governor, and weighs 3·66 grams.

REGAL TITLES

The title *al-Malik* (or prince), which occurs on the coins of the ʿUqaylids, the Marwānids, the Samānids, and the Ghaznavids during the fourth quarter of the fourth century H was also used by the Ayyūbids. The *wāzīrs* of the last Fāṭimid caliphs had the title of *al-Malik* bestowed upon them. Saladin, who was appointed as the *wāzīr* of the last caliph, al-ʿĀḍid, assumed it, but had it inscribed on his first independent coinage only in 570 H after Nūr al-Dīn ibn Zengī's death. Although I know of no written record, it seems that after Saladin had organized his family into ruling clans, every son automatically received the title *al-Malik* as an inalienable right. The title seems to mean *prince of the blood* (not *king*) in this context.

The inscriptions show that, with few exceptions, the Ayyūbid kings and princes were content to use the simple title of *al-Malik*. Saladin only once used the seemingly important but unofficial title of *Sulṭān al-Islām wa'l-Muslimīn* on his 583 H Damascus gold issue. He also used the title *Sulṭān al-Muslimīn* on his Damascus copper, beginning with 583 H. His sons, his brother, al-ʿĀdil I, and his nephews, who became overlords of the empire, were satisfied with the title *al-Malik*, as were the princes of the Jazīrah and the Yemen.

The first Ayyūbid, of whose elevation to the dignity of *sulṭān* by the caliph there is documentary evidence, is al-Ṣāliḥ Ayyūb. R. S. Humphreys underlines the fact that the policies of the caliphate were largely irrelevant to the Ayyūbids, and that the supreme lords of the Ayyūbid Empire did not consider the title *sulṭān*, dispensed by the caliph, of particular importance. Only al-Ṣāliḥ Ayyūb, the last ruler to get a firm hold on the entire Ayyūbid Empire, is known to have obtained the investiture as *sulṭān* from Caliph al-Mustaʿṣim in 643 H. Yet even al-Ṣāliḥ let four years pass before he had his new title engraved on his 647 H Damascus silver.

al-Ṣāliḥ Ayyūb's son, al-Muʿaẓẓam Tūrānshāh, who reigned for two months after his father's demise in 648 H, also used the title of sulṭān on his one issue in Damascus. It may be mentioned here that the full title for these two Egyptian rulers was *al-Sulṭān al-Malik*, as it later was for the Mamlūk rulers.

The fact that the Ayyūbid princes did not seek the official investiture as *sulṭān* by the caliph, did not mean that they disliked being addressed by that title. Indeed, in the daily official business they were almost never addressed by any other title by their courtiers, secretaries, dignitaries and generals. Whenever he is mentioned in official letters or dispatches, the ruler is referred to as *sulṭān*, even in international diplomatic correspondence.

Lapidary inscriptions on public buildings—whether pious foundations, mosques, schools, *khānkāhs*, tomb mosques or drinking fountains (*sabīls*)—are a rich source of long, sonorous, self-important protocols in which the word *sulṭān* is but the last epithet in a verbose sequence of often senseless adulation. These inscriptions on buildings do not belong to ruling princes only, but very often to princes who never had any possessions, were never in office, or who even died in tender childhood. Some modern scholars consider these lapidary inscriptions as official products, but I am convinced that the correct term would be 'adulatory inscriptions'.

I am also convinced by now that Humphreys is right and that one should not lay too much stress on the question of whether the title *sulṭān* on coins was granted by the caliph or arrogated by the prince responsible for the issue. That al-Ṣāliḥ Ayyūb obtained the caliph's investiture is not really in doubt. The matter was simply not of first importance.

al-Muẓaffar Ghāzī, governor of Mayāfāriqīn, issued copper coinage with the title *al-Sulṭān al-Malik* before 642 H. Humphreys has pointed out that my statement in *BIE* (1952) that al-Ṣāliḥ Ayyūb's silver was the first Ayyūbid issue with *sulṭān*, was 'mildly inaccurate'. al-Muẓaffar's special coinage is, of course, further proof that, in the case of the Ayyūbids, one should not draw the line too sharply between a self-adopted title and one officially bestowed by the caliph. The motivation behind al-Muẓaffar's move may well have been status to replace his waning power and increasing isolation. His son, al-Kāmil Muḥammad II, followed his father's example by including this title on his coinage.

Ḥiṣn-Kayfā is the best example of how the coinage and the royal protocol inscribed on it can contrast with the importance and power of the government that issued it. After the disappearance of the conquering Ilkhānids, Ḥiṣn-Kayfā developed an autonomous silver currency, of correct weight and good alloy, engraved with a royal protocol from which the title *sulṭān* was missing only exceptionally. Yet the entire principality consisted of barely more than the castle and its immediate neighbourhood.

The Yemeni governor, Ismā'īl b. Tughtegīn, used the title *Sulṭān al-Muslimīn* on his dirhems for some personal reason. al-Ṣāliḥ Ismā'īl inscribed the dirhem issues of Damascus between 636 and 638 H with the name of his Rūm Seljūqid ally and nominal overlord, Kaykhusraw II. Some of the dirhems have *al-Sulṭān Kaykhusraw*; others *al-Sulṭān al-A'ẓam Kaykhusraw*; and some only *al-Sulṭān al-A'ẓam*. This last obviously refers to Kaykhusraw. There are other coins on which the protocol is very much abbreviated, reading only: *al-Sulṭān*. This has been mistaken by some modern scholars for the title of the Ayyūbid prince, which it is not.

It was probably not to add an extra title, but simply to show their descent, that the Ayyūbid princes of Ḥiṣn-Kayfā began to affix the epithet 'the Ayyūbid' to their protocol on the silver coinage long after the Ayyūbid Empire had vanished and they were the only living members of their clan. There can be no doubt that their aim was to add prestige to their own status by association with the past glory of the dynasty.

INSCRIPTIONS

Ayyūbid coins always display the name of the ruler. There are no anonymous copper *fulūs* as with other dynasties. Up to the date of the destruction of the ʿAbbāsid caliphate by Hūlāgū in 656 H, the name of the caliph is also present, and only then is replaced by a religious legend.

The gold coins show, with a solitary exception (No. 62 of the Catalogue), the mint and date, as do the silver dirhems, although there are several undated half dirhems. Copper issues often have the mint and date, although some issues lack both indications. Religious legends accompany the protocol and the mint/date formula. On some issues they are on the side on which the caliph's name is written; on others around the name of the ruler or, as on the earliest gold coins of Saladin, on both sides.

The arrangement of the gold and silver coins tends to remain conservative. Whenever there is evident change, it is consequent to some political event, such as Saladin's emancipation from Zengid suzerainty, or the investitute of a new ʿAbbāsid caliph.

The name of an overlord appears on many coins issued by regional princes. The head of the Ayyūbid clan was generally recognized as the overlord by the ruling members of the family, although there were varying grades of dependency. Some princes were more allies than vassals; others were kept in subordinate positions. During the first two years of his reign Saladin held an appointment by Maḥmūd b. Zengī and his coinage reflects this status. In fact, the first coinage was in the name of the liege-lord, and Saladin's name does not even occur on the issue. Political situations, alliances, intrigues and danger of foreign or domestic military action more than once obliged an Ayyūbid prince to accept tutelage, sometimes by an outside power. Examples of a foreign sovereign recognized by an Ayyūbid prince are with the Seljūq sultan Kaykhusraw II of Asia Minor, some dirhems of al-ʿAzīz Muḥammad, and of al-Nāṣir Yusuf of Aleppo.

HUMAN AND ANIMAL FIGURES

Representations of human and animal figures are restricted to issues of al-Jazīrah (Mesopotamia)—always on copper only. Saladin's bust, crowned with a Sassanid crown, appears on large coppers struck at Niṣibīn. He is also depicted sitting on a throne on a mintless issue. al-ʿĀdil I, al-Awḥad Najm al-Dīn Ayyūb and al-Ashraf Mūsā I have bust portraits or are shown sitting in an oriental pose. Other coins of Saladin have connections with astronomy; their subjects are either the constellation of the lion, or the seated figure of the sultan (?), holding up a crescent. Obviously these issues were inṣpired by the somewhat earlier copper coins of the Zengids and Artuqids of the Jazīrah.

CALLIGRAPHIC STYLES

GOLD

Saladin's first coinage issue, struck while he was still a vassal of Nūr al-Dīn, has legends in simple *Kūfic* script with minute characters. These tiny characters are maintained during the years 570 to 575 H under Caliph al-Mustaḍī, but became larger with a few ornamental additions after the advent of Caliph al-Nāṣir. This style continued under his successors until 622 H. In 623 H al-Kāmil Muḥammad introduced a radical change: from then on all the legends on the dinar were executed in *Naskh* script.

SILVER

In Egypt, from Saladin through the year 622 H, the black dirhem dominated, with its inscriptions in a simple, unadorned *Kūfic*. From 623 H onward the globular dirhem, inscribed in bold *Naskh* characters, came into circulation. Several attempts were made to introduce the normal-flan, Syrian-style dirhems into Egypt. These coins first used a *Kūfic* script and then a *Naskh*.

Probably inspired by the new type of gold coins introduced by the Almohad, ʻAbd al-Mu'min (524 to 558 H), Saladin and his successors struck *square-in-the-circle* type dirhems in Damascus, Ḥamāh, Ḥimṣ, as well as in a few Mesopotamian cities. These 'Syrian' silver coins were inscribed in *Kūfic*, and from 623 H onwards in *Naskh*. An exception is Aleppo, where the dirhem's central legends, enclosed in a six-pointed star, were in *Kūfic* under Saladin; in *Naskh* under al-Ẓāhir Ghāzī until 598 H; changed to *Kūfic*; and finally returned to *Naskh* under al-ʻAzīz Muḥammad from 613 H.

The silver struck in the Yemen is a quite different series. At first, the inscriptions were in *Kūfic*, enclosed in an eight-pointed star or a scalloped circle; but after 612 H they were changed into flowing *Naskh* and the marginal legends were discontinued. Lastly, the dirhems issued by the Ḥiṣn-Kayfā princes, who long survived the Ilkhānid apocalypse, became Mongol in type and display their legends in the characteristic Mongol or Ilkhānid *Kūfic*.

COPPER

Egypt. Instead of introducing copper currency, Saladin maintained the fiduciary glass-paste coinage of the Fāṭimids, substituting the name of the ʻAbbāsid caliph for the protocol of the Fāṭimid caliph. His own name was omitted, as were the names of his successors, until probably some time before 622 H, when al-Kāmil Muḥammad I put his own name on the jetons. In 622 H, however, he was obliged to issue copper in Egypt. Although there is no mint name on these coins, they are easily identified from comments in the medieval Arabic literary sources cited by Hassanein Rabie, in *The Financial System of Egypt* (London, 1972), F.N. 1, p. 183; and from the names of the two consecutive caliphs: al-Ẓāhir and al-Mustanṣir. These suggest the period around 622 to 623 H and occur on the three known varieties of these copper coins. The writing on all the coins of this series is in bold *Naskh*, typical of the transition period from *Kūfic* to *Naskh*. Curiously, we have no further copper coins from al-Kāmil's successors in Egypt.

Syria. On his Damascus copper, which he issued when he was still a nominal vassal of the Zengids of Aleppo, Saladin used large, bold *Naskh* for the coin legends, interspersed with a few small ornaments. On the next series, which he struck as a sovereign ruler, the inscriptions are in *Kūfic*, of which there is a wide range of variations, the style depending on the individual die-cutter. Some coins show a few ornaments; others none. The few copper coins of al-ʿAzīz ʿUthmān are again in large *Naskh* and so are those of al-ʿĀdil I, as well as the scarce *square-in-the-circle fulūs* of al-Kāmil Muḥammad I and the similar Ḥamāh issues of al-Ṣāliḥ Ayyūb.

Aleppo had its own style. The severely ornamented *Kūfic*, with a floweret at the top and bottom of the field, introduced by Saladin, was maintained by his son, al-Ẓāhir Ghāzī, until 596 H. At that time the central legend, in an ornamented square, is in *Naskh* and the marginal inscriptions are in *Kūfic*. On the 603 H coins the style of the legends remains the same; only the square has been changed into an octagonal star. Ghāzī's son, al-ʿAzīz Muḥammad, maintained the *Naskh*, but changed the border into multilobes of varying detail. Under al-Nāṣir Yūsuf only the border was changed; the style of writing was in *Naskh* from then on.

The quasi-independent principality of Ḥamāh seems to have imitated Aleppo, in so far as the first issues are in *Naskh*; later they were in *Kūfic*, and a floweret at the top and the bottom of the field was added. The only coin struck by the first prince written in *Naskh* has no date; therefore, it is impossible to establish, at least until further specimens come to light, whether it is earlier or later than the *Kūfic* coins. The few *fulūs* of the second prince are in *Naskh*.

Mesopotamia. On Saladin's coins, whether with legends only or with figures too, the *Kūfic*, although simple enough, shows a sophisticated style. The figured coppers of his brother, al-ʿĀdil I, present quite simple *Kūfic* writing, but those which are purely inscriptional are more varied. The legends of Qalʿat Jaʿbar exhibit a curious transition from *Kūfic* to *Naskh*; the coppers from al-Ruhā and Ḥarrān display tall *Kūfic* characters ornamented halfway on their upright strokes, though some are in an undistinguished style. The few coppers of al-Kāmil I, on which a Mesopotamian mint is discernible, are in *Naskh* arranged in the *square-in-the-circle* design. *Naskh* was by then the accepted style of inscriptions on the coinage and remained so until the end of that dynasty. The only exception is the Mayāfāriqīn issue of al-Muẓaffar Ghāzī, struck before the death of Caliph al-Mustanṣir, which was inscribed in *Kūfic*.

ABBREVIATIONS AND BIBLIOGRAPHY

The authorities used for compiling this list are as follows, in the order of priority:

1. *The National Union Catalogue* of the Library of Congress.
2. The American Numismatic Society. *Dictionary Catalogue of the Library of the American Numismatic Society*. Boston, 1962.
3. The American Numismatic Society. *Numismatic Literature*. New York, 1947–.
4. Mayer, Leo A. *Bibliography of Moslem Numismatics*, 2nd ed. London, 1954.

ʿAdan Museum: Aden, People's Democratic Republic of Yemen.

Adler, Jacob Georg Christian: *Museum Cuficum Borgianum Velitris, illustravit*. Rome, 1782–92.

Album: Stephen Album collection, Santa Rosa, California.

Album, Stephen. A Hoard of Silver Coins from the Time of Iskandar Qarā-Qoyūnlū, *NC* 136 (1976), pp. 109–57.

Amedroz, Henry F. Arabic, etc. coins, *NC*, 3rd series, 13 (1893), pp. 76–9.

ANS: The American Numismatic Society collection, New York.

ANS-Artuqid Hoard: Hoard of Artuqid and other coins in the ANS collection.

ANS-Hisp.: Hispanic Society of America collection at the ANS.

ANS-56.125: ANS hoard of dirhems, 1956.

ANS-71.76: ANS hoard of dirhems, 1972.

ANS-Laties: Hoard of half dirhems examined at the ANS in June 1972.

ANSMN: American Numismatic Society Museum Notes.

ANS-UM: University of Pennsylvania Museum collection, Philadelphia, on permanent loan to the ANS.

Arigoni, Honorius. *Numismata quaedam cujuscunque formae, et metalli musei Honorii Arigoni Veneti*, t. III *Nummi Arabici*. Tarvisio, 1745.

Arri, Giovanni Antonio. Observationes in quosdam Abbasidarum numos atque in alia monumenta arabico-cufica, *Memorie della R. Accademia delle Scienze di Torino* 39 (1836), pp. 33–85.

Artuk: Artuk, İbrahim and Cevriye. *İstanbul Arkeoloji Müzeleri Teşhirdeki İslâmî Sikkeler Kataloğu I*. İstanbul, 1971.

Ashmolean: The Ashmolean Museum, Oxford.

Ashmolean-Bodleian: The Bodleian Library collection, Oxford, now in the Ashmolean Museum.

Ashmolean-Christ Church: Christ Church College collection, Oxford, now in the Ashmolean Museum. Cf. Lane-Poole, *NC* (1886).

Ashmolean-Thorburn: Ph. Thorburn collection, now in the Ashmolean Museum.

Assemani, Simone. Sopra le monete arabe effigiate, *Memorie della Academia di Scienze, Lettere ed Arti di Padova* 1 (1809), pp. 417–36.

Awad: Dr. Henri Amin Awad collection, Cairo.

Bacharach, Jere L. and Adon A. Gordus. Studies in the Fineness of Silver Coins, *JESHO* 11 (1968), pp. 298–317.

Bacharach, Jere L. and Henri Amin Awad. The Problem of the Obverse and the Reverse in Islamic Numismatics, *NC*, 7th series, 13 (1973), pp. 183–91.

Balog: Dr. Paul Balog collection, Rome.

Balog, Paul. Deux dinars inédits du dernier roi Ayoubite d'Égypte, al-Malek al-Achraf Abou'l Fath Moussa, *BIE* 31 (1949), pp. 187–90.

——. Études numismatiques de l'Égypte musulmane I, *BIE* 33 (1951), pp. 1–42.

——. Études numismatiques de l'Égypte musulmane II, *BIE* 34 (1952), pp. 17–55.

——. Études numismatiques de l'Égypte musulmane III, *BIE* 35 (1953), pp. 401–29.

——. Monnaies islamiques rares Fāṭimites et Ayoubites, *BIE* 36 (1954), pp. 327–46.

——. Dirhems Ayoubites inédits du Yemen, *BIE* 36 (1954), pp. 347–55.

——. Dinars of al-Mu'aẓẓam Shams al-Dīn Tūrānshāh and al-'Azīz Ṭughtegīn, Ayyūbid Princes of the Yemen, *ANSMN* 9 (1960), pp. 237–40.

——. History of the Dirhem in Egypt from the Fāṭimid Conquest Until the Collapse of the Mamlūk Empire, *RN* 6ᵉ serie, 3 (1961), pp. 109–46.

——. Les jetons Fāṭimites en verre, *Revue Belge de Numismatique et de Sigillographie*, 107 (1961), pp. 171–83.

——. The Ayyūbid Glass Jetons and their Use, *JESHO* 9 (1966), pp. 242–56.

——. The Fāṭimid Glass Jeton, *Annali dell' Instituto Italiana di Numismatica* 18–19 (1971–2), pp. 175–264; 20 (1973), pp. 121–212.

——. Fāṭimid and Post-Fāṭimid Glass Jetons from Sicily, *Studi Magrebini* 7 (1975), pp. 125–48.

——. Ayyūbid Divisional Currency Issued in Egypt by al-Kāmil Muḥammad I, *Gazette Numismatique Suisse* 27 (1977), pp. 62–7.

—— and Jacques Yvon. Monnaies à légendes arabes de l'orient latin, *RN* 6ᵉ serie, 1 (1958), pp. 133–68.

Bartholomaei, Ivan Alexevitch. Troisième lettre . . . à M. F. Soret, sur des monnaies koufiques inédites trouvées en Géorgie, *RNB* 3ᵉ serie, 6 (1862), pp. 23–105, 305.

Bates: Ayyūbid coin hoards in the ANS, to be published by Dr. Michael L. Bates.

Bates, Michael L. Thirteenth-Century Crusader Imitations of Ayyūbid Silver Coinage: A Preliminary Survey, *Near Eastern Numismatics, Iconography, Epigraphy and History. Studies in Honor of George C. Miles*. Eds. D. Kouymjian and J. L. Bacharach. Beirut, 1974, pp. 393–409.

Berezin, Ilia Nikolaevich. *Catalogue des monnaies et médailles du cabinet numismatique de l'Université Impériale de Casan*. Kazan, 1855.

Bergmann, Ernst Ritter, von. Zur muhammedanischen Münzkunde, *NZ* 8 (1876), 28–44.

Berlin: Bode Museum, Berlin, DDR.

Berman: Berman, Ariel. *Islamic Coins—Catalogue of the Exhibition Winter 1976, L. A. Mayer Memorial Institute for Islamic Art*. Jerusalem, 1976.

BIE: Bulletin de l'Institut d'Égypte.

Blau, Otto. *Die orientalischen Münzen des Museums der Kaiserlichen Historisch-Archäologischen Gesellschaft zu Odessa*. Odessa, 1876.

—— and Johann Gustav Stickel. Zur muhammedanischen Numismatik und Epigraphik, *ZDMG* 11 (1857), pp. 443–74.

Blochet, Edgar. *Histoire de l'Egypte de Makrizi*. Paris, 1908.

BM: British Museum (uncatalogued specimens).

BMC: Stanley Lane-Poole. *Catalogue of Oriental Coins in the British Museum*, IV and IX. London, 1879, 1889.

BMCG: Stanley Lane-Poole, *Catalogue of Arabic Glass Weights in the British Museum*. London, 1891.

Broome: Collection of Michael R. Broome, Woodley, Reading, England.

BSOAS: *Bulletin of the School of Oriental and African Studies.*

Butak: Butak, Behzad, *XI. XII. ve XIII. yüzyillarda resimli Türk paraları*. Istanbul, 1947.

——. *Resimli Türk Paralarına, Ek*. Istanbul, 1948.

——. *Resimli Türk Paralarına, Ek. II–III*. Istanbul, 1950.

Casanova, Paul. Catalogue des pièces de verre des époques byzantine et arabe de la collection Fouquet, *Mémoires de la Mission Archéologique Française au Caire* 6 (1893), pp. 337–414.

Castiglioni, Carlo Ottavio. *Monete cufiche dell' I.R. Museo di Milano*. Milan, 1819.

Çetinyalçın: Prof. Ismail Çetinyalçın collection, Istanbul.

Codrington, Humphrey William. *Catalogue of Coins in the Colombo Museum*. Hertford, 1914.

——. *Ceylon Coins and Currency. Memoirs of the Colombo Museum*. Colombo, 1924.

Codrington, Oliver. On a Hoard of Coins Found at Broach, *Journal of the Bombay Branch of the Royal Asiatic Society* 15 (1881–2, publ. 1883), pp. 339–70.

Cottevieille-Giraudet, Rémy. La collection Decourdemanche (monnaies musulmanes) au Cabinet des Médailles, *RN* 4e série, t. 37 (1934), pp. 199–219; t. 38 (1935), pp. 19–46, 197–229.

da Cunha: da Cunha, Joseph Gerson. *Catalogue of the Coins in the Numismatic Cabinet Belonging to J. Gerson da Cunha*. Bombay, 1888–9.

Damascus: al-ʿUshsh, Dr. Muḥammad Abū al-Faraj. *Preliminary Catalogue of the Ayyūbid Dirhems Struck in Ḥalab (Aleppo) Bearing Dates After the Death of al-Ẓāhir and al-ʿĀdil*. Presented (in typescript) at the Numismatic Colloquium of the World of Islam Festival, London, April 13–14, 1976, as part of a paper: *The Ayyūbid Dirhams of al-Ẓāhir Ghāzī and al-ʿĀdil Abū Bakr after their death.*

Dauwe: R. B. F. Dauwe collection, Terneuzen, The Netherlands.

Dorn: Dorn, Boris Andreevich (Bernhard). *Inventaire des monnaies des khalifes orientaux et de plusieurs autres dynasties*. St. Petersburg, 1877.

Dorn 4th fasc./Dorn IV: Dorn, Boris Andreevich and Matveĭ Avel'ich Gamazov. *Monnaies de différentes dynasties musulmanes*. St. Petersburg, 1881.

Ehrenkreutz, Andrew S. Extracts from the Technical Manual on the Ayyūbid Mint in Cairo, *BSOAS* 15 (1953), pp. 423–47.

——. The Crisis of the *Dīnār* in the Egypt of Saladin, *JAOS* 70 (1950), pp. 178–84.

——. *Saladin*. Albany, 1972.

Erdmann, Franz von. *Numi asiatici musei Universitatis Caesareae Literarum Casanensis*, Pars. I. Kazan, 1834.

Erel, Şerafettin. *Nâdir birkaç sikke*. 4 parts. Istanbul, 1963–73.

Erman, Adolf. Mittelalterliche und neuere Münzen, *Katalog der Bibliothek der Deutschen Morgenländischen Gesellschaft*, Bd. II, pp. 57–77. Leipzig, 1881.

Fahmy: Fahmī, ʿAbd al-Raḥmān Muḥammad (ed.). Ibn Baʿrah, Manṣūr al-Dhahabī al-Kāmilī, *Kitāb kashf al-asrār al-ʿilmīyah bi-dār al-ḍarb al-miṣrīyah* (followed by a catalogue of the Ayyūbid coins in the Museum of Islamic Art in Cairo). Cairo, 1385/1966.

Fasti Arabici V: Cf. Lane-Poole, Oriental Coins at Christ Church.

Fouquet: See Casanova.

Fraehn, Christian Martin Joachim. Über einige bemerkenswerte Stücke des Orientalischen Münzkabinettes der Kaiserlichen Universität zu Kiew, *Bulletin Scientifique* 4 (1838), cols. 225–8.

——. Nachricht von den verschiedenen orientalischen Münzsammlungen der Kaiserlichen Eremitage und kurze Beschreibung der unedirten Stücke der letzten derselben, *Bulletin Scientifique* 4 (1838), cols. 305–18; rpt. *Mélanges Asiatiques* t. III, pp. 149–66.

——. Bericht über eine, der Akademie aus Aegypten zugekommene Bereicherung der Numismatischen Abtheilung ihres Asiatischen Museums, *Bulletin Scientifique* 7 (1840), cols. 134–43.

Fraehn, *Nova Suppl.*: ——. *Opusculorum Postumorum Pars I, Nova supplementa ad Recensionem numorum Muhammedanorum*, ed. B. A. Dorn. St. Petersburg, 1855.

Gautier: George Gautier collection, Paris.

Ghalib: Ghalib (Edhem), Ismail. *Catalogue des monnaies turcomanes*. Constantinople, 1894.

Glidden: Dr. Harold W. Glidden collection, Washington.

Gottschalk, Hans Ludwig. *Al-Malik al-Kāmil von Egypten und seine Zeit*. Wiesbaden, 1958.

Grabar, Oleg. On Two Coins of Muẓaffar Ghāzi, Ruler of Maiyāfāriqīn (AH 617–42/AD 1220–44), *ANSMN* 5 (1952), pp. 167–80.

Grohmann: Grohmann, Adolf. Arabische Eichungsstempel, Glasgewichte und Amuletter aus Wiener Sammlungen, *Islamica* 1 (1925), pp. 145–226.

al-Hamdānī: Cf. Toll.

Hirsch: Hirsch, Berhard, *Auktionskatalog Cora-Spina*. Munich, 1958.

Horovitz: Théodore Horovitz collection, Geneva.

Humphreys, R. Stephen. *The Ayyūbids of Damascus 589–658 H/AD 1193–1260*. Ph.D. Dissertation University of Michigan, 1969. High Wycombe and Ann Arbor, 1970.

——. *From Saladin to the Mongols: The Ayyūbids of Damascus*. Albany, 1977.

Ibn al-Dawādārī, Abū Bakr ibn ʿAbd Allāh. *Durar al-tījān wa-ghurar tawārīkh al-zamān*. MS. Istanbul: Damad Ibrahim Paşa, No. 913.

Ibn Baʿrah: See Fahmy.

Ibn Shaddād, Bahāʾ al-Dīn Yusūf ibn Rāfiʿ. *al-nawādir al-sulṭānīyah wa-al-maḥāsin al-yūsufīyah —sīrat Ṣalāḥ al-Dīn*, ed. Jamāl al-Dīn Shayyāl. Cairo, 1964.

Ilisch: Lutz Ilisch collection, Billerbeck, West Germany.

Istanbul: Archeological Museum, Istanbul.

Izmir: Private collection, Izmir.

Izzet: Izzet, Holu Pacha. *Monnaies anciennes musulmanes, Catalogue d'une collection de monnaies appartenant à un amateur*. Constantinople, 1901.

JA: Journal Asiatique.

JESHO: Journal of the Economic and Social History of the Orient.

Johnston: Johnston, J. M. C. Mohammedan Coins, *NC* 3rd series, 19 (1899), pp. 265–8.

Karabacek, Joseph, Ritter von. Zur orientalischen Münzkunde, *WNM* 3 (1867), pp. 35–42.

——. Die kûfischen Münzen des steiermärkisch-ständischen Joanneums in Graz, *WNM* 4 (1868), pp. 12–82.

——. Über muhammedanische Vicariatsmünzen und Kupferdrachmen des XII.–XIII. Jahrhunderts, *NZ* 1 (1869), pp. 265–300.

Khediv: See Lane-Poole, *Catalogue* (1897).

Krehl, Ludolf. Ueber einige muhammadanische Münzen des Königlichen Münz-Cabinets zu Dresden, *ZDMG* 12 (1858), pp. 250–63.

Lagumina: Lagumina, Bartolomeo. *Catalogo delle monete arabe esistenti nella Biblioteca comunale di Palermo*. Palermo, 1892.

Lane-Poole, Stanley. *Coins of the Urtuḳí Turkumáns*. London, 1875.

——. *Catalogue of Oriental Coins*. Cf. BMC.

——. Fasti Arabici, II. Mr. Calvert's Collection, *NC* 3rd series, 5 (1885), pp. 229–36.

——. Oriental Coins at Christ Church, Oxford (Fasti Arabici V), *NC* 3rd series, 6 (1886), pp. 233–8.

——. *Catalogue of Arabic Glass Weights*. Cf. BMCG.

——. *Catalogue of the Collection of Arabic Coins Preserved in the Khedivial Library at Cairo*. London, 1897.

Launois-Maspéro: Launois, Aimée. *Catalogue des étalons monétaires et autres pièces musulmanes en verre de la collection Jean Maspéro*. Paris, 1960.

Lavoix: Lavoix, Henri. *Catalogue des monnaies musulmanes de la Bibliothèque Nationale, Vol. III, Égypte et Syrie*. Paris, 1896.

Le Strange, Guy. *The Lands of the Eastern Caliphate*. Cambridge, 1905.

Leuthold: Dr. Enrico Leuthold collection, Milan.

Leuthold, Enrico, Jr. Di un dinaro coniato alla Mecca da al-'Azîz 'Othmân, *Italia Numismatica* 20, No. 3 (March 1969), pp. 53–4.

Leuthold-Ripostiglio: ——. Monete con leggende arabo-islamiche e dei Crociati—in un Ripostiglio del XIII Secolo., *Revista italiana di numismatica* Ser. 5, 19 (1971), pp. 175–84.

Lowick: Lowick, Nicholas M. Feudalism in Syria: An Ayyūbid Silver Hoard, *Spink's Numismatic Circular* 79, No. 10 (October 1971), pp. 358–9.

Madras: Government Museum. *Catalogue of Coins in the Collection of the Government Central Museum, Madras*. Madras, 1874.

al-Maqrīzī, Aḥmad ibn 'Alī. *Shudhūr al-'uqūd fī dhikr al-nuqūd*, ed. Anastās Mārī al-Kirmilī, *al-nuqūd al-'arabīyah wa-'ilm al-nummīyāt*, pp. 21–73. Cairo, 1939; [trans. Antoine Isaac Silvestre de Sacy]. *Traité des monnoies musulmanes, traduit de l'arabe de Makrizi*. Paris, 1797; Henri Sauvaire, *Matériaux pour servir à l'histoire de la numismatique et de la métrologie musulmanes*, *JA* 7e série, 19 (1882), pp. 23–77, 97–163, 281–327.

——. *Kitāb ighāthat al-ummah bi-kashf al-ghummah*, ed. Muḥammad Muṣṭafā Ziyādah and Jamāl al-Dīn al-Shayyāl. Cairo, 1940; [trans. Gaston Wiet, Le traité des famines de Maqrīzī]' *JESHO* 5 (1962), pp. 1–90.

Markov: Markov, Alexeĭ Konstantinovich. *Inventarniy Katalog musulmanskikh monet Imperatorskavo Ermitazha*. St. Petersburg, 1896–8.

Miles-Yaman: Miles, George Carpenter. The Ayyūbid Dynasty of the Yaman and their Coinage, *NC* 5th series, 19 (1939), pp. 62–97.

Miles-Sinjār: ——. Some Coins from Sinjār, *American Journal of Semitic Languages and Literatures*, 56 (1939), pp. 244–50.

Miles-Antioch: ——. Islamic Coins in *Antioch-on-the-Orontes*, IV, Part 1, pp. 109–24. Princeton, 1948.

——. Byzantine Miliaresion and Arab Dirhem, *ANSMN* 9 (1960), pp. 189–218.

——. Some Islamic Coins in the Berne Historical Museum *Revue Suisse de Numismatique* 45 (1966), pp. 131–43.

Mingana: 37 Ayyūbid dirhems of the Dr. Mingana collection, property of Selly Oaks Colleges, Birmingham, on temporary loan to the Ashmolean Museum. Studied by Mrs. Helen Mitchell-Brown, who will publish them. Included in the present Catalogue by courtesy of Mrs. Mitchell-Brown.

Mitchell-Brown: Mrs. Helen W. Mitchell-Brown collection, Oxford.

Möller, Johann Heinrich, *De numis orientalibus in Numophylacio gothano asservatis commentatio prima*. Gotha, 1826.

München: Staatliche Münzsammlung, München.

Munzel: Kurt Munzel collection.

Munzel, Kurt. Beiträge zur Islamischen Numismatik I, *Jahrbuch für Numismatik und Geldgeschichte* 22 (1972), pp. 103–11.

Mustafa Beyram Bey. *Monnaies Orientales. Collection de Mr. Moustapha Beyram Bey.* Sales Catalogue, Amsterdam, 1909.

NC: Numismatic Chronicle.

Nicol: Dr. Norman D. Nicol collection, Seattle, Washington.

al-Nuwayrī, Aḥmad ibn ʿAbd al-Wahhāb. *Nihāyat al-ʿarab fī funūn al-adab*, Vols. 26–30. MS. Cairo: Dār al-Kutub, No. 549 *maʿārif ʿāmmah.*

NZ: Numismatische Zeitschrift.

Olivier de Beaumont: Olivier de Beaumont collection, Geneva.

Østrup: Østrup, Johannes Elith. *Catalogue des monnaies arabes et turques du Cabinet Royal des Médailles du Musée National de Copenhague.* Copenhagen, 1938.

Pakhomov VII: Pakhomov, Evgeniĭ Aleksandrovich. *Monetnye klady Azerbaidzhana i drugikh respublik kraev i oblastei Kavkaza*, VII. Baku, 1957.

Paris: Unpublished coins in the Cabinet des Médailles, Bibliothèque Nationale, Paris.

Paris-Mecca: Coins acquired by the Cabinet des Médailles, Bibliothèque Nationale, Paris, from a hoard found in Mecca, 1967. Cf. A. Launois, *Bulletin d'Études Orientales* 24 (1971), pp. 19–53, and *Coin Hoards* I (1975), No. 302.

Paris trade: Coins recorded by M. Raoul Curiel, Cabinet des Médailles, Bibliothèque Nationale, Paris, from collections offered for sale in Paris.

Paris-Vogüé: Collection de Vogüé in the Cabinet des Médailles, Bibliothèque Nationale, Paris.

Petrie: Petrie, Sir William Matthew Flinders. *Arabic Glass Weights and Stamps*. London, 1927.

Peus: Busso Peus auction catalogues.

Pietraszewski: Pietraszewski, Ignacy. *Numi mohammedani*. Berlin, 1843.

Prague: Naprstkovo Museum, Prague.

Rabie, Hassanein. *The Financial System of Egypt, AH 564–741/AD 1169–1341*. London, 1972.

Rivero, Casto Maria del. *La moneda arábigo-española; compendio de numismática musulman.* Madrid, 1933.

RN: Revue Numismatique.

RNB: Revue Numismatique Belge.

Rodgers, Charles James. *Catalogue of the Coins of the Indian Museum.* Calcutta, 1893–6.

Rogers: Rogers, Edward Thomas. Glass as a Material for Standard Coins Weights, *NC* n.s. 13 (1873), pp. 60–88.

Samir Shamma: Mr. Samir Shamma collection, Jeddah, Saudi Arabia.

Saulcy, Louis F. J. C. de. Lettre à Reinaud, *JA* 3e série, 13 (1842), pp. 315–26.

Seaby's Coin and Medal Bulletin 545 (October 1963).

Shukrī: Shukrī, Sājidah. al-dīnār al-islāmī, *Sumer* 10 (1954), pp. 129–38.

Siouffi: Siouffi, Nicolas, *Catalogue des monnaies arabes*. Mosul, 1879–80.

——. *Supplément nº 1 au Catalogue de monnaies arabes publié en 1879*. Mosul, 1891.

Soret, Frédéric Jacob. Lettre à . . . de Fraehn, *Mémoires de la Société Impériale d'Archéologie* 5 (1851), pp. 41–66, 179–214, 310–27.

——. Lettre à M. Sawelief, *RNB* 2e série, 4 (1854), pp. 273–99, 377–416.

——. Lettre à . . . de Dorn, *RNB* 2e série, 6 (1856), pp. 1–41, 129–77.

——. Lettre à . . . de Bartholomae, *RNB* 3e série, 2 (1858), pp. 105–39, 217–60, 476.

——. Lettre à . . . L. Krehl, *ZDMG* 19 (1865), pp. 544–61.

Sourdel, Dominique. Inventaire des Monnaies Musulmanes Anciennes du Musée de Caboul. Damascus, 1953.

Spinks Numismatic Circular (October 1945).

Tewhid: Ahmed Tewhid collection now in the Archeological Museum, Istanbul.

Tewhid-Bruxelles: Tewhid, Ahmed. Monnaies des Ayoubites de Hisn-Keïfa, *Procès-Verbaux et Mémoires du Congrès International de Numismatique et d'Art de la Médaille Contemporaine*, pp. 493–505. Bruxelles, 1910.

Tiesenhausen, Vladimir Gustavovich. Mélanges de numismatique orientale, *RNB* 31 (1875), pp. 189–214, 329–79.

Toll, Christopher. *Kitâb al-ǧauharatain al-ʿatîqatain al-mâʾiʿatain as-ṣafrâ waʾl-baiḍâʾ. Die Beiden Edelmetalle Gold und Silber von al-Hamdânî*. Uppsala, 1968.

Vollers, Karl. Das orientalische Münzkabinett der Universität Jena im Jahre 1906, *Blätter für Münzfreunde* 41 (1906), cols. 3515–20, 3522–4, 3529–37.

Wakin, Jeanette. *Catalogue of Ayyūbid coins at the American Numismatic Society* (manuscript). New York, 1963.

Webdale: C. M. Webdale collection, Bedford, England.

Weyl: Weyl, Adolph. *Verzeichnis von Münzen und Denkmünzen . . . verschiedener mohammedanischer Dynastien der Jules Fonrobert'schen Sammlung*. Berlin, 1878.

Wien: Kunsthistorisches Museum, Vienna.

Windisch-Graetz: Zambaur, Eduard Karl Max von. *Kollektion Ernst Prinz zu Windisch-Grätz. Orientalische Münzen*, Bd. VII, Teil 1. Vienna, 1906.

WNM: Wiener Numismatische Monatshefte.

Yapı-Kredi: Yapı ve Kredi Bankası collection, Istanbul.

Zambaur-*Contrib.* (I and II): Zambaur, Eduard Karl Max von. Contributions à la numismatique orientale, *NZ* 36 (1904), pp. 43–122; 37 (1905), pp. 113–98.

Zambaur-N.C.: ——. Nouvelles contributions à la numismatique orientale, *NZ* 47 (1914), pp. 115–90.

——. *Manuel de généalogie et de chronologie pour l'histoire de l'Islam*. Hannover, 1927.

——. *Die Münzprägungen des Islams*. Wiesbaden, 1968.

ZDMG: Zeitschrift der Deutschen Morgenländischen Gesellschaft.

ZfN: Zeitschrift für Numismatik.

Ziya: Ziya, Ahmet. *Meskûkât-ı islâmîye takvîmî*. Istanbul, 1328/1910.

CATALOGUE

THE AYYŪBIDS OF EGYPT

AL-NĀṢIR ṢALĀḤ AL-DĪN YŪSUF IBN AYYŪB

I. As Vassal of Nūr al-Dīn Maḥmūd ibn Zengī
[567–569 H = 1171–1173 AD]

II. As Nominal Vassal of al-Ṣāliḥ Ismāʿīl ibn Maḥmūd
[570–571 H = 1174 AD]

III. As Independent Ruler and Head of the Ayyūbid Family
[570–589 H = 1174–1193 AD]

I. AS VASSAL OF NŪR AL-DĪN MAḤMŪD IBN ZENGĪ

Saladin's first gold and silver issues do not bear his name, only that of Maḥmūd ibn Zengī. Nevertheless, they are Saladin's coinage and not that of the Aleppo Zengid. It was a cautious political move by Saladin, and after Maḥmūd died in 569 H, Saladin issued new coins in his own name.

GOLD

1. *Cairo—567 H*

On both sides: border of plain circle, in which counterclockwise marginal legend:

بسم الله الرحمن الرحيم ضرب هذا الدينر بالقاهرة سنة سبع وستين وخمسمائة   محمد رسول الله ارسله بالهدى ودين الحق ليظهره على الدين كله

Second circle, then second counterclockwise circular legend:

لا اله الا الله وحده لا شريك له ابو محمد   محمد رسول الله صلى الله عليه وعلى اله

Third circle and third counterclockwise circular legend:

وسلم تسليماً الملك العادل

Centre:

عال
محمود
بن زنكي
غاية

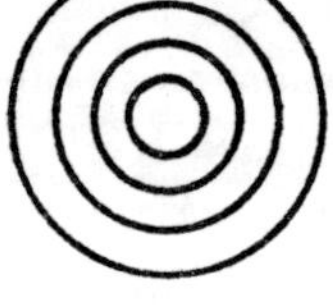

المستضي بامر الله امير المؤمنين

Centre:

الامام
الحسن

Izzet 243. Leuthold (21, 4.42). Khediv., p. 345.

2. *Cairo—568 H*

As above, but the following date:

سنة ثمان وستين وخمسمائة

Kurt Munzel, *Jahrbuch f. Num. u. Geldgeschichte*, 1972. No. 19 (22, 4.50, ill.).

3. *Cairo—569 H*

As above, but the following date:

سنة تسع وستين وخمسمائة

ANS (20, 4.11). Balog (21, 4.28, ill.). BMC 597 (22, 4.37, ill.). Samir Shamma (21, 4.15).

4. *Alexandria—567 H*

As above, but the following mint and date:

بالاسكندرية سنة سبع وستين وخمسمائة

ANS (21, 4.51). Ashmolean-Thorburn (22, 3.94, ill.). Balog, *BIE* XXXVI, 1953 (22, 4.53, ill.). BMC 596 (23, 4.97) [ستمأة instead of ستمائة].

5. *Alexandria—568 H*

As above, but the following date:

سنة ثمان وستين وخمسمائة

Balog (22, 4.79, ill.).

6. *Alexandria—569 H*

As above, but the following date:

سنة تسع وستين وخمسمائة

Centre:

محمود

بن زنكي

Without:

عال
—
غاية

Kurt Munzel, *Jahrbuch f. Num. u. Geldgeschichte*, 1972. No. 20 (22, 4.589, ill.). Paris (21, 3.82, ill.). Paris–Mecca (22, 4.03).

SILVER

7. *Black Dirhems*

The silver coins are in the shape of small square or oblong pieces, cut with a cold chisel from cast ribbon-like ingots and struck without sufficient heating. Because of the reduced size of the flan, the marginal legends are always missing, as is part of or the entire second circular legend. Some times even the inner circular legend is off the flan. The legends are similar to those on the gold coins, but without عال/غاية in the obverse centre. They were minted in Cairo or Alexandria.

External (actually second) circle on both sides.

Counterclockwise circular legend on both sides:

لا اله الا الله وحده لا شريك له ابو محمد

محمد رسول الله صلى الله عليه وعلى اله

Middle (actually third) circle on both sides.

Counterclockwise circular legend on both sides:

المستضي بامر الله امير المؤمنين

وسلم تسلماً الملك العادل

Inner circle on both sides:

Centre:

محمود

بن زنكي

Centre:

الامام

الحسن

The circular legends have been reconstructed with the help of the similar gold coins.

Balog, *BIE* XXXV, 1953. 1: (7 × 8, 0.69, ill.); 2: (8 × 8, 0.82, ill.); 3: (11 × 11, 1.33, ill.); 4: (9 × 12, 1.20); 5: (8 × 12, 0.92).

II. As Nominal Vassal of al-Ṣāliḥ Ismā'īl ibn Maḥmūd ibn Zengī

COPPER

8.

Damascus—570 H

Type A

[Legends in this series are in tall *Naskh*]

Border on both sides: dotted circle. Counterclockwise marginal legend on both sides:

ضرب هذا الفلس بدمشق سنة سبعين

Inner dotted circle.

On both sides arabesque flowers sprout from the top of the inner circle, above the legend:

Centre:

*

الملك الناصر

* يوسف

Centre:

الملك الصالح

|

اسمعيل

Balog (24, 4.97).

9.

Type B

Marginal legends (as far as on the flan), as above.

Inner dotted circle.

Centre:

الملك الناصر

* يوسف

Centre:

الملك الصالح

○ * ○

اسمعيل

Paris (23, 5.15; 23, 4.83; 23, 3.96; 23, 4.91).

10.

Type C

Marginal legends:

لا اله الا الله محمد رسول الله

ضرب هذا الفلس بدمشق سنة سبعين وخمسمائة

Inner circle of dots.

Centre:

* يو *

الملك الناصر

* سف

Centre:

ܓ

الملك الصالح

اسمعيل

BMC 6080 (28, 5.46, ill.). Khediv. 1464 (Obverse centre: يو / الملك النا / سف). Soret, letter to Krehl, *ZDMG*, 1865, No. II. München (28, —, ill.). Ilisch No. 8 (23, —).

11. *Damascus—571 H*

Obverse marginal legend missing.

Counterclockwise marginal legend:

ضرب . . . . سنة احد

Inner dotted circle, from the top of which an arabesque floweret hangs down on both sides.

Centre:	Centre:
الملك الناصر	الملك الصالح
يوسف *	اسمعيل
	*

ANS-UM (24, 5.69, ill.).

III. As Independent Ruler

A. With Caliph al-Mustaḍī bi-Amr Allāh

[570–575 H = 1174–1179 AD]

GOLD

[*Egypt Only*]

12. *Cairo—570 H*

Border on both sides-plain circle.

Counterclockwise marginal legend on both sides:

بسم الله الرحمن الرحيم ضرب هذا الدينر بالقاهرة سنة سبعين وخمسمائة   محمد رسول الله ارسله بالهدى ودين الحق ليظهره على الدين كله

Second circle on both sides. Counterclockwise circular legend on both sides:

لا اله الا الله وحده لا شريك له ابو محمد   ولو كره المشركون صلى الله عليه وعلى اله

Third circle on both sides. Counterclockwise circular legend on both sides:

المستضى بامر الله امير المؤمنين   عال الملك غاية الناصر

Fourth circle on both sides:

Centre:	Centre:
يوسف	الامام
بن ايوب	الحسن

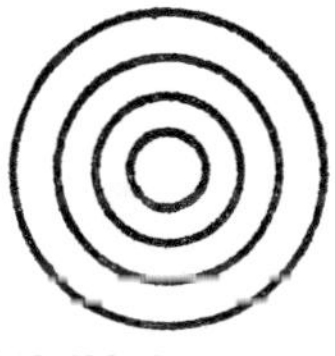

ANS-UM (21, 4.11). Balog (21, 4.24, ill.). BMC 243 (20, 3.45). Fahmy 1 (21, 4.24). Khediv. 1301 (—, 4.70). Lavoix 454 (21, 4.62). Yapı-Kredi (22, 4.30).

13. *Cairo 571 H*

As above, but the following date:

سنة ا عدى وسبعين وخمسمائة

ANS-UM (22, 4.01). Balog (21, 4.37). BMC 243 (21, 3.45). da Cunha II 1455 (18, 4.13). Fahmy 2 (21, 3.90). Khediv. 1303; 1304 (digit of date: احد). München 94066 (21, 4.929; digit of date: احد). Paris (21, 4.45). Samir Shamma (20, 3.90).

14. *Cairo—572 H*

As above, but the following date:

سنة اثنين وسبعين وخمسمائة

ANS-UM (20, 3.75). Balog (22, 3.72, ill.; 20, 4.15). Berlin 96/1898 (20, 5.11). BMC 244 (20, 4.54; In mint/date formula: هذ [*sic*], and in the third obverse circular legend عال and غاية transposed). Khediv. 1305. Munzel (22, 4.25). Paris–Mecca (21, 4.50). Paris trade (—, 3.23).

15. *Cairo—573 H*

As above, but the following date:

سنة ثلث وسبعين وخمسمائة

Artuk 710 (20, 3.75). Balog (20, 4.50, ill.). BMC 245 (21, 4.65; dated ثلث وسبعين وخمس مائة). Izzet 257. Khediv. 1306. Lavoix 455 (20, 4.58). Paris (20, 3.62). Paris trade (—, 4.68; —, 4.15). Paris–Mecca (20, 4.56). Siouffi, p. 17. Ziya 1613 (22, —).

16. *Cairo—574 H*

As above, but the following date:

سنة اربع وسبعين وخمسمائة

Lavoix 456 (21, 3.95). Leuthold (20, 4.51). Paris (21, 4.63). Paris–Mecca (21, 4.51). Samir Shamma (20.5, 5.00; digit of date ابع [*sic*]).

17. *Cairo—575 H*

As above, but the following date:

سنة خمس وسبعين وخمسمائة

ANS-UM (20, 3.86). Ashmolean-A. C. Kay (21, 3.80). Balog (21, 3.88, ill.). Berman 171 (21, 3.97). BMC 247 (20, 4.70; عال and غاية in the third obverse circular legend transposed). Fahmy 3 (20, 4.44); 4 (20, 5.53); 5 (20, 3.69). Lavoix 457 (21, 2.98). Leuthold (21, 4.46). Paris–Mecca (20, 4.38; 22, 5.00). Paris trade (—, 3.56; —, 4.01).

18. *Miṣr—573 H*

As above, but the following mint and date:

بمصر سنة ثلث وسبعين وخمسمائة

Balog (20, 3.87, ill.). BMC 246 (20, 3.90). Siouffi, p. 17. Yapı-Kredi (20, 4.00).

19. *Alexandria—570 H*

As above, but the following mint and date:

بالاسكندرية سنة سبعين وخمسمائة

ANS-UM (21, 4.11). Fahmy 86 (20, 3.72); 87 (20, 4.12). Khediv, 1302 (—, 4.00; date with query). Leuthold (22, 4.16, ill.). Paris–Mecca (21, 4.25).

20. *Alexandria—571 H*

As above, but the following date:

سنة احدى وسبعين وخمسمائة

ANS-UM (22, 4.01). Coll. R. B. F. Dauwe, Terneuzen, Holland. Leuthold (20, 4.12). Paris–Mecca (20, 3.36).

21. *Alexandria—572 H*

As above, but the following date:

سنة اثنين وسبعين وخمسمائة

ANS-UM (20.5, 3.72). Leuthold 1 (22, 5.82); 2 (20, 4.07). Samir Shamma (20, 5.05; *Iskandarīyah* written without the *yā*). Wien 6363 (21, 4.12).

22. *Alexandria—573 H*

As above, but the following date:

سنة ثلث وسبعين وخمسمائة

Paris-Mecca (21, 4.06). Paris trade (—, 4.06). Samir Shamma (20, 5.15; *Iskandarīyah* written without the *yā*).

23. *Alexandria—574 H*

As above, but the following date:

سنة اربع وسبعين وخمسمائة

Paris-Mecca (20, 4.32).

24. *Alexandria—575 H*

As above, but the following date:

سنة خمس وسبعين وخمسمائة

ANS-UM (20, 3.86). Ashmolean-A. C. Kay (16, 4.04, ill.). Berlin-Guthrie (20, 4.65). Fahmy 88 (21, 4.26). Khediv. 1307. Paris-Mecca (21, 4.62). Paris trade (—, 3.85).

SILVER

25. *Egypt—Undated*

The Egyptian silver coins are small, square or oblong flan *black dirhems*. The reading is reconstructed from several specimens, but even so, the mint, Cairo or Alexandria, is missing. The century and decade of the date are present on some specimens, but the digit is missing.

Border on both sides: plain circle. Counterclockwise marginal legend on both sides:

بسم الله ضرب هذا الدرهم . . . ستين خمسمائة　　　محمد رسول الله صلى الله عليه وعلى اله

Second circle on both sides. Counterclockwise circular legend on both sides:

ابو محمد المستضي بامر الله امير المؤمنين　　　وسلم تسليماً الملك الناصر

Inner circle on both sides.

Centre:
يوسف
بن ايوب

Centre:
الامام
الحسن

ANS-Newell (9 × 12, —). Balog 1 (5 × 7, 0.38);* 2 (6 × 11, 0.77, ill.); 3 (7 × 7, 0.80); 4 (10 × 10, 0.93, ill.); 5 (5 × 10, 0.98, ill.); 6 (9 × 11, 1.06, ill.); 7 (8 × 11, 1.15, ill.); 8 (9 × 13, 1.16); 9 (6 × 12, 1.16, ill.); 10 (10 × 13, 1.18, ill.); 11 (9 × 9, 1.20); 12 (9 × 13, 1.28); 13 (10 × 10, 1.33); 14 (9 × 12, 2.31).

---

*The date (5)67 H, سبع ستين is legible on the reverse of this specimen.

DIVISIONAL CURRENCY

The question of the use of glass jetons in Fāṭimid and Ayyūbid society has become the subject of a lively scholarly debate. My own position has been spelled out in a number of articles, including:

—'Les Jetons Fatimites en Verre,' *Revue Belge de Numismatique*, Vol. 107 (1961);

—'The Fāṭimid Glass Jeton,' *Annali dell'Instituto Italiano di Numismatica* 18–19 (1971–72) and 20 (1973);

—'The Ayyūbid Glass Jetons and their Use,' *JESHO* 9 (1966);

—'Fāṭimid and Post-Fāṭimid Glass Jetons from Sicily,' *Studi Magrebini* 7 (1975); and

—'Ayyūbid Divisional Currency Issued in Egypt by al-Kāmil Muḥammad I,' *Gazette numismatique suisse* 27 (1977).

In a forthcoming issue of *JESHO* my good friend, Dr. Michael Bates, will take issue with my interpretations in an article entitled, 'Were the Fāṭimid and Ayyūbid Glass Weights Used as Currency?' The editors of *JESHO* have been kind enough to agree to publish my response, 'Fāṭimid Glass Jetons: Token Currency or Coin Weights?' What follows is a summary of my views:

The Fāṭimids, at the beginning of their rule, used glass discs or glass jetons as coin weights, as had been done in Egypt and occasionally in Syria and Tunisia (Ifrīqīyah) since the time of Caliph 'Abd-al-Mālik.

At the beginning of al-Ḥākim's reign the number of glass jetons suddenly increased and remained very high under Caliphs al-Ẓāhir and al-Mustanṣir. As the number of jetons vastly exceeded the number needed as coin weights, they may have served as a fiduciary divisional currency. Not only do they still exist in huge numbers in modern collections—a fact which indicates that at the time of their circulation there must have been many times more—but often they have been found in hoards. Only money is hoarded; there would be no purpose in hiding large numbers of coin weights.

The almost total absence of copper coinage also seems to indicate that the glass jetons replaced the copper as currency. Copper had to be imported at high cost; whereas glass was cheap to produce, as the raw materials abound in Egypt.

The Umayyad and 'Abbāsid coin weights always show the denomination and it is clearly stated that they are a *dinar* weight, *dirhem* weight or a *fals* weight. The Fāṭimid jetons, with very few exceptions, never show a denomination—only the caliphal protocol, religious legends, and sometimes a date. Even when the value *dinar* is mentioned, the word *weight* is never used.

Finally, for every three or four genuine Fāṭimid jetons, there is one contemporary forgery. Some of these counterfeits are cleverly done, with legends more or less well-written, but with errors which do not occur in genuine pieces produced by skilled engravers. Others are clumsy imitations of the authentic government-issued jetons and could have circulated only among a largely illiterate population. Counterfeit coins have been manufactured for illicit gain in all periods, but it is difficult to believe that coin weights should have been imitated in such large quantities.

The Ayyūbids inherited from the Fāṭimids a well-functioning, highly developed government run by competent officials. They also inherited their mint and the monetary, as well as their ponderal system.

It is no surprise then that Saladin did not strike copper coins in Egypt at the beginning of his career, but, on the other hand, continued to issue glass jetons. Yet there are differences between the Fāṭimid jetons and those produced by Saladin and his successors, who, until al-Kāmil Muḥammad, never put their own names on the jetons—only those of the 'Abbāsid caliphs. The jetons struck in the name of Caliph al-Mustaḍī, from the years between 567 and 575 H, clearly belong to Saladin. After 575 H the jetons bear the name or short protocol of Caliph al-Nāṣir, who reigned from 576 until 622 H. Therefore, these jetons could have been issued by Saladin; his son, al-ʿAzīz ʿUthmān; his grandson, al-Manṣūr Muḥammad; or his brother, al-ʿĀdil I. As we have no means of attributing them to any one of these reigns, they will be listed under Saladin's reign.

The other difference between Fāṭimid and Ayyūbid jetons is in the raw material used. The early Fāṭimid jetons consist of transparent glass of poorer quality than that of their Umayyad and ʿAbbāsid precursors. There are, from the reign of al-Ḥākim, a few opaque glass-paste jetons, while under al-Mustanṣir they became a little more frequent, yet transparent glass still prevailed. Then, during the later periods of Fāṭimid rule, the transparent glass disappeared and was replaced by harder, more resistant opaque glass-paste jetons.

The Ayyūbid jetons, on the other hand, are, from the beginning, exclusively made of hard, resistant opaque glass-paste. This is of some importance because we can accept the actual weight of the Ayyūbid jetons as their original weight at the time of their emission; whereas the transparent Fāṭimid glass has often lost some of its superficial layers.

The colouring of the Ayyūbid jetons is of a limited range: from white, off-white, light grey, grey or grey-green, to pale blue and blue. The inscriptions on the jetons, with the caliph's name, are always in *Kūfic* and no date is present.

GLASS-PASTE JETONS

Caliph al-Mustaḍī

26.

Border: plain circle.

Centre:

الله

الامام

المستضي بامر

امير المؤمنين

ANS (30, 8.60, turquoise blue, ill.; 29, 8.58, turquoise blue). Balog (31, 8.42, blue; 31, 8.21, light green).

27.

Border: Plain Circle

الله

الامام

المستضي

بامر

ANS (24, 6.04, grey-white; 25, 6.09, light grey, ill.; 22, 2.96, pale brown). Balog (25, 5.87, light grey; 25, 5.87, yellowish-grey; 25, 5.68, yellowish-grey; 25, 6.03, light grey; 25, 5.98, yellowish-white; 22, 2.96, grey; 19, 2.93, light grey; 22, 2.07, pale green, ill.; 21, 2.94, light grey; 23, 2.97, light green; 21, 2.71, light grey). BMCG 58 (24, 5.70, white); 58a (22, 5.77, white); 59 (21, 4.93, white); 60 (21, 6.03, white). Launois-Maspéro 117 (26, 6.00, white/blue patches); 118 (26, 6.05, blue-white); 119 (26, 6.05, white); 120 (26, 6.05, off-white). Petrie 632 (—, 60.4); 633 (—, 6.04); 634 (—, 5.96); 635 (—, 5.98; all Petrie's jetons are 'milky'). Viré 165 (25, 5.83).

28. *No Border*

الله

المستضي

بامر

BMCG 64 (19, 2.98, white). Fouquet, p. 402, Nos. 239–240 (no weights given and inscriptions misread).

Syria

All the Syrian *silver* issues are on a normal-size round flan.

29. *Damascus—571 H*

On both sides: a plain within a dotted square, enclosed by a circle of dots. This arrangement will be designated as the *square-in-the-circle* type. Any variation from this composition will be fully recorded. For example, there is a linear square in a linear circle, and a square of dots in a circle of dots. These slightly different *square-in-the-circle* types are found on some copper issues. Counterclockwise marginal legends contained within the segments surrounding the square:

يوسف بن ايوب|ضرب بدمشق|سنة احدو|سبعين وخمسمائة

Centre:

صر

الملك النا

صلاح الد

نيا والدين

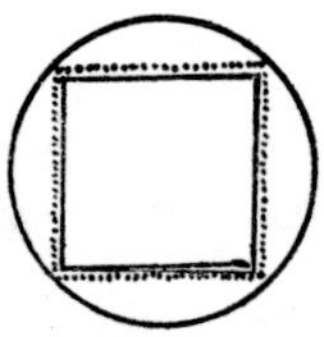

لا اله الا|الله وحده|محمد رسول|الله

Centre:

الامام

المستضي

بامر الله ا

مير المؤمنين

Pietraszewski 406.

30. *Damascus—573 H*

Square-in-the-circle type.

Border Segments:

يوسف بن ايوب|ضرب بدمشق|سنة ثلاث و|سبعين وخمسمائة

Centre:

صر

الملك النا

صلاح الد

نيا والدين

Border Segments:

لا اله الا|الله وحده|محمد رسو|ل الله الامام

Centre:

المستضي

بامر الله ا

مير المؤمنين

ANS (22, 2.92, ill.; 22, 2.924). Berlin-Guthrie (20, —). Berman 172 (19, 2.70). BMC 260 (20, 2.82; century of the date without the *alif*). Peus 1873. Lavoix 478 (19. 2.90). Leuthold-Ripostiglio 31 (—, 2.91). Weyl 6500 (20, 2.60). Casto Mario del Rivero, *La Moneda arábigo-española*, p. 140, No. 68.

31. *Damascus—575 H*

As above, but the following date:

سنة خمس وسبعين وخمسمائة

ANS (20.5, 2.96). K. Vollers, Das Orientalische Münzkabinett der Universität Jena im Jahre 1906, *Blätter für Münzfreunde*, 1906. 18 (photograph only).

Half Dirhem
Damascus—Undated
Type A

32.
Square-in-the-circle type.

Border Segments:
يوسف | بن ايوب | ضرب | بدمشق
Centre:
الملك النا
صر صلاح
الدين

Border Segments:
لا اله ا | لا الله | محمد رسو | ل الله الامام
Centre:
المستضي
بامر الله
امير المؤمنين

ANS (15, —, ill.). Berlin 627/1896 (14, 1.18). Paris (15, 1.42, ill.).

Type B

33.
Square-in-the-circle type.

Border Segments:
يوسف | بن ايوب | ضرب | بدمشق
Centre:
الملك النا
صر صلاح
الدين

Border Segments:
لا اله | الا الله | محمد رسو | ل الله
Centre:
الامام
المستضي
بامر الله

Album. ANS-Torrey (16, 1.28, ill.). Ashmolean-Thorburn (14, 1.38). BMC 261 (14, 1.47). Berman 173 (13, 0.95). Khediv. 1332. New York trade (14, 1.39).

Quarter Dirhem
Damascus—Undated

34.
Square-in-the-circle type.

Border Segments:
يوسف | بن ايوب | ضرب | بدمشق
Centre:
الملك
الناصر

Border Segments:
لا اله الا | الله وحده | محمد رسو | ل الله
Centre:
المستضي
بامر الله

Artuk 700 (10, 0.60). Ashmolean-Sir C. Warren (11, 0.68). Paris (10, 0.73).

Half Dirhem
Ḥamāh—Undated

35.
Square-in-the-circle type.

Border Segments:
يوسف | بن ايوب | ضرب | بحماه
Centre:
الملك
O
الناصر

Border Segments:
لا اله | الا ا | لله و | حده
Centre:
المستضئ
بامر الله

ANS-UM (14, 1.493, ill.). Khediv. 1333.

COPPER

There are no known copper coins struck by Saladin with the name of Caliph al-Mustaḍī.

B. With Caliph al-Nāṣir li-Dīn Allāh
[575–589 H = 1179–1193 AD]

Egypt

GOLD

36. *Cairo—576 H*

Border on both sides—plain circle. Counterclockwise marginal legend on both sides:

بسم الله الرحمن الرحيم ضرب هذا الدينر بالقاهرة سنة ست وسبعين وخمسمائة

محمد رسول الله ارسله بالهدى ودين الحق ليظهره على الدين كله

Double circle on both sides. Counterclockwise circular legend on both sides:

لا اله الا الله ابو العباس الناصر لدين الله امير المؤمنين

عال الملك غاية صلاح الدين

Inner circle on both sides.

Centre:

الامام
•
احمد

Centre:

يوسف
بن ايوب

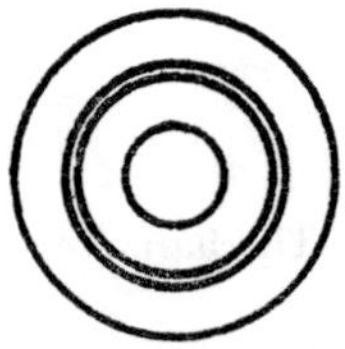

ANS-UM (20, 5.213). Fahmy 6 (20, 3.56); 7 (19, 3.73); 8 (19, 3.30). Khediv. 1308 (—, 4.60). Lavoix 458 (20, 4.40, ill.). Samir Shamma (20, 4.10). Yapı-Kredi (19, 3.65).

37. *Cairo—577 H*

As above, but the following date:

سنة سبع وسبعين وخمسمائة

Artuk 711 (19, 4.35). Balog (19, 5.29). Khediv. 1309. Leuthold (19, 4.60). Paris (20, 6.63, ill.). Samir Shamma (19, 4.10; 21, 5.70).

38. *Cairo—578 H*

As above, but the following date:

سنة ثمان وسبعين وخمسمائة

ANS-UM (19.6, 3.736). Codrington, *Ceylon Coins and Currency*. Fahmy 9 (20, 4.64). Khediv. 1310. Paris-Mecca (18, 5.46; 18, 4.08). Paris trade (—, 4.47; —, 3.32). Samir Shamma (19, 4.85). Wien 7719 (19, 4.00).

39. *Cairo—579 H*

As above, but the following date:

سنة تسع وسبعين وخمسمائة

ANS-UM (19.5, 4.169; 19, 3.766). Balog (20, 4.15). Fahmy 10 (20, 4.44); 11 (20, 4.14); 12 (19, 4.33). Khediv. 1312. Leuthold (19, 4.18). Munzel (19, 3.82). Yapı-Kredi (20, 4.25).

40. *Cairo—580 H*

As above, but the following date:

سنة ثمانين وخمسمائة

ANS-UM (19.5, 3.79). BMC 249 (20, 4.04, ill.; century of the date: خمس مائة). BM (—, 5.15). Fahmy 13 (19, 4.62); 14 (19, 3.70); 15 (18, 4.97); 16 (18, 1.93); 17 (20, 4.37). Khediv. 1315. Leuthold (19, 4.75). Paris-Mecca (19, 4.71; 18, 4.64; 20, 4.78; 19, 4.72; 19, 2.86; 19, 4.02). Paris trade (—, 4.74; —, 3.94; —, 4.56; —, 4.47; —, 3.65). Samir Shamma (20, 4.30). Siouffi, p. 17.

41. *Cairo—581 H*

As above, but the following date:

سنة احدى وثمانين وخمسمائة

ANS-UM (20, 4.86). Fahmy 18 (19, 4.66); 19 (19, 3.29). Khediv. 1319. Lavoix 459 (20, 4.08, ill.). Leuthold (19, 3.58). Paris-Mecca (20, 4.36; 18, 2.58). Paris trade (—, 3.41; —, 4.70). Samir Shamma (20, 4.75). Siouffi, p. 17.

42. *Cairo—582 H*

As above, but the following date:

سنة اثنين وثمنين *or* ثمانين وخمسمائة

ANS-UM (19.5, 5.53; 19.5, 4.70). Berlin 607/1892 (20, 4.06; the digit of the date: اثنتين). BMC 251 (19, 4.39; ornaments over عال and غاية). Mitchell-Brown (20, 5.93; decade of the date with an *alif*). Fahmy 20 (20, 4.24); 21 (20, 4.57); 22 (20, 4.32); 23 (20, 4.64); 24 (20, 4.83); 25 (20, 6.45); 26 (20, 4.43); 27 (18, 4.15); 28 (19, 3.62). Khediv. 1382. Leuthold (20, 4.18; 19, 3.62; 18, 3.84). Paris-Mecca (20, 5.69; 20, 5.46; 20, 5.41). Paris trade (—, 3.73; —, 3.71; —, 3.96; —, 3.20). Samir Shamma (19, 4.60; 19, 4.67; 18, 3.95; 19, 3.15). Siouffi, p. 17. Yapı-Kredi (20, 4.17).

43. *Cairo—583 H*

As above, but the following date:

سنة ثلث وثمانين وخمسمائة

Floweret over عال and غاية.

ANS-UM (20, 3.98). Balog (20, 4.42, ill.). BMC 253 (20, 4.16). Dorn, *Inventaire*, 4th fasc., No. 1. Fahmy 29 (20, 4.78); 30 (20, 3.85); 31 (19, 3.69); 32 (19, 3.90); 33 (20, 4.85); 34 (20, 5.07); 35 (20, 3.55); 36 (20, 5.15); 37 (19, 4.43); 38 (19, 4.45); 39 (20, 4.14). Khediv. 1322. Leuthold (20, 4.18; 19, 4.34). Munzel (20, 5.42). Paris-Mecca (20, 5.80; 20, 4.06; 20, 5.25, 20, 4.43, 20, 4.40). Paris-RN 1935 (20, 3.78). Paris trade (—, 5.02; —, 3.60; —, 4.07; —, 4.58; —, 4.29). Samir Shamma (19, 4.00). Siouffi, p. 17.

44. *Cairo—584 H*

As above, but the following date:

سنة اربع وثمانين وخمسمائة

Ornament over عال and غاية.

ANS-UM (20, 4.58). Balog (20, 4.87). Fahmy 40 (19, 4.12). Khediv. 1324. Lavoix 460 (19, 4.10). Leuthold (20, 4.08). Samir Shamma (18.5, 4.37). Siouffi, p. 17.

45. *Cairo—585 H*

As above, but the following date:

سنة خمس وثمنين وخمسمائة

Ornament over عال and غاية.

ANS-UM (19, 4.41). Artuk 712 (19, 4.80). BMC 255 (19, 2.77; century of the date: خمس مائة). Fahmy 41 (19, 4.77); 42 (20, 6.57); 43 (20, 6.47); 44 (20, 5.37); 45 (20, 4.32); 46 (20, 4.02). Izzet 258. Leuthold (20, 4.16). München 82625 (20, 3.763; decade: ثمانين). Paris-Mecca (20, 4.48; 20, 4.58). Paris trade (—, 4.07; —, 3.48). Pietraszewski 411 (2 specimens); 412. Siouffi, p. 17.

46. *Cairo—586 H*

As above, but the following date:

سنة ست وثمانين وخمسمائة

Floweret over عـــال and غـــاية.

ANS-UM (20, 3.46). Balog (20, 3.63, ill.). Berlin 236/1881 (20, 5.00). BMC 256 (18, 3.23; ringlet over المؤمنين). Fahmy 47 (19, 4.65); 48 (20, 4.76); 49 (20, 7.37); 50 (20, 5.06); 51 (20, 4.90); 52 (20, 5.49). Khediv. 1326. Lavoix 461 (20, 4.34); 462 (20, 4.30). Leuthold (20, 4.60; 18, 3.10). Paris-Mecca (19, 4.60; 21, 5.49; 19, 4.11; 19, 3.83). Paris trade (—, 3.79; —, 4.41; —, 3.68; —, 4.22; —, 3.84; —, 4.33; —, 4.02; —, 4.27). Samir Shamma (19, 4.55). Yapı-Kredi (20, 4.10).

47. *Cairo—587 H*

As above, but the following date:

سنه سبع وثمنين وخمسمائة

Floweret over عـــال and غـــاية.

ANS-UM (20, 3.47). Artuk 713 (20, 3.75). Ashmolean-A. C. Kay (20, 3.914). Balog (20, 4.55). BMC 257 (20, 4.54; century of the date written: خمس مائة); 258 (20, 4.53; annulet over عليه at the end of the obverse marginal legend). Fahmy 53 (20, 3.53); 54 (20, 3.47); 55 (19, 2.71); 56 (20, 3.92); 57 (20, 4.17); 58 (20, 4.17); 59 (20, 5.07); 60 (19, 4.44); 61 (20, 5.09); 62 (21, 6.81); 63 (20, 3.85); 64 (20, 4.47). Khediv. 1328. Leuthold (20, 3.62; 19, 3.76). Munzel (20, 3.43). Paris-Mecca (20, 4.17; 20, 3.55; 19, 3.76; 20, 3.34; 19, 2.82; 20, 4.56, ill.). Paris trade (—, 3.85; —, 3.76; —, 3.18; —, 3.65; —, 3.27; —, 4.17; —, 3.80; —, 4.23; —, 3.83). Peus 1878. Samir Shamma (20, 4.3; 20, 3.93). Siouffi, p. 17. Yapı-Kredi (20, 4.14). Wien 12324 (21, 4.15; 20, 3.20); 7548 (20, 2.57).

48. *Cairo—588 H*

As above, but the following date:

سنة ثمان وثمانين وخمسمائة

Floweret over عـــال and غـــاية.

ANS-UM (20.5, 3.50). Artuk 714 (20, 3.40). Balog (19, 3.97, ill.). Berlin-Guthrie (21, 3.65; ringlet over المؤمنين). BMC 259 (20, 4.76). da Cunha 1457 (18, 4.65). Fahmy 65 (19, 4.15); 66 (20, 3.64); 67 (20, 4.18); 68 (20, 5.19); 69 (20, 3.95); 70 (20, 4.38); 71 (20, 5.50); 72 (20, 5.36); 73 (20, 5.36); 74 (20, 3.21); 75 (19, 4.02); 76 (20, 3.89); 77 (19, 3.37); 78 (19, 3.68); 79 (20, 4.60). Khediv. 1329. Lavoix 463 (20, 2.60). Leuthold (21, 3.46; 20, 3.99). Markov, p. 355, No. 8. Munzel (20, 5.16). Østrup 1555 (—, 3.03). Paris-Mecca (20, 3.66; 20, 4.66; 19, 3.08; 20, 3.33; 20, 4.73; 20, 4.72; 20, 3.12). Paris-Vogüé 1538 (20, 3.95). Paris trade (—, 4.14; —, 3.28; —, 4.63; —, 3.63; —, 3.72; —, 3.74; —, 4.30; —, 4.24; —, 3.61; —, 3.58; —, 4.35; —, 3.27). Samir Shamma (20, 4.60; 20, 4.70). Siouffi, p. 17. Yapı-Kredi (20, 4.30).

49. *Cairo—589 H*

As above, but the following date:

سنة تسع وثمنين وخمسائة

da Cunha 1458 (18, 5.06). Fahmy 80 (20, 4.42); 81 (19, 4.68). Khediv. 1330, 1331. Leuthold (20, 5.31). Paris-Mecca (20, 2.41; 21, 4.20). Paris trade (—, 4.52; —, 3.75; —, 3.00). Samir Shamma (19, 3.35; 20, 4.30). Siouffi, p. 17.

50. *Alexandria—576 H*

As above, but the following mint and date:

بالاسكندرية سنه ست وسبعين وخمسائة

Balog (20, 4.04, ill.). Paris-Mecca (21, 4.88).

51. *Alexandria—578 H*

As above, but the following date:

سنة ثمان وسبعين وخمسائة

Khediv. 1311. Leuthold (18, 4.29). Samir Shamma (19, 4.30). Siouffi, p. 17.

52. *Alexandria—579 H*

As above, but the following date:

سنة تسع وسبعين وخمسائة

ANS-UM (20, 4.26). BMC 248 (20, 3.55). Fahmy 89 (20, 4.85); 90 (20, 4.25); 91 (20, 3.45); 92 (20. 4.73); 93 (19, 3.25). Khediv. 1313, 1314. Leuthold (20, 4.00). Paris-Mecca (19, 2.49; 20, 4.28). Paris trade (—, 4.00; —, 4.35; —, 4.09; —, 3.84). Samir Shamma (20, 5.15).

53. *Alexandria—580 H*

As above, but the following date:

سنة ثمانين وخمسائة

ANS-UM (21, 4.53). Artuk 708 (20, 4.40). Balog (19, 3.82), ill.). BMC 250 (19, 3.29). da Cunha 1456 (18, 4.96). Fahmy 94 (19, 3.98); 95 (20, 4.82); 96 (20, 4.84). Khediv. 1316, 1317, 1318. Lavoix 451 (20, 4.18). Leuthold (19, 4.29). Munzel (19, 4.29). Paris-Mecca (20, 4.88; 20, 449). Paris trade (—, 4.33). Samir Shamma (19, 4.25). Siouffi, p. 17.

54. *Alexandria—581 H*

As above, but the following date:

سنة احدى وثمنين وخمسائة

ANS (19, 4.46). ANS-UM (19, 3.21). BM-Prideaux 151 (20, 5.84). Codrington, *Ceylon Coins and Currency*. Leuthold (19, 3.83). Paris-Mecca (19, 4.21, 19, 5.00; 19, 4.54). Paris trade (—, 4.01; —, 5.41; —, 3.81). Pietraszewski 409. Samir Shamma (19.5, 4.55). Siouffi, p. 17.

55. *Alexandria—582 H*

As above, but the following date:

سنة اثنتين وثمانين وخمسائة

[*sic*]

ANS-UM (20, 3.89). Balog (19, 3.41). Berlin-Gotha 177/1935 (20, 6.01). BMC 252 (19, 4.32; ornaments over عال and غاية). Fahmy 97 (19, 3.54); 98 (20, 4.16); 99 (20, 4.19); 100 (20, 4.23); 101 (20, 4.86). Khediv. 1321. Leuthold (19, 4.16). Paris-Mecca (19, 4.60; 19, 4.71). Paris trade (—, 4.51; —, 4.39; —, 4.64; —, 4.67).

56. *Alexandria—583 H*

As above, but the following date:

سنة ثلث وثمانين وخمسمائة

ANS-UM (20, 4.33). Artuk 709 (20, 4.35). Balog (18, 4.20, ill.). BMC 254 (20, 4.49). Fahmy 102 (19, 4.05); 103 (20, 4.45). Khediv. 1523. Lavoix 452 (19, 3.95). Leuthold (20, 5.53; 19, 3.70). Paris-Mecca (20, 4.19).

57. *Alexandria—584 H*

As above, but the following date:

سنة اربع وثمانين وخمسمائة

Leuthold (20, 6.72; 19, 3.76). Pietraszewski 411 (2 specimens). Siouffi, p. 17.

58. *Alexandria—585 H*

As above, but the following date:

سنة خمس وثمانين وخمسمائة

Balog (21, 3.65, ill.). Fahmy 104 (20, 3.88); 105 (20, 3.73). Khediv. 1325. Leuthold (21, 5.94).

59. *Alexandria—586 H*

As above, but the following date:

سنة ست وثمنين وخمسمائة

Fahmy 106 (19, 3.66). Leuthold (18, 4.67). Markov, p. 355, No. 4.

60. *Alexandria—588 H*

As above, but the following date:

سنة ثمان وثمنين وخمسمائة

ANS (19, 6.07). Fahmy 107 (19, 4.59); 108 (19, 3.63). Leuthold (20, 5.02). Siouffi, p. 17.

61. *Alexandria—589 H*

As above, but the following date:

سنة تسع وثمنين وخمسمائة

Fahmy 109 (20, 3.79). Leuthold (20, 4.96; 19, 3.89). Siouffi, p. 17.

$\frac{1}{8}$ Dinar—No Mint

62. *Egypt—Undated*

Border on both sides, plain circle. Counterclockwise marginal legend on both sides:

صلاح الدنيا والدين يوسف بن ايوب	ابو العباس احمد امير المؤمنين

Plain circle on both sides.

Centre:	Centre:
الملك	الامام
الناصر	الناصر

Artuk 697 (10, 0.40, ill.). Paris (10, 0.41).

SILVER

Black Dirhems

The black dirhems weigh, as a rule, less than one-half dirhem. The majority are well under 1·50 grams and only a few reach two grams. Their diameters are small and they are either roughly square or oblong, the centre of the design being present on most coins. The marginal legends are either off the flan, or are only partially preserved. On some specimens the century and the decade of the date are preserved, but the digit has been read on only one specimen. Three types can be distinguished on the basis of the circular patterns dividing the legends. Naturally, no chronological order can be attempted until more dated black dirhems come to light. For all three varieties, the reading is reconstructed from several coins:

A. Border: plain circle. Second circle: double. Inner circle: simple.
B. Border: plain circle. Second and inner circles: simple.
C. Border: plain circle. Second circle: simple. Inner circle: double.

63. *Cairo—576 H*

Type A

Border on both sides: plain circle. Counterclockwise marginal legend on both sides:

بسم الله ضرب . . . بالقاهرة سنة ست وسبعين وخمسمائة | محمد رسول الله ارسله بالهدى ودين الحق ليظهره

Double circle on both sides. Counterclockwise circular legend on both sides:

ابو العباس الناصر لدين الله امير المؤمنين | على الدين كله الملك صلاح الدين

Inner circle on both sides.

Centre:	Centre:
الامام	يوسف
احمد	بن ايوب

Balog, *BIE*, XXXV (1953) (7 × 11, 1.07, ill.).

The date is missing on the following specimens, but must be 576 H:

ANS (7 × 8, —). ANS-Newell (9 × 10, —). Balog, *BIE*, XXXV (1953), 1 (9 × 9, 0.91); 2 (9 × 13, 1.70); 3 (8 × 14, 2.02).

64. *Cairo—Date Missing*

Type B

Border: plain circle. Second and inner circles: simple.

ANS (8 × 12, 1.66; 9 ×9, —; 9 × 10, —; 9 ×12, —; 7 × 9, —; 7 × 7, —). Ashmolean (11 × 12, 1.90; 8 × 9, 1.30). Balog, *BIE*, XXXI (1949), pp. 21–22 and *BIE*, XXXV (1953), pp. 412–413 [In this article the name of Caliph al-Nāṣir Aḥmad has erroneously been substituted for that of his predecessor, Caliph al-Haṣan al-Mustaḍī] 1 (8 × 9, 0.67); 2 (9 × 9, 0.90); 3 (8 × 9, 0.89); 4 (9 × 9, 1.24); 5 (8 × 12, 1.50); 6 (8 × 10, 1.01); 7 (7 × 9, 1.02); 8 (8 × 10, 1.07); 9 (8 × 11, 1.18, ill.); 10 (9 × 11, 1.27, ill.); 11 (9 × 10, 1.28, ill.); 12 (6 × 13, 1.35); 13 (8 × 14, 1.45, ill.); 14 (7 ×9, 0.71); 15 (8 ×9, 0.97); 16 (7 × 12, 0.82); 17 (8 × 8, 0.70); 18 (7 × 10, 0.75); 19 (8 × 8, 0.86); 20 (8 × 11, 0.94); 21 (10 × 12, 1.38, ill.); 22 (10 × 12, 2.17); 23 (9 × 13, 1.99, ill.); 24 (10 × 14, 1.76, ill.). BM (7 × 11, 0.99; 8 × 11, 1.25; 10 × 10, 0.75, ill.). München 92495 (7 × 10, 1.286).

65. *Cairo—Date Missing*
Type C

Border: plain circle. Second circle: simple. Inner circle: double.

ANS (8 × 14, —; 9 × 14, —). ANS-Newell (10 × 12, —). Balog, *BIE*, XXXV (1953), p. 413, 1 (5 × 8, 0.55); 2 (9 ×9, 0.60); 3 (8 × 10, 0.68); 4 (8 × 9, 0.68); 5 (7 × 8, 0.69); 6 (8 × 12, 0.67); 7 (6 × 9, 0.80); 8 (6 × 12, 1.00); 9 (9 × 9, 1.02); 10 (7 × 13, 1.08); 11 (7 × 10, 1.12); 12 (10 × 11, 1.14, ill.); 13 (8 × 9, 1.29, ill.); 14 (9 × 15, 1.34); 15 (9 × 11, 1.36, ill.); 16 (9 × 10, 1.36); 17 (9 × 10, 1.41); 18 (9 × 11, 1.47); 19 (9 × 11, 1.78); 20 (7 × 11, 1.96).

Normal-Size, Round-Flan Dirhems

According to al-Maqrīzī, Saladin introduced a sweeping reform in 583 H. He had the black dirhems melted down, subsequently issuing round-flan dirhems of 50-percent fine silver. The first two years are not yet represented in modern collections, which may be due to a considerable delay before Saladin's order was carried out. The few known specimens may be a sign that the experiment had to be suspended because of a lack of bullion in Egypt. A similar coinage reform was instituted under al-ʿĀdil I; although he reigned from 596 H until 615 H, specimens for only 598 H, 600 H, 601 H and 605 H are known.

66. *Cairo—585 H*

Square-in-the-circle type.

Border Segments:

يوسف بن ايوب|ضرب بالقاهرة|سنة خمس ثما|نين وخمسمائة

Centre:

الملك الناصر
صلاح الد
نيا والدين

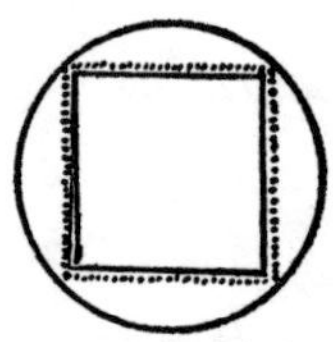

Border Segments:

لا اله الا|الله وحده|محمد ر|سول الله

Centre:

الامام النا
صر لدين الله
امير المؤمنين

Private collection, New York (23, 2.34).

67. *Cairo—586 H*

As above, but the following date:

سنة ستّ وثما|نين وخمسمائة

ANS (20, 2.83, ill.). Album 33 (21, 2.97). Artuk 715 (20, 2.85—date misprinted). Balog (20, 2.90, ill.). BM (22, —, ill.). Leuthold-Ripostiglio 21 (21, 2.98).

DIVISIONAL CURRENCY

68.

COPPER

A unique small copper coin, roughly square, is the only evidence that Saladin issued copper coins in Egypt after 576 H. On the reverse the Caliph al-Nāṣir's name can be read. The little coin was struck without heating and is similar to the black dirhems. The marginal legend is missing on both sides and much of the second circular legend is missing on the reverse. However, it is possible to reconstruct the legend sufficiently to recognize that it contains the two qualifying words, عال غاية, characteristic of the gold coins.

Border and marginal legend missing on both sides. Second, counterclockwise circular legends (reconstructed):

عال الملك (غاية صلاح الدين)	(لا اله الا الله ابو العباس الناصر لدين الله) امير المؤمنين

Inner circle.

Centre:	Centre:
يوسف	الامام
بن ايوب	احمد

Balog (10 × 11, 2.04, ill.).

GLASS-PASTE JETONS

69.

Caliph al-Nāṣir li-Dīn Allāh

In contrast to the almost non-existent copper coins, glass-paste jetons, which served as a fiduciary currency, continued to be issued in large numbers.

Border: Plain circle

Centre:
الامام
الناصر لدين
الله امير
المؤمنين

Balog 16 (32, 8.72, deep turquoise blue, ill.); 17 (26, 3.55, blue-green, ill.).

70. *Border: Plain Circle*

Centre:
الامام
الناصر
لدين الله

ANS 8 (22, 3.06, grey green). Balog 1 (26, 3.76).

71. *No Border*

Centre:

الله
الامام
الناصر
لدين

ANS 7 (20, 3.01, pale turquoise). Balog 14 (20, 2.92, light grey); 15 (25, 2.85, grey, ill.); 18 (26, 6.01, light grey); 20 (25, 5.88, grey); 22 (24, 5.80, yellowish-white); 23 (24, 6.07, grey, ill.); 24 (21, 2.80, grey); 25 (21, 2.93, green); 26 (21, 3.06, grey); 27 (24, 5.85); 30 (30, 2.94, light grey). BMCG 70 (19, —, white). Grohmann, p. 205, Nos. 155 (25, 5.08, light green); 156 (26, 6.01). Horovitz 2 (21, 2.90, light grey); 3 (20, 2.86, light grey); 4 (21, 2.96, light grey). Petrie 636 (—, 6.11, greenish, milky). Rogers 132 (20, 2.98); 133 (20, 5.84, greenish-white). Viré 167 (24, 5.83, grey-white); 168 (21, 2.98, grey-white); 169 (20, 2.97, grey-white).

72. *No Border*

Centre:

الامام
الناصر لدين
الله امير

Balog 28 (26, 5.80, blue, ill.).

73. *No Border*

Centre:

الله
الامام احمد
لدين

Balog 19 (26, 5.85, grey-green, ill.). BMCG 69 (22, 2.98, green; misread).

74. *No Border*

Centre:

الامام
الناصر
لدين له [*sic*]

BMCG 65 (22, 5.86, green); 66 (22, 5.77, green).

75. *No Border*

Centre:

الله
الاما النا
م صر

BMCG 71 (20, 3.05, white; the last line: لدين is missing).

76. *No Border*

Centre:

الامام

الناصر

ANS 10 (16, 1.51, greenish-white); 11 (25, 5.99, turquoise blue). Balog 32 (15, 1.43, white, ill.); 33 (15, 1.42, light grey); 33a (24, 6.00, grey, ill.). BMCG 67 (21, 5.85, green). Fouquet, *Suppl.* 2 and 3. Launois-Maspéro 121 (25, 6.65, green); 122 (25, 6.05, white/blue patches); 123 (25, 6.05, white); 124 (20, 3.02, white); 125 (22, 3.10, blue); 130 (13, 1.50, off-white); 131 (13, 1.50, off-white); 132 (13, 1.50, off-white). Viré 171 (15, 1.51, greenish-white).

77. *No Border*

Centre:

الامام

احمد

Horovitz 5 (21, 2.90, light grey); 6 (22, 3.02, light grey). Launois-Maspéro 126 (25, 6.05, white/blue patches); 127 (22, 2.95, white/blue patches); 128 (25, 6.05, white/blue patches); 129 (21, 2.00, off-white).

78. *No Border*

Centre:

الناصر

Balog (12, 0.75, off-white).

Syria

GOLD

79. *Damascus—583 H*

This is Saladin's only gold minted in Syria. It was probably issued to mark the conquest of Jerusalem and the defeat of the Crusaders in that year. One may attribute the exalted title used on the coin, *Sulṭān al-Islām wa'l-Muslimīn*, to Saladin's role as Defender of the Faith against the Franks. However, he issued copper coins as early as 580 H, which already featured the title of *Sulṭān al-Muslimīn*.

Border on both sides, plain circle. Counterclockwise marginal legend on both sides:

بسم الله ضرب هذا الدينر بدمشق سنة ثلث وثمنين وخمس مائة	ارسله بالهدى ودين الحق ليظهره على الدين كله ولوكره المشركون

Second circle on both sides. Counterclockwise circular legend on both sides:

صلاح الدنيا والدين سلطان الاسلام والمسلمين	لا اله الا الله وحده لا شريك له محمد رسول الله

Inner circle on both sides.

Centre:	Centre:
الملك الناصر	الامام الناصر
يوسف بن ايوب	امير المؤمنين

Ashmolean-Rev. G. J. Chester (22, 4.00, ill.). Balog (21, 4.07, ill.). BMC 254a (22, 3.79). Pietraszewski 410. Siouffi, p. 17.

The coins of this issue are of rather pale gold, which would suggest a lower-than-usual gold content.

SILVER

80. *Damascus—575 H*

Square-in-the-circle type.

Border Segments:

يوسف بن ايوب|ضرب بدمشق|سنة خمس و|سبعين وخمسمائة

Centre:

صر
الملك النا
صلاح الد
نيا والدين

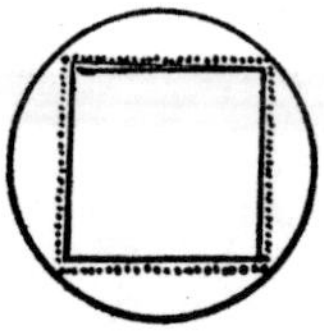

Border Segments:

لا اله الا|الله وحده|محمد رسو|ل الله

Centre:

الامام النا
صر لدين الله
ع
امير المؤمنين

ANS (20. 5, 2.96). Balog (20, 2.93, ill.). Lavoix 479 (22, 2.94). Leuthold-Ripostiglio 32 (21, 2.85). Paris (21, 2.93). Peus 1874. Ziya 1615 (19, —).

Erroneous Type

81. *Damascus—575 H*

Border Segments:

يوسف بن ايوب|ضرب بدمشق|سنة خم . . .|. . . سين وخمس . . .

Centre:

الملك النا
صر لدين الله
امير المؤمنين

Border Segments:

لا اله ا|لا الله|محمد رسو|ل الله

Centre:

الامام النا
صلاح الد
نبا والدين

The anomalous central legends on both sides are evidently due to an engraver's error.

Ilisch 3 (20.5, —).

82. *Damascus—576 H*

As No. 80, but the following date:

سنة ستة و|سبعين وخمسمائة

ANS (22.5, 3.015; 22, 2.89). Ashmolean-A.C. Kay (23, 2.86, ill.). Leuthold-Ripostiglio 33 (—, 2.97). München 91845 (19, 2.957). Pietraszewski 407. Yapı-Kredi (21, 2.75). Ziya 1916 (19, —).

83. *Damascus—577 H*

As above, but the following date:

سنة سبع وسبع|ين وخمسمائة

ANS 54119 (21, 2.964). Ashmolean-Thorburn (22, 2.97, ill.). Pietraszewski 408. Prague 92/63-892.

Damascus—578 H

84. *Type A*

As above, but the following date:

سنة ثمان|سبعين وخمسمائة

ANS-Laties (20, 2.63). Balog (20, 2.98). Çetinyalçın (21, —). Khediv. 1334. Østrup 1556 (—, 2.78).

85. *Type B*

As above, but the

Obverse Centre:	Reverse Centre:
الملك الناصر	الامام النا
صلاح الد	صر لدين الله
نيا والدين	امير المؤمنين
	Floral Sprig Across Bottom Line

ANS-Laties (21, 2.88).

Damascus—579 H

86. *Type A*

As above, but the following date:

سنة تسع و|سبعين وخمسمائة

Centre:	Centre:
صر	الامام النا
الملك النا	صر لدين الله
صلاح الد	
نيا والدين	امير المؤمنين

ANS (21.5, 2.92). Berlin-Guthrie (20, 2.80; Date: سنئة تسع|سبعين خمسمائة). BMC 262 (20, 2.93). Paris (20, 2.91). Siouffi, p. 17 (variety not stated). Tewhid (21, —; 21, —; 20, —; variety not stated).

87. *Type B*

As above, but

Centre:	Centre:
الملك النا	الامام النا
صر صلاح الد	صر لدين الله
نيا والدين	
	امير المؤمنين

Lavoix 480 (18, 2.95, ill.). Paris (20, —, ill.).

88. *Damascus—580 H*

Square-in-the-circle type.

Border Segments:	Border Segments:
سنة ثمنين و|خمسمائة	لا اله الا|الله|محمد رسو|ل الله
Centre:	Centre:
الملك النا	الامام النا
صر صلاح الد	صر لدين الله
نيا والدين	امير المؤمنين

ANS-UM (19, 2.73). Lowick (20, 2.92). München 85181 (20, 2.87). Tewhid (21, —; 22, —).

89. *Damascus—581 H*

As above, but

Obverse Border Segments:
سنة احدى و | ثمنين وخمسمائة

Reverse Border Segments:
لا اله الا ا | لله وحده | محمد رسو | ل الله

Album. ANS (20, 2.95). Balog (20, 2.95; 20, 2.96). BMC 263 (19, 2.95). Glidden. Lavoix 481 (19, 2.95, ill.). Østrup 1557 (—, 2.71). Peus 1875.

90. *Damascus—582 H*

As above, but the following date:

سنة اثنين و | ثمانين وخمسمائة

Ashmolean-A. C. Kay (22, 2.77). Artuk 701 (22, 2.65). BMC 262a (20, 2.98); 263a (20, 3.00; date written: سنة اثنين | وثمان وخمسمائة [*sic*]). Çetinyalçın (21, —). Khediv. 1335. Leuthold-Ripostiglio 34 (21, 2.87). Lowick (22, 2.98). Paris-Vogüé (22, 2.87, ill.). Yapı-Kredi (22, 2.66).

Half Dirhem

91. *Damascus—582 H*

Square-in-the-circle type.

Border Segments:
ضرب | بدمشق | سنة اثنتين و | ثمانين وخمسمائة

Centre:
صر
الملك النا
صلاح الد
نيا والدين

Border Segments:
لا اله ا | لا الله | محمد رسو | ل الله

Centre:
الامام النا
صر لدين الله
امير المؤمنين

Berlin-Guthrie (16, 1.45). BM (14, 1.46).

Damascus—583 H

92. *Type A*

Square-in-the-circle type.

Border Segments:
يوسف بن ايوب | ضرب بدمشق | سنة ثلث وثما | نين وخمسمائة

Centre:
الملك الناصر
صلاح الد
نيا والدين

Border Segments:
لا اله ا | لا الله | محمد رسو | ل الله

Centre:
الامام الناصر
لدين الله

امير المؤمنين

[Small floral sprig over المؤمنين, to the left]

ANS-Laties (20.5, —; mule of two obverses). Artuk 702 (21, 2.80). Ashmolean-Bodleian 131 (22, 2.86, ill.; date: سنة ثلث و | ثمانين وخمسمائة Berlin 137/1904 (21, 2.96). Lavoix 482 (21, 2.95). Siouffi, p. 17. Yapı-Kredi (21, 3.00; 21, 2.88).

93. *Type B*

As above, but

Border Segments:

. . . | . . . . محمد رس | الله وحده | اله الا

Centre:

الملك النا

صر صلاح الد

نيا والدين

Centre:

الامام النا

صر لدين الله

امير المؤمنين

Album.

94. *Damascus—584 H*

As No. 92, but the following date and centre inscriptions:

سنة اربع وثما | نين وخمسمائة

Centre:

صر

الملك النا

صلاح الد

نيا والدين

Centre:

الامام النا

صر لدين الله

امير المؤمنين

[Small floral sprig over المؤمنين, to the right]

Berlin (21, 2.62).

Damascus—585 H

95. *Type A*

As above, but the following date:

سنة خمس وثمنين | وخمسمائة

Album (but date: سنة خمس وثما | نين). Balog (23, 2.89, ill.; 20, 2.84, ill.). Berlin-Guthrie (22, 2.86). Izzet 258. Leuthold-Ripostiglio 35 (—, 2.83).

96. *Type B*

Same date, but

Border Segments:

الاسلام والمسلمين | ضرب بدمشق | سنة خمس ثما | نين وخمسمائة

Centre:

يوسف بن ايوب

صلاح الدنيا و

الدين سلطان

Border Segments:

لا اله الا الله | محمد رسول ا | الله وحده ا | بو نصر محمد

Centre:

الامام الناصر

لدين الله امير

المؤمنين ولى

[Floweret at the end of the last line]

ANS-Laties (22, 2.785). Paris (22, 2.75, ill.).

It is noteworthy that, from 580 H on the Damascus copper, Saladin is already styled *Sulṭān al-Islām wa-al-Muslimīn*. Yet, this title does not appear on his Damascene gold until the unique issue of 583 H, and on the silver only in 585 H.

Damascus—586 H

97. *Type A*

Square-in-the-circle type.

Border Segments:

يوسف بن ايوب|ضرب بدمشق|سنة ست ثما|نين وخمسمائة

Centre:

صر
الملك النا
صلاح الد
نيا والدين

Border Segments:

لا اله ا|لا الله|محمد رسول|الله

Centre:

الامام النا
صر لدين الله
امير المؤمنين

Album 22. ANS (23, 2.89). Balog (23, 2.81, ill.). Berlin (23, 2.89). Berlin-Mordtmann 1933 (22, 2.89). BMC 266 (23, 2.96). BM-Sir R. Burn (22, 2.72). Çetinyalçın (20, —). Lavoix 482 (22, 2.95). Leuthold-Ripostiglio 36 (—, 2.85). Lowick (21, 2.75; 21, 2.85).

98. *Type B*

As above, but no annulet above لا الله.

Centre:

الملك الناصر
صلاح الد
نيا والدين

Centre:

الامام النا
صر لدين الله
امير المؤمنين

[Tendril between the second and third lines]

ANS-Ebeyan (22, 2.94). ANS-Newell (23, 2.98). ANS-Hisp. BMC 267 (20, 2.81). Lowick (22, —). Markov, p. 355, No. 6. Siouffi, p. 17. Yapı-Kredi (24, 2.95; 22, 2.75).

Damascus—587 H

99. *Type A*

Square-in-the-circle type, with date:

سنة سبع ثما|نين خمسمائة

Obverse Centre:

صر
الملك النا
صلاح الد
نيا والدين

ANS (23, 2.97; 21, 2.99). Balog (20, 2.45, ill.). Markov, p. 355, No. 7. Yapı-Kredi (23, 2.92).

100. *Type B*

As above, but

Border Segments:

ضرب بد|مشق سنة|سبعة و|ثمانين خم . .

Centre:

الملك النا
صر صلاح الد
نيا والدين

Border Segments:

لا اله|الا الله|محمد رسو|ل الله

Album.

Damascus—588 H

101. *Type A*

As No. 99, but with the following date:

سنة ثمان و|ثمنين وخمسمائة

ANS (22, 2.99).

102. *Type B*

As above, but the date is written:

سنة ثما|ن وثمنين

ANS-Newman 71.316 (23, 2.97, ill.).

103. *Damascus—589 H*

As above, but

Border Segments:
(*sic*) سنة تسع وثما|نين وخمسمئة
Centre:
صر
الملك النا
صلاح الد
نيا والدين

Border Segments:
لا اله ا|لا الله|محمد رسو|ل الله
Centre:
الامام النا
صر لدين الله
امير المؤمنين

Album.

Half Dirhem

Damascus—Undated

104. *Type A*

All varieties square-in-the-circle type.

Border Segments:
يوسف|بن ايوب|ضرب|بدمشق
Centre:
الملك النا
صر صلاح
الدين

Border Segments:
لا اله|الا ا|الله|وحده
Centre:
الامام لنا
صر لد
ين الله

Berlin-Guthrie (14, 1.28). Berlin 627/1896 (15, 1.27; 17, 1.45; 15, 1.46); 626/1896 (15, 1.40). Lavoix 484 (14, 1.50). Paris (15, 1.28, ill.). Tewhid (14, —). Yapı-Kredi (16, 1.30).

105. *Type B*

As above, but the reverse:

Border Segments:
لا اله ا|لا الله|محمد رسو|ل الله
Centre:
الامام النا
صر لدين
الله

Album. ANS-Newell (16, 1.28). Ashmolean-Thorburn (15, 1.41, ill.).

106. *Type C*

As above, but the reverse:

Border Segments:
لا اله|الا الله|محمد رسو|ل الله
Centre:
الامام النا
صر لدين الله
امير المؤمنين

ANS-Newell (15, 1.46). Ashmolean-Christ Church 226 (15, 1.45).

Half Dirhem

107. *Ḥamāh—57x H*

Square-in-the-circle type.

Border Segments:
يوسف بن ايوب|ضرب بحماه|سنة . . .|سبعين
Centre:
الملك النا
صر صلاح الد
نيا والدين

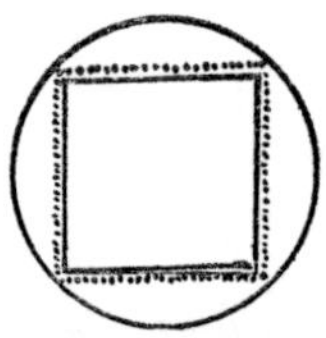

Border Segments:
لا اله ا|لا (الله|محمد) رسو|ل الله
Centre:
الامام النا
صر لدين الله
امير المؤمنين

Lavoix 486 (15, 1.73).

108. *Ḥamāh—580 H*

As above, but with the following date:

سنة ثمنين|وخمسمائة

Reverse Border Segments:
لا اله ا|لا الله|محمد رسو|ل الله

Lavoix 472 (20, 2.95, ill.).

Half Dirhem

109. *Ḥamāh—580 H*

Square-in-the-circle type.

Border Segments:
يوسف|ضرب|بحماه|سنة ثمانين
Centre:
الملك النا
صر صلاح
الدين

Border Segments:
لا اله|الا ا|لله|وحده
Centre:
الامام لنا
صر لد
ين الله

Leuthold-Ripostiglio 16 (15, 1.37).

Ḥamāh—582 H

110. *Type A*

Square-in-the-circle type.

Border Segments:

يوسف بن ايوب|ضرب بحماه|سنة اثنين و|ثمانين وخمسمائة

Centre:

صر
الملك النا
صلاح الد
نيا والدين

Border Segments:

لا اله ا|لا الله|محمد رسو|ل الله

Centre:

الامام النا
صر لدين الله
امير المؤمنين

BMC 263d (22, 2.72, ill.).

111. *Type B*

As above, but decade of date:

ثمنين

Centre:

الملك النا
صر صلاح الد
نيا والدين

Reverse Border Segments:

لا اله الا ا|لله وحده|محمد رسو|ل الله

Centre:

[As above, but tendril through last line]:

امير المؤمنين

ANS 72.75 (21, 2.966, ill.).

Ḥamāh—583 H

112. *Type A*

As above, but the following date and obverse centre inscription:

سنة ثلث و|ثمانين وخمسمائة

Centre:

صر
الملك النا
صلاح الد
نيا والدين

ANS-Ebeyan (21, 2.99; 22, 2.99). Ashmolean-Bodleian. BMC 264 (22, 2.92); 265 (20, 2.90; mule; date in the obverse segments ends without the century). BM-Davies-Sherborne 1931 (21, 2.94). Glidden. Lavoix 473 (19, 2.43). Olivier de Beaumont. Paris (21, 2.64). Khediv. 1336 (22.5, 2.90: Ḥamāh, not Damascus).

113. *Type B*

As above, but

Centre:

الملك الناصر
صلاح الد
نيا والدين

Centre:

الامام الناصر
لدين الله
امير المؤمنين

[Tendril over المؤمنين]

Paris (20, 2.86).

Half Dirhem
Ḥamāh—583 H
Type A

114.

Square-in-the-circle type.

Border Segments:
ضرب|بحماه|سنة ثلث|ثمنين
Centre:
الملك لنا
صر صلاح
الدين

Border Segments:
لا اله|الا ا|الله|محمد
Centre:
الامام لنا
صر لد
ين الله

Lavoix 474 (15, 1.49).

Type B

115.

As above, but the border segments:

يوسف|ضرب|بحماه|سنة ثلث

لا اله|الا ا|الله|وحده

ANS 51.108 (16, 1.46, ill.).

Ḥamāh—584 H

116.

Square-in-the-circle type.

Border Segments:
يوسف بن ايوب|ضرب بحماه|سنة اربع|ثمانين وخمسمائة
Centre:
الملك النا
صر صلاح الد
نيا والدين

Border Segments:
لا اله ا|لا الله|محمد رسو|ل الله
Centre:
الامام النا
صر لدين الله
امير المؤمنين

Paris (20, 2.89).

Ḥamāh—585 H
Type A

117.

As above, but the following date and centre inscriptions:

يوسف بن ايوب|ضرب بحماه|سنة خمس وثما|نين وخمسمائة

Centre:
الملك النا
صر صلاح الد
نيا والدين

Centre:
الامام النا
صر لدين الله
امير المؤمنين

Ashmolean-Thorburn (22, 2.79, ill.). Ilisch (23.5, —; tiny ornaments on reverse).

Type B

118.

As above, but segmented differently and the decade of the date is without the *alif*:

ضرب بحماه سنة|خمس وثمنين|وخمسمائة

Album 34. ANS-Terry (22, 2.195, ill.). Lavoix 475 (22, 2.95).

119. *Type C*

Border on both sides of pointillate circle. Counterclockwise marginal legend on both sides:

ضرب بحماه سنة خمس وثمانين وخمسمائة

ارسله بالهدى ودين الحق ليظهره على الدين كله

Pointillate circle on both sides.

Centre:

الملك الناصر

يوسف بن ايوب

Centre:

الله

الناصر لدين

امير المؤمنين

Paris (19, 2.58, ill.). Yapı-Kredi (20, 2.60).

On the Paris specimen the digit of the date (خمس) is clear, and on the specimen of the Yapi ve Kredi Bankası the century and decade are also clearly legible.

M. R. Broome, Woodley (12, 1.39; half dirhem—brockage).

119a. Same as 119 but for date (only 7 legible).

Private coll., Geneva (27, —).

Ḥamāh—587 H

120. *Type A*

Square-in-the-circle type.

Border Segments:

يوسف بن ايوب|ضرب بحماه|سنة سبع و|ثمانين وخمسمئة

Centre:

صر

الملك النا

صلاح الد

نيا والدين

Border Segments:

لا اله الا|الله وحده|محمد رسـ|ول الله

Centre:

الامام النّا

صر لدين الله

امير المؤمنين

ANS-Ebeyan (21, 3.01, ill.).

121. *Type B*

As above, but:

Border Segments:

ضرب بحماه سنة|سبع وثمنين|وخمسمائة

Centre:

الملك النا

صر صلاح الد

نيا والدين

Border Segments:

لا اله ا|لا الله|محمد رسول|الله

Centre:

الامام النا

صر لدين الله

امير المؤمنين

Leuthold-Ripostiglio 17 (—, 2.90).

Half Dirhem

122. *Ḥamāh—Undated*

Square-in-the-circle type.

Border Segments:

يوسف | بن ايوب | ضرب | بحماه

Centre:

الملك لنا

صر صلاح

الدين

Border Segments:

لا اله ا | لا ا | الله | احمد

Centre:

الامام لنا

صر لد

ين الله

Berlin-Guthrie (15, 1.25). Lavoix 477 (15, 1.39, ill.).

123. *Ḥimṣ—577 H*

Square-in-the-circle type.

Border Segments:

يوسف بن ايوب | ضرب بحمص | سنة سبع | سبعين وخمسمائة

Centre:

الملك النا

صر صلاح الد

نيا والدين

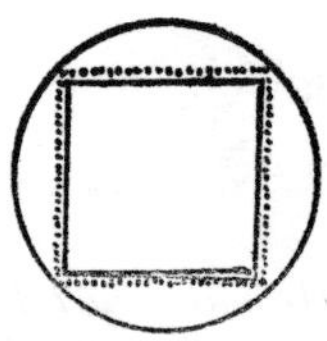

Border Segments:

لا اله ا | لا الله | محمد رسول | الله

Centre:

الامام النا

صر لدين الله

امير المؤمنين

Leuthold-Ripostiglio 29 (22, 2.88).

Half Dirhem

124. *Ḥimṣ—Undated*

Square-in-the-circle type.

Border Segments:

يوسف | بن ايوب | ضرب | بحمص

Centre:

الملك النا

صر صلاح

الدين

Border Segments:

لا اله ا | لا ا | الله احمد

Centre:

الامام النا

صر لد

ين الله

Leuthold-Ripostiglio 30 (16, 1.46, ill.).

125. *Ḥimṣ—578 H(?)*

Square-in-the-circle type.

Border Segments:

يوسف (بن ايوب) | ضرب بحمص | (سنة) ثمانية | . .

Centre:

الملك الناصر

صلاح الد

نيا والدين

Border Segments:

. . . . | . . . . | محمد ر | سول الله

Centre:

الامام النا

صر لدين الله

امير المؤمنين

Album 35 [the badly preserved date is uncertain].

126. *No Mint—Undated*

Square-in-the-circle type.

Border Segments:
لا اله الا ا|لله وحده|محمد رسو|ل الله
Centre:
الملك الناصر
صلاح الد
نيا والدين

Border Segments:
لا اله الا ا|لله وحده|محمد رسو|ل الله
Centre:
الامام النا
صر لدين الله
امير المؤمنين

Leuthold (22, 2.88, ill.; segments partly reconstructed).

Aleppo

Saladin acquired Aleppo from ‘Imād al-Dīn Zengī II in 579 H and began to mint dirhems from 579 H. Copper and silver issues in his name continued until his death in 589 H. Background details can be found in the introductory Historical Outline.

The Aleppo silver has a characteristic design in the form of a six-pointed star. It consists of a line of dots between two plain lines and this star is organically linked with the similarly constructed border. We shall refer to this hexagram, composed of a line of dots between two plain lines, as a *six-pointed star.* There are also six-pointed stars consisting of a single plain line or a line of dots found on copper coins. These will always be designated as ‘linear’ or ‘pointillate’ six-pointed stars.

Although the six-pointed star is characteristic of the Aleppo silver, it also occurs on some Mesopotamian dirhems of Saladin and was adopted by the Artuqid princes of Mārdīn and Ḥiṣn-Kayfā.

With the exception of the next coin, all but a few Aleppo dirhem issues are of the *six-pointed star* type. In 654 H the last Ayyūbid of Aleppo, al-Nāṣir Yūsuf, issued a square-in-the-circle type of dirhem in Aleppo.

127. *Aleppo—579 H*

Six-pointed star.

Border Segments:
ضرب|بحلب|سنة|تسع|وسبعين|وخمسمائة
Centre:
الملك
الناصر صلاح
الدين يوسف بن
ايوب

Border Segments:
لا اله|الا ا|لله|محمد|رسول|الله
Centre:
الامام
الناصر لدين
الله امير المؤ
منين

Balog (21, 2.88). Berlin 608/1909 (21, 3.00). Paris (20, 2.90; 20, 2.77, ill.). ***Seaby's Coin and Medal Bulletin,*** **Sept. 1972, W-530.**

128. *Aleppo—580 H*

As above, but the following date:

سنة | ثمنين | وخمس | مائة

ANS (19.5, 2.61). ANS-Wood (19, 2.613), Berlin 608/1909 (20, 3.00). BMC 268 (19, 2.70). Glidden. Ilisch 7 (20.5, —). Lavoix 464 (19, 2.70); 465 (20, 2.95). Lowick (20, 2.89; 20, 2.92). Paris (20, 2.91; 20, 2.97, ill.). Prague 92/63–893. Siouffi, p. 17. Tewhid (20, —). Yapı-Kredi (21, 2.80; 20, 2.55; 19, 2.63). Ziya 1618 (21, —); 1619 (20, —); 1620 (22, —).

Half Dirhem

129. *Aleppo—580 H*

Six-pointed star.

Border Segments:
صلا | حا | لد | ين | يو | سف
Centre:
الملك
الناصر

Border Segments:
ضر | ب | بحلب | في | سنة | ثمنين
Centre:
الامام
الناصر

[Note that mint/date formula is in the reverse segments]

ANS (16, 1.42; 16, 1.39; 14.5, 1.477). ANS-Wright 49.163 (16, 1.425). Artuk 705 (15, 1.85). Berlin-Guthrie (14, 1.48). BM-S. Johnston 14 (13, 1.47). Izzet 261. Lavoix 466 (14, 1.24). Paris (14, 1.39, ill.). Yapı-Kredi (14, 1.40).

130. *Aleppo—581 H*

As No. 128, but the following date:

سنة | احدى | وثمنين | وخمسمائة

ANS (20, 2.97). Berlin 130/1904 (20, 2.98). Berlin-Mordtmann 1933 (21, 2.66). BMC 268c (21, 2.85). Lavoix 467 (20, 2.90); 468 (20, 3.00). Markov, p. 355, No. 2. München 91846 (19, 3.018). Paris (20, 2.99; 19, 2.86). Paris-Vogüé 1539 (19, 2.72). Tiesenhausen, *RNB*, XXXI (1875), p. 368, No. 160. Yapı-Kredi (19, 2.85; 19, 2.75; 20, 2.95).

Half Dirhem

131. *Aleppo—581 H*

Six-pointed star.

Border Segments:
صلا | حا | لد | ين | يو | سف
Centre:
الملك
الناصر

Border Segments:
ضر | ب | بحلب | سنة | احدى | وثمنين
Centre:
الامام
الناصر

ANS (14, 1.366). Lavoix 469 (14, 1.43, ill.).

132. *Aleppo—582 H*

As No. 128, but the following date:

سنة | اثنتين | وثمنين | وخمسمائة

Berlin 608/1909 (20, 2.87); 610/1909 (20, 2.98). Berman 174 (20, 2.92). BMC 269 (20, 2.94). Paris (20, 2.97; 20, 2.98). Casto Maria del Rivero, *La Moneda arábigo-española*, p. 141, No. 69.

133. *Aleppo—583 H*

As above, but the following date:

سنة | ثلث | وثمنين | وخمسمائة

ANS-Newell (21, 2.736). Balog (20, 2.90, ill.). BMC 270 (19, 2.67). Lavoix 470 (21, 2.99). München 85260 (20, 2.876). Paris (20, 2.69). Yapı-Kredi (20, 2.75). Ziya 1622 (28, —).

134. *Aleppo—584 H*

As above, but the following date:

سنة | اربع | وثمنين | وخمسمائة

Album. Berlin 608/1909 (21, 2.99). Lavoix 471 (21, 2.72). Tewhid (20, —). Yapı-Kredi (20, 2.92; 20, 2.92).

135. *Aleppo—585 H*

As above, but the following date:

سنة | خمس | وثمنين | وخمسمائة

ANS-Newell-Newman (21.5, 2. 873); 72.75 (21, —). ANS-UM (20.5, 2.758). BMC 271 (21, 2.35). Glidden. Lowick (21, 2.94). München 85011 (21, 2.994). Paris (21, 2.82). Paris-Vogüé 1547 (21, 2.95). Soret à Dorn, *RNB* (1856), No. 63. Yapı-Kredi (21, 2.92).

136. *Aleppo—586 H*

As above, but the following date:

سنة | ست | وثمنين | وخمسمائة

Album. ANS 48.102 (22.5, 2.968; 21, 2.79). Ashmolean-Baldwin 16.7.51 (22, 2.80). Lagumina, p. 64, No. 1 (20, 2.26). Lowick (21, 2.96). Paris (22, 2.91). Yapı-Kredi (21, 2.90; 21, 2.80). Ziya 1624 (31, —).

Half Dirhem

137. *Aleppo—586 H*

Obverse segments off the flan, but must be similar to No. 129.

Centre:

الملك
ناصر صلاح
الدين يوسف (بن)
ايوب

Reverse Segments:

بحلب | سنة | ستة | وثمنين | وخمس | مائة

Centre:

الامام
الناصر

Ashmolean-Thorburn (15, —).

138. *Aleppo—587 H*

As No. 128, but the following date:

سنة | سبع | وثمنين | وخمسمائة

ANS-Newell (21.5, 2.604).

139. *Aleppo—588 H*

As above, but the following date:

سنة | ثمان | وثمنين | وخمسمائة

ANS (21, 2.997). Paris (21, 2.59). Soret à Fraehn, *Mémoires de la Soc. Imp. d'Archéol.*, V (1851), No. 103.

140. *Aleppo—589 H*

As above, but the following date:

سنة | تسع | وثمنين | وخمسمائة

Album 36. Paris (20, 2.90). Yapı-Kredi (20, 2.90).

Half Dirhem

141. *Aleppo—589 H*

Border Segments:

صلا | حا | لد | ين | يو | سف

Centre:

الملك
الناصر صلاح
الدين يوسف (بن)
ايوب

Border Segments:

ضر | ب | بحلب | في | سنة | تسع

Centre:

الامام
النا
صر

Soret à Dorn, *RNB* (1856), No. 65 (15, 1.50).

142. *Aleppo—579 H or 589 H (?)*

The Lutz Ilisch collection contains a half dirhem of the usual stellate design, with exactly the same marginal legends, the reverse formula ending with the digit تسع, just as the above coin described by Soret. The important difference resides in the central legend on both sides, which shows the well-known abbreviated protocol:

Obverse:

الملك
الناصر

Reverse:

الامام
الناصر

Ilisch.

There is no indication of the date on this half-dirhem, other than the digit. The only guideline may be the fact that Saladin's earlier half dirhem issues from Aleppo (580 H and 581 H) show the abbreviated royal protocol; whereas, the later half dirhems (586 H and probably 589 H) present the full royal protocol.

142a. *Aleppo—'592' H (?posthumous issue)*

As No. 127 but the following date:

سنة | اثنين | تسعين | وخمسمائة

BM (19.5, 2.89).

The date may be an engraver's error for 582.

COPPER

[The caliph's name is normally not found on this series]

143. *Damascus—583 H*

Border of pellets on both sides. Counterclockwise marginal legend on both sides:

صلاح الدنيا والدين سلطان المسلمين — ضرب بدمشق سنة ثلث ثمنين وخمسمائة

Circle of pellets on both sides.

Centre:	Centre:
الملك	يوسف
الناصر	بن ايوب

ANS-Newell (13, 3.00).

144. *Damascus—584 H*

As above, but the following date:

سنة اربع ثمنين وخمسمائة

ANS (25, 4.64).

145. *Damascus—585 H*

As above, but the following date:

سنة خمس وثمنين وخمسمائة

Album (reverse ornaments:). ANS-Wood (26, 5.18, ill.). Ashmolean-Bodleian 133 (26, 6.46, ill.; reverse ornaments:). Berlin (23, 6.82; obverse ornaments: ; reverse ornaments:); (21, 4.46; obverse ornaments: ; reverse ornaments: none); 121/1927 (25, 5.68; ornaments not recorded). Guthrie (23, 5.76); (24, 5.98; ornaments on both Guthrie coins not recorded); Mordtmann 1933 (24, 5.06; obverse ornaments: ; reverse ornaments:); (23, 5.16; obverse ornaments: ; reverse ornaments:). Ilisch, No. 9 (26, —; reverse ornaments: small star over and under the central legend).

146. *Damascus—586 H*

As above, but the following date:

سنة ستة وثمنين وخمسمائة

Ornaments:

Centre:	Centre:
	يوسف
الملك	بن ايوب
الناصر	

Album (one as above; a second specimen without star in reverse exergue). Ashmolean-Sir C. Warren (24, 4.27; century with an *ālif*); (24, —, century without an *alif*). Ashmolean-A. C. Kay (24, —). Ashmolean-Bodleian 135 (23, 5.81; century without an *ālif*). Ashmolean-Thorburn (23, 5.76). BM-A. N. Clemonger (23, 5.29). Bulak I, p. 106, No. 118 (no star in the reverse exergue). Gautier (21, 4.71, ill.). Ilisch, No. 10 (23–26, —; ornament on the reverse over the legend). Lagumina, p. 65, No. 2 (18, 3.42). Østrup 1562. Prague 92/63–895. Yapı-Kredi (23, 4.20; 24, 4.35).

147. *Damascus—587 H*

As above, but the following date:

سنة سبع وثمنين وخمسمائة

Ornaments:

Centre:	Centre:
⚘	⋀
الملك	يوسف
●	بن ايوب
الناصر	✱

Artuk 703 (24, 6.00). Ashmolean-A. C. Kay (25, —; 23, 5.68). Berman 176 (22, 5.54). BMC 279 (22.5, —); 280 (26, —); 281 (24.5, —); 282 (24, —). BM-A. N. Clemenger (25, 5.58). Khediv. 1340, 1341. Paris (25, 4.71). Wien 7812 (24, —). Yapı-Kredi (20, 2.62).

148. *Damascus—589 H*

As above, but the following date:

سنة تسع وثمنين وخمسمائة

ANS (25, 5.08).

- - - - - - -

Same series, but mint and/or date missing, or the digit of the date is missing.

ANS-Newell (26, —; no reverse ornaments). ANS-Wood (2 specimens; no reverse ornaments). ANS-Sobernheim. Paris (23, —, ill.; reverse ornaments: —/✱); (24, —, ill.; obverse ornaments: ⚘/—; reverse ornaments: ⋀/—/ᔓᔕ). BMC 280 (24, —, ill.; obverse ornaments: ⚘/—; reverse ornaments: ⋀/—). BMC 281 (24, —, ill.; obverse ornaments: ⚘/—; reverse ornaments: ⋀/—/∴). Balog (24, 3.92, ill.; obverse ornaments: ⚘/—/ᔓᔕ; reverse ornaments: ⋀/—/∴).

149. *Damascus—584 H*

Border of small pellets on both sides. Counterclockwise marginal legend on both sides:

ضرب بدمشق سنة اربع ثمنين وخمسمائة	لا اله الا الله وحده محمد رسول الله

Circle of small pellets on both sides.

Centre:	Centre:
الملك الناصر	يوسف بن ا
	يوب

Ornaments: over and under legend, fair-sized floweret, flanked by two equal-sized, six-petaled rosettes.	Ornaments: over legend only, fair-sized floweret, flanked by two equal-sized, six-petaled rosettes.

ANS-Wood (24, 4.647, ill.). Ashmolean-Thorburn (24, 5.37, ill.). Berman 177 (23, 5.15).

150. *Damascus—Date Missing*

Marginal legend in *Naskh*, centre in tall, fluid *Naskh*. Pointillate border on both sides. Counterclockwise marginal legend on both sides:

(لا اله) الا الله وحده لا (شريك له محمد رسول الله) — ضرب بدمشق . . . .

Pointillate circle on both sides.

Centre:

يوسف
الملك النا ﺻ
بن ايوب

Centre:

الدنيا
صلاح
والدين

ANS 71.89 (23, —, ill.).

151. *Damascus—Undated*

Pointillate square in a pointillate circle.

Border Segments:

صلاح | الدين | يوسف | بن ايوب

Centre:

الملك
الناصر

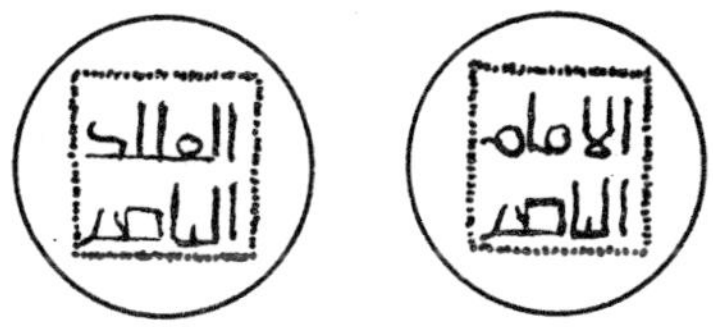

Border Segments:

لدين | الله | امير | المؤمنين

Centre:

الامام
✳
الناصر

The obverse marginal legends are read with difficulty. Note that the name of Caliph al-Nāṣir appears on this issue, but that the mint name does not.

Album (small star on obverse above the *rā*ʾ of al-Nāṣir). Artuk 697 (20, —, ill.). Ashmolean-Thorburn (21, 3.26). Lagumina, p. 66, No. 5 (19, 4.70; small star in the reverse centre on both sides of the legend).

152. *Ḥamāh—583 H*

Pointillate border on reverse, off flan on obverse. Counterclockwise marginal legend on both sides:

ارسله بالهدى ودين الحق ليظهره على الدين — . . . . (اه؟) سنة ثلاث وثمنين . . . .

Centre:

يوسف
بن ايوب

Centre:

الملك النا ﺻ

Album.

153. *Ḥamāh—585 H*

Pointillate border on both sides. Counterclockwise marginal legend on both sides:

. . . . . ارسله بالهدى ودين الحق — بسم الله ضرب بحماه سنة خمس وثمانين وخمسمائة

Pointillate circle on both sides.

Centre:

الملك
الناصر

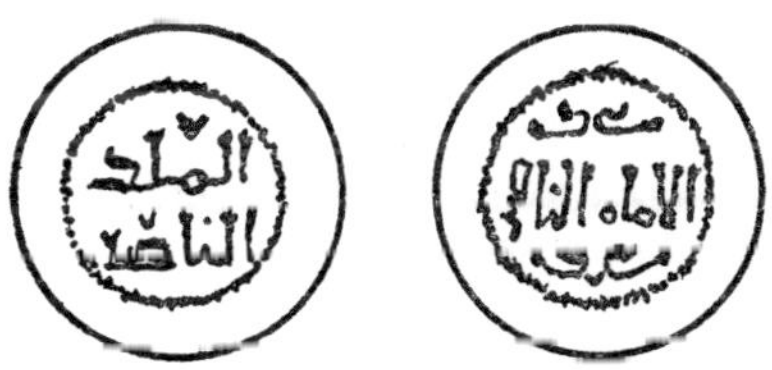

Centre:

الامام النا ﺻ

This copper *fals* is similar to the 585 H silver coin of Ḥamāh (No. 135), except that the dirhem has two horizontal legends in the centre. Note that the caliph's name appears on this coin.

ANS 71.89 (20, 2.77). Balog (22, 1.65, ill.).

154. *Ḥamāh—Undated*

Pointillate border (?). Counterclockwise marginal legend on both sides:

صرب بحماه	[illegible]

Pointillate circle on both sides.

Centre:	Centre:
يوسف	الملك النا ؟
بن ايوب	[Ornament unclear]

Album.

155. *Aleppo—584 H*

Although silver coins from the Aleppo mint are known dating from 579 H, copper issues are known only from the year 584 H on.

Pointillate border on both sides. Counterclockwise marginal legend on both sides:

. . . . يوسف بن	. . . . . — ب سنة اربع و . . . .

Pointillate circle on both sides.

Centre:	Centre:
الملك	الامام
الناصر	الناصر

Album.

Aleppo—585 H

156. *Type A*

Pointillate border on both sides. Counterclockwise marginal legends on both sides:

صلاح الدنيا والدين يوسف بن ايوب	ضرب بحلب سنة خمس وثمانين وخمسائة

Pointillate circle on both sides.

Centre:	Centre:
الملك	الامام
الناصر	الناصر

Ornaments on both sides; above the legends: floweret; beneath the legends: small double scroll.

Album (2 specimens). BMC 284a (20, 2.80, ill.); 284b (22, 2.86, ill.). Ilisch (20, —; reverse top ornament:). Paris (19, 0.69).

157. *Type B*

As above, but the ornaments in the obverse and reverse centres are; a small six-pointed star above and beneath the legends.

Centre:	Centre:
الملك	الامام
الناصر	الناصر

BMC 284 (20, 2.48); 284ba (22, 2.80). Ilisch, No. 12 (23, —; the digit of the date is missing).

158. *Aleppo—Date Incomplete*

This coin, although there are no ornaments in the centre and the digit of the date is missing, belongs to the same series.

Pointillate border on both sides. Counterclockwise marginal legends on both sides:

صلاح الدنيا والدين يوسف بن ايوب	ضرب بحلب سنة . . . ثمنين وخمسمائة

Pointillate circle on both sides.

Centre:	Centre:
الملك الناصر	الامام الناصر

Ashmolean-Christ Church 231 (21, 2.00). Berlin (21, 3.096, ill.).

159. *Aleppo—587 H*

Lineate circular border on both sides. No marginal legend.

Centre:	Centre:
ضر ب بن الملك الناصر حلب (سنة)	سبع ثمنين الامام الناصر وخمس مائة

Note that, with this issue, a new series of Aleppo *fulūs*, without a marginal legend, commences.

Album 31.

160. *Aleppo—588 H*

Border of pellets between two lineate circles on both sides. No marginal legend.

Centre:	Centre:
ضر ب الملك الناصر بحلب سنة	ثمان ثمانين الامام الناصر وخمس ماية

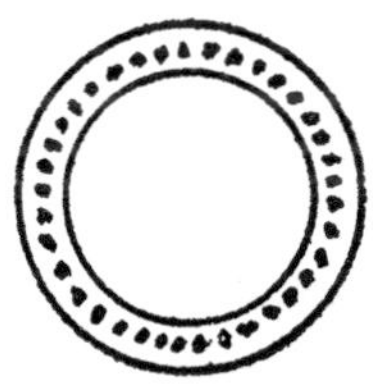

Arabesque ornaments above and beneath the central legend divide the first and third lines in two.

ANS Wood (23, 5, 4.17). BMC 284c (27, 4.80). Fraehn, *Nova Suppl.*, p. 89, No. 1 (probably belongs here). Lagumina, p. 65, No. 3 (21, 3.35); No. 4 (21, 3.27). München 36385 (23, 5.225, ill.); unnumbered (23, 4.003). Paris (23, 4.13, ill.).

161. *Aleppo—589 H*

As above, but the following date:

تسع ثمنين

ANS (25, 5.08). Ashmolean-Christ Church 232 (20, 4.35, ill.). Berlin (24, 4.70). Miles, *Some Islamic Coins in the Berne Historical Museum*, No. 13. München (22, 4.954, ill.).

Syrian Type

162. *Mint and Date Missing*

Border missing on both sides. Counterclockwise marginal legend:

Traces:	[Missing]
ضرب . . . . خمسمائة	

Pointillate circle on both sides.

Centre:	Centre:
الملك الناصر	الله
يوسف بن ايوب	الناصر لدين
	امير المؤمنين

[Obverse: Arabesque floweret above and beneath legend]

Butak I, p. 105, No. 116.

Syrian Type(?)

163. *Mint and Date Missing*

Border and marginal legend missing on both sides. Linear circle on both sides.

Centre:	Centre:
[Vertically Elongated *Kūfic*]	[Similar *Kūfic*]
✳	✳
الملك الناصر	يوسف بن ايوب
✳	✳

Ashmolean-Chester (23, —, ill.). München (21, —, ill.).

Palestine

SILVER

164. *al-Ramlah—580 H*

Pointillate border on both sides. Counterclockwise marginal legends:

[Obverse legend missing]	ضرب بالرملة سنة ثمانين (وخمسمائة)

Pointillate circle on both sides.

Centre:	Centre:
الملك	يوسف
الناصر	بن ايوب

Tewhid (22, —).

Mesopotamia
SILVER

165. *Mārdīn—581 H*

Six-pointed star.

Border Segments:		Border Segments:
ضرب | بماردين | سنة | احد | ثمانين | وخمسمائة		لا اله | الا ا | لله | محمد | رسول | الله
Centre:		Centre:
الملك الناصر صلاح الدين يوسف ايوب		الامام الناصر لدين الله امير المؤ منين

[No بن between يوسف and ايوب]

München 85034 (21, 2.824, ill.). Soret, *RNB* (1858), 112, *IVe lettre à Bartholomaei.*

It would seem that, after Saladin's conquest of Mayāfāriqīn in 581 H, the Artuqids of Mārdīn also accepted Saladin, at least for the time being, as their overlord.

166. *Mayāfāriqīn—589 H*

Six-pointed star.

Border Segments:	Border Segments:
ضرب | بميفرقين | سنة | تسع | ثمنين | وخمسمائة	لا اله | الا ا | لله | محمد | رسول | الله
Centre:	Centre:
الملك الناصر صلاح الدين يوسف بن ايوب	الامام الناصر لدين الله امير المؤ منين

Album 12 (date written: تسعة/و; mint written: بمفرقين). Berlin (20, —, ill.). BM (20, —, ill.).

COPPER
Mayāfāriqīn—581 H

167. *Type A*

Obverse:	Reverse:
Border linear circle; double linear hexagon, with annulets in the six corners. Traces of legend or ornaments in segments between border and hexagon.	Border pointillate circle.
Centre: الملك الناصر صلاح الدين يوسف بن ايوب	Centre: الامام الناصر لدين الله امير المؤمنين
Circular legend around central legend: محي | دولة | امير | المؤمنين	Circular legend around central legend: ضرب ميفرقين | سنة | احد وثمنين | وخمسمائة

Berlin-Guthrie (26, 6.93, ill.; 28, 9.45).

168. *Type B*

Border of pellets on both sides.

Centre:	Centre:
الملك الناصر	الامام الناصر
صلاح الدين	لدين الله
يوسف بن ايوب	امير المؤمنين
Circular legend around central inscription:	Circular legend around central inscription:
محي | دولة | امير | المؤمنين	رسم بميفرقين | سنة | احد وثمنين | وخمسمائة

Album (2 specimens). ANS-Paul Kelly (24, —). ANS-Wright (24.5, 7.06). BMC 272 (33, 14.48, ill.; reverse partly double-struck). Leuthold (26, 8.93, ill.). München 85988 (25, 6.949). Tewhid (27, —). Zambaur-N.C. 507 (26, 11.80); 508 (27, 10.25).

169. *Type C*

Although the mint name is not in evidence, the issue is identical with the above, and there is little doubt that it was struck in Mayāfāriqīn.

Pointillate border on both sides.

Circular legend as above:	Circular Legend:
محي | دولة | امير | المؤمنين	سنة | احد وثمنين | وخمسمائة

Butak I, p. 106, No. 119 (circular legends incomplete). Yapı-Kredi (25, 8.08; 22, 9.58).

Mayāfāriqīn—587 H

170. *Type A*

Obverse

Pointillate border, pointillate square inside:

Border Segments:

ضرب | سنة سبع | وثمانين | وخمسمائة

Centre:

الملك الناصر

صلاح الدين

يوسف بن ايوب

Reverse

Pointillate border. Counterclockwise marginal legend:

الملك الناصر صلاح الدنيا والدين يوسف بن ايوب

Centre:

Sultan crowned, sitting cross-legged and holding crescent. Between the crescent and head, counterclockwise:

Left:	Right:
بميافرقين	ضرب

[Star under each elbow]

BM-Amedroz (23, 5.85). Butak I, p. 104, No. 114.

171. *Type B*

As above, but the mint in the top obverse segment is: ضرب بميفر (قين)

ANS-Wood (25, 6.025). Berman 178 (24, 6.46).

Niṣibīn belonged to ʿImād al-Dīn Zengī, of whom there exist copper *fulūs* dated 577 H. Saladin occupied Niṣibīn in 578 H and issued a new type of copper coinage, very large and heavy, on which was placed his facing bust, adorned with a Sassanian crown. The prototype for this coin is the mintless copper of the Artūqid prince Najm al-Dīn Alpī of Mārdīn, struck in 558 H.

Niṣibīn—578 H

172. *Type A*

Pointillate circular border on both sides.

Obverse:
Pointillate square.
Border Segments:
يوسف بن|ايوب محي|دولة امير|المومنين
Centre:

الملك الناصر
صلاح الدنيا وا
لدين سلطان
الاسلام ابو المظفر

Reverse:
Counterclockwise marginal legend:
ضرب بنصيبين سنة ثمانية وسبعين وخمسمائة
Centre:
Sultan's facing bust, crowned with a three-pointed Sassanian crown without the Sun disk. The face is beardless, the hair hangs down in two lateral curls, ending in minute pellets. The eyes are beady, the chin weak. Right and left of the face two words are written horizontally:

Left: لله — Right: الملك

⌊al-Muẓaffar, one of Saladin's sons, is mentioned only on these coins.⌉

Artuk 716 (33, 21.70, ill.; courtesy of Ībrahim Artuk; overstruck on an older coin).

173. *Type B*

As above, but obverse centre:

الملك الناصر
صلاح الد
نيا والدين
ابو المظفر

ANS (33, 13.34, ill.).

174. *Type C*

As above, but on the reverse the two words flanking the face are written vertically, counterclockwise:

Left: لله — Right: الملك

ANS (34, 16.06, ill.; 34, 17.92, ill.; one ANS specimen is double-struck on an unidentified earlier coin. The decade is erroneously written 90: تسعين). BM (33, 16.96, ill.; 34, 15.80, ill.). Yapı-Kredi (35, 16.9).

175. *Ḥarrān—586 H*

Obverse:

Fine pointillate border with fine pointillate square inside.

Border Segments:

ضرب بحران|سنة ستة|وثما نين|وخمسمائة

Centre:

الملك الناصر
صلاح الدين
يوسف بن ايوب

Reverse:

Fine pointillate border. Counterclockwise marginal legend:

(محي دولة) امير المؤمنين

Centre:

Sultan facing, sitting cross-legged, holding up crescent with both hands. Star under each elbow.

Album (1 specimen with الله to right of figure; another specimen, mint uncertain, with الله to right of figure and الملك ال . . . . to left). Windisch-Graetz 163 (26, —).

176. *No Mint—582 H*

Constellation of the Lion type; Mesopotamian style. Pointillate circular border on both sides. Counterclockwise marginal legend on both sides:

الملك الناصر صلاح الدنيا والدين يوسف بن ايوب محي دولة امير المؤمنين

ضرب هذا الدرهم سنة اثنين وثمنين وخمسمائة

Pointillate circle on both sides.

Centre:

Seated lion facing left, surrounded by four stars.

Centre:

الامام
الناصر لدين
الله امير
المؤمنين

Yapı-Kredi (29, 12.30).

177. *No Mint—583 H*

As above, but the following date:

سنة ثلثة وثمنين وخمسمائة

Album (3 specimens). ANS-Proskey (28, —). Artuk 698 (29, 13. 65). Ashmolean-Rev. Neesan (28, 13.82, ill.; no floweret over the reverse legend, but a star to the right). Ashmolean-Thorburn (28, 11.30). BMC 273 (25, —); 274 (26, —). Hirsch 2079 (26, —). Leuthold (29, 10.25). München 85679 (30, 13. 232). Lavoix 491 (27, 11.22); 492 (29, 11.45, ill.); 493 (28, 14.10). Paris (28, 11.93). Peus 1876.

178. *No Mint—584 H*

As above, but the following date:

سنة اربع وثمنين وخمسمائة

ANS (34, 11.01). Paris (28, 11.97). Yapı-Kredi (28, 11.10; 27, 10.18).

179. *No Mint—586 H*

As above, but the following date:

سنة ست وثمنين وخمسمائة

Yapı-Kredi (27, 11.80).

180. *No Mint—587 H*

As above, but the following date:

سنة سبع وثمنين وخمسمائة

Yapı-Kredi (28, 10.00).

181. *No Mint—589 H*

As above, but the following date:

سنة تسع ثمانين وخمسمائة

Butak I, p. 104, No. 114. According to Butak, the obverse marginal legend ends with: محمد ما امام امو اله, but it almost certainly reads: محي دولة امير المؤمنين, as on all the other coins of this series. His attribution of the coin to Mayāfāriqīn is also questionable.

No Mint—586 H

Type of turbaned sultan sitting cross legged on a low throne. Mesopotamian style.

182. *Type A*

Obverse:

Linear circular border. Counterclockwise marginal legend:

الملك الناصر صلاح الدنيا والدين يوسف بن ايوب

Centre:

Turbaned sultan sitting cross-legged on a low throne with square back, which is surmounted by two pinnacles at upper corners.

Reverse:

Pointillate circular border.

Centre:

الامام النا
صر لدين الله
امير المؤمنين

Ornaments above and below

Counterclockwise circular legend around the centre:

ضرب هذا الدرهم سنة ستة ثمنين وخمسمائة

ANS (30, 12.62; 29, 10.52; 28, 8.48; 30, 9.80). ANS-UM (30, 12.97; 29, 10.39). Artuk 699 (29, 12.60). Ashmolean-Christ Church 228 (29, 11.36, ill.). Berlin IV.76.A.1 (26. 9.38). Berlin-Guthrie (31, 11.40). BMC 275 (29, 12.31); 276 (28, —); 278 (20, 10.78). Ghalib 188 (29, —); 189 (29, —). Butak I, p. 103, No. 113. Paris (26, —, ill.). Tewhid (27, —).

183. *Type B*

As above, but on the reverse a circular legend, reading counterclockwise from the left:

ضرب هذا | الدرهم سنة | ستة ثمنين | وخمسمائة

ANS (27, 10.72). BMC 277 (31, —). Izzet 262, 263. Lavoix 494 (29, 11.40); 495 (27, 9.80). Østrup 1562. Peus 1877. Rogers, Indian Museum (27, 10.19). Yapı-Kredi (32, 10.90).

* * *

It cannot be ascertained to which variety the following specimens belong:

Adler II, p. 89, No. LXII-B. Pietraszewski 413.

AL-'AZĪZ 'IMĀD AL-DĪN ABŪ AL-FATH 'UTHMĀN IBN YŪSUF

Ruler of Egypt [589–592 H = 1193–1195 AD]

Sultan of the Empire [592–595 H = 1195–1198 AD]

Egypt

GOLD

184. *Cairo—589 H*

Border on both sides: plain circle. Counterclockwise marginal legend on both sides:

لا اله الا الله محمد رسول الله ارسله بالهدى ودين الحق ليظهره على الدين كله	بسم الله الرحمن الرحيم ضرب هذا الدينر بالقاهرة سنة تسع وثمانين وخمسمائة

Double circle on both sides. Counterclockwise circular legend on both sides.

غال الملك غاية العزيز	ابو العباس الناصر لدين الله امير المؤمنين

Inner circle on both sides.

Centre:	Centre:
عثمان	الامام
بن يوسف	احمد

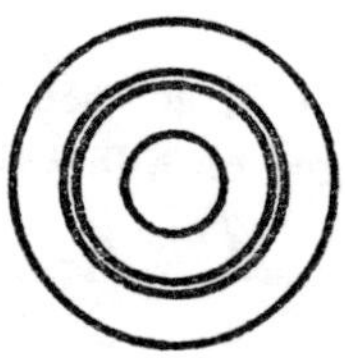

ANS-UM (20, 4.024). Ashmolean-A. C. Kay (21, 3.47). Balog (20, 4.71, ill.; 20, 4.07). Berlin-Guthrie (20, 3.70). BMC 287 (20, 3.32); 288 (20, 3.56). da Cunha 1458 (18, 5.06). Fahmy 114 (19, 4.17); 115 (19, 3.71); 116 (20, 3.72); 117 (20, 4.15); 118 (20, 6.29); 119 (20, 5.07); 120 (20, 4.30); 121 (20, 3.38); 122 (19, 3.91); 123 (20, 3.12); 124 (20, 3.87); 125 (20, 4.84); 126 (21, 4.46); 127 (20, 4.62); 128 (20, 4.67); 129 (19, 3.32); 130 (20, 3.09); 131 (20, 5.01); 132 (20, 4.53). Khediv. 1342 (—, 4.30). Lavoix 502 (21, 5.10); 503 (21, 5.80). Leuthold (20, 5.56; 20, 3.86; 19, 3.28). Paris-Mecca (20, 4.72; 20, 3.72; 19, 3.76; 20, 2.48; 21, 3.35; 20, 5.22; 20, 2.87; 19, 4.05). Paris trade (—, 5.03; —, 4.92; —, 3.93; —, 3.79; —, 4.38; —, 4.22; —, 4.78; —, 4.14; —, 4.33; —, 3.92; —, 4.66). Samir Shamma (20, 3.20; 20, 4.85; 20, 3.35; 20, 4.20; 20, 4.60). Yapı Kredi (20, 4.80; 21, 3.80).

185. *Cairo—590 H*

As above, but the following date:

سنة تسعين وخمسمائة

ANS-Newell (21, 3.967). ANS-UM (21, 4.533). Ashmolean-A. C. Kay (20, 3.79). Berlin-Guthrie (20, 3.76). BMC 290 (20, 4.69). Fahmy 133 (20, 4.22); 134 (20, 4.71); 135 (20, 3.54); 136 (19, 4.34); 137 (19, 4.41); 138 (19, 3.42). Khediv. 1345. Leuthold (21, 2.54). Munzel (20, 2.70). Paris-Mecca (20, 4.46; 20, 3.38; 20, 4.45). Paris trade (—, 4.66; —, 3.98). Ziya 1663 (20, —).

186. *Cairo—591 H*

As above, but the following date:

سنة احدى وتسعين وخمسمائة

Balog (20, 4.65, ill.). Khediv. 1347. Østrup 1566 (—, 4.15). Paris (20, 4.85). Paris-Mecca (20, 4.61). Pietraszewski 417. Siouffi, p. 17. Yapı-Kredi (20, 3.50).

187. *Cairo—592 H*

As above, but the following date:

سنة اثنين وتسعين وخمسمائة

ANS-UM (21, 4.836; 20, 5.42). Balog (20, 5.64, ill.; 20, 4.95). BM (21, 5.96). Mitchell-Brown (21, 4.74). Fahmy 139 (20, 3.40); 140 (20, 5.05). Khediv. 1349. Leuthold (18, 3.75; 19, 5.46). Paris-Mecca (19, 3.86; 19, 6.01; 20, 6.35). Paris trade (—, 4.08; —, 4.63; —, 4.43; —, 4.13). Samir Shamma (20, 5.85; 19, 4.68, century of date written: خمسا).

188. *Cairo—593 H*

As above, but the following date:

سنة ثلث وتسعين وخمسمائة

ANS-UM (20, 5.88; 21, 5.41; 21, 5.48). BMC 294c (20, 5.96). Fahmy 141 (19, 4.89); 142 (18, 2.69); 143 (19, 4.97); 144 (20, 5.91); 145 (19, 4.16); 146 (20, 5.04). Lavoix 503 *bis* (20, 3.72). Munzel (20, 4.15). Leuthold (20, 4.92). Paris-Mecca (20, 4.35). Paris trade (—, 3.77; —, 2.80). Samir Shamma (19, 5.17). Siouffi, p. 17.

189. *Cairo—594 H*

As above, but the following date:

سنة اربع وتسعين وخمسمائة

ANS-UM (20, 4.98). Artuk 721 (19, 5.20). Balog (21, 5.84, ill.). Fahmy 147 (18, 4.46); 148 (18, 3.53); 149 (19, 4.28); 150 (18, 3.65). Khediv. 1352. Leuthold (18, 4.46; 19, 5.84; 20, 3.28; 20, 5.40). Paris-Mecca (18, 2.95; 19, 6.11; 19, 3.98). Paris trade (—, 3.52; —, 4.90; —, 3.67; —, 4.23; —, 3.49; —, 4.98; — 3.57). Samir Shamma (19, 5.55; 19, 7.10). Siouffi, p. 17. Yapı-Kredi (19, 3.35).

190. *Cairo—595 H*

As above, but the following date:

سنة خمس وتسعين وخمسمائة

Paris-Mecca (20, 3.21, ill.).

191. *Alexandria—589 H*

Border on both sides, plain circle. Counterclockwise marginal legend on both sides:

بسم الله الرحمن الرحيم ضرب هذا الدينر بالاسكندرية سنة تسع وثمنين وخمسمائة	لا اله الا الله محمد رسول الله ارسله بالهدى ودين الحق ليظهره على الدين كله

Double circle on both sides. Counterclockwise circular legend on both sides:

ابو العباس الناصر لدين الله امير المؤمنين	عال الملك غاية العزيز

Inner circle on both sides.

Centre:	Centre:
الامام	عثمان
احمد	بن يوسف

ANS-UM (21, 4.644). Balog (20, 4.69). Berlin-Guthrie (21, 3.32; ثمانين with an *alif*). BMC 289 (20, 3.77; ثمانين with an *alif*). Fahmy 153 (19, 4.36; the author gives the date as 587 H and believes that al-ʿAzīz ʿUthmān struck gold coins in Alexandria in 587 H, and in Cairo in 588 H while Saladin was still alive!); 154 (19, 3.70); 155 (20, 4.06); 156 (18, 5.36); 157 (20, 3.87); 158 (19, 5.22); 159 (19, 5.16); 160 (20, 4.64); 161 (19, 3.74). Khediv. 1343 (—, 3.9); 1344. Paris (19, 5.13). Paris-Mecca (20, 4.17; 19, 5.23; 20, 4.77; 20, 5.03; 20, 6.41; 20, 4.12). Paris trade (—, 3.36; —, 4.24; —, 4.25; —, 4.67; —, 3.52; —, 3.83; —, 4.43; —, 3.25; —, 4.57; —, 3.97; —, 3.94; —, 4,47). Pietraszewski 415. Samir Shamma (19, 4.47; 19, 5.60).

192. *Alexandria—590 H*

As above, but the following date:

سنة تسعين وخمسمائة

Markov, p. 355, No. 14.

193. *Alexandria—593 H*

As above, but the following date:

سنة ثلث تسعين وخمسمائة

Berman 180 (20, 4.90). BMC 294e.

193a. *Alexandria—594 H*

As above, but the following date:

سنة اربع وتسعين وخمسما (*sic*)

BMC 294K.

194. *Miṣr—590 H*

As above, but the following mint and date:

بمصر سنة تسعين وخمسمائة

Markov, p. 355, No. 14.

Fractional (1/10?) Dinar

195. *Mint and Date Missing*

As above, but the outer reverse legend is:

بسم الله الرحمن الرحيم . . . .

And the inner obverse legend is:

كله ○ عال ○ الملك غاية

Note that the last word of the obverse marginal legend [كله] has been transposed to the beginning of the second circular legend.

Samir Shamma (12.5, 0.43, ill.; In all probability this coin is from the Cairo mint. Similar small fractions had been struck in Cairo under the Fāṭimids).

SILVER

Black Dirhems

On one specimen the mint *Alexandria* is legible. On all the others the mint is missing; it may be either *Cairo* or *Alexandria.* al-'Azīz 'Uthmān's black dirhems are similar to those of Saladin. They are found in three varieties, the difference being only the inner circle. The marginal and second circular legends are reconstructed.

196. *Type A*

Border on both sides, plain circle. Counterclockwise marginal legend on both sides:

بسم الله ضرب هذا الدرهم بالقاهرة / بالاسكندرية سنة . . . .

لا اله الا الله محمد رسول
الله ارسله بالهدى ودين الحق ليظهره

Plain circle on both sides. Counterclockwise circular legend on both sides.

ابو العباس الناصر لدين الله امير المؤمنين

على الدين كله الملك العزيز ابو الفتح

Plain inner circle on both sides.

Centre:		Centre:
عثمان بن يوسف		الامام احمد

ANS-Wood (10 × 11, —). Balog (10 × 12, 1.20, ill.; on this specimen the mint is clearly recognizable: (بالا) سكند (رية); i.e., *Alexandria*). On the following the mint is missing: Balog, *BIE*, XXXV (1953), p. 414, 1 (9 × 10, 0.79, ill.); 2 (6 × 7, 0.84); 3 (11 × 11, 1.21, ill.). München 92492 (8 × 10, 1.459).

197. *Type B*

As above, but the inner circle is a *double* circular line.

ANS (8 × 9.5, —). Ashmolean (7 × 10, 1.09). Balog, *BIE*, XXXV (1953), p. 414, 1 (9 × 9, 0.49); 2 (9 × 10, 0.85); 3 (6 × 10, 0.84); 4 (7 × 9, 0.93); 5 (7 × 10, 1.08); 6 (10 × 10, 1.22); 7 (7 × 14, 1.22, ill.); 8 (9 × 10, 1.23); 9 (8 × 10, 1.32); 10 (9 × 10, 1.47, ill.); 11 (9 × 10, 1.59, ill.); 12 (7 × 12, 1.60, ill.). BM (7 × 12, —).

198. *Type C*

As above, but the inner circle consists of a pointillate circle within a linear circle.

Balog, *BIE*, XXXV (1953), p. 414, 1 (8 × 9, 0.79); 2 (9 × 9, 0.97); 3 (7 × 12, 1.32); 4 (7 × 11, 1.36); 5 (10 ×11, 1.30, ill.); 12 (10 × 11, 1.76, ill.). München 92493 (8 × 9, 0.767).

Round-Flan Quarter Dirhems
Mint and Date Missing

199. *Type A*

As above, but the inner circle is a *double* circular line.

Balog (16, 0.59, ill.).

200. *Type B*

As above, but the inner circle is composed of a pointillate circle within a linear circle.

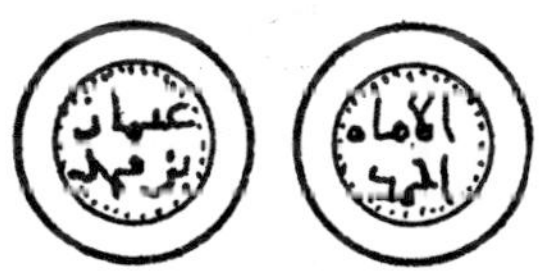

Balog (17, 0.68, ill.).

The above round-flan quarter dirhems appear to have been struck by the same dies as the second and third types of black dirhems.

DIVISIONAL CURRENCY

There are no Egyptian copper coins of al-ʿAzīz ʿUthmān, but it seems probable that the glass jetons struck in the name of Caliph al-Nāṣir continued to serve as fiduciary coinage.

Syria

GOLD

There is no gold coinage of this ruler from Syria proper, but one dinar struck in *Filasṭīn* is in the Horovitz collection. Although only the lower half of the letters are on the flan, the mint name *Filasṭīn* is clearly indicated.

201. *Filasṭīn—592 H*

Border on both sides, plain circle. Counterclockwise marginal legends on both sides:

لا اله الا الله محمد رسول الله ارسله بالهدى ودين الحق ليظهره على الدين كله

بسم الله الرحمن الرحيم ضرب هذا الدينر بفلسطين سنة اثنين وتسعين وخمسمائة

Double circle on both sides. Counterclockwise circular legends on both sides:

عال الملك غاية العزيز

ابو العباس الناصر لدين الله امير المؤمنين

Inner circle on both sides.

Centre:
عثمان
بن يوسف

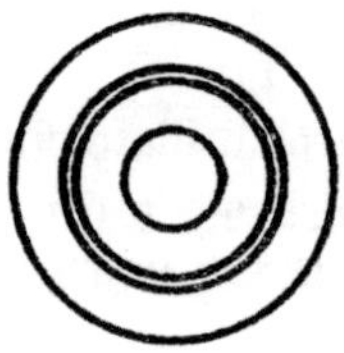

Centre:
الامام
احمد

Horovitz (20, 4.18, ill.).

SILVER

202. *Damascus—590 H*

Square-in-the-circle type.

Border Segments:
ضرب | بدمشق | سنة تسعين | وخمسمائة
Centre:
الملك العز
يز عثمان
بن يوسف

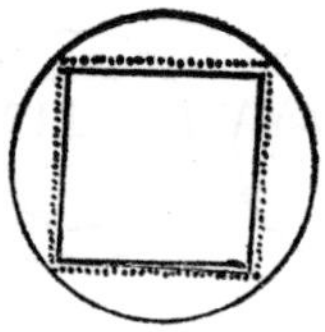

Border Segments:
لا اله | الا ا | لله | وحده
Centre:
الامام النا
صر لدين
الله

[Date has been proposed with some reservation]

ANS (20, 5, 2.914). Weyl 6506 (23, 2.70).

203. *Damascus—591 H*

As above, but the following date:

ضرب بدمشق|سنة احدى و|تسعين|وخمسمائة

Østrup 1567 (—, 2.75).

Half Dirhem

204. *Damascus—591 H*

As above, but the border segments:

ضرب بدمشق|سنة احد|وخمسمائة

لا اله|الا ا|لله و|حده

BM-F. W. Hasluck (17, 1.46, ill.).

Damascus—593 H

205. *Type A*

Square-in-the-circle type.

Border Segments:

بن يوسف ضرب|بدمشق سنة|ثلث وتسعين|وخمسمائة

Centre:

الملك العزيز
عماد الدنيا و
الدين عثمان

Border Segments:

لا اله|الا ا|لله|وحده

Centre:

الامام الناصر
لدين الله ا
مير المؤمنين

[Fluid but clumsy *Naskh*]

Album 50. München 85075 (23, 2.633, ill.; published by Soret in *RNB* (1856), No. 66).

206. *Type B*

As above, but the obverse bottom segment ثلاث وتسعين [three ثلاث with an *ālif*]. *Naskh* drawn in good calligraphy.

ANS-Laties (22, 2.903, ill.).

Half Dirhem

Damascus—593 H

207. *Type A*

Square-in-the-circle type.

Border Segments:

ضرب|بدمشق|سنة|ثلاث [*sic*]

Centre:

الملك العز
يز عثمان
بن يوسف

Border Segments:

لا اله|الا ا|لله و|حده

Centre:

الامام النا
صر لدين
الله

München (15, 1.504, ill.; published by Soret in *RNB* (1856), No. 67).

208. *Type B*

As No. 206, but a half dirhem with the date missing.

Paris (16, 1.46, ill.).

Damascus—594 H

209. *Type A*

Square-in-the-circle type.

Border Segments:
ضرب بد|مشق سنة|اربعة وتسع|ين وخمسمائة
Centre:
الملك العز
يز عماد الدنيا
والدين عثمان

Border Segments:
لا اله ا|لا الله|محمد رسو|ل الله
Centre:
الامام النا
صر لدين الله
امير المؤمنين

BMC 294t (23, 2.91, ill.). Leuthold-Ripostiglio 37 (—, 2.92). Yapı-Kredi (22, 2.9).

210. *Type B*

As above, but:

Border Segments:
(ضرب بدمشق)|سنة|اربع و|تسعين وخمسمائة
Centre:
الملك العز
يز بن الملك
الناصر عثمان

Border Segments:
لا اله الا|الله|محمد ر|سول الله
Centre:
الامام النا
صر لدين الله
امير المؤمنين

ANS-Laties (21, 2.493; 21, 2.87—digit missing, but the same variety and identical reverse die).

211. *Type C*

As above, but:

Border Segments:
بن يوسف ضرب|بدمشق سنة|اربع وتسعين|وخمسمائة
Centre:
الملك العزيز
عماد الدنيا و
الدين عثمان

Border Segments:
لا اله ا|لا الله|محمد رسو|ل الله
Centre:
الامام الناصر
لدين الله ا
مير المؤمنين

[All legends in *Naskh* script]

ANS-Laties (21, 2.711, ill.). Artuk 718 (22, 2.85). Balog (20, 2.32).

212. *Damascus—595 H*

As above, but the following date:

بدمشق|سنة خمس|وتسعين وخمسمائة

[All legends in *Naskh* script]

Berlin 428/1892 (21, 2.87). Pakhomov VII, p. 54, No. 493 (23, —).

Half Dirhem

213. *Damascus—595 H*

As above, but:

Obverse Segments:

ضرب بدمشق|سنة خمس|تسعين|وخمسمائة

Reverse Centre:

الامام الناصر

لدين الله

امير المؤ منين

All legends in *Naskh* script. Tendril across centre bottom line.

Lavoix 504 (17, 1.50).

Damascus—Undated

214. *Type A*

Square-in-the-circle type.

Border Segments:

بسم|الله|ضرب|بدمشق

Centre:

الملك

العزيز

Border Segments:

لا اله|الا الله|محمد رسو|ل الله

Centre:

الامام

الناصر

[Centres only in *Naskh* script]

Paris (14, 1.30).

215. *Type B*

As above, but the border segments, both sides:

عثمان بن|يوسف|ضرب|بدمشق

لا اله|الا ا|لله و|حده

[In *Naskh* script]

BMC 295 (15, 1.41, ill.).

216. *Type C*

As above, but the reverse border segments:

لا اله|الا ا|لله|وحده

[In *Naskh* script]

ANS-Laties (15, 1.43, ill.).

217. *Ḥamāh—594 H*

Square-in-the-circle type.

Border Segments:

ضرب|بحماه|سنة اربع و|تسعين

Centre:

الملك العزيز

عماد الدنيا

والدين عثمان

Border Segments:

لا اله ا|لا الله|محمد رسو|ل الله

Centre:

الامام النا

صر لدين الله

امير المومنين

Leuthold-Ripostiglio 18 (21, 2.93, ill.).

Ḥamāh—595 H

218. *Type A*

As above, but the border segments:

ضرب | بحماه | سنة خمس | تسعين وخمسمائة

لا اله ا ∴ | لا الله | محمد رسو | ل الله

Leuthold-Ripostiglio 19 (20, 2.96).

219. *Type B*

As above, but:

Reverse Border Segments:

لا اله | الا ا | لله | وحده

الملك العزيذ
عماد الدنيا
والدين عثما [*sic*]

Album.

220. *Ḥimṣ—592 H*

Square-in-the-circle type.

Border Segments:

ضرب | بحمص سنة | ثنتين وتسعين | (وخمسمائة)

Centre:

الملك العزيز
عماد الدنيا و
الدين عثمان

Border Segments:

لا اله الا ا | (لله وحده) | محمد رسو | ل الله

Centre:

الامام الناصر
لدين الله ا
مير المؤمنين

[Centres only in *Naskh* script]

ANS-Laties (21, 2.784).

221. *Undetermined Silver Brockage*

Border: Traces of Thin Circle

Centre:

الملك الناص(ر)
يوسف بن ايو(ب)

Border: Missing

Centre:

Incuse image of the obverse.

M. R. Broome (16, 1.39).

COPPER

222. *Damascus—594 H*

Border on both sides, pointillate circle. Counterclockwise marginal legend on both sides:

ضرب بدمشق سنة اربع وتسعين وخمسمائة

لا اله الا الله وحده محمد رسول الله

Pointillate circle on both sides.

Centre:

عثمان
الملك العزيز

Centre:

سف
بن الملك النا ؟
يو

[All legends in *Naskh* script]

ANS (24.5, 5.22). Artuk 719 (23, 5.80). Ashmolean (25, —). Berman 181 (23, 6.12). BMC 297 (23, 6.87); 298 (20, 4.59). Ilisch 14 (23, —); 15 (23, —). Lavoix 505 (25, 5.92, ill.). Østrup 1568 (seems to belong here). Wien 644 (24, —). Yapı-Kredi (24, 4.93).

223. *Damascus—595 H*

As above, but the following date:

سنة خمس وتسعين وخمسمائة

Album (2 specimens). ANS-Wood (24, —; 26, —). ANS Kelly (24, —). Ashmolean-Thorburn (25, 6.14). Balog (23, 6.95; 24, 5.14, ill.). Berlin (23, 4.80; 24, 4.94). Lavoix 506 (23, 5.50). Paris (25, 4.91, ill.; 23, 4.97; 23, 5.00). München 86011 (24, 6.24). Windisch-Graetz 164 (24, —); 165 (22, —); 166 (23, —).

224. *Aleppo—Date Missing*

The border margins seem to consist of a plain circle. Some trace of missing date present on the reverse. No circular legends.

بحلب سنه	(ضر) ب
الملك العزيز	الامام الناصر

[*Kūfic* Script]

Album (obverse bottom line: ب لا.; i.e., ثلاث?; top reverse line: له لا). Paris (20, —, ill.).

This *fals* bears the name of the overlord, al-ʿAzīz ʿUthmān of Egypt, without that of the prince of Aleppo, al-Ẓāhir Ghāzī. On his silver struck in 593 and 594 H, Ghāzī mentions al-ʿAzīz ʿUthmān. Therefore, the present *fals* may have been issued between 593 and 594 H.

Arabia

GOLD

225. *Mecca—594 H*

As the dinars of Cairo, but the following mint and date formula:

بمكة سنة اربع وتسعين وخمسمائة

Balog (19, 4.21, ill.). Gautier (20, 4.15). Leuthold, *Italia Numismatica* 3 (1969) (20, 4.16). Paris-Mecca (19, 4.57; 19, 4.30; 19, 4.28; 19, 4.39, ill.; 19, 4.34; 19, 3.69; 19, 4.49). Paris trade (—, 4.34; —, 4.49; —, 3.69). Samir Shamma (20, 3.80).

No political event is known which would explain the recognition of al-ʿAzīz ʿUthmān at Mecca, even for a brief period. Enrico Leuthold, Jr. in *Italia Numismatica* 3 (1969), relates that the unpopular Sharīf of Mecca, of the Banū Fulaytah (Hawāshim), aroused the animosity of a brother of Saladin's who, on his way to South Arabia, passed through Mecca. He must have been the future governor of the Yemen, Shams al-Dīn Tūrānshāh I. He intended to abolish the sharifate, but accepted instead, leadership of the yearly pilgrimage by an Ayyūbid and the inclusion of the Ayyūbid sultan's name in the *khuṭbah*. It would seem that the present issue is only a pious offering to the holy city, struck at the Cairo mint, but bearing the mint name of Mecca.

AL-MANṢŪR MUḤAMMAD IBN AL-ʿAZĪZ ʿUTHMĀN

Ruler of Egypt and Nominal Sultan of the Empire

[595–596 *H* = 1198–1199 AD]

Egypt

GOLD

226. *Cairo—595 H*

Border on both sides, plain circle. Counterclockwise marginal legend on both sides:

بسم الله الرحمن الرحيم ضرب هذا الدينر بالقاهرة سنة خمس
وتسعين وخمسمائة

لا اله الا الله محمد رسول الله ارسله بالهدى ودين الحق ليظهره
على الدين كله

Double circle on both sides. Counterclockwise circular legend on both sides.

ابو العباس الناصر لدين الله امير المؤمنين

عال الملك غاية المنصور

Inner circle on both sides.

Centre:
الامام
احمد

Centre:
محمد
بن عثمان

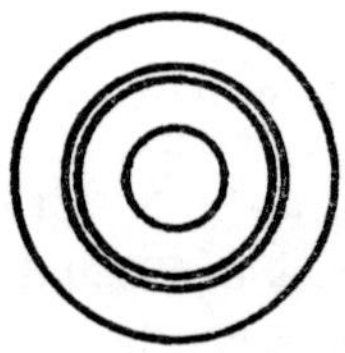

ANS-UM (19, 4.68). Balog (19, 5.27, ill.; 19, 4.44, ill.). Berman 182 (18, 4.49). BMC 299 (21, 6.05). Fahmy 221 (19, 3.71); 222 (21, 4.50); 223 (18, 3.76). Khediv. 1355. Lavoix 507 (20, 4.00). Leuthold (19, 4.04). Paris-Mecca (20, 4.69).

227. *Cairo—596 H*

As above, but the following date:

سنة ست وتسعين وخمسمائة

ANS-UM (19.5, 4.00). Balog (20, 6.21, ill.). Fahmy 224 (19, 4.34). Leuthold (16, 3.96). Paris-Mecca (20, 3.95; 20, 3.46, ill.). Yapı-Kredi (19, 6.20).

228. *Alexandria—595 H*

As above, but the following mint and date formula:

بالاسكندرية سنة خمس وتسعين وخمسمائة

Ashmolean-Thorburn (20, 4.40, ill.). BMC 299 (20, 6.05). Fahmy 226 (19, 3.58); 227 (19, 5.04); 228 (20, 4.47); 229 (19, 3.65); 231 (19, 3.45; according to Fahmy, the word *dirhem* is substituted for *dinar* on this coin). Khediv. 1355 (20, 4.97). Leuthold (20, 5.10). Paris-Mecca (19, 4.41; 19, 5.28). Paris trade (—, 4.22; —, 3.31; —, 3.43). *Spinks Num. Circ.*, Oct. 1945, No. 33301.

229. *Alexandria—596 H*

As above, but the following date:

سنة ست وتسعين وخمسمائة

ANS-UM (19.5, 4.00; 19, 3.85). Paris-Mecca (21, 5.41). Paris trade (20, 4.69; 20, 4.51). Siouffi, p. 17.

SILVER

Black dirhems, mint and date missing, but most likely Cairo or Alexandria. Circular legends reconstructed from various coins.

230. *Type A*

Border on both sides, plain circle. Counterclockwise marginal legend on both sides:

لا اله الا الله محمد رسول الله ارسله بالهدى ودين الحق ليظهره   بسم الله ضرب هذا الدرهم . . . . .

Second plain circle on both sides. Counterclockwise circular legend on both sides.

على الدين كله الملك المنصور   ابو العباس الناصر لدين الله امير المؤمنين

Pointillate circle in plain circle on both sides.

Centre:		Centre:
محمد بن عثمان		الامام احمد

Balog, *BIE*, XXXV (1953), p. 415, 1 (8 × 9, 0.82, ill.); 2 (8 × 9, 1.15); 3 (8 × 10, 1.21, ill.); 4 (8 × 9, 1.41). München 92494 (7 × 10, 1.518).

231. *Type B*

As above, but the inner circle is:

Double on obverse. Pointillate circle in plain circle on reverse.

Balog, *BIE*, XXXV (1953), p. 415, (9 × 9, 1.30, ill.).

232. *Type C*

As above, but plain inner circle on both sides.

Balog, *BIE*, XXXV (1953), p. 415, (8 × 8, 1.25).

AL-ʿĀDIL SAYF AL-DĪN ABŪ BAKR MUḤAMMAD I IBN AYYŪB

Governor of Aleppo (No Coinage) [579–592 H = 1183–1195 AD]

Governor of Karak (No Coinage) [584–592 H = 1188–1195 AD]

Lord of Ḥarrān [589–591 H = 1193–1194 AD]

Governor of Mayāfāriqīn and Sinjār [591–596 H = 1194–1199 AD]

Lord of Damascus (No Coinage) [592–596 H = 1195–1199 AD]

Sultan of the Empire [596–615 H = 1199–1218 AD]

Egypt
GOLD

A new type of gold coinage was introduced by al-ʿĀdil, with a counterclockwise marginal legend and a central inscription consisting of several horizontal lines. Besides this new type, he maintained—but only for a few issues—the earlier type of two concentric legends around a short central inscription. The new type (Type A) was issued beginning in 596 H, and for each of the following years—when there are dinars known—until 612 H, and then again in 615 H. The traditional type (Type B) is known from the years 597 H and 610 H, when the new type was struck also, and from 613 and 614 H without the new type. The year 615 H is exceptional, because the Cairo mint issued both types; Alexandria struck only the old type. Type B always contains the protocol of al-Kāmil Muḥammad, the heir apparent.

Cairo—596 H

233. *Type A*

Border on both sides, plain circle. Counterclockwise marginal legend on both sides:

لا اله الا الله محمد رسول الله ارسله بالهدى ودين الحق ليظهره على الدين كله

بسم الله الرحمن الرحيم ضرب هذا الدينر بالقاهرة سنة ستة وتسعين وخمسمائة

Double circle on both sides

Centre:

عال
الملك العادل
ابو بكر محمد بن ايوب
وولي عهده محمد
الملك الكامل
غاية

Centre:

الامام احمد
ابو العباس
الناصر لدين الله
امير المؤمنين

[Ornaments above and beneath reverse centre: ∴ ∵]

Artuk 727 (21, 3.45). Berlin-Gotha 178/1935 (21, 4.75). Berlin-Guthrie (20, 3. 60). Fahmy 232 (20, 5.14); 233 (21, 2.72); 234 (21, 4.93); 235 (21, 4.92). Paris (19, 5.04). Paris-Mecca (20, 4.37). Samir Shamma (22, 4.55).

234. *Cairo—597 H*

As above, but the following date:

سنة سبع وتسعين وخمسمائة

Balog (20, 6.83, ill.). BMC 342 (22, 3.79); 343 (18, 3.82). Fahmy 236 (19, 3.35); 237 (20, 5.38); 238 (20, 4.15); 239 (20, 5.00); 240 (20, 4.44); 241 (19, 3.00); 242 (20, 5.05); 243 (20, 3.95). Khediv. 1357a. Leuthold (20, 5.50). Paris-Mecca (20, 3.90). Pietraszewski 420.

235. *Type B*

Border on both sides, plain circle. Counterclockwise marginal legend on both sides:

لا اله الا الله محمد رسول الله ارسله بالهدى ودين الحق ليظهره على الدين كله

بسم الله الرحمن الرحيم ضرب هذا الدينر بالقاهرة سنة سبع وتسعين وخمسمائة

Double circle on both sides. Counterclockwise circular legend on both sides:

الملك العادل ولي عهده الملك الكامل

Centre:

ابو بكر
بن ايوب

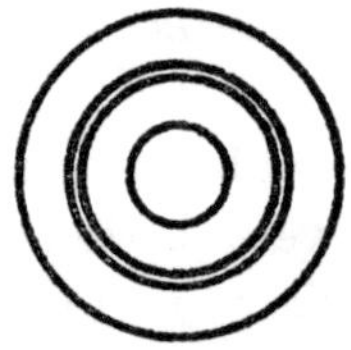

ابو العباس الناصر لدين الله امير المؤمنين

Centre:

الامام
احمد

Samir Shamma (20, 5.25).

236. *Cairo—599 H*
Type A

As No. 234, but the following date:

سنة تسع وتسعين وخمسمائة

ANS-UM (19, 3.82). Fahmy 244 (20, 4.21); 245 (20, 3.92); 246 (20, 3.78); 247 (20, 6.53); 248 (20, 4.64). Khediv. 1359.

237. *Cairo—600 H*
Type A

As above, but the following date:

سنة ستمائة

Ornaments above and beneath the reverse centre: $\frac{\therefore}{\because}$, but on some specimens, only above the reverse centre: $\overset{\therefore}{-}$.

ANS-UM (21.5, 4.80). Balog (19, 3.62, ill.). BMC 345 (20, 3.84). Fahmy 260 (19, 5.04); 261 (20, 5.97); 262 (19, 3.71); 263 (20, 5.21); 264 (19, 5.14). Leuthold (20, 4.86; 18, 3.98; 20, 3.04). Paris-Mecca (20, 4.86). Pietraszewski 421. Yapı-Kredi (20, 3.80).

238. *Cairo—601 H*
Type A

As above, but the following date:

سنة احدى وستمائة

Pietraszewski 423.

239. *Cairo—602 H*
Type A

As above, but the following date:

سنة ثنتين وستمائة

[Ornaments above and beneath the reverse centre: $\frac{\therefore}{\because}$]

Lavoix 587 (20, 6.75).

240. *Cairo—603 H*
Type A

As above, but the following date:

سنة ثلث وستمائة

Pietraszewski 424.

241. *Cairo—606 H*
Type A

As above, but the following date:

سنة ست وستمائة

ANS (20, 3.734). Artuk 728 (20, 4,40). BMC 346 (20, 4.70). Fahmy 281 (20, 4.57). Horovitz (20, 3.47, ill.). Yapı-Kredi (19, 3.45; 19, 3.90).

242. *Cairo—607 H*

Type A

As above, but the following date:

سنة سبع وستمائة

BMC 347 (20, 3.00). Khediv. 1362. Markov, p. 356, No. 20. Paris (19, 4.82). Yapı-Kredi (21, 4.17; 20, 4.45).

243. *Cairo—608 H*

Type A

As above, but the following date:

سنة ثمان وستمائة

Balog (22, 4.17, ill.). Fahmy 282 (20, 5.46). Horovitz (20, 4.60). Markov, p. 356, No. 21. Prague 92/63–896.

244. *Cairo—609 H*

Type A

As above, but the following date:

سنة تسع وستمائة

ANS-UM (20, 6.307). Balog (21, 7.00, ill.). Yapı-Kredi (20, 5.50).

245. *Cairo—610 H*

Type A

As above, but the following date:

سنة عشرة وستمائة

Balog (22, 4.12, ill.).

246. *Type B*

As No. 235, but the following date:

سنة عشر وستمائة

Horovitz (21, 4.18, ill.). J. M. C. Johnston, *NC*, 3rd Ser., XIX (1899), p. 267. Yapı-Kredi (20, 4.05).

247. *Cairo—612 H*

Type A

As No. 245, but the following date:

سنة اثنين وعشر وستمائة

Munzel (20, 6.41).

248. *Cairo—613 H*

Type B

As No. 246, but the following date:

سنه ثلث وعشر وستمائة

ANS (20, —). BMC 349 (20, 3.71); 350 (20, 4.34; on both coins the century of the date is written: ستما ئة); 351 (20, 3.86). Hirsch 2081 (—, 4.10). Horovitz (20, 4.38, ill.). Leuthold (20, 4.95). Markov, p. 356, No. 23.

249. *Cairo—614 H*

Type B

As above, but the following date:

سنة اربع عشرة وستمائة

Awad. BMC 352 (23, 4.36). Yapı-Kredi (21, 6.50).

250. Deleted.

251. *Type B*

As No. 249, but the following date:

سنة خمس عشرة وخمسمائة

Balog (21, 4.04, ill.). BMC 354 (22, 2.98). Khediv. 1364 (—, 5.10). Horovitz (21, 3.18; 20, 3.96). Lavoix 588 (21, 3.70).

252. *Alexandria—596 H*

Type A

As No. 235, but the following mint and date:

بالاسكندرية سنة ست وتسعين وخمسمائة

[Ornament above the reverse centre: ∴]

ANS-UM (22, 5.148). Balog (21, 4.70, ill.). BMC 341 (22, 5.43). Fahmy 305 (20, 5.12); 306 (22, 3.62); 307 (21, 5.14); 308 (21, 3.47); 309 (20, 4.07). Khediv. 1357. Lavoix 579 (21, 4.50); 580 (19, 5.20). Leuthold (22, 3.47). Paris-Mecca (22, 5.40; 20, 4.07). Paris-trade (—, 4.55). Samir Shamma (21, 5.17; 22, 4.62). Yapı-Kredi (20, 4.25).

253. *Alexandria—597 H*

Type A

As above, but the following date:

سنة سبع وتسعين وخمسمائة

[Ornament beneath the reverse centre: ⋯̲]

ANS-UM (20.5, 4.97). Artuk 724 (21, 4.65). BMC 344 (22, 4.60, ill.). Mitchell-Brown (20, 4.49). Fahmy 319 (21, 4.58); 320 (21, 3.69); 321 (20, 4.97); 322 (20, 4.62); 323 (20, 4.12). Leuthold (19, 4.50). Paris-Mecca (21, 6.03). Samir Shamma (19, 5.28). Siouffi, p. 17.

254. *Type B*

As No. 251, but the following mint and date:

بالاسكندرية سنه سبع وتسعين وخمسمائة

Samir Shamma (21, 5.85).

255. *Alexandria—598 H*
Type A

As No. 253, but the following date:

سنة ثمان وتسعين وخمسمائة

[Ornaments above and beneath reverse centre: ⁘]

Artuk 725 (19, 3.70). Berlin-Guthrie (21, 5.55). Fahmy 330 (21, 5.09); 331 (21, 5.65); 332 (20, 5.35); 333 (20, 5.40); 334 (20, 4.74); 335 (20, 5.03); 336 (20, 5.65). Khediv. 1358 (—, 4.50). Paris-Mecca (19, 4.77; 20, 3.79; 20, 2.94).

256. *Alexandria—599 H*
Type A

As above, but the following date:

سنة تسع وتسعين وخمسمائة

ANS (20, 4.08. ANS-UM (20, 4.39). Leuthold (20, 3.74). Markov, p. 356, No. 18. Paris-Mecca (20, 6.60; 18, 2.65). Paris trade (—, 4.52). Siouffi, p. 17, Yapı-Kredi (20, 3.95).

257. *Alexandria—600 H*
Type A

As above, but the following date:

سنة ستمائة

ANS (20, 5.088). Fahmy 341 (20, 5.50); 342 (20, 3.82); 343 (19, 5.77); 344 (19, 3.57); 345 (20, 5.24). Khediv. 1360. Yapı-Kredi (20, 5.40).

258. *Alexandria—601 H*
Type A

As above, but the following date:

سنة احدى وستمائة

[No ornaments above or beneath the reverse centre]

Balog (21, 4.92). Berlin-Guthrie (20, 4.29). Fahmy 357 (20, 3.07); 358 (20, 5.30). Lavoix 581 (21, 5.53; erroneously identified as *AE*).

259. *Alexandria—602 H*
Type A

As above, but the following date:

سنة اثنين وستمائة

Fahmy 359 (20, 3.89); 360 (19, 4.85); 361 (20, 4.18); 362 (20, 5.17); 363 (20, 4.84). Lavoix 582 (20, 5.92). Munzel (20, 4.59). Paris-Mecca (21, 4.01; 20, 5.47; 20, 4.02). Paris trade (—, 3.73; —, 4.71; —, 3.42; —, 4.26; —, 3.48; —, 4.75).

260. *Alexandria—603 H*
Type A

As above, but the following date:

بالاسكندرة (*sic*) سنة ثلث وستمائة

BM-Lowick (23, 5.75, ill.).

261. *Alexandria—604 H*

Type A

As above, but the following date:

بالاسكندرية سنة اربع وستمائة

ANS 62.16 (20, 4.995). Fahmy 383 (20, 5.03). Leuthold (21, 4.15).

262. *Alexandria—605 H*

Type A

As above, but the following date:

سنة خمس وستمائة

[Ornaments above and beneath reverse centre: ∴̣ ÷]

Lavoix 583 (21, 5.92). Siouffi, p. 77.

263. *Alexandria—606 H*

Type A

As above, but the following date:

سنة ست وستمائة

[No ornaments]

ANS-UM (20, 6.316). Khediv. 1361. Lavoix 584 (20, 4.80). Leuthold (20, 5.00). Samir Shamma (19, 4.85). Yapı-Kredi (20, 3.12).

264. *Type B*

As No. 251, but the following date:

سنة ست وستمائة

Wien 645 (20, 4.15).

265. *Alexandria—607 H*

Type A

As No. 263, but the following date:

سنة سبع وستمائة

ANS 62.126 (19, 5.02).

266. *Alexandria—608 H*

Type A

As above, but the following date:

سنة ثمان وستمائة

[Ornaments above and beneath reverse centre: ∴̣ ÷]

ANS 62. 126 (22, 4.53). Dorn IV, p. 67, No. 2. Fahmy 384 (20, 5.69). Lavoix 582 (19, 5.92; attributed to 602 H). Siouffi, p. 17. Yapı-Kredi (19, 5.16).

267. *Alexandria—609 H*

Type A

As above, but the following date:

سنة تسع وستمائة

ANS 62.126 (21, 4.26). ANS-UM (20, 6.31). Khediv. 1363. München 94069 (21, 4.891, ill.).

268. *Alexandria—610 H*

Type A

As above, but the following date:

سنة عشر وستمائة

Markov. p. 356, No. 22.

269. *Alexandria—611 H*

Type A

As above, but the following date:

سنة احدى عشر وستمائة

Samir Shamma (19, 5.15).

270. *Alexandria—613 H*

Type B

As No. 264, but the following date:

سنة ثلث عشرة وخمسمائة

ANS (20.5, 4.51). Artuk 726 (20, 4.20). Horovitz (20, 4.95). Lavoix 585 (20, 5.30, ill.; erroneously numbered 576, between Nos. 584 and 586). Leuthold (20, 5.02). Markov, p. 356, No. 24. Munzel. Paris (20, 3.99). Pietraszewski 425. Samir Shamma (20, 4.60; 18, 3.65; 19, 4.95; 20, 3.60; 19, 3.62).

271. *Alexandria—614 H*

Type B

As above, but the following date:

سنة اربع عشرة وستمائة

ANS (20, 5.661). Balog (21, 3.52, ill.). BMC 353 (22, 5.33). Lavoix 586 (21, 4.10). Samir Shamma (19, 4.12; 19, 4.95; 20, 4.77; 18, 6.27; 18, 5.55; 19, 4.17; 19, 6.25; 18, 5.38; 19, 5.82; 18, 3.62; 18, 4.10). Yapı-Kredi (20, 3.90).

272. *Alexandria—615 H*

Type B

As above, but the following date:

سنة خمس عشرة وستمائة

Balog (21, 4.48).

Yearly distribution of dinars, Types A and B, of al-ʿĀdil I:

Year	Cairo	Alexandria
596 H	Type A	Type A
597	A and B	A and B
598	—	A
599	A	A
600	A	A
601	A	A
602	A	A
603	A	A
604	—	A
605	—	A
606	A	A
607	A	A
608	A	A
609	A	A
610	A and B	A
611	—	A
612	A	—
613	B	B
614	B	B
615	A and B	B

Type A was introduced in 596 H under al-ʿĀdil I. It has a single marginal legend and a central legend on several horizontal lines, with غاية/عال at the top and bottom. Type A is, however, only a revival of the very common type introduced by the Fāṭimid Caliph al-Mustanṣir, and issued by several of his successors.

In 597 H the old B-type, with two concentric legends appeared again, but was then abandoned for 12 years. It was brought back, on and off, during the last years of al-ʿĀdil's reign. His successor, al-Kāmil Muḥammad I, minted Type A exclusively.

SILVER

Black Dirhems

On all of the following black dirhems, the mint and date are missing. They may be attributed to either Cairo or Alexandria.

273. *Type A*

The legends of al-ʿĀdil's small, Type A, black dirhems can be only partially reconstructed. Until more complete specimens are discovered, the following reconstruction is tentative. There appears to be a strong similarity to the Type A dinars.

The border and the marginal legends are missing on both sides.

Centre:

?عال؟
الملك العادل سيف
الدين ابو بكر محمد
ولي عهد الملك
?الكامل محمد بن ايوب؟
?غاية؟

Centre:

الامام احمد
ابو العباس
الناصر لدين الله
امير المؤمنين

Balog, *BIE*, XXX (1951), pp. 23–24, 1 (7 × 10, 0.76, ill.); 2 (7 × 12, 1.14, ill.); 3 (7 ×8, 0.99, ill.).

274. *Type B*

Similar to the dinar of Type B, but the marginal legend is missing on both known specimens. Border and marginal legend missing on both sides. Counterclockwise circular legend on both sides:

الملك العادل ولي عهده الملك الكامل

ابو العباس الناصر لدين الله امير المؤمنين

Inner circle on both sides.

Centre:

ابو بكر
بن ايوب

Centre:

الامام
احمد

ANS-UM (10 × 10, 1.467, ill.). Awad.

Round-Flan Dirhems

The coins of this series are all of the square-in-the-circle type and of normal dimensions.

275. *Cairo—598 H*

Border Segments (Beginning from Left):

ضرب بالقاهرة|سنة ثمان و|تسعين وخمسما|ئة محمد بن ايوب

Centre:

الملك العادل
ولي عهده
الملك الكامل

Border Segments (Beginning at Top):

لا اله الا|الله وحده|محمد ر|سول الله

Centre:

الامام النا
صر لدين الله
امير المؤمنين

[*Kūfic* script]

ANS (21, 2.93, ill.). Ashmolean-Griffith (20, —). Balog (20, 2.71, ill.).

276. *Cairo—600 H*

Border Segments:

محمد بن ايوب|ضرب بالقا|هرة سنة ستمائة

Border Segments:

لا اله الا|الله وحده|محمد رسو|ل الله

Centres as above, on both sides.

Glidden (21, —). Lavoix 608 (21, 2.55, ill.). Tewhid (20, —).

277. *Cairo—601 H*

As above, but the following date:

ضرب بالقاهرة|سنة احدى|وستمائة

Album 28 (variety with reverse last segment: سول الله). Berlin-Guthrie (20, 2.78). München 85017 (20, 2.964, ill.).

278. *Cairo—605 H*

As above, but the following date:

سنة خمس | وستمائة

ANS (20.5, 2.93).

Fiduciary divisional currency

We have no copper coins for Egypt from al-ʿĀdil's reign; instead, there is a fragment of a glass-paste jeton which may belong to him. The Caliph's name does not appear on the fragment, but from the existing half, it would seem that only his title was given. However, the pleasing Kūfic and the presence of the heir's name after the title of the prince seems to point to al-ʿĀdil, who used to name al-Kāmil on the coins.

279. Border: plain circle

مولانا

وسيدنا (وولي)

عهد

Balog 30,—turquoise blue.

SYRIA

Silver

Under Saladin the silver issues of Damascus, as well as those of Ḥamāh and Ḥimṣ, become stereotyped as the 'square in the circle', that is, a thin linear square, surrounded by a square of dots, which is enclosed in a plain circle surrounded by a border of dots. The marginal legends are placed in the segments between the square and the circle, the royal protocol in the centre of the obverse, and that of the Caliph in the centre of the reverse. The script on these coins is always Kūfic.

Al-ʿAzīz ʿUthmān maintained the 'square in the circle' type for his Syrian issues but also used Naskhi script for some of his silver.

When al-Afḍal ʿAlī started to strike silver, he introduced a completely new type, the main feature of which was a linear octalobe in an octalobe of dots.

Al-ʿAdīl I introduced other dirhem types in Damascus. His first issue in 598 H was of the 'festooned double trefoil' design. This consists of two interlaced trefoils, with a small arch connecting the taller arches of each trefoil. The trefoils are not simple linear constructions, but consist of two lines with a line of dots or small pellets between them. It is an intricate pattern and at first glance gives the impression of a double six-foil. The double-trefoil type was in use from 508 H until 610 H without interruption. The sole exceptions are one dirhem of 600 H and some ½ dirhems of 600, 603, 606 and 610 H, showing the six pointed star. This star, which is already known from Saladin's Aleppo dirhems, also consists of two plain lines and a line of dots between the two. It is typical of Aleppo until the end of the Ayyūbid dynasty, but did appear occasionally at Damascus as well as on some rare dirhems of Khilāt, and in Mesopotamia (al-Ruhā, Harrān, Mayāfāriqīn).

In 610 H, the 'double trefoil' gave way to a simplified variant, the 'festooned six-foil' which is composed of six lobes, each with a line of dots between two plain lines. Each such section meets the next with a pointed end. The dirhem of this type exists only with the date 610 H, and there are many $\frac{1}{2}$ dirhems, on which the date is unfortunately missing. But in the same year 610 H, the six-pointed star type appears also and is the only type from now onwards, except in 612 H, when the 'six-foil' is used once more, beside the star type.

The following table illustrates the pattern of types in Damascus, between 598 and 615 H:

Year	Pattern
598 H	Double Trefoil
599	Double Trefoil
600	Double Trefoil
600	Six-Pointed Star
600*	Six-Pointed Star
601	Double Trefoil
602	Double Trefoil
603	Double Trefoil
603*	Six-Pointed Star
604	Double Trefoil
605	Double Trefoil
606	Double Trefoil
606*	Double Trefoil
606*	Six-Pointed Star
607	No Coins
608	Double Trefoil
609	Double Trefoil
610	Double Trefoil
610	Six-foil Type
610*	Six-Pointed Star
611	Six-Pointed Star
612	Six-foil Type
612*	Six-Pointed Star
613	Six-Pointed Star
613*	Six-Pointed Star
614	Six-Pointed Star
615	Six-Pointed Star

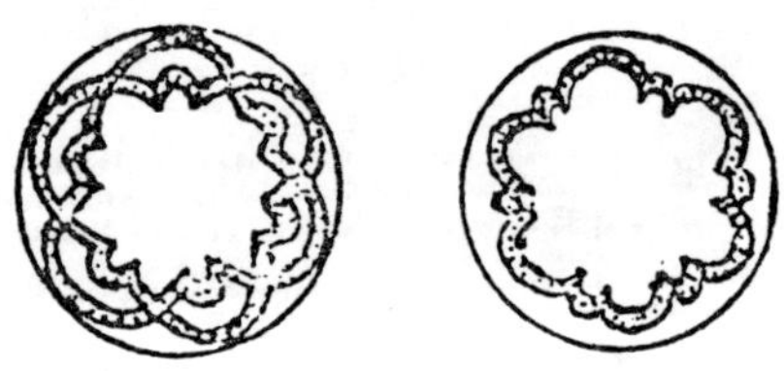

" Double Trefoil " and " Six-foil "

The double trefoil and the six-foil dirhems are engraved in Naskhi, but the writing on the six-pointed star coins is in a rather ornate Kūfic, with the terminal letters often ending in a minute scroll or a plant-leaf. It was Dr. Michael Bates of the ANS who drew my attention to the differences between the double trefoil and the sixfoil.

280. *Damascus—598 H*

Festooned double trefoil.

Border Segments:	Border Segments:
ضرب | بد | مشق | سنة | ثمان | وتسعين	لا اله | الا | الله | محمد | رسول | الله
Centre:	Centre:
الدين	منين
الملك العادلى	الامام الناصر
ابو بكر بن ايوب	لدين الله امير
سيف	المؤ

ANS (22, 3.00, ill.). Lowick (22, 2.88; 20, 2.96). Siouffi, p. 17. Berlin-Dahlem J. 20/71 (21, 2.855).

281. *Damascus—599 H*

Festooned double trefoil.

Border Segments:	Border Segments:
ضرب | بد | مشق | سنة | تسع و | تسعين	لا اله | الا | الله | محمد | رسول | الله
Centre:	Centre:
الدين	المؤ
الملك العادل	الامام الناصر
ابو بكر بن ايوب	لدين الله امير
سيف	منين

Lowick (20, 2.82; 20, 2.96, ill.). Yapı-Kredi (21, 2.95).

Damascus—600 H

282. *Type A*

As above, but obverse border segments:

ضر \| ب \| بد \| مشق \| سنة \| ستمائة

ANS (20, 2.94). Lowick (19, 2.97; 20, 3.00). Pietraszewski 422. Ziya 1627 (20, —).

283. *Type B*

Six-pointed star.

Border Segments:	Border Segments:
ضر | ب | بد | مشق | سنة | ستمائة	لا اله | الا ا | لله | محمد | رسول | الله
Centre:	Centre:
الامام	الملك
الناصر لدين	العادل سيف
الله امير المؤ	الدين ابو بكر بن
منين	ايوب

ANS-Lowell (20, 2.997).

284. *Half Dirhem*

Six-pointed star.

Border Segments:
ضر | ب | بد | مشق | سنة | ستمائة
Centre:
○
الملك
العادل
○

Border Segments:
لا | اله | الا | الله | محمد | رسوله
Centre:
○
الامام
الناصر
○

BMC 357 (14, 1.41). Lowick (13, 1.39, ill.; mint/date formula: ضر | ب | بد | مشق | ستة | مائة).

285. *Damascus—601 H*

As No. 280, but obverse border segments:

ضرب | بد | مشق | سنة | احد و | ستمائة

Album 40 (date written: احدى/وستمائة). ANS (20, 2.98). Artuk 722 (20, 3.00). Wien (19, —, ill.).

286. *Damascus—602 H*

Type A

As above, but obverse:

Border Segments:
ضرب | بد | مشق | سنة | اثنين و | ستمائة
Centre:
سيف
الملك العادل
ابو بكر بن ايوب
الدين

Album. ANS 72.75 (21, 2.987, ill.).

287. *Type B*

Six-pointed star.

Border Segments:
ضرب | بد | مشق | سنة | اثنتين | ستمائة
Centre:
سيف
الملك العادل
ابو بكر ابن ايوب
الدين

Border Segments:
لا اله | الا | الله | محمد | رسول | الله
Centre:
الامام
الناصر لدين
الله امير المؤ
منين

Album.

Damascus—603 H

288. *Type A*

As No. 286, but obverse border segments:

ضرب | بدمشق | سنة | ثلث | ستة | مائة

BM (21, —, ill.). Yapı-Kredi (20, 2.95).

289. *Type B*

Festooned double trefoil.

Border Segments:	Border Segments:
ضرب | بد | مشق | سنة | ثلاث | ستمائة	لا اله | الا | الله | محمد | رسول | الله
Centre:	Centre:
سيف	منين
الملك العادل	الامام الناصر
ابو بكر بن ايوب	ادين الله امير
الدين	المؤ

Album 24.

290. *Half Dirhem*

As No. 284, but border segments:

ضر | ب | بد | مشق | سنة | ثلث — لا اله | الا ا | لله | محمد | رسو | ل الله

Berlin 710/1903 (14, 1.41). Horovitz (14, 1.46, ill.).

291. *Damascus—604 H*

As No. 289, but obverse border segments:

ضرب | بد | مشق | سنة | اربع | وستمائة

ANS-Laties (19, —). Berlin 806/1904 (21, 1.89). Nicol (20.2, 2.955).

292. *Damascus—605 H*

As above, but the following date:

خمس | ستمائة

ANS-Laties (21, —). BMC 358 (20, 2.92). Markov, p. 356, No. 19.

293. *Damascus—606 H*

As above, but the following date:

ست | ستمائة

Album. ANS-Laties (20, —; date ست/وستماية). Ashmolean-Bodleian 147 (20, 2.77, ill.). Balog (21, 2.86, ill.).

Half Dirhem

294. *Type A*

Festooned double trefoil.

Border Segments:
ضر | ب | بدمشق | سنة | ست و | ستمائة
Centre:
الدين
الملك العادل
سيف

Border Segments:
لا اله | الا ا | لله | محمدر | سول | الله
Centre:
الله
الامام الناصر
لدين

Ashmolean-Bodleian.

295. *Type B*

As No. 284, but the following date:

سنة | ست

Horovitz (16, 1.44).

296. *Damascus—608 H*

Festooned double trefoil.

Border Segments:
ضرب بد | مشق | سنة | ثمان | ست | مائة
Centre:
الدين
الملك العادل
⊙
ابو بكر بن ايوب
سيف

Border Segments:
لا اله | الا | الله | محمد | رسول | الله
Centre:
المؤ
الامام الناصر
⊙ ومن
لدين الله امير
منين

Album (date not clear). ANS 72.75 (23, —). Ashmolean-Thorburn (23, 2.91, ill.). BM-Rev. Chester (23, 2.97). Lavoix 596 (22, 2.93, ill.; Lavoix did not read the date). Paris (23, 2.99, ill.).

297. *Damascus—609 H*

As above, but:

Obverse Border Segments:
ضرب | بد | مشق | سنة | تسع or سبع ؟ | ستمائة

Reverse Centre:
المؤ
الامام الناصر
⊙
لدين الله امير
منين

ANS-Laties (19.5, —). Paris (20, 2.95).

Damascus—610 H

298. *Type A*

Festooned six-foil.

Border Segments:
ضرب | بد | مشق | سنة | عشر | وستمائة
Centre:
الملك العادل
سيف الدين
ابو بكر بن ايوب

Border Segments:
ابو | العباس | احمد | امير | المو | منين
Centre:
الله
لا اله الا الله
محمد رسول الله
الامام الناصر
لدين

[Floweret above and beneath obverse centre]

BMC 364 (20, 2.44; the date is missing, but the legends are found only on this year's issue). Glidden (22, 2.90, ill.). Lavoix 590 (21, 2.90. ill.). Siouffi, p. 17 (probably this issue). Yapı-Kredi (21, 2.80).

299. *Type B*

As No. 289, but the following date:

عشر | وستمائة

ANS (21, —, ill.). Berman 186 (21, 2.95).

300. *Type C*

Six-pointed star.

Border Segments:
ضرب | بد | مشق | سنة | عشر | وستمائة
Centre:
الملك العادل
سيف الدين
ابو بكر بن ايوب

Border Segments:
ابو | العباس | احمد | امير | المو | منين(؟)
Centre:
الله
لا اله الا الله
محمد رسول الله
الامام الناصر
لدين

ANS (21, 2.941). Khediv. 1365.

301. *Damascus—611 H*

Six-pointed star.

Border Segments:
ضرب | بد | مشق | سنة | احد عشر | ستمائة
Centre:
سيف
الملك العادل
ابو بكر ابن ايوب

Border Segments:
لا اله | الا | الله | محمد | رسول | الله
Centre:
الامام
الناسر لدين
الله امير المؤ
منين

Ashmolean-Thorburn (22, 2.95). BMC 365 (20, 2.99). Peus 1886. Yapı-Kredi (20, 2.75).

Damascus—612 H

302. *Type A*

Festooned six-foil.

Border Segments:
ضرب | بدمشق | سنة | اثني | عشر | ستمائة
Centre:
الملك العادل
ابو بكر بن ايوب

Border Segments:
لا اله | الا | الله | محمد | رسول | الله
Centre:
المؤ
الامام الناصر
لدين الله امير
منين

Khediv. 1367. Yapı-Kredi (19, 3.08; 20, 2.80).

303. *Type B*

Six-pointed star.

Border Segments:
ضرب | بدمشق | سنة | اثنين | عشر | ستمائة
Centre:
الملك
العادل سيف
الدين ابو بكر بن
ايوب

Border Segments:
لا اله | الا ا | الله | محمد | رسول | الله
Centre:
الامام
الناصر لدين
الله امير المؤ
منين

ANS-UM (19, 2.75). ANS 72.75 (19.5, —). ANS-Laties (18, —; date in *Naskh*). BM-Spinks (20, 2.92, ill.). München 91847 (20, 2.982, ill.).

304. *Half Dirhem*

As No. 284, but border segments:

ضرب | بد | مشق | سنة | اثني | عشر

لا اله | الا ا | الله | محمد | رسول | الله

[No annulets above and beneath both centre areas]

Khediv. 1368.

Damascus—613 H

305. *Type A*

As No. 303, but the following date:

ثلث | عشر | ستمائة
٣

Ashmolean-Thorburn (19, 2.95). Balog (21, 2.93, ill.). Yapı-Kredi (19, 2.95; 19, 2.90).

306. *Type B*

As above, but:

In date, but no ٣ under عشر.

Centre:
سيف
الملك العادل
ابو بكر ابن ايوب
الدين

Album 39. ANS-Wood (19, 2.885). BMC 360 (20, 2.81). Khediv. 1369. Lavoix 602 (20, 2.95).

307. *Half Dirhem*

As No. 304, but the following date:

ضرب|بد|مشق|سنة|ثلث|عشر

[Annulets above and beneath both centre areas]

BMC 367 (14, 1.45; obverse segments: [*sic*] (سنة|ثلث|عشر|مف|ضرب|(بدمشق)). Lavoix 606 (14, 1.40).

308. *Damascus—614 H*

As No. 306, but the following date:

اربع|عشر و|ستمائة

ANS-Laties (20, —, ill.). Berlin-Guthrie (21, 2.97, ill.). Berman 184 (19, 2.90). BMC 366 (21, 2.94; dated 613 H by Lane-Poole). Markov, p. 356, No. 25. Peus 1887. Prague 898 (19, 2.90). Yapı-Kredi (20, 2.50).

309. *Damascus—615 H*

As above, but the following date:

ضرب|بدمشق|سنة|خامس (*sic*)|عشر و|ستمائة

Album. ANS-Newell (20, 2.92; 20, 2.90). ANS-Laties (20, —; digit of the date: خمس). BMC 367a (19, 2.87, ill.). Ilisch 17 (20, —). Lavoix 602 (19, 2.95); 603 (18, 2.52). Paris (20, 3.00. ill.). Siouffi, p. 77. Tewhid (20, —).

Half Dirhems—Date Missing

310. *Type A—59x H*

Festooned six-foil.

Border Segments:

ضرب|بد|مشق|سنة . . . . . |وتسعين|خمسمائة

Centre:

الدين

الملك العادل

سيف

Border Segments:

لا اله|الا ا|لله|محمد|رسول|الله

Centre:

الله

الامام الناصر

لدين

ANS-Boyd (13, 1.315). ANS-Newell (12, —; 12, —). ANS-UM (8, —). ANS-Wright (13, 1.419). Ashmolean-Thorburn (14, 1.48, ill.). Ashmolean-Rev. Chester (14, 1.42). Ashmolean-Griffith (13, 1.39). Berlin 438/1911 (15, 1.41). Berman 187 (13, 1.50). BMC 356 (13, 1.43). BM 1962 (13, 1.45). Lavoix 591 (14, 1.42); 592 (12, 1.46); 593 (14, 1.46); 594 (13, 1.35, ill.).

311. *Type B*

Festooned double trefoil. Border segments on both sides, as above.

Centre:

سيف

الملك العادل

ابو بكر بن ايوب

الدين

Centre:

منين

الامام الناصر

لدين الله امير

المؤ

Balog (13, 1.35). BMC 355 (14, 1.44). Lavoix 601 (13, 1.42, ill.). Paris (12, 1.30, ill.).

312. *Type C*

Six-pointed star.

Border segments missing almost entirely.

Centre:

سيف
الملك العادل
ابو بكر بن ايوب
الدين

Border Segments (Reconstructed).

لا اله | الا | الله | محمد | رسول | الله

Centre:

الامام
الناصر لدين
الله امير المؤ
منين

ANS-Laties (13, 1.50, ill.). Berman 185 (13, 1.85). Lavoix 607 (13, 1.43, ill.).

313. *Ḥamāh—597 H*

Square-in-the-circle type.

Border Segments:

ضرب بحماه | سنة تسع | وتسعين | خمسمائة

Centre:

الملك العادل
سيف الدين
ابو بكر بن ايوب

Border Segments:

لا اله الا | الله وحده | محمد رسو | ل الله

Centre:

الامام الناصر
لدين الله
امير المؤمنين

[*Kūfic* script]

Lavoix 589 (20, 2.83). Leuthold-Ripostiglio 21 (21, 2.98).

314. *Ḥimṣ—598 H*

Border on both sides: thin linear circle within pointillate circle. Counterclockwise marginal legend on both sides:

بسم الله ضرب بحمص سنة ثمانيه وتسعين وخمسمائة

لا اله الا الله وحده لا شريك له محمد رسول الله صلى الله

Linear octalobe within pointillate octalobe.

Centre:

الملك العاد
ل ولى عهده ا
لملك الكامل

Centre:

الامام النا
صر لدين الله ا
مير المؤمنين

[Marginal legends in *Kūfic*; centre in *Naskh*]

Berman 188 (22, 2.87). Tewhid (21, —).

315. *Ḥimṣ—599 H*

As above, but the following date:

سنة تسع وتسعين وخمسمائة

BM (20, 2.63, ill.

316. *Mint and Date Missing*

Festooned double trefoil.

Obverse	Reverse
Border Segments:	Border Segments:
[Missing]	لا اله | الا ا | لله | محمد | رسول | الله
Centre:	Centre:
الملك	المؤ
الملك العادل	الامام الناصر
ابو بكر بن ايوب	لدين الله امير
الكامل	منين

[*Naskh* script]

The traces of festooned double trefoil margin suggest the mint of Damascus.

ANS-Laties (21, —; 19, —, ill.). ANS-Starosselsky (17, 1.432, ill.).

COPPER

317. *Damascus—596 H*

Border of small beads on both sides. Counterclockwise marginal legend on both sides:

Obverse	Reverse
ضرب هذا الفلس بدمشق سنة ست وتسعين وخمسمائة	ضرب هذا الفلس بدمشق سنة ست وتسعين وخمسمائة

Circle of small beads on both sides.

Obverse	Reverse
Centre:	Centre:
* سيف *	* *
الملك العادل	ابو بكر ايوب
* الدين *	بن
	* *
Small six-pointed star in the four corners.	Small six-pointed star in the four corners. Intricate arabesque knot above and beneath the legend.

[The inscriptions on all the coins of this series are in *Naskh*]

Zambaur, *Contrib.* II, 276.

Damascus—598 H

318. *Type A*

As above, but the following date:

سنة ثمان تسعين وخمسمائة

Ashmolean-Thorburn (23, 4.54, ill.; 23, 5.56). Berlin 629/1896 (24, 4.82). BMC 369b (23, 4.81); 369c (23, 6.74); 369d (24, 4.62). Prague 61/66–1. Windisch-Graetz 173 (24, —).

319. *Type B*

As above, but the obverse centre:

الدين

الملك العادل

سيف

Glidden.

320. *Damascus—599 H*

As No. 318, but the following date:

سنة تسع وتسعين وخمسمائة

Ashmolean-Bodleian 150 (23, 5.52, ill.). Berlin 631/1896 (25, 5.55; 23, 6.10). Berlin-Dahlem J. 19/71 (20, 5.39).

321. *Damascus—599 H Mule*

[Mule of Obverse of 598 H with Reverse of 599 H]

As all the above coins, but the two marginal legends:

ضرب هذا الفلس بدمشق سنة ثمان وتسعين وخمسمائة — ضرب هذا الفلس بدمشق سنة تسع وتسعين وخمسمائة

Ashmolean-Griffith (21, 5.82, ill.).

322. *Damascus—608 H*

Border of small beads on both sides. Counterclockwise marginal legend on both sides:

ضرب هذا الفلس بدمشق سنة ثمان وستمائة — ضرب هدا الفلس بدمشق سنة ثمان وستمائة

Circle of small beads on both sides.

Centre:

※ الدين ※
الملك العادل
※ سيف ※

Arabesque knot in the four corners.

Centre:

※
* *
ابو بكر بن ايوب
* *
※

Small six-pointed star in the four corners. Arabesque knot above and beneath legend.

ANS (25, 4.70). Ashmolean-Bodleian 149 (25, —). Ashmolean-A. C. Kay (23, 4.67, ill.). Berman 190 (23, 5.50). BMC 372 (23, 4.36; reverse central legend has the last letter in a lower line: ابو بكر بن ايو / ب). 372b (24, 4.94). Horovitz (22, 4.86). Khediv. 1385; 1388 (both coins probably belong here). Lagumina, p. 81, No. 47, (21, 5.72; probably belongs here).

323. *Damascus—609? H*

Outer borders off flan. Counterclockwise marginal legends on both sides:

. . . . ضرب . . . . . سع وستمائة — [Reverse legend illegible]

Centre:

* الدين *
الملك العادل
. . . .

Centre:

* ※ *
ابو بكر بن ايو
* ب *

Album.

324. *Damascus—610 H*

As No. 322, but the following date:

سنة عشر وستمائة

The reverse central legend has the last letter in a lower line: ابو بكر بن ايو / ب

ANS (27, 4.36; 24, 5.64; 23, 5.28, ill.; the last specimen has a digit partly visible that seems to be خمس. In this case the date is 615 H).

Damascus—No Date

325. *Type A*

As above, but the date is missing.

BM (22, —). Lavoix 612 (24, —); 613 (22, —). Prague 901 (23, —). Yapı-Kredi (23, 5.68).

326. *Type B*

Border of pellets on both sides. Counterclockwise marginal legend:

[Obverse legend illegible] ضرب هذا الفلس سنة . . . . .

Circle of pellets on both sides.

Centre:	Centre:
❋ ✤ ❋	ابو بكر
الملك العادل	بن ايوب
❋ ✤ ❋	

Star in each of the four corners.

[*Kūfic* Script]

Lavoix 614 (25, 5.35).

Ḥamāh—Date Missing

327. *Type A*

Border on both sides: plain circle within pointillate circle, within which is a double concave-sided pointillate hexagon, each point linked with the border by a small loop.

Border Segments:	Border Segments:
ضرب | بحماه | سنة | . . . | . . . | . . .	لا الله | (الا) | (الله) | محمد | رسول | الله
Centre:	Centre:
الملك	احمد
العادل	الامام
ابو بكر	الناصر
بن ايوب	

[*Kūfic* Script]

Ashmolean-Bodleian 148 (20, 4.186, ill.). Ashmolean-Christ Church 252 (20, 3.93, ill.).

328. *Type B*

As above, but the following obverse centre:

ابو
المالك
العادل
بكر

ANS (20, —).

Mint and Date Missing

329. *Type A*

Border and marginal legends, if any, missing on both sides. Pointillate circle on both sides.

Centre:

ب
الملك
العادل

Centre:

الامام
الناصر

Album (trace of date in obverse margin: ضر . . . . ين وخمسمائة). Lagumina, p. 83, No. 51, (19, 2.62).

330. *Type B*

Border missing on both sides. Counterclockwise marginal legend on both sides:

العادل ابو بكر سيف الدين

Centre:

الملك

الناصر لدين الله امير المؤمنين

Centre:

الامام

Khediv. 1386.

Mesopotamia

SILVER

331. *al-Ruhā—605 H*

Six-pointed star.

Border Segments:

ضرب | بالرها | سنة | خمس | . . . | . . .

Centre:

الملك
العادل سيف
الدنيا والدين بن
ايوب

Border Segments:

لا له | الا ا | لله محمد | رسول | الله

Centre:

الامام
الناصر لدين
الله امير المؤ
منين

Ilisch 16 (21, —). München 94399 (20, 2.726).

Although the decade is missing, this coin should be assigned to 605 H, because the arrangement of the central legends is different on the 615 H dirhem.

332. *al-Ruhā—611 H*

Six-pointed star.

Border Segments:

ضرب | بالرها | سنة ا | حد عشرة | وست | مائة

Centre:

سيف
الملك العادل
ابو بكر بن ايوب
الدين

Border Segments:

لا اله | الا ا | لله | محمد | رسول | الله

Centre:

الامام
الناصر لدين
الله امير المؤ
منين

Tewhid (19, —, ill.).

al-Ruhā—615 H

333. *Type A*

As above, but the following date:

سنة | خمس | عشر و | ستمائة

and above Reverse Centre:

ↄc

الناصر لدين

ANS-Laties (19, —; 20, —).

334. *Type B*

As above, but the reverse centre:

الامام
الناصر لدين
الله امير . . . .

Album 2.

335. *Aleppo (?)—607 H*

Six-pointed star.

Border Segments:
ضرب | بحلب ؟ | سنة | سبع | وستة | مائة
Centre:
الملك
العادل ابو بكر بن
ايوب

Border Segments:
لا اله | الا | الله | محمد | رسول | الله
Centre:
الامام
الناصر لدين الله
امير المؤمنين
احمد

Izzet 303.

Holu Izzet Pasha read the mint as *Ḥalab.* However, Aleppo is a highly improbable mint for al-ʿĀdil. al-Ẓāhir Ghāzī was the uncontested ruler of Aleppo since Saladin's death in 589 H and struck silver in that city continuously from the beginning of his reign until he died in 613 H. al-ʿĀdil's name is mentioned on the reverse of al-Ẓāhir's coins, under the caliph's protocol, as overlord from 596 H onward, almost without interruption. The entire obverse field is, nevertheless, inscribed with al-Ẓāhir's own name and protocol as Lord of Aleppo. Furthermore, there is a dirhem issue, in al-Zāhir's name and with al-ʿĀdil as overlord, for the year 607 H.

The present location of the Izzet specimen is unknown to me, so that a re-examination is not possible. Based on similar silver dirhems of the six-pointed star arrangement, it would seem more likely that the mint is one of the Mesopotamian localities, such as Ḥarrān or al-Ruhā .

336. *No Mint—Undated*

Border on both sides, plain circle. Counterclockwise marginal legends on both sides:

سيف الدين ابو بكر بن ايوب

الناصر لدين الله امير المومنين

Pointillate circle on both sides.

Centre:
الملك

Centre:
الامام

[This coin may have been struck in Syria]

BM (12, —, ill.; cast of coin only; weight not recorded).

COPPER

Mayāfāriqīn—591 H

337. *Type A*

Border is a plain circle in pointillate circle on both sides.

Counterclockwise marginal legend:
ضرب هذا الدرهم بميفرقين سنة احد

Plain circle.

Centre:

Bust of prince facing, wearing headdress and cloak with three folds around shoulders. Cloak held together by clasp in front loosely hanging down; two horizontal folds shown on sides of cloak's open edge. Hair hangs in loose waves. No beard, no moustache. Right and left of head, counterclockwise legend:

Left: خمسائة Right: وتسعين

Bust is based at lower border of coin, so that marginal legend starts at right side of bust, ending at its left side.

Counterclockwise legend around centre:
الملك العادل سيف الدين ابو بكر بن ايوب

Centre:
لا اله الا الله
محمد رسول
الله الامام
الناصر لدين
الله امير
المؤمنين

Album. ANS (32.5, 11.00, ill.; 28.5, 10.45; 28, 10.45). ANS-UM (28, 9.12, ill.; تسعين is written without the preceding و). Artuk 730 (27, 9.40). Berman 189 (30, 12.50). BMC 368 (30, 14.80, ill.). Butak I, p. 108, No. 121. Ghalib 192 (28, —). Izzet 306, 307, 308, 309. Prague 38/68–21 (29, —). Tewhid (28, —; 28, —; 28, —). Yapı-Kredi (32, 12.55; 30, 9.00; 29, 10.12; 30, 13.00; 29, 10.85).

338. *Type B*

As above, but:

Counterclockwise marginal legend:
الملك العادل سيف الدين ابو بكر بن ايوب

Counterclockwise legend, right and left of head:

Left: احد تسعين Right: ضرب سنة :

Counterclockwise circular legend around central legend:
ضرب علله بميافارقين

Centre:
لا اله الا الله
وحده لا شر
يك له الامام
الناصر لدين
الله امير المؤ
منين

ANS (28, 9.90; 33, 11.993). Ashmolean-Christ Church (28, —). Berlin-Guthrie (30, 11.021, ill.). BM-Amedroz (30, 9.65). Butak I, p. 107, No. 120. Castiglioni CLXXVIII, No. 5 (28, —, ill.). Izzet 310, 311, 312. Prague 900 (28, —). Ziya 1635 (30, —); 1636 (30, —).

339. *Type C*

As above, but the circular legend around the reverse central inscription:
ضرب هذا الفلس بمافرقين

Ghalib 191 (28, —).

340. *Type D*

As No. 337, but the date to the left and right of the head:

Left:	Right:
(و) تسعين خما	سنة احد

ANS-Dumbarton Oakes (32, 10.997, ill.). Berlin (27, 10.65). Izmir (28, —, ill.).

341. *Mayāfāriqīn—592 H*

As No. 337, but the counterclockwise marginal legend on the obverse:

ضرب هذا الدرهم بميفرقين سنة اثنين

and the legend to the left and right of the head:

Left:	Right:
وخمسمائة	تسعين

Album. ANS-Wright (27, —). Bartholomaei à Soret, *RNB* (1862), p. 59, No. 60 *bis*. Ziya 1637 (28, —); 1638 (28, —).

342. *Mayāfāriqīn—595 H*

As above, but the following obverse marginal legend:

ضرب هذا الدرهم بميفرقين

The legend to the left and right of the head:

Left:	Right:
وتسعين	سنة خمس

Lavoix 623 (30, 9.80).

343: *Mayāfāriqīn—596 H*

As above, but the following obverse marginal legend:

ضرب هذا الدرهم بميافرقين سنة ستة

The legend to the left and right of the head:

Left:	Right:
وخمسمائة	تسعين

München 85668 (28, 9.59, ill.).

344. *Mayāfāriqīn—601 H*

As No. 338, but the legend to the left and right of the head:

Left:	Right:
سنة احد وستمائة	ضرب بميفرقين

Castiglioni CLXXXI (Castello Sforzesco Museum new No. 384).

345. *Mayāfāriqīn—608 H*

As above, but the legend to the left and right of the head:

Left:	Right:
ستمائة	سنة ثمان و

Paris (30, 12.14; 31, 13.85).

Qalʿat Jaʿbar—601 H

346. *Type A*

Border on both sides: circle of pellets.

Centre:	Centre:
سنة احد	بقلعت
الملك العادل	ابو بكر بن ايوب
وست	جعبر
مائة	ضرب

[Central legend is in *Kūfic*; upper and lower lines, both sides, are in *Naskh*]

Artuk 729 (20, 3.00). Ashmolean-Thorburn (24, 2.76, ill.).

347. *Type B*

Border of pellets on both sides within a plain circle.

Centre:	Centre:
سنة احد	ضرب بقلعة
الملك العادل	ابو بكر بن ايوب
وستمائة	جعبر

[Central legend is in *Kūfic*; upper and lower lines are in *Naskh*]

Artuk 729 (20, 3.00, ill.). Lavoix 619 (23, 2.75) ill.). München 86992 (22, 2.353, ill.).

348. *Qalʿat Jaʿbar—602 H*

As above, but the top line of the obverse centre:

سنة اثنان [*sic*]

Album.

349. *al-Ruhā—602 H*

Border on both sides: plain circle in circle of pellets.

Centre:	Centre:
ضرب بالرها	اثنين
الملك العادل	ابو بكر بن ايوب
سنة	ستمائة

The central legend is in *Qarmāṭī Kūfic*; the upper and lower lines are in *Naskh*.

München 86377 (20, 4.081, ill.).

350. *al-Ruhā—603 H*

As above, but the obverse and reverse centres:

Obverse:	Reverse:
ثلاث و	ضرب بالر
الملك العادل	ابو بكر بن ايوب
ستمائة	ها سنة

Album. Castiglioni, Plate X, No. 9. Lavoix 615 (22, 3.80, ill.).

351. *al-Ruhā—604 H*

As above, but the obverse and reverse centres:

Centre:	Centre:
ضرب بالرها	اربع و
الملك العادل	⚜
سنة	ابو بكر بن ايوب
	ستمائة

Album 21. ANS (22, 4.17; 21.5, 3.38; 21.5, 3.39; 23, 4.76; 20.5, 4.26; 21, 3.324). Arri, p. 40. Berlin (21, 4.88). Berlin 1137/1898 (22, 4.87). Berlin-Guthrie (22, 4.31; 20, 3.90). BMC 369e (19.5, 3.10); 369f (20, 4.02). Castiglioni CXC, Plate X, No. 9 (From the illustration, the coin seems to belong to 604 H). Ghalib 193b (23, —). Lagumina, p. 82, No. 49, (20, 4.32). Lavoix 616 (20, 3.55); 617 (22, 4.21). München 86002 (23, 3.831, ill.); 88190 (21, 3.663). Peus 1885. Tewhid (22, —). Wien 651 (24, —, ill.).

352. *al-Ruhā—605 H*

As above, but the obverse and reverse centres:

Centre:	Centre:
ضرب بالرها	خمس
الملك العادل	⚜
(ornament) سنة (ornament)	ابو بكر بن ايوب
	وستمائة

Album 17. ANS-Newell (20, 4.304; 20, 3.493; 20, 3.754). Lavoix 618 (20, 4.65). Paris (20, 3.81, ill.).

al-Ruhā—611 H

353. *Type A*

Pointillate border on both sides. On both sides concave-sided plain linear hexagon, in which is a similar pointillate hexagon, ending at each point in a loop. The loops touch the border.

Border Segments:	Border Segments:
ضرب | بالرها | سنة | احدى | عشرة | وستمائة	لا اله | الا ا | لله | محمد | رسول | الله
Centre:	Centre:
الملك	احمد
العادل	الامام
	الناصر

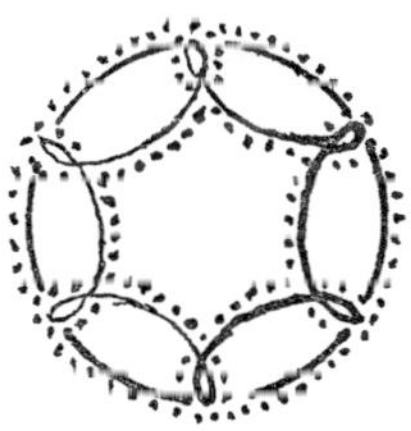

[*Kūfic* script]

Album. Berlin-Guthrie (23, 4.24, ill.). Istanbul (21, —, ill.). Soret à Fraehn (1851), No. 105. Yapı-Kredi (21, 3.70).

354. *Type B*

As above, but the obverse and reverse centres:

بكر	احمد
الملك	الامام
العادل	الناصر
ابو	

Album. ANS (20, 4.09). München 88168 (21, 4.996).

355. *Type C*

As above, but the obverse and reverse centres:

ابو	احمد
الملك	الامام
العادل	الناصر
بكر	

ANS (20, 3.78); (19, 4.75; date missing, but belongs to this variety, and is either 611 or 612 H). BM (21, —, ill.). Khediv. 1387.

356. *al-Ruhā—612 H*

Border of pellets on both sides. Plain linear concave-sided hexagon with a loop at each point. The loops touch the border.

Border Segments:	Border Segments:
ضرب | بالرها | سنة | اثنتى | عشر | وستمائة	لا اله | الا | الله | محمد | رسول | الله
Centre:	Centre:
الملك	احمد
العادل	الامام
ابو بكر بن ا	الناصر
يوب	

[*Kūfic* script]

BMC 370 (19, 4.98); 371 (19, —; the *alif* of ايوب is at the beginning of the last line).

357. *al-Ruhā—614 H*

As above, but the obverse:

Border Segments:

ضرب | بالرها | سنة | اربع | عشر | وستمائة

Centre:

الملك

العادل

Çetinyalçın (21, —).

Ḥarrān—589 H

358. *Type A (Hexalobe)*

Pointillate border on both sides. Linear hexalobe with a ringlet at the top of each convexity. The ringlets touch the border.

Border Segments:

ضرب | بحران | سنة | تسع | وثمانين | وخمسمائة

Centre:

ابو بكر
الملك العادل
سيف الدين
ابن ايوب

Border Segments:

لا اله | الا | الله | محمد | رسول | الله

Centre:

الله
الامام
الناصر لدين
امير المؤمنين

[*Kūfic* script]

Ashmolean (21, 3.18). Ashmolean-Christ Church 253 (20, 3.40, ill.). Berlin 429/1892 (20, 2.78, ill.). Lagumina, p. 84, Nos. 52, 53 and 54 (all three: diameter 20, weight between 2.30–2.55). Lavoix 625 (18, 2.60); 626 (19, 2.40, ill.).

359. *Ḥarrān—590 H*

As above, but the following date:

ضر | ب | بحران | سنة | تسعين | وخمسمائة

Ashmolean-Mrs. Muirbank (18, 2.44).

360. *Ḥarrān—591 H*

As above, but the following date:

ضرب | بحران | سنة | احد | وتسعين | وخمسمائة

BM (22, 2.48, ill.). BMC 369a (20, 2.89, ill.).

Ḥarrān—596 H

361. *Type A*

Border on both sides: pointillate circle within lineate circle.

Centre:

وتسعين
الملك العادل
وخمسمائة

Centre:

ضرب بحران
ابو بكر بن ايوب
ϒ ϒ
سنة ستة

[Central line in *Qarmāṭī Kūfic*; upper and lower legends in *Naskh*]

ANS (25.5, 4.42; digit of the date: ست). Ashmolean-Christ Church (22, —). Balog (23, 5.47, ill.). Lavoix 609 (23, 4.65). Wien (24, —, ill.). Yapı-Kredi (23, 5.85).

362. *Type B*

As above, but the obverse and reverse centres:

ضرب بحران
الملك العادل
سنة ستة

وتسعين
ابو بكر بن ايوب
وخمسمائة

Zambaur, *Contrib.* I, p. 80, No. 75.

363. *Ḥarrān—598 H*

As above, but the following date arrangement:

Centre:	Centre:
تسعين	ضرب بحران
الملك العادل	ابو بكر بن ايوب
وخمسمائة	سنة ثمان

Album. ANS (25, 6.42; 19.5, 3.94). Arri, p. 71, Tav. 1. Artuk 723 (22, 5.00). Ashmolean-Thorburn (22, 4.74). Ashmolean-Morgan (24, 5.636). Berlin-Gagarin (22, 4.50). BMC 438 (24, 3.79. ill.; attributed to al-Ṣāliḥ Ismāʿīl). BM-Amedroz (22, 5.64. ill.; 23, 5.56). Butak I, p. 108, No. 122. Ghalib 193a (22, —; identical with Artuk 723. Istanbul (20, —; 23, —). Lavoix 610 (23, 5.08, ill.); 611 (22, 6.14). Miles-Sinjār 36 (21, —; date missing, but this type). Paris (21, 4.54; 23, 4.06; 23, 5.42). Siouffi, p. 17 (misread the mint as Naḥrān). Ziya 1634 (22, —).

AL-KĀMIL NĀṢIR AL-DĪN ABŪ AL-MAʿĀLĪ MUḤAMMAD I IBN AL-ʿĀDIL I

Ruler of Egypt [615–635 H = 1218–1237 AD]

Lord of Palestine and South Syria [625–635 H = 1227–1237 AD]

Sultan of the Empire [Nominal Overlord from 625 H = 1227 AD, but Effective Master from 634 H = 1236 AD until 635 H = 1237 AD]

Egypt

GOLD

All the issues struck with the name of the Caliph al-Nāṣir (615–622 H), and with that of Caliph al-Ẓāhir (622–623 H), are in *Kūfic*. From 624 H onward all the dinars are engraved in *Naskh*. al-Kāmil's successors all used *Naskh* on their gold coins.

364. *Cairo—616 H*

Border on both sides: plain circle. Counterclockwise marginal legend on both sides:

لا اله الا الله محمد رسول الله ارسله بالهدى ودين الحق ليظهره على الدين كله	بسم الله الرحمن الرحيم ضرب هذا الدينر بالقاهرة سنة ست عشرة وستمائة

Double circle on both sides.

Centre:	Centre:
الملك الكامل	الامام احمد
ابو المعالي	ابو العباس
محمد بن ابي بكر	الناصر لدين الله
∴ بن ايوب ∴	امير المؤمنين

Balog (21, 4.64, ill.). Berlin 237/1881 (22, 3.41). BMC 373 (22, 3.69). Markov. p. 356, No. 28. Samir Shamma (20, 4.50; 22, 5.30; date not certain). Weyl 6517 (22, 3.69).

365. *Cairo—618 H*

As above, but the following date:

سنة ثمان عشرة وستمائة

Trefoil above the obverse and reverse central legends: ჻.

Balog (22, 4.60, ill.). Wien (20, 4.35).

366. *Cairo—619 H*

As above, but the following date:

سنة تسع عشر وستمائة

ANS (22, 5.82). Markov, p. 356, No. 29.

Cairo—620 H

Fahmy described a dinar (No. 483) for this year, but he misread the mint/date legend; and his coin, written in *Naskh*, contains the name of Caliph al-Mustanṣir, so that the dinar must have been struck in or after 623 H. The illustration, wrongly numbered 383, is illegible.

367. *Cairo—621 H*

As No. 366, but the following date and centre legends:

سنة احد عشرين وستمائة

Centre:	Centre:
غاية	الامام احمد
الملك الكامل	ابو العباس الناصر
ابو المعالي محمد	لدين الله امير
ابن ابي بكر بن	المؤمنين
ايوب عال	

ANS-UM (24, 5.16). Balog (23, 6.95, ill.). Horovitz (21, 5.72). Østrup 1575 (—, 4.21). Samir Shamma (21, 6.30).

368. *Cairo—622 H*

As above, but the following date:

سنة اثنين وعشرين وستمائة

Trefoil above the reverse legend only: ჻.

Artuk 736 (21, 3.90). Ashmolean-A. C. Kay (22, 4.61). Balog (21, 4.92). da Cunha II, 1458 (18, 6.11). Horovitz (21, 4.20). Khediv. 1390. Munzel (21, 5.10). *Seaby's Coin and Medal Bulletin*, Oct. 1963, G-2278 (—, 5.07).

Cairo—623 H

369. *Type A*

As above, but the following date and centre legends:

سنة ثلث وعشرين وستمائة

Centre:	Centre:
الملك الكامل	عال
ابو المعالى محمد	الامام محمد
ابن ابى بكر بن	ابو نصر الظاهر
ايوب	بامر الله امير
	المؤمنين
	غاية

[Last issue with *Kūfic* script]

Horovitz (20, 5.30, ill.).

370. *Type B*

As above, but with the reverse centre:

الامام
المنصور ابو
جعفز المستنصر
بالله امير المؤمنين

Pietraszewski 426.

371. *Cairo—624 H*

As above, but the following date and centre legends:

سنة اربع وعشرين وستمائة

Obverse:	Reverse:
∴	∴
ايوب	الامام
الملك الكامل	المنصور ابو
ابو المعالي محمد	جعفز المستنصر
ابن ابي بكر بن	بالله امير المؤمنين

Trefoil above the obverse and reverse central legends: ∴.

Horovitz (22, 5.80, ill.). Khediv. 1393, 1394. Pietraszewski 427.

372. *Cairo—625 H*

As above, but the following date:

سنة خمس وعشرين وستمائة

No trefoil on this or any subsequent Cairo dinars.

ANS-UM (20, —). Artuk 737 (20, 5.40). Balog (22, 5.15, ill.). BMC 376 (21, 5.28); 377 (20, 4.45); 378 (21, 5.15); 379 (22, 4.66). Fahmy 484 (20, 5.06); 485 (21, 5.06); 486 (20, 4.64). Istanbul (21, —). Khediv. 1395. Lavoix 630 (20, 4.73). Markov, p. 356, No. 30. Munzel (21, 4.72). Paris (21, 3.86). Pietraszewski 428. Samir Shamma (21, 5.75). Wien 7549 (20, —, ill.). Ziya 1670 (20, —).

373. *Cairo—626 H*

As above, but the following date:

سنة ست وعشرين وستمائة

ANS-UM (21, —; 21, —). Artuk 738 (22, 7.30). Balog (21, 4.25, ill.; 21, 5.35). Berlin-Guthrie (22, 6.25). Berman 191 (21, 6.40). BMC 380 (21, 3.31); 381 (19, 3.31). Fahmy 487 (20, 5.22); 488 (21, 7.30). Fraehn, *Nova Suppl.*, p. 90 (2 coins). Horovitz (20, 7.40; 21, 5.44; 20, 3.22). Istanbul (21, —). Khediv. 1396. 1397. Munzel (20, 4.48). Markov, p. 356, No. 31. Paris (21, 5.78, ill.). Peus 1894 (626 H?). Samir Shamma (20, 4.80; 21, 5.30). Yapı-Kredi (22, 4.15; 19, 2.72).

374. *Cairo—627 H*

As above, but the following date:

سنة سبع وعشرين وستمائة

ANS-UM (21, 3.94). Artuk 739 (20, 6.10). Balog (22, 6.50, ill.; 21, 4.40; 22, 5.87; 21, 2.13). BMC 383 (21, 4.02); 383a (21, 3.95). Dorn IV, p. 67, No. 3. Fahmy 489 (21, 4.49); 490 (20, 4.98). Hirsch 2082 (—, 6.35). Horovitz (21, 5.80; 22, 3.65). Istanbul (21, —). Lavoix 631 (20, 5.07). Markov, p. 356, No. 32. München 82626 (22, 6.203). Munzel (21, 5.14). Peus 1895. Pietraszewski 429. Samir Shamma (20, 4.50; 20, 4.88; 19, 3.63). Yapı-Kredi (21, 6.75; 22, 5.12; 21, 5.00; 22, 4.50; 21, 4.45).

375. *Cairo—628 H*

As above, but the following date:

سنة ثمان وعشرين وستمائة

ANS (21.5, 2.91). ANS-UM (22, 5.78; 22, 5.03). Artuk 740 (21, 4.30). Ashmolean-J. Schulman (20, 4.05). Balog (21, 3.92; 21, 4.13, ill.). Berlin-Guthrie (21, 3.74; 21, 3.87). BMC 384 (21, 4.83); 385 (21, 4.78); 386 (20, 5.21); 387 (21, 5.39); 388 (21, 6.01). Fahmy 491 (21, 5.10); 492 (20, 4.59); 493 (20, 5.31); 494 (20, 5.21); 495 (20, 5.63). Horovitz (21, 4.75; 22, 3.40). Markov, p. 356, No. 33. Munzel (21, 7.06). Khediv. 1398. Paris (21, 6.30). Pietraszewski 430. Samir Shamma (21, 5.17). Yapı-Kredi (21, 5.30; 22, 5.05; 21, 3.80; 23, 4.20; 21, 3.52; 21, 3.90).

376. *Cairo—629 H*

As above, but the following date:

سنة تسع وعشرين وستمائة

ANS-Newell (21, —). Artuk 741 (20, 4.50). Balog (22, 4.50). BMC 389 (21, 3.45); 390 (21, 4.01); 391 (21, 4.42); 392 (22, 3.92); 383b (22, 4.47; listed under 627 H). Fahmy 500 (20, 5.29); 501 (22, 5.94); 502 (22, 5.30); 503 (21, 6.37). Horovitz (23, 5.10, ill.). Istanbul (24, —). Khediv. 1399. Paris (22, 6.78). Paris-Vogüé (22, 5.56). Markov, p. 357, No. 34. Yapı-Kredi (21, 7.00; 21, 5.95; 21, 4.64).

377. *Cairo—630 H*

As above, but the following date:

سنة ثلثين وستمائة

ANS (21.5, 4.75). Artuk 742 (21, 4.95). Balog (21, 2.30, ill.). Fahmy 510 (22, 7.60); 511 (19, 4.12); 512 (20, 6.82). Horovitz (21, 6.20). Khediv. 1400. Lavoix 632 (23, 5.05); 633 (21, 6.13). Munzel (21, 4.48). Paris-R. N. 1935 (21, 4.52). Peus 1896. Pietraszewski 431. Samir Shamma (21, 3.95; 21, 3.85; 21, 2.90). Siouffi, p. 77. Yapı-Kredi (22, 4.12).

378. *Cairo—631 H*

As above, but the following date:

سنة احدى وثلثين وستمائة

Artuk 743 (20, 4.40). BMC 394 (21, 4.98); 395 (21, 7.06, ill.). Fahmy 513 (20, 4.89); 514 (21, 5.48). Horovitz (22, 6.20). Khediv. 1401. Munzel (22, 4.80). Paris (22, 7.24). Paris-R.N. 1935 (22, 4.17). Soret à Dorn, *RNB* (1856), No. 69. Yapı-Kredi (20, 4.70; 21, 4.54). Ziya 1671 (22, —).

379. *Cairo—632 H*

As above, but the following date:

ستة اثنين وثلثين وستمائة

ANS-UM (22, —). Artuk 744 (21, 5.85). Ashmolean-A. C. Kay (24, 4.37). Balog (23, 4.46; 22, 6.84). BMC 374 (23, 7.43; definitely this date, but was erroneously dated by Lane-Poole as 622 H); 396 (22, 5.33); 397 (23, 5.80, ill.). Fahmy 515 (22, 4.34); 516 (21, 4.80); 517 (21, 5.26); 518 (20, 3.70). Horovitz (23, —; 22, 5.95; 20, 2.85). Khediv. 1402. Markov, p. 357, No. 35. Munzel (22, 6.60). Paris-R.N. 1935 (22, 6.11). Peus 1897. Pietraszewski 432; digit of the date: اثنتين). Samir Shamma (21, 3.90). Yapı-Kredi (20, 3.35).

380. *Cairo—633 H*

As above, but the following date:

سنة ثلث وثلثين وستمائة

ANS (22, 4.79). ANS-Bruce (21, —). Balog (22, 6.21; 22, 5.68, ill.). Berlin-Guthrie (22, 7.61). BMC 398 (21, 5.78, ill.); 399 (22, 3.92). Fahmy 519 (22, 4.70). Horovitz (22, 5.90). Paris (23, 6.16). Pietraszewski 433; decade of the date with an *alif*: ثلاثين).

381. *Cairo—634 H*

As above, but the following date:

سنة اربع وثلثين وستمائة

Artuk 745 (21, 4.30). Balog (22, 5.68, ill.; 22, 4.13). BMC 400 (22, 4.49); 401 (21, 4.56); 402 (22, 5.20). Fahmy 520 (23, 6.96); 521 (22, 3.96). Horovitz (21, 3.80; 21, 6.91). Mitchell-Brown (22, 3.67). Markov, p. 357, No. 36. Samir Shamma (21, 4.17). Yapı-Kredi (22, 5.55; 21, 4.25).

382. *Cairo—635 H*

As above, but the following date:

سنة خمس وثلثين وستمائة

ANS-Hirsch (22, —). ANS-Newell (21, —). ANS-UM (21, —). Balog (23, 5.71, ill.). BMC 403 (22, 3.03); 404 (22, 6.01). Horovitz (21, 5.95). Lavoix 634 (22, 5.10). Østrup 1576 (—, 3.71). Yapı-Kredi (22, 5.65).

383. *Miṣr—623 H*

As above, but the following mint/date and centre legends:

بمصر سنة ثلاث وعشرين وستمائة

Centre:	Centre:
الملك الكامل	٧
ابو المعالي محمد	الامام المنصور
ابن ابي بكر بن ايوب	ابو جعفر المستنصر
	بالله امير المؤمنين

Berlin-Guthrie (20, 3.39). Yapı-Kredi (20, 5.50).

384. *Miṣr—624 H*

As above, but the following date:

سنة اربع وعشرين وستمائة

Small trefoil above both central legends: ⁘.

ANS (22, 5.77). ANS-UM (20, 4.34; 24, 5.77, ill.). BMC 375 (22, 6.33). Horovitz (24, 6.00, ill.). Khediv. 1392. Yapı-Kredi (23, 6.00).

385. *Miṣr—62x H*

As above, but the digit of the date is missing.

Fahmy 524 (21, 4.28).

386. *Alexandria—617 H*

As above, but the following mint/date and centre legends:

بالاسكندرية سنة سبع عشرة وستمائة

Centre:	Centre:
O	O
الملك الكامل	الامام احمد
ابو المعالي	ابو العباس
محمد بن ابو بكر	الناصر لدين الله
بن ايوب	امير المؤمنين

Ringlet above obverse and reverse central legends; *Kūfic* script.

Khediv. 1389 (—, 4.70).

387. *Alexandria—618 H*

As above, but the following date:

سنة ثمان عشرة وستمائة

ANS (21, 6.04, ill.). BMC 373k (22, 6.29). Siouffi, p. 17.

388. *Alexandria—619 H*

As above, but the following date:

سنة تسع عشرة وستمائة

Fahmy 525 (21, 6.00). Siouffi, p. 17.

Alexandria—623 H

389. *Type A*

As above, but the following date and centre legends:

سنة ثلاث وعشرين وستمائه

Centre:	Centre:
الملك الكامل	الامام محمد
ابو المعالي محمد	ابو نصر الظاهر
ابن ابي بكر بن	بامر الله امير
ايوب	المؤمنين

[*Kūfic* script]

ANS (20, —). Fahmy 526 (20, 4.63).

390. *Type B*

As above, but the obverse central legend:

الملك الكامل
ابو المعالي
محمد بن ابي بكر بن
ايوب

Khediv. 1391.

391. *Alexandria—624 H*

As above, but the following date and centre legends:

سنة اربعة وعشرين وستمائة

Centre:

∴
الملك الكامل
ابو المعالي محمد
ابن ابي بكر

Centre:

∴
الامام المنصور
ابو جعفر المستنصر
بالله امير المؤمنين

[Trefoil above both central legends]

Naskh script on this and all subsequent issues.

BMC 375c (23, 5.59, ill.; the digit of the date is written: اربعة, and the last word of the obverse central legend is in *Kūfic*: بكر). Siouffi, p. 17.

392. *Alexandria—625 H*

As above, but the following date and centre legends:

سنة خمس وعشرين وستمائة

Centre:

ايوب
الملك الكامل
ابو المعالي محمد
ابن ابي بكر بن

Centre:

الامام
المنصور ابو
جعفر المستنصر
بالله امير المؤمنين

ANS-UM (22, 3.25). Balog (20, 4.33, ill.; 22, 6.09). BM (22, 4.65, ill.). Horovitz (23, 4.95). Lavoix 627 (24, 6.58). Siouffi, p. 17. Yapı-Kredi (21, 4.05).

393. *Alexandria—626 H*

As above, but the following date:

سنة ست وعشرين وستمائة

Balog (20, 3.15, ill.).

394. *Alexandria—627 H*

As above, but the following date:

سنة سبع وعسرين وستمائة

ANS (21, —; the date is not quite clear; it could be 7: سبع, as well as 9: تسع). Siouffi, p. 17.

395. *Alexandria—628 H*

As above, but the following date:

سنة ثمان وعشرين وستمائة

ANS-UM (21, 5.48). Artuk 734 (21, 5.00). Balog (21, 4.01, ill.). Horovitz (21, —). Lavoix 628 (21, 6.77); 629 (22, 4.64). Yapı-Kredi (20, 5.10).

396. *Alexandria—629 H*

As above, but the following date:

سنة تسع وعشرين وستمائة

Fahmy 527 (20, 6.68). Siouffi, p. 17. Yapı-Kredi (22, 5.75).

397. *Alexandria—630 H*

As above, but the following date:

سنة ثلثين وستمائة

BMC 393 (22, 5.98). Yapı-Kredi (20, 4.50).

398. *Alexandria—632 H*

As above, but the following date:

سنة اثنين وثلثين وستمائة

ANS (22, 5.45). Artuk 735 (21, 3.85). Berlin 238/1881 (23, 6.31). BMC 374 (23, 7.43). Fahmy 528 (22, 7.58).

399. *Alexandria—634 H*

As above, but the following date:

سنة اربع وثلثين وستمائة

BM (23, 5.18, ill.). Dorn IV, p. 68, No. 4. Fahmy 529 (20, 6.50). Siouffi, p. 17.

400. *Alexandria—635 H*

As above, but the following date:

سنة خمس وثلثين وستمائة

ANS-UM (22, 7.95). Yapı-Kredi (22, 5.95).

401. No coin.

SILVER

402. *Black Dirhems*

These small, irregularly square or oblong coins, struck after insufficient heating, are more or less well-centered, but contain only fractions of the inner circular legends and none of the marginal inscriptions. Only the central legends can be reconstructed accurately, but there is no doubt that the coins were struck in Egypt, either in Cairo or Alexandria.

Centre:	Centre:
الملك الكامل	الامام احمد
ابو المعالي	ابو العباس
محمد بن ابي بكر	الناصر لدين الله
بن ايوب	امير المؤمنين

[Legends in minute *Kūfic* script]

Balog, *BIE* XXXIII (1951); 1 (10 × 10, 0.76, ill.); 2 (9 × 11, 1.17); 3 (8 × 12, 1.11); 4 (8 × 10, 1.25, ill.); 5 (7 × 12, 1.36); 6 (8 × 13, 1.81).

al-Kāmil Muḥammad's Monetary Reforms

In Dhū al-Qaʿdah 622 H, al-Kāmil was obliged, by the ever-increasing dissatisfaction of the public over the persistent economic difficulties, to introduce a radical monetary reform. According to al-Maqrīzī, this reform consisted of a new silver currency supposed to be an improvement upon the old *black dirhem*. According to that medieval historian, the Kāmilī dirhems had two-thirds fine silver content and only one-third copper. The new coin, contrary to the *black dirhem*, was produced by a different technique (see: A. S. Ehrenkreutz, *Extracts from the Technical Manual . . . of Ibn Baʿrah* and the Arabic text of *Ibn Baʿrah*, edited by ʿAbd al-Raḥmān Fahmī Muḥammad: *Kashf al-asrār al-ʿilmīyah bi-dār al-ḍarb al-miṣrīyah*, Cairo, 1966). The new dirhems were small, thick, globular coins; many were round, others oval or deformed.

Our own experience, based on repeated chemical assays, showed that the new, globular *round dirhems* were, in fact, in no way better than the old, unpopular *black dirhems*. Therefore, the reform was a fictitious improvement, extending only to the outward appearance of the coins and not to their intrinsic value.

Al-Kāmil's reform coinage belongs to three distinct chronological groups:

—The first issue was struck in 622 H and bears the name of Caliph al-Nāṣir;

—The second, between 622 and 623 H, under Caliph al-Ẓāhir; and

—The third was issued with the name of Caliph al-Mustanṣir.

Other than the name of the caliph, there are distinct differences in the style of calligraphy among the three issues. The legends have been reconstructed.

403. *Cairo—622 H*

Caliph: al-Nāṣir

Border on both sides: plain circle. Counterclockwise marginal legend on both sides:

لا اله الا الله محمد رسول الله ارسله بالهدى ودين الحق ليظهره
على الدين كله

بسم الله ضرب بالقاهرة سنة اثنين عشرين وستمائة

Inner circle on some coins; on others there is none.

Centre:
الملك الكامل
ابو المعالي محمد
بن ابي بكر بن
ايوب

Centre:
الامام
ابو العباس
الناصر لدين الله
امير المؤمنين

[All Legends in *Kūfic* script]

Ashmolean (10, 1.16). Ashmolean-Thorburn (9, 1.15). Awad (13, 2.70; 10, 0.90). Balog, *BIE* XXXV (1953), pp. 417–418 1 (9, 0.68); 2 (9, 0.70, ill.); 3 (8, 0.77); 4 (8, 0.90); 5 (10, 1.15, ill.); 6 (11, 1.50); 7 (11 × 16, 1.56, ill.); 8 (10 × 12, 1.64, ill.); 9 (9 × 14, 1.68, ill.); 10 (12, 1.84, ill.); 11 (11, 1.91, ill.); 12 (12, 2.26); 13 (13, 2.96); 14 (14 × 18, 4.32, ill.). München 92503 (17, 4.378); 92504 (10, 1.477).

404. *Cairo—622 or 623 H*

As above, but the following date and reverse centre legend:

سنه اثنين / ثلث عشرين وستمائة

Inner circle on both sides.

Reverse:
الامام
ابو نصر الظاهر
بامر الله
امير المؤمنين

[Marginal legends are in small *Kūfic*; centre is in simple *Naskh*]

Although the date is missing on all specimens, it must be either 622 or 623 H because of the Caliph's name.

ANS 56.52 (11, —; 9, —; 6, —; 11, —; 11, —). Awad (13, 3.45). Balog, *BIE* XXXV (1953), p. 419, 1 (6, 0.41); 2 (6, 0.48); 3 (8, 0.70, ill.); 4 (7, 0.72); 5 (9, 0.95); 6 (8, 0.99); 7 (10, 1.31); 8 (10, 1.46, ill.); 9 (10, 1.57, ill.); 10 (11, 1.78, ill.).

405. *Cairo—625 H*

Border on both sides: plain circle. Counterclockwise marginal legend on both sides:

لا اله الا الله محمد رسول الله ارسله بالهدى ضرب هذا الدرهم بالقاهرة سنة خمس وعشرين وستمائة

Plain circle on both sides.

Centre:
الملك
الكامل

Centre:
الامام
٧
المستنصر

Legends in the margin and in the centre are in large flowing *Naskh*, similar to the writing on the gold coins after 623 H, bearing the name of Caliph al-Mustanṣir.

ANS 56.52 (11 × 13, —; 12, —; 8, —; 10, —; 10, —; 7, —). Balog, *BIE* XXXV (1953), pp. 419–420, 1 (8, 0.54); 2 (9, 0.45). Lavoix 641 (16, 2.84).

406. *Cairo—626 H*

As above, but the following date:

سنة ست وعشرين وستمائة

Balog, *BIE* XXXV (1953), pp. 419–420. 1 (8, 0.75); 2 (14, 3.36).

407. *Cairo—632 H*

As above, but the following date:

سنة اثنين و(ثلثين وستمائة)

Balog, *BIE* XXXV (1953), pp. 419–420. (13, 1.87, ill.).

408. *Cairo—623 or 633 H*

As above, but the following date:

سنة ثلاث (وعشرين) (وثلثين)

Ashmolean-A. C. Kay (12, 1.72).

409. *Cairo—635 H*

Square-in-the-circle type.

Border Segments:	Border Segments:
. . ./. . ./لا شر . ./محمد رسول الله	ضرب با (لقاهرة)/سنة خمس و/ثلاثين/. . .
Centre:	Centre:
الملك الكامل	الامام المنصور
ناصر الدنيا وا	ابو جعفر المستنصر
لدين محمد بن ابي بكر	بالله امير المؤمنين

[*Naskh* script]

Album (2 specimens from same dies). Although the mint name is unclear, several reasons, according to Album, permit a Cairo attribution:

1. The beginning of the article in mint name;
2. The placement of the mint/date on the reverse, as on Egyptian dinars and round-flan dirhems dated 645 H;
3. The protocol of caliph; i.e., the arrangement of parts of his name.
4. General style, which is similar to early Mamlūk dirhems of Cairo.

410. *Date Missing*

As No. 408, but the date is off the flan.

ANS (6 specimens). Ashmolean (10, 1.37; 13, 1.58). Awad (10 × 20, 3.95; 10, 2.70). Balog, *BIE* XXXV (1953), pp. 419–420. 1 (14, 3.12, ill.); 2 (12, 2.54); 3 (11, 2.22, ill.); 4 (14, 1.91); 5 (12, 2.10); 6 (12, 2.00); 7 (11, 1.94); 8 (12, 1.75); 9 (15, 0.99, ill.); 10 (8 × 19, 1.57); 11 (11, 0.98); 12 (9, 0.95); 13 (10, 0.90); 14 (10, 0.87); 15 (10, 0.57); 16 (7, 0.44, ill.). BMC 408 (10 × 13, 1.89); 408a (14, 1.91). Lavoix 642 (10, 1.25); 643 (12, 1.62); 644 (10, 1.05); 645 (12, 1.26); 646 (10, 1.75).

It is evident that the black dirhems have no fixed weight, so that they had to be accepted by weight and not by tale. This irregularity of weight stems from the particular technique of their manufacture. The globular reform silver coins of al-Kāmil also lack a relationship to a regular weight system. In fact, practically no two globular Kāmilī dirhems have the same weight (Ref. Balog, *History of the Dirhem*, pp. 116 ff.).

Divisional Currency Issued in Egypt by al-Kāmil Muḥammad I

We have mentioned already that there was a practical reason for the presence of glass-paste jetons and the lack of copper coinage in Egypt during the reign of the first Ayyūbid rulers. Hundreds of copper coins struck by the early Ayyūbids have been studied up-to-date. Surprisingly, not one coin can be attributed to an Egyptian mint and whenever a mint name is preserved, it is invariably a Syrian or Mesopotamian location. Also, all the *fulūs*, mintless or with mint missing, are typical Syrian or Mesopotamian issues. Up to now only two coins, much worn, can be attributed to some Yemeni mint. Of all these Ayyūbid coppers there is only one assignable to Egypt—a small, irregularly square copper of Saladin—probably struck in his early years with the dies of a black dirhem. As no second specimen seems to have ever been found, one may assume it to have been an experimental issue that had to be abandoned for lack of copper bullion in Egypt, to leave the field open for the abundant glass-paste jeton circulation.

The total lack of copper currency in early Ayyūbid Egypt is corroborated in Hassanein Rabie's outstanding monograph,[1] where he points out:

That according to Maqrīzī copper *fulūs* were in circulation in Egypt until 622/1255 as a local currency for the purchase of cheap goods, but were not legal tender in the same sense as dinars and dirhems. It appears that their circulation was limited, as the coining of the *fulūs* was in the hands of the local *Walīs*, without centralised control. After 622/1225, copper *fulūs* attained the status of official currency. According to Ibn al-Dawadārī and Nuwayrī, Sulṭān al-Kāmil ordered copper *fulūs* to be struck in Cairo and Miṣr (Fusṭāṭ) and they became valid currency.

I cannot agree with Maqrīzī that there was ever any copper coinage issued by the local *walīs* of the Ayyūbid period, struck privately or semi-officially, and tolerated by the central government. No coin is known with the name of an Egyptian local governor of the Ayyūbids or any anonymous *fals* that could point to such an issue. On the contrary, all the Ayyūbid *fulūs* found in Egypt come from Syria and Mesopotamia. They must have reached Egypt privately in the purses of traders and other travellers, and were accepted by the local population willingly. However, they were not sufficient to satisfy the needs of the Egyptian market. These, being unfamiliar coins to the Egyptians, may have been the *fulūs* described by Ibn al-Dawadārī and Nuwayrī.

The statements of Ibn al-Dawadārī and Nuwayrī, that no Ayyūbid copper was minted in Egypt prior to 622 H, can be accepted, therefore, as correct. Yet the Egyptian economy needed some kind of divisional currency beside the insufficient and irregularly imported Syrian and Mesopotamian copper *fulūs*. It would seem that Saladin simply continued to issue glass-paste jetons as fiduciary money, the use of which he inherited, together with the practice of issuing *black dirhems*, from the Fāṭimids.[2] It is well-known that the earlier Ayyūbid glass-paste jetons do not include the Ayyūbid sultan's name—only that of the reigning ʿAbbāsid caliph (al-Mustaḍī from 567 until 575 H, and al-Nāṣir from 575 to 622 H). These jetons represent the reigns of Saladin, al-Azīz ʿUthmān, al-Manṣūr Muḥammad, and the first seven years of al-Kāmil.

Only in 622 H did al-Kāmil replace the caliph's protocol with his own. Although the glass jetons bearing his name also lack mint and date, they can safely be attributed to the beginning of the 622 H Cairo coin reform because they clearly present the characteristic process of transformation of the style of writing that can be seen on al-Kāmil's gold and silver coinage starting in the same year.

The lack of locally produced copper, the scarcity of imported foreign *fulūs*, and the inferior quality of the Egyptian Ayyūbid silver (black dirhems) inconvenienced the economic life in Egypt to such an extent that in 622 H al-Kāmil was obliged to introduce a much publicized currency reform.[3] On the gold the innovation was purely morphological, since, instead of the traditional *Kūfic*, the new legends were engraved skillfully in a pleasing and distinctive *Naskh* script. The gold content, which was still high, remained at the same level. In any transaction, the gold coins to be weighed, as conformity to a weight standard was no longer observed and there were no more true dinars of one *mithqāl* (or 4·25 grams)—only coin-shaped gold ingots of differing worth.

[1]*The Financial System of Egypt*, Oxford University Press, 1972, pp. 181 and f.n. Maqrīzī, *Ighāthah*, pp. 66–67; trad. Wiet, pp. 65–66; *idem Shudhūr*, pp. 67–68; trad. S. de Sacy, p. 182, f.n. 3; Ibn al-Dawadārī, *Durār*, fol. 200r; and Nuwayrī, XXVII, fol. 27.

[2]Paul Balog, 'Les Jetons Fatimites en Verre,' *RBN* (1961); Balog, 'The Ayyūbid Glass Jetons and their Use,' *JESHO* 9 (1966).

[3]Paul Balog, 'Études Numismatiques de l'Égypte Musulmane, III,' *BIE* XXXV (1952).

The second part of al-Kāmil's monetary reform, concerning the silver coinage of Egypt, was a colossal fraud. In spite of the sultan's protestations that the new 'round' dirhem (*dirham mustadīrah*) contained a much higher proportion of fine silver than the unpopular, customary, crudely manufactured 'black' dirhems (*dirham waraq*), the new issue contained about the same percentage as the one abandoned. The difference between the old and new Egyptian silver currency was purely superficial. This fraudulent pseudo-reform passed undetected until modern times, when it was discovered during a series of chemical tests carried out by the present author.[4]

We have now further proof that, until the reform of 622 H, no Ayyūbid copper was minted in Egypt and it is even more certain than hitherto that the non-existant copper divisional currency was replaced by a fiduciary coinage made of glass-paste. The following pages of this catalogue describe a distinctive series of copper coins which, although mintless, can be seen to represent the various phases of the monetary development that took place in Egypt between 622 and 623 H by virtue of

—a gradual change in the style of writing,
—the naming of three caliphs who succeeded each other, and
—the resemblance of the legends to those of the gold coins.

OPAQUE GLASS-PASTE JETONS

411. *Type A*

No border, with the following centre legend:

محمد
الملك الكامل

ANS (21, 2.97; white). ANS (22, 3.02; yellowish-green with blue-green, ill.; ex-Balog collection).

412. *Type B*

No border, with the following centre legend:

الملك
الكامل
محمد

ANS (26, 5.96; ex-Balog collection; pale yellow, streaked with brown, ill.).

413. *Type C*

No border, with the following centre legend:

ايوب
الملك الكامل
محمد بن ابي بكر
ابن

ANS (30, 8.55; turqouise blue, ill.).

---

[4]P. Balog, 'History of the dirhem in Egypt from the Fāṭimid conquest until the collapse of the Mamlūk empire,' *RN* (1961), pp. 109–146. J. L. Bacharach and A. Gordus, 'Studies on the Fineness of Silver Coins,' *JESHO* XI (1968), pp. 298–317.

414. *Type D*

Border: plain circle, with following centre legend:

الملك
الكامل

ANS (27, 5.73; ex-Balog collection; pale honey colour).

415. *Type E*

No border, with the following centre legend:

(الملك؟) الكامل

Only the last two letters of *al-Kāmil* are on the flan. The name may have been preceded by the title *al-Malik*.

ANS (10, 0.48; ex-Balog collection; turquoise blue, ill.).

COPPER

[*With Caliph al-Nāṣir (Before 30 Ramaḍān 622 H)*]

The only specimen recorded was published by Zambaur, *Contrib. II*, No. 279 (8, 0.68). Its small diameter and the distribution of the legends indicate that it must have been a globular silver dirhem and not a copper *fals*. It was probably completely covered by a layer of verdegris. Nearly all the globular dirhems that I have seen were in a similar condition before cleaning, and are deceptively similar to coppers.

[*With Caliph al-Ẓāhir (1 Shawwāl 622–14 Rajab 623 H)*]

Zambaur describes another coin (*Contrib. II*. No. 281) with a diameter of 10 mm. Judging from his description—neither this coin nor the other one was illustrated—this is also a copper-encrusted silver globular dirhem of al-Kāmil. The following coins belong to the series of coppers issued by al-Kāmil from 622 H. There is no marginal legend on any of the issues:

416. *Type A*

Border on both sides: plain circle in circle of pellets.

Centre:	Centre:
بن ايوب	محمد امير
الملك الكامل	الامام الظاهر
بن ابي بكر	المؤمنين

Zambaur, *Contrib. II*, No. 282. No diameter or weight. Zambaur noted the similarity of the script to that of the Cairo dinars after 622 H.

417. *Type B*

Border as above.

Centre:	Centre:
محمد بن	امير
الملك الكامل	الامام الظاهر
ابي بكر	المؤمنين

Album (2 specimens). Ashmolean-Thorburn (16, 3.34). Balog (19, 2.80). München 88154 (19, 2.42). Paris (22, 4.41, ill.; 21, 3.84; 16, 2.42, ill.).

[*With Caliph al-Mustanṣir* (*After Rajab 623 H*)]

418. *Type A*

Border as above.

Centre:
محمد بن
الملك الكامل
ابي بكر

Centre:
بالله
المستنصر
الامام المنصور
امير المؤمنين

Lavoix 658 (16, 2.34).

419. *Type B*

Border as above.

Centre:
محمد بن
الملك الكامل
ابي بكر

Centre:
ابو جعفر
الامام المنصور
امير المؤمنين

Album (caliph named only as: المنصور). Balog (18, 2.74); 19, 3.35).

420. *Type C*

Border on both sides: plain circle enclosing linear tetrafoil with pointed arches. In the small segments between the plain border and the tetrafoil:

R Upper R Lower L Lower L Upper
(لا اله الا الله) محمد ر سو ل الله

Centre:
محمد بن
الملك الكامل
ابي بكر

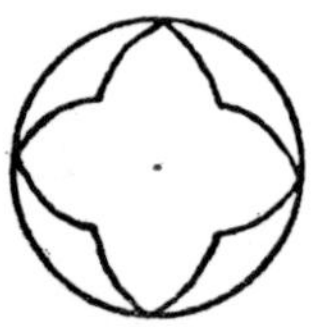

R Upper R Lower L Lower L Upper
ابو جعفر امير ا لمؤمنين

Centre:
بالله
الامام المنصور
المستنصر

Album 4 (2 specimens). ANS (20, —). ANS-Chimirri (24, —, and 4 other specimens). ANS-Wood (26, —). Ashmolean-Bodleian 153 (24, 4.30). Ashmolean-A. C. Kay (23, 3.20). Ashmolean-Thorburn (23, 3.81). Balog (22, 4.06; 23, 4.99; 24, 4.10, ill.; 25, 4.37, ill.). BMC 418 (23, 3,46). Fahmy 553–562 (23, 3.20; 22, 3.20; 21, 4.35; 21, 3.80; 20, 3.20; 23, 4.30; 17, 2.02; 15, 1.52; 19, 2.25; 23, 3.70). Wien 7736 (22, —).

421. *Type D*

Border on both sides as above. In the small segments there are illegible remains of an inscription.

Centre:
محمد بن
الملك الكامل
ابي بكر

Centre:
ابو جعفر
الامام المنصور
امير المؤمنين

BMC 416 (17, 2.95); 417 (17, 1.33). Fahmy 563 (17, 2.95); 564 (23, 3.70). Khediv. 1425–1427. München 88153 (26, 4.486); 86412 (23, 2.541); 92444 (22, 2.483). Windisch-Graetz 175 (17, —).

Syria

SILVER

All the Syrian silver coins of al-Kāmil are of the square-in-the-circle type, struck on normal-size flans, and the inscriptions are always in *Naskh*.

Damascus—615 H

422. *Type A*

Border Segments:
بن ابى بكر|ضرب بدمشق|سنة خمس|عشرة وستمائة
Centre:
الملك الكامل
ناصر الدنيا
والدين محمد

Border Segments:
لا اله ا|لا الله و|حده محمد|رسول الله
Centre:
الامام الناصر
لدين الله
امير المؤمنين

ANS-Newell (22, 2.90; obverse top segment: بن ابو بكر). BM-Sir R. Burn (21, 2.99; mint missing, but there is no doubt that it is Damascus). On the following specimens the type is not known: Khediv. 1407. Østrup 1577 (—, 3.00). Peus 1892. Tewhid (22, —).

423. *Type B*

Border Segments:
بسم الله|ضرب بدمشق|سنة خمس|عشرة ستمائة
Centre:
الملك الكامل
ناصر الدنيا وا
لدين محمد بن ابي بكر

Border Segments:
لا اله الا ا|لله وحده|لا شريك له|محمد رسول الله
Centre:
الامام الناصر
لدين الله امير
المؤمنين احمد

ANS-Laties (21, —). Balog (21, 2.58, ill.). Berlin (20, 2.43); 632/1896 (20, 3.20). BMC 406 (22, 3.02). Khediv. 1406; date written: سنة خمسة|عشرة وستمائة). Paris (21, 3.00). Siouffi, p. 17. Weyl 6515 (22, 3.00).

Half Dirhem

424. *Damascus—615 H*

Border Segments:
ضرب بد|مشق سنة|خمس عشرة|ستمائة
Centre:
الملك
الكامل

Border Segments:
لا اله|الا الله|محمد رسو|ل الله
Centre:
الامام
الناصر

Album 47. ANS 72.75 (15, —; 6 other specimens from Laties hoard). Artuk 731 (14, 1.35). BM-Sir R. Burn (16, 1.50). BMC 405 (15, 1.45, ill.). Horovitz (15, 1.47, ill.). Weyl 6516 (22, 1.60; in the Weyl catalogue: 11.60, and the coin is registered as a dirhem?).

425. *Damascus—616 H*

Border Segments:
بسم الله|ضرب بدمشق|سنة ست|عشرة و ستمائة
Centre:
الملك الكامل

ناصر الدنيا وا
لدين محمد بن ابي بكر

Border Segments:
لا اله الا |الله وحده|لا شريك له|محمد رسول الله
Centre:
الامام الناصر
لدين الله امير
المؤمنين احمد

Album 46. ANS 72.75 (22, —). ANS-Avery (21, 2.91). ANS-Newell (22, 2.93). Artuk 732 (21, 3.00). Balog (21, 3.00, ill.). Berlin-Guthrie (21, 3.20). Berman 192 (21, 2.85). BMC 406 (22, 2.97, ill.). BM-G. I. Chester (22, 2.98, ill.). Khediv. 1408–12. Paris (21.5, 2.99). Siouffi, pp. 17, 77. Wien (21, 2.90).

Half Dirhem

426. *Damascus—616 H*

Border Segments:
ضرب بد|مشق سنة|ست عشر|وستمائة
Centre:
الملك
الكامل

Border Segments:
لا اله ا|لا الله|محمد رسو|ل الله
Centre:
الامام
الناصر

ANS (15, 1.47, ill.). ANS-Laties (15, —; 15, —). Zambaur, *Contrib. II*, No. 277 (13, 1.44; the decade of the date is: عشرة).

Damascus—617 H

427. *Type A*

Border Segments:
بسم الله|ضرب بدمشق|سنة سبع|عشرة وستمائة
Centre:
الملك الكامل

ناصر الدنيا وا
لدين محمد بن ابي بكر

Border Segments:
لا اله الا |الله وحده|لا شريك له|محمد رسول الله
Centre:
الامام الناصر
لدين الله امير
المؤمنين احمد

Album. ANS-Newell (21, 2.94). ANS-UM (22, 2.99). Balog (21, 2.78, ill.; 21, 2.84, ill.). BMC 407 (21, 3.02). Glidden. Khediv. 1413, 1414. Lavoix 635 (20, 2.82). Lowick (22, 3.01). München 85290 (22, 2.869).

428. *Type B*

As above, but obverse border segments and reverse centre legend:

ضرب هذا الد|رهم بدمشق|سنة سبع|عشرة ستمائة

الامام الناصر
ولي عهده عدة
الدنيا والدين محمد

Ashmolean-Thorburn (22, 2.99, ill.). Balog (20, 2.88). Peus 1893. Yapı-Kredi (21, 2.95; 21, 3.00; 21, 2.95; 21, 2. 85).

429. *Half Dirhem*

Border Segments:
ضرب بد|مشق سنة|سبع عشرة|ستمائة
Centre:
الملك
الكامل

Border Segments:
لا اله|الا الله|محمد رسو|م الله
Centre:
الامام
الناصر

ANS-Laties (14, —; 14, —). BM-R. H. Dundar (14, 1.46). Khediv. 1415. Siouffi, p. 17.

430. *Damascus—618 H*

Border Segments:
بسم الله|ضرب بدمشق|سنة ثمان|عشرة وستمائة
Centre:
الملك الكامل
ناصر الدنيا وا
لدين محمد بن ابي بكر

Border Segments:
لا اله الا ا|لله وحده لا|شريك له|محمد رسول الله
Centre:
الامام الناصر
لدين الله امير
المؤمنين احمد

Album. ANS-Newell (20, 2.99). Ashmolean-Thorburn (22, 2.97, ill.). Balog (22, 2.95; 21, 2.97, ill.). Khediv. 1417. Paris (21, 2.80). Paris-R.N. 1935 (21, 2.95). Siouffi, p. 17. Weyl 6519 (20, 2.90).

431. *Half Dirhem*

As No. 429, but with the following date:
ثمان عشرة|وستمائة

ANS-Laties (15, —). ANS-Wood (16, 1.43). Yapı-Kredi (14, 1.47).

Damascus—619 H

432. *Type A*

Border Segments:
بسم الله|ضرب بدمشق|سنة تسع|عشرة ستمائة
Centre:
الملك الكامل
ناصر الدنيا وا
لدين محمد بن ابي بكر

Border Segments:
لا اله الا ا|لله وحده|لا شريك له|محمد رسول الله
Centre:
الامام النا[illegible] (*sic*)
لدين الله امير
المؤمنين احمد

Balog (20, 2.97, ill.).

433. *Type B*

Border Segments:
ضرب هذا الد|رهم بدمشق|سنة تسع|عشرة وستمائة
Centre:
الملك الكامل
ناصر الدنيا وا
لدين محمد بن ابي بكر

Border Segments:
لا اله الا ا|لله وحده لا شريك|له محمد|رسول الله
Centre:
الامام الناصر
ولى عهده عدة
الدنيا والدين محمد

Album. ANS-Newell (21, 2.98; 22, 2.93). Balog (20, 2.60). Lavoix 636 (20, 3.00, ill.). Weyl 6520 (20, 2.80).

434. *Half Dirhem*

As No. 429, but the following date:

تسع عشر . . . | . . . .

The date can only be 619 H because Caliph al-Nāṣir died in 622 H.

Berman 193 (15, 1.38).

435. *Damascus—620 H*

As No. 433, but the following obverse segments:

بسم الله | ضرب بد مشق | سنة عشرين وستمائة |

Yapı-Kredi (22, 2.60). Ziya 1676 (22, —).

Damascus—621 H

436. *Type A*

As above, but the following date:

سنة احد عشرين | وستمائة

Yapı-Kredi (21, 2.95).

437. *Type B*

As No. 433, but the following date:

سنة احد | وعشرين | وستمائة

ANS-Laties (21, —).

438. *Damascus—622 H*

As above, but the obverse and reverse border segments:

ضرب بدمشق سنة | اثنين | وعشرين | وستمائة

لا اله الا ا | لله وحده | لا شريك له | محمد رسول الله

ANS-Newell (21, 2.83, ill.; 20.5, 2.48). Ashmolean (22, —, ill.). Khediv. 1418. Lavoix 637 (21, 2.91, ill.). Sioufﬁ, p. 17. Yapı-Kredi (20, 2.82; 21, 2.95).

439. *Half Dirhem*

Border Segments:

ضرب بد | مشق سنة ا | ثنين وعشرين | وستمائة

Centre:

الملك

الكامل

Border Segments:

لا اله ا | لا الله | (محمد رسو) | (ل الله)

Centre:

الامام

الناصر

ANS-Newell (15.5, 1.47).

440. *Half Dirhem—Date Missing*

As No. 424, but the date in the obverse segments is incomplete.

Ashmolean-Keble College (12, 1.23, ill.). Ashmolean-Thorburn (14, 1.49). Lavoix 638 (13, 1.45). Østrup 1581 (—, 1.37). Prague 904 (14, 1.40).

441. *Damascus—623 H*

Border Segments:	Border Segments:
ضرب بدمشق|سنة ثلث|وعشرين|وستمائة	لا اله الا ا|لله وحده|لا شريك له|محمد رسول الله
Centre:	Centre:
الملك الكامل	الامام الظاهر
٧	بامر الله ابو نصر
ناصر الدنيا وا	محمد امير المؤمنين
لدين محمد بن ابي بكر	

ANS 56.125 (23, 2.976). ANS 72.75 (1, —). Hirsch 2083. Siouffi, p. 17. Zambaur *Contrib. II*, No. 280.
A dirhem in the Ashmolean, dated 623 H, has the protocol of Caliph al-Nāṣir and his heir on the reverse. The only explanation is that an old reverse die was used by mistake.

442. *Half Dirhem*

Border Segments:	Border Segments:
ضرب بد|مشق سنة|ثلث وعشرين|وستمائة	لا اله ا|لا الله|محمد رسو|ل الله
Centre:	Centre:
الملك	الامام
الكامل	الظاهر

ANS-Laties (15, —).

443. *Half Dirhem—Date Missing*

As above, but the date is either 622 or 623 H because of the caliph's name:

اثنين / ثلث عشرين|وستمائة

Ashmolean-A. C. Kay (16, —). Khediv. 1420.

444. *Damascus—623 H*

Border Segments:	Border Segments:
ضر(ب) بدمشق|سنة ثلث|وعشر(ين)|. . . .	. . .|. . .|(لا) شريك له|محمد رسول الله
Centre:	Centre:
الملك الكامل	الامام
الناصر الدنيا وا	المستنصر
لدين محمد بن ابي بكر	بالله ابو جعفر
	المنصور امير المؤمنين

Album.

445. *Damascus—624 H*

Border Segments:
ضرب بدمشق|سنة اربع|وعشرين|وستمائة
Centre:
الملك الكامل
ناصر الدنيا وا
لدين محمد بن ابي بكر

Border Segments:
لا اله الا ا|لله وحده|لا شريك له|محمد رسول الله
Centre:
الامام
المستنصر
بالله ابو جعفر
المنصور امير المؤمنين

Album. ANS 72.75 (23, —). Balog (22, 3.00, ill.; 21, 2.94, ill.; although only the digit of the date is on the last coin, the reverse centre after 628 H is different. So the date cannot be 634 H). Tewhid (22, —).

446. *Half Dirhem*

Border Segments:
ضرب بدمشق|سنة اربع|وعشرين|وستمائة
Centre:
الملك
الكامل

Border Segments:
لا اله ا|لا الله|محمد رسو|ل الله
Centre:
الامام
المستنصر

ANS-Laties (15, —). Ilisch 25 (15, —; digit and decade of the date seem to be in the same segment on the obverse).

447. *Damascus—626 H*

As No. 445, but the following date:

ضرب بد|مشق سنة|ست وعشرين|وستمائة

Album 45 [obverse segments: . . . بدمشق/سنة ست/عشر; reverse is incuse of obverse (brockage); a second Album specimen is a normal coin]. ANS-Newell (23, 2.96). Yapı-Kredi (20, 2.80).

448. *Damascus—627 H*

As above, but the following obverse segments:

بسم الله|ضرب بدمشق|سنة سبع عشرين|وستمائة

ANS (21, —). Yapı-Kredi (20, 2.80).

449. *Damascus—628 H*

As above, but the following obverse segments and reverse centre legend:

ضرب بدمشق|سنة ثمان|وعشرين|وستمائة

الامام المستنصر
بالله ابو جعفر
امير المؤمنين

Album. ANS-Laties (21, 2.824).

450. *Damascus—629 H*

Border Segments:
ضرب بدمشق|سنة تسع|وعشرين|وستمائة
Centre:
الملك الكامل
ناصر الدنيا وا
لدين محمد بن ابى بكر

Border Segments:
لا اله الا|الله وحده|لا شريك له|محمد رسول الله
Centre:
الامام المستنصر
بالله ابو جعفر
المنصور امير المؤمنين

ANS (23, 2.94). Ashmolean-Thorburn (21, 2.91).

Half Dirhem
Damascus—62x H

451. *Type A*

Border Segments:
ضرب بد|مشق سنة. . . . عشرين|وستمائة
Centre:
الملك
الكامل

Border Segments:
لا اله الا|الله محمد|رسول|الله
Centre:
الامام
المستنصر

Balog (15, 1.43, ill.).

452. *Type B*

Border Segments:
ضرب بد|مشق سنة|. . . . عشرين|وستمائة
Centre:
الملك
الكامل

Border Segments:
لا اله ا|لا الله|محمد رسو|ل الله
Centre:
الامام
المستنصر

Ashmolean-Thorburn (15, 1.41). Balog (15, 1.43; 15, 1.43; 15, 1.46). Paris (15, 1.49).

453. *Damascus—630 H*

As No. 450, but the border segments, both sides, are:
ضرب بد|مشق سنة|ثلاثين|وستمائة
لا اله الا ا|لله وحده لا|شريك له محمد|رسول الله

ANS-Newell (22, 2.926). ANS 56 125 (22, 2.019).

454. *Half Dirhem*

Border Segments:
(ضرب بد|مشق سنة)|ثلاثين|(وستمائة)
Centre:
الملك
الكامل

Border Segments:
لا اله الا|الله|محمد ر|سول الله
Centre:
الامام
المستنصر

ANS-Boyd (15, —). ANS-Newell (15, —).

455. *Damascus—631 H*

As No. 450, but the following obverse border segments:

ضرب بد|مشق سنة|احدى ثلاثين|وستمائة

Balog (22, 2.99). Yapı-Kredi (23, 2.85).

456. *Half Dirhem*

As No. 454, but the obverse and reverse border segments:

ضرب بد|مشق سنة|احد ثلثين|وستمائة

لا اله|الا الله|محمد رسو|ل الله

ANS-Newell (16, 1.46).

457. *Damascus—632 H*

As No. 450, but the following date:

اثنين وثلاثين|(وستمائة)

ANS 56.125 (22, 2.956).

458. *Half Dirhem*
Damascus—632 H

Border Segments:

. . .|مشق سنة|اثنين و|. . .

Centre:

الملك
الكامل

Border Segments:

. . .|. . .|. . .|ل الله

Centre:

الامام
المستنصر

Album.

459. *Damascus—633 H*

As No. 450, but the following date:

ثلاث وثلثين|وستمائة

Yapı-Kredi (20, 2.95).

460. *Half Dirhem*

As No. 454, but the obverse and reverse border segments:

ضرب|بدمشق|سنة ثلاث|وثلاثين

لا اله الا|الله . . .|. . .|. . .

ANS (15, 1.484, ill.; 12, 1.42, ill.). ANS-Laties (16, —).

461. *Damascus—634 H*

As No. 459, but the following date:

اربعة وثلث|ين وستمائة

ANS Newell (21, 2.892).

462. *Half Dirhem*

Border Segments:

. . . | . . . | اربعة و | ثلا . . .

Centre:

الملك

الكامل

Border Segments:

[Illegible]

Centre:

الامام

المستنصر

Album.

Half Dirhem

463. *Damascus—63x H*

Border Segments:

ضرب بد | . . . . | . . . . | ثلاثين ستة

Centre:

الملك

الكامل

Border Segments:

لا اله الا | . . . . | . . . . | الله

Centre:

٧

الامام

المستنصر

Ashmolean (16, —, ill.).

COPPER

[Caliph's Name Not Mentioned]

464. *Damascus—631 H*

Square-in-the-circle type.

Segments beginning at bottom:

ضر | ب بد | مشق | . . .

Centre:

الملك الكا

مل ناصر الدين

Border Segments beginning at top:

احدى | وثلاثين | ست | . . .

Centre:

محمد بن ابي

بكر بن ايوب

[Tall *Naskh*]

The above legends were reconstructed from both specimens.

Album 5 (2 specimens).

465. *Damascus—6[3]3 H*

Square-in-the-circle type.

Border Segments:

لا اله الا الله | وحده لا شريك له |

محمد رسول الله | صلى الله عليه

Centre:

الملك الكا

مل ناصر الدين

Border Segments:

ضرب بد | مشق | سنة ثلثة | (ثلاثين؟) وستمائة

Centre:

محمد بن ابي

بكر بن ايوب

[Tall *Naskh*]

Ashmolean (23, 3.71). Ashmolean-Thorburn (23, 4.90; on both Ashmolean specimens the legends on the reverse segments start at the left). Balog (21, 4.20, ill.; 21, 3.99). BMC 419 (22, 3.16). Çetinyalçın (21, —). München 85966 (19, 3.943, ill.). Prague 907 (20, —).

[With Caliph al-Mustanṣir]

Damascus—62x H

466. *Type A*

Square-in-the-circle type.

Border Segments:

لا اله الا الله|وحده لا شريك له|محمد رسول الله|صلى الله عليه

Centre:

الامام

المستنصر

بالله امير المؤمنين

Border Segments:

ضرب بدمشق|سنة . . . .|وعشرين|وستمائة

Centre:

الملك الكامل

محمد بن ابي بكر

BMC 415 (20, 2.55); 415a (23, 3.40). Çetinyalçın (21, —; obverse segments: . . . .|. . . .|مشق سنة|ضرب بد).

Damascus—Date Missing

467. *Type B*

Square-in-the-circle type.

Border Segments:

(لا اله الا اله)|(وحده لا شر)|يك له محمد ر|سول الله

Centre:

الامام المستنصر

بالله ابو جعفر

المنصور امير المؤمنين

Border Segments:

(بسم الله)|ضرب بدمشق|. . . .|. . . .

Centre:

الملك الكامل

ناصر الدنيا وا

لدين محمد بن ابي بكر

Horovitz (20, 2.74, ill.).

Half *Fals*

468. *Damascus—633 H*

Square-in-the-circle type.

Border Segments:

. . . .|. . . .|لا شريك له|. . . .

Centre:

الامام

المستنصر

Border Segments:

(ضرب بد)|(مشق سنة)|ثلث وثلثين|. . . .

Centre:

الملك

الكامل

ANS-UM (16, —, ill.).

Palestine

SILVER

Ghazzah—624 H

469. *Type A*

Square-in-the-circle type.

Border Segments:

بسم الله|ضرب بغزة|سنة اربع و|عشرين وستمائة

Border Segments:

لا اله الا|الله وحده|لا شريك له|محمد رسول الله

Centre:	Centre:
	٢
الملك الكامل	الامام المنصور
ناصر الدنيا وا	ابو جعفر المستنصر
لدين محمد بن ابي بكر	بالله امير المؤمنين

Album 7. ANS (21, —; the digit is scarcely legible; it is either 4 or 5; 21, —). Ashmolean-A. C. Kay (21, 2.68). Balog. *BIE* XXXVI (1955), p. 343, 1 (21, 2.83, ill); 2 (21, 2.84).

470. *Type B*

Border Segments:	Border Segments:
لا اله الا | الله وحده | لا شريك له | محمد رسول الله	ضرب بغزه | سنة اربع | وعشرين | وستمائة
Centre:	Centre:
الملك الكامل	الامام المنصور
ابو المعالي	ابو جعفر المستنصر
محمد بن ابي بكر	بالله امير المؤمنين

Balog, *BIE* XXXVI (1955) (20, 2.88, ill.).

471. *Type C*

Border Segments:	Border Segments:
ضرب بغزه | سنة اربع | وعشرين | وستمائة	لا اله الا ا | لله وحده | لا شريك له | محمد رسول الله
Centre:	Centre:
الملك الكامل	الامام
ناصر الدنيا وا	المستنصر
لدين محمد بن ابي بكر	بالله ابو جعفر
	المنصور امير المؤمنين

Balog (22, 3.00). Lowick (22, 2.87; date missing, but this variety).

472. *Ghazzah—625 H*

As No. 469, but the following date:

سنة خمس و \| عشرين وستمائة

[No ٢ above المنصور]

Balog, *BIE* XXXVI (1955), a(22, 2.86, ill.); b(22, 2.81, ill.; the date is missing on (b), but it is the same type and is likely the same date).

473. *Ghazzah—634 H*

As above, but the following date and centre legends:

ضرب هذا الدر \| هم بغزه سنة \| اربع وثلثين \| وستمائة

Centre:	Centre:
الملك الكامل	الامام المنصور
ابو المعالي	ابو جعفر
محمد بن ابي	المستنصر بالله
بكر بن ايوب	امير المؤمنين

Dr. Michael Bates, ANS, drew my attention to this late issue.

ANS-Newell (20, 2.899, ill.; 22, 3.039).

Mesopotamia

SILVER

474. *Mayāfāriqīn—617 H*

Square-in-the-circle type.

Border Segments:

بسم الله | بميا فرقين | سنة سبع | (عشرة) وستمائة

Centre:

الملك الكامل

ناصر الدنيا وا

لدين محمد بن ابي بكر

Border Segments:

لا اله الا | الله وحده | لا شريك له | محمد رسول الله

Centre:

الامام الناصر

لدين الله امير

المؤمنين احمد

Soret à Fraehn, No. 106 (Soret did not identify the mint, though there is no doubt that it is Mayāfāriqīn. The decade must be عشرة, as the caliph is al-Nāṣir).

Half Dirhem

475. *Mayāfāriqīn—Date Missing*

Six-pointed star.

Border Segments:

ضرب | بمياف | رقين | سنة | . . . | . . .

Centre:

الملك

الكامل محمد

بن ابو بكر بن

ايوب

Border Segments:

لا اله | الا ا | لله | محمد | رسول | الله

Centre:

الامام

الناصر لدين

الله امير المؤ

منين

[*Kūfic* Script]

Ashmolean (15, —). Ashmolean-Thorburn (13, 1.13).

Ḥarrān—623 H

476. *Type A*

Square-in-the-circle type.

Border Segments:

بسم الله | ضرب بحران | سنة ثلث و | عشرين وستمائة

Centre:

الملك الكامل

ناصر الدنيا وا

لدين محمد بن ابي بكر

Border Segments:

لا اله الا ا | لله وحده | لا شريك له | محمدرسول الله

Centre:

الامام المستنصر

بالله امير المؤ

منين المنصور

[*Naskh* Script]

ANS (22, 2.75; date missing, but the same legends). Khediv. 1421.

477. *Type B*

As above, but the reverse:

. . . | . .الله | محمد رسو | ل الله

Centre:

الامام المستنصر

بالله ابو جعفر

المنصور امير المؤمنين

Album.

Half Dirhem

478. *Ḥarrān—623 H*

Square-in-the-circle type.

Border Segments:

. . . ان سنة | ثلث وع . . . |

Centre

الملك

الكامل

Border Segments:

. . . الله | محمد رسو | ل الله . . .

Centre

الامام

المستلصر

[*Naskh* Script]

ANS-Laties (15, —, ill.).

479. *Ḥarrān—624 H*

Square-in-the-circle type.

Border Segments:

ضرب بحران سنة | اربعة و | عشرين | وستمائة

Centre:

الملك الكامل

ناصر الدننا وا

الدين محمد بن ابو بكر

Border Segments:

لا اله الا ا | لله وحده | محمد رسو | ل الله

Centre:

الامام المستنصر

بالله ابو جعفر

المنصور امير المؤمنين

[*Naskh* Script]

Album. ANS 72.75 (23, 2.75, ill.; probably this date, but the decade and digit are missing). *Seaby's Coin and Medal Bulletin*, Sept. 1972, W-532 (21, —, ill.; courtesy of Peter Seaby).

al-Ruhā Silver : see nos. 490-91

COPPER

The copper coins of Ḥarrān are all of the square-in-the-circle type. There is always, on both sides in the centre, a central pellet flanked by two ringlets. All the coins in this series are in *Naskh* script.

[With Caliph al-Ẓāhir]

480. *Ḥarrān—Date Incomplete (622/623 H)*

Square-in-the-circle.

Border Segments:

ضرب بحران|سنة . . . |وعشرين|ستمائة

Centre:

الملك الكامل

○ ○ ○

محمد بن ابي بكر

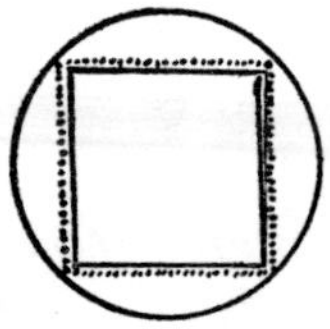

Border Segments:

لا اله|الا الله|جعفر محمد|رسول الله

Centre:

الامام الظاهر

○ ○ ○

بامر الله محمد

ANS (several specimens). BMC 409 (23, 5.76).

[With Caliph al-Mustanṣir]

481. *Ḥarrān—623 H*

As above, but the following date and reverse centre legend:

سنة ثلاثة|وعشرين|وستمائة

الامام

المستنصر

○ ○ ○

بالله امير المؤمنين

Album (2 specimens). Lagumina, p. 86, No. 57 (20, 5.36). Paris (21, 6.70, ill.; digit of date: ثلاث). Lavoix 650 (24, 7.67); 656 (—, 4.65, ill.) is probably also Ḥarrān, but with a different arrangement of the reverse centre:

لاامـام المستنصر.

○ امير ○

بامر الله المؤمنين

Note: *al-Mustanṣir bi-Amr Allāh.*

482. *Ḥarrān—624 H*

As above, but the following date:

سنة اربع|وعشرين|وستمائة

Album (2 specimens; one with reverse segments: لا اله /الا الله). Artuk 733 (22, 5.70). Berlin (23, 5.43). Berman 194 (22, 6.40). BMC 412 (24, 4.76, ill.). Lavoix 654 (23, 5.73; mint missing, but the pellets in the centre belong to the Ḥarrān issues); 646 (22, 5.17).

483. *Ḥarrān—625 H*

As above, but the following date:

سنة خمس|وعشرين|وستمائة

Paris (23, 5.90).

484. *Ḥarrān—627 H*

As above, but the following date:

سنة سبع|وعشرين|وستمائة

ANS (20, —; the last letter of the digit is off the flan, but it may be ستة or سبع). Çetinyalçın (21, —).

Ḥarrān—628 H

485. *Type A*

As above, but the following date:

سنة ثمان|وعشرين|وستمائة

ANS-Greenwood (20, —).

486. *Type B*

Border Segments:

سنة ثمان|. . . . .|. . . . .|ضرب بحران

Centre:

الملك الكامل

○ ○ ○

محمد بن ابي بكر

Border Segments:

لا اله الا ا|لله وحده|(محمد رسو)|ل الله

Centre:

الامام

المستنصر

○ ○

بالله امير المؤمنين

Ashmolean-Christ Church (22, —, ill.).

487. *Ḥarrān—632 H*

As above, but the following date:

ضرب بحران|سنة اثنين|ثلاثين|وستمائة

Yapı-Kredi (21, 5.50).

488. *Ḥarrān—634 H*

As above, but the following date:

سنة اربع|ثلثين و|ستمائة

Ashmolean-Christ Church 256 (21, 4.57). München 85990 (22, 5.686).

489. *Ḥarrān—Date Missing*

As above, but date is off the flan or illegible.

Album 42 (xx3 H). ANS (21, —; 20, —; 21, —). Ashmolean-Bodleian 151 (23, —). Balog (23, 7.06, ill.; 21, 5.10). BMC 410 (23, 4.75); 411 (23, 4.26). Lavoix 653 (22, 5.03) ill.). Østrup 1583, 1584.

SILVER

490. *al-Ruhā—616 H*

Six-pointed star.

Border Segments:

ضرب|بالرها|سنة|ست|عشر و|ستمائة

Centre:

الملك

الكامل محمد

ابن ابي بكر بن

ايوب

Border Segments:

لا اله|الا ا|لله|محمد|سول|الله

Centre:

الامام

الناصر لدين

الله امير المؤ

منين

[*Kufic* Script]

Album 48 (reverse segments written correctly). ANS-Laties (21, 2.691, ill.; 18, 2.888). BM (21, —, ill.). Broome (—, 2.66).

491. *al-Ruhā—617 H*

As above, but the following date:

سنة|سبع|عشر و|ستمائة

ANS-Laties (20, 2.834, ill.).

COPPER

The Niṣibīn copper coins of al-Kāmil are marked by three—and in one case, by two—distinctive small six-pointed stars, placed in a horizontal row between the legends of the obverse and reverse centres. Niṣibīn was handed over to al-Kāmil's lieutenant and son, al-Ṣāliḥ Ayyūb, in 632 H by the son of al-Ṣāliḥ Ismāʿīl, who inherited it from al-Ashraf Mūsā. The date 631 H on the first issue may indicate either an engraver's error, or some inexactitude of the dating in the chronicles. All coins in this series are the square-in-the-circle type.

492. *Niṣibīn—631 H*

Square-in-the-circle type.

Border Segments:
ضرب|بنصبين|سنة احد و|(ثلثين وستمائة)
Centre:
الملك الكامل
* * *
محمد بن ابي بكر

Border Segments:
لا اله الا ا|لله وحده|محمد رسو|ل الله
Centre:
الامام
المستنصر
* * *
بالله امير المؤمنين

[3 stars in each centre; segments have been reconstructed]

BMC 415a (21.5, —).

493. *Niṣibīn—632 H*

As above, but the following date:

سنة اثنين|ثلثين وستمائة

[Three stars in each centre]

Ashmolean-Baldwin (20, 4.33). BM-Amedroz (20, —). Ilisch 33 (21, —); 34 (23, —; on these 2 specimens the letter *wāw* between اثنتين and ثلثين is apparently present). Lavoix 651 (21, 5.60, ill.). Paris (21, 4.04, ill.).

494. *Niṣibīn—634 H*

As above, but the following date and centre legends:

سنة اربع|(ثلثين وستمائة

Centre:
الملك الكامل
* *
محمد بن ابي بكر

Centre:
الامام
المستنصر
* *
بالله امير المؤمنين

[Only two stars in each centre]

ANS-Wood (22, 4.341 ,ill.).

495. *Niṣibīn—Date Missing*

The three stars indicate that these coins may belong to either 631 or 632 H.

Album 18 (2 specimens). ANS-Henry Field (9 specimens). BMC 413 (22, —); 414 (22, —); 415 (22, —). Izzet 351–355 (gives no details; may belong to Damascus or any of the Mesopotamian mints). Lavoix 659 (21, 5.45). Østrup 1585 and 1596.

Qalʿat Jaʿbar—Date Missing (623–9 H)

Square-in-the-circle type with a thin plain line in a line of pellets.

496. *Type A*

Border Segments:
ضرب بقلعة|(جعبر سنة . . . .|وعشرين|(وستمائة)
Centre:
الملك الكامل
محمد بن ابي بكر

Border Segments:
لا اله|الا الله|محمد رسو|ل الله
Centre:
الامام المستنصر
O
بامر الله امير المؤمنين

Only one pellet or annulet in the reverse centre; none in the obverse.

Album 44. Lagumina, p. 85, No. 55 (22, 4.90).

497. *Type B*

As above, but the reverse centre:

✤ الامام ✤
المستنصر
●
بالله امير المؤمنين

BMC 415 (19, 2.56, ill.).

498. *Qalʿat Jaʿbar—629 H*

As above, but the following date and reverse centre:

ضرب بقلعت|جعبر سنة|تسع وعشرين|وستمائة

الامام
المستنصر
O
بالله امير المؤمنين

Album (reverse segments: بسم الله|لا اله الا|. . . .|رسول الله). Ashmolean-Thorburn (22, 3.37, ill.). Bergmann, Zur muhammedanischen Münzkunde, *NZ* (1876), p. 39. Berlin (21, 3.56; 17, 2.08). Wien (21, 2.62, ill.).

499. *Qalʿat Jaʿbar—631 H*

Border Segments:
ضرب بقلت|جعبر سنة|احد وثلا . .| . . .

Border Segments:
لا اله الا الله|وحده لا شر . .|. . محمد رسو . . .|صلى الله عليه

Centre:
الملك الكامل
محمد بن ابي بكر

Centre:
الامام
المستنصر
بالله امير المؤمنين

[Appears not to have a central annulet on the reverse]
Album. BMC 415a.

500. *Qalʿat Jaʿbar—634 H*
As No. 498, but the following date:
اربع ثلثين | (وستمائة)
ANS (21, —).

501. *Mint Missing—635 H*
Border: circle in circle of pellets, within which is a linear square in a square of pellets.

Border Segments:
. . . | . . . سنة | خمس وثلاثين | (وستمائة
Centre:
الملك الكامل
ناصر الدنيا وا
لدين محمد بن ابي بكر

Border Segments:
(لا) اله (الا) | (الله وحده) | (محمد) | رسول الله
Centre:
الامام المستنصر
بالله ابو جعفر
المنصور امير المؤمنين

Balog (21, 4.85, ill.).

502. *al-Ḥiṣn—632 H*
Square-in-the-circle type.

Border Segments:
. . . بالحصن | سنة اثنتى | . . . | . . .
Centre:
(الم)لك الكامل
(محمد) بن ابي بكر

Border Segments:
لا اله | . . . | . . . | . . .
Centre:
الامام
المستنصر
بالله امير المؤمنين

Album 41 (2 specimens, one of which has faulty last line in reverse centre: امير المؤ).

503. *al-Ḥiṣn—Date Missing*
Square-in-the-circle type.

Border Segments:
. .ب بالحصن | سنة ا . . | . . . | ستمائة
Centre:
الملك الكامل
* * *
محمد بن ابي بكر

Border Segments:
لا اله | . . . | . . . | سول الله
Centre:
الامام
المستنصر
* * *
بالله امير المؤمنين

[Unlike issues of Niṣibīn, stars are small]
Album.

AL-ʿĀDIL SAYF AL-DĪN ABŪ BAKR II IBN AL-KĀMIL MUḤAMMAD I

Lord of Damascus [635–636 H = 1237–1238 AD]

Ruler of Egypt/Sultan of the Empire [635–637 H = 1237–1239 AD]

Egypt
GOLD

504. *Cairo—635 H*

Border on both sides: plain circle. Counterclockwise marginal legend on both sides:

بسم الله الرحمن الرحيم ضرب هذا الدينر بالقاهرة سنة خمس وثلثين وستمائة

لا اله الا الله محمد رسول الله ارسله بالهدى ودين الحق ليظهره على الدين كله

Double circle on both sides.

Centre:	Centre:
الامام!	محمد
المنصور ابو	الملك العادل
جعفر المستنصر	سيف الدين ابو بكر بن
بالله امير المؤمنين	الملك الكامل

ANS-UM (23, 6.35). Artuk 747 (21, 5.35). Awad (20, 4.10; 20, 6.00). Balog (22, 4.08, ill.; 22, 5.70; 22, 6.66). Berlin 623a/1876 (20, 4.66). BMC 420 (22, 5.11). Fahmy 283 (21, 5.40); 284 (22, 4.35; both coins are erroneously listed under al-ʿĀdil I). Horovitz (22, 5.30; 21, 4.56). Khediv. 1428 (—, 7.50). Leuthold (21, 6.06). Markov, p. 357, No. 44. Paris (22, 3.97; 22, 5.12). Samir Shamma (20, 3.95). Yapı-Kredi (22, 5.15; 21, 4.23).

505. *Cairo—636 H*

As above, but the following date:

سنة ست وثلثين وستمائة

ANS-UM (23, 5.79). Artuk 748 (21, 3.40). Awad (20, 5.70). Balog (21, 4.94; 22, 7.28, ill.; 22, 5.90, ill.; 22, 4.23). BMC 421 (21, 3.80). Fahmy 285 (21, 6.54); 286 (21, 4.65; both coins erroneously listed under al-ʿĀdil I). Horovitz (22, 6.45). Khediv. 1429 (—, 4.20). Leuthold (22, 10.90; 22, 10.00; 22, 5.42). Munzel (22, 5.67). Østrup 1590 (—, 3.51). Samir Shamma (21, 5.86). Weyl 6529 (22, 3.50).

506. *Cairo—637 H*

As above, but the following date:

سنة سبع وثلثين وستمائة

ANS (24, 4.94). ANS-UM (21.5, 5.51). Balog (22, 4.47, ill..; 22, 3.70). Fahmy 287 (22, 6.23); 288 (21, 7.25; both coins erroneously listed under al-ʿĀdil I).

507. *Alexandria—636 H*

As above, but the following mint/date formula:

بالاسكندرية سنة ست وثلثين وستمائة

Artuk 746 (21, 5.40). Leuthold (22, 6.80; 22, 6.40). Yapı-Kredi (22, 7.35).

508. *Alexandria—637 H*

As above, but the following date:

سنة سبع وثلثين وستمائة

BM-N.Q. (23, 4.09).

Syria
SILVER

509. *Damascus—635 H*

Square-in-the-circle type.

Border Segments:	Border Segments:
ضرب بد|مشق سنة|خمس وثلاثين|وستمائة	لا اله الا الله|وحده لا شر|يك له محمد|رسول الله
Centre:	Centre:
الملك العادل	الامام المستنصر
سيف الدين	بالله ابو جعفر
ابـو بكر ابن محمد	المنصور امير المؤمنين

[All silver coins of al-ʿĀdil II are in *Naskh* script]

ANS (24, 2.90). ANS 56.125 (23, 3.02; 25, 2.89; 23, 2.989; 23, 2.986). Balog (22, 2.88, ill.; 22, 2.95, ill.; 21, 2.96). Berman 195 (23, 2.85). BM-Amedroz (24, 3.02). Yapı-Kredi (22, 3.00; 21, 2.90).

Half Dirhem

510 *Damascus—635 H*

Border Segments:	Border Segments:
ضرب|بدمشق|سنة خمس|وثلثين	لا|اله|الا|الله
Centre:	Centre:
الملك	الامام
العادل	المستنصر

ANS-Newell (15, 1.42; 15, —; the reading of the digit of the date is not quite certain on these 2 coins). Berlin 633/1896 (16, 1.40, ill.).

511. *Damascus—636 H*

Border Segments:	Border Segments:
ضرب بد|مشق سنة|ستة ثلاثين|وستمائة	لا اله الا ال|له لا شر|يك له محمد|رسول الله
Centre:	Centre:
الملك العادل	الامام المستنصر
سيف الدين	بالله ابو جعفر
ابـو بكر ابن محمد	المنصور امير المؤمنين

ANS (21, 2.91). ANS 56.125 (23, 2.95). Ashmolean-Thorburn (24, 2.92). Balog (22, 2.72, ill.). New York trade (—, 3.01).

Damascus—637 H

512. *Type A*

Border Segments:	Border Segments:
؟(ضرب)|(بدمشق سنة)|سبع وثلاثين|وستمائة	لا اله الا ا|لله وحده|محمد ر|سول الله
Centre:	Centre:
الملك العادل	الامام المستنصر
سيف الدين	بالله ابو جعفر
ابـو بكر ابن محمد	المنصور امير المؤمنين

Album 49. ANS (21, 2.91; 24, 2.71; 25, —). ANS 56. 125 (23, —). ANS-Newell (22, 2.59; 23, 2.914, ill.). Yapı-Kredi (20, 2.95).

513. *Type B*

Border Segments:	Border Segments:
بسم الله|ضرب بدمشق|سنة سبع و|ثلاثين وستمائة	لا اله الا ا|لله وحده|لا شريك له|محمد رسول الله
Centre:	Centre:
[As above]	الامام المستنصر بالله ابو جعفر المنصور امير المؤمنين

ANS 56.125 (23, —). ANS-Newell (21, —, ill.; 23, —). BMC 421m (21, 2.92; mint missing, probably Damascus). Lavoix 659 (22, 3.10); 660 (20, 3.10; small writing, similar to the later dirhems of al-Ṣāliḥ Ismāʿıl. The decade of the date is: ثلثين). Nicol (21.2, 2.791).

514. *Type C*

As above, but the obverse segments and reverse centre:

(بسم الله ضرب)|بد مشق سنة|سبع وثلاثين|وستمائة	الامام المنصور المستنصر (بالله ابو جعفر) (امير المؤمنين)

[Coin is double struck]

ANS-Newell (23, —).

515. *Damascus—Date Missing*

ANS (21, —). ANS-Newell (23, —; 21, —). ANS-UM (23, —). Balog (22, 2.79; 21, 2.76). Berman 196 (13, 1.52, half dirhem). BM-Spink (23, 2.90).

AL-ṢĀLIḤ NAJM AL-DĪN AYYŪB IBN AL-KĀMIL MUḤAMMAD I

Lord of Āmid and Ḥiṣn-Kayfā [629–636 H = 1231–1238 AD]

Lord of Damascus, First Rule (636 H = 1238 AD]

Ruler of Egypt/Sultan of the Empire [637–647 H = 1239–1249 AD]

Lord of Damascus, Second Rule [643–647 H = 1245–1249 AD]

Egypt

GOLD

516. *Cairo—637 H*

Border on both sides: plain circle. Counterclockwise marginal legend on both sides:

لا اله الا الله محمد رسول الله ارسله بالهدى ودين الحق ليظهره على الدين كله	بسم الله الرحمن الرحيم ضرب هذا الدينر بالقاهرة سنة سبع وثلثين وستمائة

Double circle on both sides.

Centre:	Centre:
محمد الملك الصالح نجم الدين ايوب بن الملك الكامل	الامام المنسور ابو جعفر المستنصر بالله امير المؤمنين

Berman 197 (22, 5.40). BMC 422 (23, 6.37, ill.). Shukrī, p. 135, No. 4286 (22.3, 4.318).

517. *Cairo—638 H*

As above, but the following date and centre legends:

سنة ثمان وثاثين وستمائة

Centre:

● محمد
الملك الصالح
نجم الدين ايوب بن
الملك الكامل
● ●

Centre:

الامام
المنصور ابو
جعفر المستنصر
بالله امير المؤمنين
● ●

BMC 423 (23, 4.23). Fahmy 530 (21, 6.45). Horovitz (24, 3.96). Khediv. 1430 (—, 4.20). Pietraszewski 434. Yapı-Kredi (23, 5.55).

518. *Cairo—639 H*

As above, but the following date:

سنة تسع وثلثين وستمائة

ANS (21, —). ANS-UM (22, 4.32). Balog (23, 4.36, ill.). Fahmy 531 (22, 4.31). Khediv. 1431 (—, 4.20).

Half Dinar

519. *Cairo—639 H*

Border on both sides: plain circle. Counterclockwise marginal legend on both sides:

As on full dinars, but end with ليظهره.

بسم الله الرحمن الرحيم ضرب بالقاهرة سنة تسع وثلثين وستمائة

Centre:

محمد
الملك الصالح
نجم الدين ايوب
ابن

Centre:

الامام
˅
المنصور ا
بو جعفر امير
المؤمنين

BMC 424 (19, 2.14).

520. *Cairo—640 H*

As No. 516, but the following date:

سنة اربعين وستمائة

Two pellets under امير ●● in the reverse central legend.

Ashmolean-A. C. Kay (22, 4.08). Balog (22, 4.17). BMC 425 (22, 4.30); 426 (22, 4.18). Khediv. 1432. Paris (22.5, 4.24, ill.).

521. *Cairo—641 H*

As above, but the following date and reverse centre legend:

سنة احدى واربعين وستمائة

الامام
˅ ˅
المستعصم
بالله ابو احمد عبد
الله امير المؤمنين

Artuk 752 (22, 4.50). BMC 426d (22, 4.23). Østrup 1592 (—, 4.30). Wien 629 (21, 4.30).

522. *Cairo—642 H*

As above, but the following date:

سنة اثنين واربعين وستمائة

Artuk 753 (23, 4.25). Balog (22, 4.28). BMC 426k (23, 4.21, ill.). Leuthold (24, 4.28).

523. *Cairo—643 H*

As above, but the following date:

سنة ثلث واربعين وستمائة

Awad (21, 4.10). Balog (23, 4.38, ill.; 23, 4.30, ill.; 23, 4.35). Berlin 239/1881 (23, 4.30). BMC 427 (23, 4.30). Horovitz (24, 4.20). Paris (24, 4.28). Pietraszewski 435. Weyl 6532 (23, 8.70). Yapı-Kredi (23, 4.05).

Half Dinar

524. *Cairo—643 H*

As No. 519, but the following date and reverse centre legend:

سنة ثلث واربعين وستمائة

Double circle on both sides.

Centre:
الامام
ヾ ヾ
المستعصم
بالله امير المؤ
منين

Balog (20, 2.13, ill.).

525. *Cairo—644 H*

As No. 521, but the following date:

سنة اربع واربعين وستمائة

Awad (23, 4.00). BMC 428 (22, 4.34). Fahmy 532 (21, 4.19). Samir Shamma (22, 4.35).

Half Dinar

526. *Cairo—644 H*

As No. 519, but the following date:

سنة اربع واربعين وستمائة

Samir Shamma (18.5, 2.15).

527. *Cairo—645 H*

As No. 521, but the following date:

سنة خمس واربعين وستمائة

Two pellets beneath the obverse and reverse central legends.

Balog (23, 4.14, ill.; 22, 4.33). da Cunha 1460 (18, 4.85).

Half Dinar

528. *Cairo—645 H*

As No. 519, but the following date:

سنة خمس واربعين وستمائة

Balog (20, 2.21, ill.).

529. *Cairo—646 H*

As No. 521, but the following date:

سنة ست واربعين وستمائة

Two pellets beneath the obverse and reverse central legends.

Balog (22, 4.30, ill.). BMC 429 (22, 4.37, ill.).

Half Dinar

530. *Cairo—646 H*

As No. 519, but the following date:

سنة ست واربعين وستمائة

Artuk 754 (18, 2.10).

531. *Cairo—647 H*

As No. 521, but the following date:

سنة سبع واربعين وستمائة

da Cunha 1461 (18, 4.85). Fahmy 533 (22, 4.14).

Half Dinar

532. *Cairo—647 H*

As No. 519, but the following date:

سنة سبع واربعين وستمائة

Hirsch 2084 (18, 2.10). Munzel (19, 2.15, ill.).

533. *Alexandria—Date Missing*

As No. 521, but the following mint and centre legends:

بالاسكندرية سنة . . . .

Centre:

• محمد •
الملك الصالح
نجم الدين ايوب بن
الملك الكامل

Centre:

الامام
المستعصم
بالله ابو احمد عبد
الله امير المؤمنين

Fahmy 536 (20, 5.07).

SILVER

A. Globular Dirhems and Dirhem Fractions

534. *Cairo—Date Missing*

Border on both sides: plain circle. Counterclockwise marginal legend on both sides (reconstructed):

لا اله الا الله محمد رسول الله | ضرب بالقاهرة سنة . . . ين وستمائة

Inner circle on both sides.

Centre:	Centre:
الملك	الامام
الصالح	م
	المنصور

[*Naskh* script]

Balog (13, 1.84, ill.; 9, 1.02).

535. *Cairo—641 H*

As above, but the following date and centre legends:

سنة احدى واربعين وستمائة

Centre:	Centre:
الملك	الامام
	م
الصالح	المستعصم

BM (17 × 21, 5.08; oval flan).

536. *Cairo—645 H*

As above, but the following date:

سنة خمس واربعين وستمائة

Balog, *BIE* XXXV (1953), p. 421 (13, 0.76, ill.).

537. *Cairo—Date Missing*

As above, but date is not present.

Ashmolean-Thorburn (11, 1.63). Balog, *BIE* XXXV (1953) and unpublished specimens, 1 (13, 2.20); 2 (10, 0.96); 3 (10, 1.32); 4 (12, 2.40); 5 (12, 2.00); 6 (10, 0.98); 7 (9, 0.76, ill.); 8 (9, 0.76); 9 (11, 1.82); 10 (9, 1.82).

B. Normal Round-Flan Dirhems

The normal-size round dirhems of the Cairo mint, struck by al-Ṣāliḥ Ayyūb, belong to the square-in-the-circle type characteristic of the Damascus issues. They can be easily recognized by the special style of writing, which is a little angular, less flowing than the mostly elegant *Naskh* of the Damascene engravers.

538. *Cairo—645 H*

Square in the circle.

Border Segments:
محمد رسول|الله ارسله|بالهدى|ودين الحق
Centre:
الملك الصالح
نجم الدين ايوب بن
الملك الكامل

Border Segments:
بسم الله ضرب|بالقاهرة سنة|خمس واربعين|وستمائة
Centre:
الامام
المستعصم
بالله ابو احمد عبد
الله امير المؤمنين

Balog, *BIE* XXXIV (1952), 1 (21, 2.36, ill.); 2 (22, 2.89). BM (20, 2.32: date missing).

Half Dirhem

539. *Cairo—645 H* (?)

Even when only the last digit of the date is on the flan, the date must be 645 H, because of Caliph al-Mustaʿṣim's name. No normal-size, round-flan silver from Cairo is known earlier than 645 H.
Balog, *BIE* XXXIV (1952), 1 (15, 1.62, ill); 2 (13, 1.44, ill.). Balog (18, 1.65; 17, 1.43, ill.; 14, 1.42, ill.).

540. *Cairo—646 H*

As No. 538, but the following date:
ضرب بالقا|هرة سنة|ست اربعين|وستمائة
Balog, *BIE* XXXIV (1952), 1 (23, 2.73); 2 (20, 2.75).

COPPER

541. *Cairo—640 H*

Square-in-the-circle type (thin plain line in a line of dots).

Border Segments:
(بسم الله)|ضرب بالقاهرة|سنة اربعين|وستمائة
Centre:
الملك الصالح
نجم الدنيا والدين
ايوب بن محمد

Border Segments:
لا اله الا|الله وحده|لا شريك له|محمد رسول الله
Centre:
الامام
المستنصر
بالله ابو جعفر
المنصور امير المؤمنين

ANS (22, 2.56). Balog (21, 1.65, ill.; 20, 2.06, ill.).

542. *Cairo—Date Missing*

Square-in-the-circle type.

Border Segments Beginning at Right:
لا اله الا|الله محمد|. . .|. . .
Centre:
الملك الصالح
نجم الدين ايوب
بن الملك الكامل

Border Segments:
بسم الله|ضرب بالقا (هرة)|(سنة) . . .|وستمائة
Centre:
الامام
المستعصم
بالله ابو احمد عبد
الله امير المؤمنين

ANS-Wood (22, —).

Syria

SILVER

Damascus—636 H

543. *Type A*

Square-in-the-circle type.

Border Segments:

بسم الله|ضرب بدمشق|سنة ست ثلاثين|وستمائة

Centre:

الملك الصالح
نجم الدنيا والدين
ايوب ابن محمد

Border Segments:

لا اله الا|الله وحده|لا شريك له|محمد رسول الله

Centre:

الامام
المستنصر
بالله ابو جعفر
المنصور امير المؤمنين

ANS (22.5, 2.82). Balog (22, 2.69, ill.). Yapı-Kredi (25, 2.85; 20, 2.20).

544. *Type B*

Border Segments:

ضرب بدمشق|سنة ستة|وثلاثين|وستمائة

Centre:

الملك الصالح
نجم الدنيا والدين
ايوب ابن محمد

Border Segments:

لا اله الا الله|وحده لا شريك له|محمد رسو|ل الله

Centre:

الامام المستنصر
بالله ابو جعفر
المنصور امير المؤمنين

Album. ANS (22, —). ANS-Newell (21, —; 22.5, —; 21, —; 22, —). Balog, *BIE* XXXIV (1952), (21, 2.82, ill.). Berman 198 (23, 2.80). Lavoix 661 (24, 3.00; reverse segments: لا اله الا|الله وحده|محمد ر|سول الله).

545. *Type C*

As above, but the obverse segments begin at the left:

ضرب بدمشق|سنة ستة|وثلاثين|وستمائة

Balog, *BIE* XXXIV (1952), (21, 2.55).

Half Dirhem

546. *Damascus—636 H*

Square-in-the-circle type.

Border Segments:

ضرب|بدمشق|سنة ست ثلثين|وستمائة

Centre:

الملك
الصالح

Border Segments:

لا اله الا|الله|محمد رسو|ل الله

Centre:

الامام
المستنصر

Balog (10 × 12, 1.45). Glidden (15, 1.42, ill.)

Half dirhems of the square-in-the-circle type, with the date missing and with the name of Caliph al-Mustanṣir, bear only the name al-Ṣāliḥ [الصالح] and so may belong to al-Ṣāliḥ Ayyūb, as well as to al-Ṣaliḥ Isma'il. Only when the date is present, can a precise attribution be made. It must be also borne in mind that Dr. Michael Bates, in an extensive study of large numbers of such half dirhems, was able to show that many of these coins are Crusader imitations.

Damascus—644 H

547.

Type A

Border on both sides: circle of dots between two plain circles. Counterclockwise marginal legend on both sides:

ضرب بدمشق سنة اربعة واربعين وستمائة | لا اله الا الله وحده لا شريك له محمد رسول الله

On both sides linear *dodekalobe*, with a small pellet between each of the arches.

Centre:	Centre:
الملك الصالح	الامام
نجم الدنيا والدين	المستعصم
ايوب ابن محمد	بالله ابو احمد
	امير المؤمنين

This new type was probably designed purposely to change the style of the coins after the expulsion of al-Ṣāliḥ Ismāʿīl. However, from 645 H the square-in-the-circle type was struck once again so that both types occurred simultaneously.

Album (2 specimens). ANS-Newell (23, 2.83). ANS-Newman (21, —). ANS 71.76 (21, 2.88). Balog, *BIE* XXXIV (1952), 1 (20, 2.80, ill.); 2 (20, 2.80, ill.); 3 (20, 2.78); 4 (20, 2.79). Berlin 635/1896 (21, 2.90). Leuthold-Ripostiglio 39 (20, 2.83).

548.

Type B

As above, but the obverse marginal legend is:

ضرب هذا الدرهم بدمشق سنة اربع واربعين وستمائة

Balog (21, 2.80, ill.; 20, 2.80).

Half Dirhem

549.

Damascus—644 H

Dodekalobe type. As above, but the following marginal legends:

ضرب بدمشق سنة اربع واربعين وستمائة | لا اله الا الله وحده لا شريك له محـا (*sic*)

On both sides linear *dodekalobe* without pellets.

Centre:	Centre:
الملك	الامام
	المستعصم
الصالح	

ANS 71.76 (16, —). Balog (16, 1.38, ill.). Leuthold (14, 1.42; 15, 1.42, ill.). Zambaur, *Contrib. II*, No. 284 (14, 1.30; probably this date).

Damascus—645 H

550.

Type A

Dodekalobe type. As No. 547, but the following date:

سنة خمس اربعين وستمائة هجرية

ANS-Newell (20, 2.887). ANS 71. 76 (21, —). Balog (20, 2.90, ill.; 20, 2.84; 21, 2.86, ill.).

551. *Type B*

Square-in-the-circle type.

Border Segments:	Border Segments:
ضرب بدمشق|سنة خمس|واربعين|وستمائة	لا اله الا|الله وحده|لا شريك له|محمد رسول الله
Centre:	Centre:
الملك الصالح	الامام
نجم الدنيا وا	المستعصم
لدين ايوب بن محمد	بالله ابو احمد
	امير المؤمنين

Album (2 specimens, same obverse dies). Berman 200 (19, 2.23; date missing). Ilisch 37 (20. 5, —). Istanbul (20, 2.80). Yapı-Kredi (22, 3.02; 22, 2.95; 19, 2.90; 19, 2.90).

Half Dirhem

Damascus—645 H

552. *Type A*

Dodekalobe type. As No. 547, but the following date:

سنة خمس واربعين وستمائة

Balog (13, 1.28, ill.).

553. *Type B*

Square-in-the-circle type.

Border Segments:	Border Segments:
ضرب بد|مشق سنة|خمس ار|بعين ستمائة	لا اله الا|الله|محمد|رسول الله
Centre:	Centre:
الملك	الامام
الصالح	المستعصم

Ahmed Tewhid (17, —).

554. *Damascus—646 H*

Dodekalobe type. As No. 547, but the following date:

سنة ست واربعين وستمائة

ANS (22, 2.68; 22, 2.87). ANS 71.76 (20.5, —; 22, —; several other specimens). Artuk 751 (22, 2.85). Balog, *BIE* XXXIV (1952), 1 (23, 2.95, ill.); 2 (22, 2.93; 3 (23, 2.88, ill.); 4 (23, 2.90); 5 (22, 2.70, ill.); 6 (22, 2.76); 7 (22, 2.65).

Half Dirhem

Damascus—646 H

555. *Type A*

Dodekalobe type. As No. 547, but the following date:

سنة ست اربعين وست(مائة)

ANS 71.76 (15, —). Ilisch 38 (16, —).

556. *Type B*

Square-in-the-circle type.

Border Segments:
بسم الله|ضرب بدمشق|سنة ست و|اربعين
Centre:
الملك
الصالح

Border Segments:
لا اله الا|الله وحده|لا شريك|له محمد رسول الله
Centre:
الامام
●
المستعصم

Gautier (10 × 14, 1.47). Peus 1900 (attributed to al-Ṣāliḥ Ismāʿīl, but belongs here).

557. *Damascus—647 H*

Square-in-the-circle type.

Border Segments:
ضرب بدمشق|سنة سبع|واربعين|وستمائة
Centre:
السلطان الملك
الصالح نجم الدنيا
والدين ايوب بن
محمد بن ابي بكر

Border Segments:
لا اله الا|الله وحده|لا شريك له|محمد رسول الله
Centre:
لا اله الا الله
محمد رسول الله
الامام المستعصم
بالله امير المؤمنين

Album. ANS-Newell (22, 2.87). ANS-UM (22.5, 2.93). Balog, *BIE* XXXIV (1952, 1 (23, 2.82, ill.); 2 (21, 2.83, ill.); 3 (23, 2.80); 4 (23, 2.86); 5 (23, 2.77); 6 (22, 2.84, ill.); 7 (23, 2.87); 8 (22, 2.90); 9 (24, 2.68, ill.); 10 (23, 2.79); 11 (23, 2.90). BM (23, —).

Half Dirhem

558. *Damascus—647 H*

Dodekalobe type. Marginal legends on both sides:

ضرب بدمشق سنة سبع واربعين وستمائة
Centre:
الملك
الصالح

لا اله الا الله وحده لا شريك له محمد
Centre:
الامام
المستعصم

ANS 71.76 (several specimens). Leuthold (14, 1.42).

Half Dirhem

Damascus—Date Missing

559. *Type A*

Dodekalobe type as above, but date is not present.

ANS 71.76 (several specimens). Berman 201 (14, 1.20).

560. *Type B*

Square-in-the-circle type.

Border Segments:

ضرب|بدمشق|سنة . . . .|. . . .

Centre:

الملك

الصالح

Border Segments:

لا اله الا|الله وحده|لا شريك له|(محمد رسول الله)

Centre:

الامام

المستعصم

ANS 71.76 (13, 1.46; 14, 1.28).

561. *Type C*

Segments partly reconstructed.

Border Segments:

. . . .|. . . .|وار بعين|(وستمائة)

Centre:

الملك الصالح

نجم الدين

Border Segments:

لا اله الا ا|لله وحده|لا شريك له|محمد رسول الله

Centre:

الامام

المستعصم

ANS 71.76 (15, 1.51). Paris (11 × 16, 1.46, ill.). Yapı-Kredi (11, 1.40; 16, 1.45).

562. *Ḥamāh—645 H*

The square-in-the-circle type of the Ḥamāh silver consists of a thin plain line in a line of dots.

Border Segments:

ضرب بحماه|سنة خمس|وار بعين|وستمائة

Centre:

الملك الصالح

نجم الدننا وا

لدين ايوب بن محمد

Border Segments:

لا اله الا|الله وحده|لا شريك له|محمد رسول الله

Centre:

الامام

المستعصم

بالله ابو احمد

امير المؤمنين

Album. ANS-Newell (21, 2.87; 21, 2.83; 20, —). ANS 71.76 (20, —; 20, —). Balog, *BIE* XXXIV (1952), 1 (21, 2.77, ill.); 2 (20, 2.82); 3 (21, 2.79, ill.); 4 (20, 2.86); 5 (21, 2.68); 6 (21, 2.92, ill.); 7 (20, 2.61); 8 (22, 3.01); 9 (21, 2.82, ill.); 10 (21, 2.42); 11 (20, 2.93); 12 (23, 2.65); 13 (20, 2.75). Leuthold (21, 2.82). Leuthold-Ripostiglio 22 (—, 2.83); 23 (—, 2.85).

563. *Ḥamāh—646 H*

Border Segments:

ضرب بحماه|سنة ست|وار بعين|وستمائة

Centre:

الملك الصالح

نجم الدنيا وا

لدين ايوب بن محمد

Border Segments:

لا اله الا ا|لله وحده|لا شريك له|محمد رسول الله

Centre:

الامام

المستعصم

٢

بالله ابو احمد

امير المؤمنين

Balog, *BIE* XXXIV (1952), (21, 2.79, ill.; segments partly reconstructed).

COPPER

564. *Damascus—64x H*

Square-in-the-circle type: thin plain line in line of small pellets.

Border Segments:	Border Segments:
ضرب بدمشق | . . . | اربعين | وستمائة	[Traces of legend]
Centre:	Centre:
الملك	الامام
الصالح	المستعصم

The attribution is tentative. This *fals* may belong to al-Ṣāliḥ Ismāʿīl.

Balog (14, 1.51, ill.).

565. *Damascus 'the Guarded'—Date Missing*

Border on both sides, plain circle. Counterclockwise marginal legend on both sides:

(ضرب) بدمشق المحروسة	[Traces of legend]

Circle of dots on both sides.

Centre:	Centre:
الملك الصالح	بالله
نجم الدبن ابن الملك	الامام المستعصم
. . . (محمد) بن ايوب	امير المؤمنين

Traces of overstriking on the reverse. المحروسة is exceptional on the Ayyūbid coins; it appears more often on the Mamlūk coinage.

Ashmolean-Thorburn (23, 3.88, ill.).

566. *Ḥamāh—641 H*

Square of dots in a circle of dots.

Border Segments:	Border Segments:
ضرب بحماه | سنة احد | واربعين | (وستمائة)	(لا اله) | (الا الله) | محمد رسو | ل الله
Centre:	Centre:
الملك الصالح	الامام
نجم الدين ايوب	المستعصم
	بالله امير المؤمنين

ANS (18, —, ill.). Ashmolean-Institute of Archaeology, University of London (17, —, ill.). Balog (19, 1.92, ill.). Berlin (22, 1.92). Berlin-Guthrie (18, 2.74, ill.). BMC 431 (18, 1.62). Lavoix 663 (18, 2.10, ill.). Paris (19, —, ill.).

Mesopotamia

SILVER

567. *Ḥarrān—634 H*

Square-in-the-circle type.

Border Segments:	Border Segments:
ضرب بحران سنة | اربع و | ثلاثين | وستمائة	لا اله الا | الله وحده | لا شريك له | محمد رسول الله

Centre:	Centre:
الملك الصالح	الامام
نجم الدنيا والدين	المستنصر
ايوب بن محمد	بالله ابو جعفر
	المنصور امير المؤمنين

Yapı-Kredi (22, 2.75).

COPPER

568. *Āmid—636 H*

Border on both sides; plain circle in circle of pellets, within which is a six-pointed star with convex sides. In the segments between border and star:

لا اله | الا الله | محمد | رسو | ل ا | لله	ضرب | بامد | سنة | ستة | ثلثين | ستمائة
Centre:	Centre:
	م
الملك الصالح	الاما
ايوب بن محمد	المستنصر بالله
	امير المؤمنين

Arabesque floweret above obverse legend. Arabesque floweret in the reverse exergue.

Ashmolean-Thorburn (23, 4.07, ill.; 21, 3.19). Lavoix 664 (22, 3.22, ill.).

569. *Āmid—637 H*

As above, but the following date:

سنة | سبع | ثلثين | ستمائة

Yapı-Kredi (21, 4.70).

570. *[Āmid—63]8 H*

Six-pointed star with convex sides, within a plain circle on both sides.

Border Segments:	Border Segments:
ضرب | . . . | . . . | ثمان | . . . | . . .	. . . | الا | الله | محمد | . . . | . . .
Centre:	Centre:
	م
الملك الصالح	الاما
ايوب بن محمد	المسصر (*sic*) بالله
O	امير المؤمنين

The mint is off the flan and the decade of the date is not clear, but the general type, as well as the inscription, enable this coin to be assigned to the present series of Āmid issues.

Album (2 specimens).

571. *Āmid—Date Missing*

ANS (23, 3.80; 19, 2.42; 4 other specimens). ANS-Hisp. (21.5, 4.26). ANS-UM (23, 3.83). BMC 433a (22, 4.17, ill.). Fraehn, *Nova Suppl.*, p. 90. Yapı-Kredi (21, 3.50; 22 × 29, 4.55).

572. *Mint Missing—640 H*

Square-in-the-circle type; thin plain line in a line of dots.

Border Segments:

بسم الله|صرب . . .|سنة اربعين|وستمائة

Centre:

الملك الصالح
نجم الدنيا وا
لدين ايوب بن محمد

Border Segments:

لا اله الا|الله وحده|لا شريك له|محمد رسول الله

Centre:

الامام
المستنصر
بالله امير المؤمنين

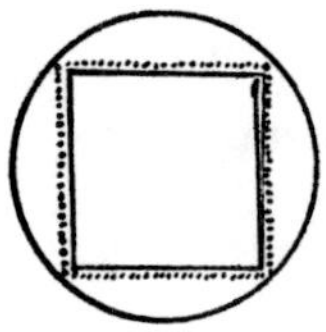

Balog (20, 2.70).

573. *Mint Missing—64x H*

Square of dots in a circle of dots.

Border Segments:

الملك لله|ضرب . . . .|. . . .|واربعين وستمائة

Centre:

الملك الصالح
نجم الدين
ايوب ابن (محمد)

Border Segments:

● لا اله الا ●|(الله وحده)|لا شريك له|محمد رسول الله

Centre:

الامام
المستعصم
بالله ابو احمد
امير المؤمنين

Ashmolean-Bodleian 154 (21, 2.86).

574. *Mint and Date Missing*

Border on both sides; circle of pellets.

Centre:

محمد
الملك الصالح
نجم الدين ايوب
بن

Centre:

. . . . .
المنصور . . .
امير المؤمنين

Ashmolean-Thorburn (18, 2.31; legends much effaced).

575. *Mint and Date Missing*

This coin is identical with the Ḥamāh *fulūs*, but the obverse segments are missing, the mint and date having been obliterated.

ANS (17, —).

AL-MU'AZZAM GHIYĀTH AL-DĪN TŪRĀNSHĀH IV IBN AL-ṢĀLIḤ AYYŪB

[His name, Tūrānshāh, is always written without the و and ا = ترنشاه]

Lord of Ḥiṣn-Kayfā and Āmid [636–647 H = 1238–1249 AD]

Sultan of the Empire [647—Muḥarram 648 H = 1249–1250 AD]

SILVER ONLY

Egypt

576. *Cairo—647 H* (?)

Globular dirhem. Border on both sides, plain circle. Counterclockwise marginal legend on both sides:

لا اله الا الله محمد رسول الله ارسله بالهدى	بسم الله ضرب بالقاهرة سنة (سبع واربعين وستمائة)

On both sides a plain circle.

Centre:	Centre:
الملك المعظم	الامام المستعصم

[*Naskh* Script]

Balog, *BIE* XXXV (1953), 1 (18 × 13, 2.73); 2 (13, 2.40); 3 (13 × 10, 1.77, ill.); 4 (12 × 10, 1.67), 5 (10, 0.73, ill.).

Syria

Normal-Size, Round-Flan Dirhems

577. *Damascus: 647 H*

Square-in-the-circle type.

Border Segments:	Border Segments:
ضرب بدمشق | سنة سبع | واربعين | وستمائة	لا اله الا الله | وحده | لا شريك له | محمد رسول الله الامام
Centre:	Centre:
الملك المعظم غياث الدنيا وا لدين ترنشاه بن ايوب	المستعصم بالله ابو احمد امير المؤمنين

Album 3. ANS (20, —). ANS-Newell (21, —). ANS-Starosselsky (21, —; 20, —).

Half Dirhem

578. *Damascus—647 H*

Square-in-the-circle type.

Border Segments:	Border Segments:
(ضرب بدمشق | سنة سبع) | اربعين | وستمائة	لا اله | الا الله | محمد رسو | ل الله
Centre:	Centre:
الملك المعظم	الامام المستعصم

ANS (14, 1.36). Balog (15, 1.51, ill.). Paris (12 × 18, 1.46, ill.).

579. *Damascus—648 H*

Square-in-the-circle type.

Border Segments:	Border Segments:
ضرب بد|مشق سنة|ثمان واربعين|وستمائة	لا اله الا|الله وحده|لا شر|يك له
Centre:	Centre:
السلطان الملك	لا اله الا الله
المعظم غياث	محمد رسول الله
الدين ترنشاه	الامام المستعصم
ابن ايوب بن محمد	بالله امير المؤمنين

Album. ANS (22, 2.91; 22, 2.02; 22, 2.74). ANS 71.76 (22, 2.98; 22.5, —). ANS-Newell (22, —; 22, —; 23, —; 22, —; 21, —; 21, —). ANS-Wood (21, —; 24, —). Ashmolean (22, —). Balog, *BIE* XXXV (1953), 1 (22, chipped, ill.); 2 (24, 2.73, ill.); 3 (22, 2.85, ill.); 4 (23, 2.68, ill.); 5 (23, 2.87); 6 (21, 2.90); 7 (22, 2.99, ill.); 8 (22, 2.90); *9 (22, 2.91); 10 (23, 2.73); 11 (23, 2.23); 12 (21, 2.78); 13 (22, 2.77); 14 (22, 2.77). BM (22, —). Leuthold-Ripostiglio 40 (22, 2.87). Yapı-Kredi (22, 2.95). (*Has reverse segments [لا اله الا\|الله وحده\|لا شريك له\|محمدرسول الله] Reverse die of No.549.

580. *Ḥamāh—647 H*

Square-in-the-circle type.

Border Segments:	Border Segments:
ضرب بحماه|سنة سبع|واربعين|وستمائة	لا اله الا الله|وحده|لا شريك له|محمد رسول الله
Centre:	Centre:
الملك المعظم	الامام
غياث الدنيا وا	المستعصم
لدين ترنشاه بن ايوب	بالله ابو احمد
	امير المؤمنين

ANS (21, —; date missing, but this is only a one-year issue). Ashmolean (21, —). Balog, *BIE* XXXV (1953), 1 (22, 2.95, ill.); 2 (21, 2.80); 3 (21, 2.81); 4 (21, 2.73); 5 (22, 2.41, ill.); 6 (22, 2.79); 7 (21, 2.81). München 92471 (20, 2.97; date missing, but belongs to this issue). Yapı-Kredi (20, 2.85).

PRINCIPALITY OF ALEPPO

AL-ẒĀHIR GHIYĀTH AL-DĪN GHĀZĪ IBN ṢALĀḤ AL-DĪN

[582–613 H = 1186–1216 AD]

Endowed with Aleppo in 579 H (1183 AD), but deprived of it soon after. Although he was installed by Saladin in Aleppo in 582 H (1186 AD), Saladin continued to issue coins there until his death; thus, al-Ẓāhir's first coinage dates only from 589 H.

SILVER

581. *Aleppo—589 H*

Diamond-in-the-circle type.

Border:
Circle of dots between two plain circles, within which is a similar circle with four loops pointing outwards. In the second circle a concave-sided diamond of the same composition, the points of which touch the border.

Border:
Circle of dots in which there is a concave-sided diamond of dots; the points touch the border. Between the two there is a circle of dots with four loops that also touch the border.

In the segments between border and the looped circle on both sides:

ضر | ب | بحلب | سنة | تسع | ثمنين | وخمس | مائة

لا ا | اله ا | الا ا | الله | محمد | رسو | ل ا | الله

The decade and digit of the date are difficult to read and there is some doubt about them.

Centre:
الملك
الظاهر بن
الملك النا
صر

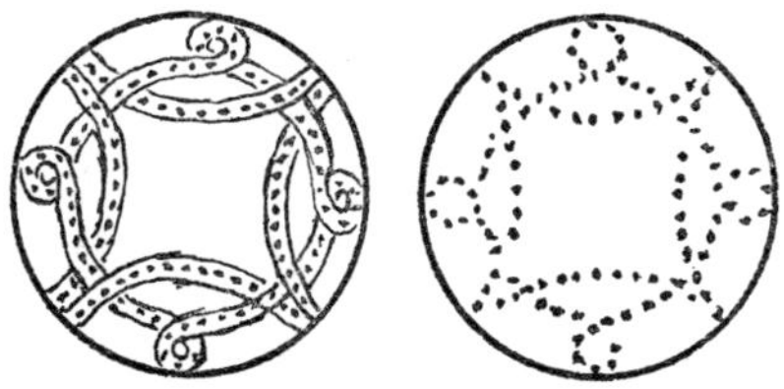

Centre:
الامام
الناصر
امير المؤ
منين

Kūfic script.

Berlin-Guthrie (23, 2.74, ill.). Yapı-Kredi (20, 2.95; 20, 2.90).

582. *Aleppo—589 H*

Six-pointed star type.

Border Segments:
ضرب | بحلب | سنة | تسع | وثمنين | وخمسائة ◦

Centre:
الملك
الظاهر غازى
الملك النا
صر

Border Segments:
لا اله | الا ا | الله | محمد | رسول | الله

Centre:
الامام
الناصر لدين
الله امير المؤ
منين

[Segments in *Kūfic*; centres in *Naskh* script]

ANS (21, 2.97). Berlin-Mordtmann 1933 (20, 2.89).

583. *Aleppo—590 H*

As above, but the following date and obverse centre legend:

سنة | تسعين | وخمس | مائة
غازي ظهر
الملك الظاهر
ابن الملك الناصر
يوسف

Album. BMC 300 (22, 3.00. ill.).

584. *Aleppo—591 H*

As above, but the following date:

سنة | احدى | تسعين | وخمسمائة

No floral ornament to left of غـازى on obverse centre. An *iḥmāl* [^v^] above al-Nāṣir on reverse of some specimens.

ANS (21, 2.979). BMC 301 (22, 3.00). Lavoix 510 (20, 2.80, ill.); 511 (20, 2.75). Lowick (20, 2.93). New York trade (20, 2.93). Paris (21, 2.92). Yapı-Kredi (21, 2.99).

Half Dirhem

585. *Aleppo—591 H*

Six-pointed star.

Obverse	Reverse
Border Segments:	Border Segments:
[Traces only]	ضر | ب | بحلب | سنة | احـ | د
Centre:	Centre:
الملك الظا	^v^
هر غازي	الامام
	الناصر

[Segments in *Kūfic*; centre in *Naskh* Script]

Probably 591 H, because on the 601 H half dirhem, the inscriptions are entirely in *Kūfic* script.

ANS (15, 1.337).

Aleppo—593 H

586. *Type A—No Overlord*

As No. 584, but the following date:

سنة | ثلث و | تسعين | وخمسمائة

ANS (20.5, 2.88). Artuk 761 (20, 2.80). BMC 301a (20, 2.74); 302a (19, 2.79); 302b (20, 2.85). Lavoix 512 (20, 2.95, ill.). Leuthold-Ripostiglio 1 (—, 2.95). Prague 913 (20, 3.00).

587. *Type B*

Overlord: al-ʿAzīz ʿUthmān

As above, but the reverse centre legend:

احمد

^v^

الامام الناصر

الملك العزيز

عثمن

ANS-Newell (20, 2.88). Lavoix 513 (20, 1.92, ill.). München 85361 (21, 2.996, ill.); 85036 (20, 3.01). Peus 1903.

On 27 Rabīʿ II 593 H, an agreement was reached in which al-Ẓāhir Ghāzī acknowledged al-ʿAzīz ʿUthmān as his overlord—a fact reflected on the Aleppo coinage. The 593 H and 594 H Aleppo dirhems bear al-ʿAzīz ʿUthmān's name. He died in Muḥarram 595 H.

Half Dirhem

588. *Type A—No Overlord*

Six-pointed star.

Border Segments:	Border Segments:
ضرب | بحلب | سنة | ثلث و | تسعين | وخمسمائة	لا اله | الا ا | لله | محمد | رسول | الله
Centre:	Centre:
⚜	⚜
الملك	الامام
الظاهر	الناصر
⚜	⚜

[Segments in *Kūfic*; centre in *Naskh* script]

Gautier (16, 1.51, ill.).

589. *Type B*

Overlord: al-ʿAzīz ʿUthmān

As above, but the obverse and reverse centre legends:

ɔc	صر
الملك الظاهر	الامام النا
ɔc	الملك العز
	يز

ANS-Hisp. (16, 1.453).

590. *Aleppo—594 H*

As No. 587, but the following date:

سنة \| اربع و \| تسعين \| وخمسمائة

[No ornament above الناصر on reverse]

Album 25 (2 specimens: one with date written تسعين و / خمسمائة). ANS (20, 2.978). ANS-UM (20, 2.847). Artuk 762 (21, 2.95, ill.). Ashmolean-Bodleian 137 (20, 2.75, ill.). Berlin-Gagarin 320/1885 (20, 2.84). Berlin-Sobernheim 474/1908 (20, 2.84). Berman 203 (20, 2.95; date missing). Lavoix 514 (20, 3.00). Lowick (20, 2.78). Leuthold-Ripostiglio 2 (—, 3.00). Paris (20, 2.93). Tewhid (20, —; 20, —). Yapı-Kredi (20, 2.98; 21, 2.95). Ziya 1664 (20, —; listed under al-ʿAzīz ʿUthmān).

Half Dirhem

591. *Aleppo—594 H*

All legends as above, except date is written:

(ضرب) \| (بحلب) \| اربع \| تسعين \| وخمس \| مائة

Ashmolean-Thorburn (16, 1.46, ill.)

Aleppo—595 H

592. *Type A—No Overlord*

As No. 587, but the following date and centre legends:

سنة \| خمس \| وتسعين \| وخمسمائة

Centre:	Centre:
غازي	المؤ
الملك الظاهر	الامام الناصر
غياث الدنيا و	لدين الله امير
الدين	منين

ANS (20.5, 2.64). Lowick (20, 2.86). Paris (20, 2.94, ill.). Zambaur-N.C. 509 (21. 2.97).

593. *Type B—No Overlord*

As above, but the obverse segments and centre legend:

ضرب | بحلب | سنة | خمس و | تسعين | خمسمائة

غا
الملك الظاهر غيا
ث الدنيا والدين
زي

Tewhid (21, 2.88).

594. *Type C—Overlord: al-ʿĀdil I*

As above, but the following obverse and reverse centre legends:

يوسف	احمد
الملك الظاهر	الامام الناصر
غيات الدين غازي	الملك العادل
ابن	ابو بكر

Lowick (20, 2.94, ill.; explaining al-Ẓāhir's recognition of al-ʿĀdil in terms of a pact contrived between the two rulers towards the end of 595 H.).

Aleppo—596 H

595. *Type A—Overlord: al-Afḍal ʿAlī*

As above, but the following date and centre legends:

سنة | ست و | تسعين | وخمسمائة

Centre:	Centre:
علي	المؤ
الملك الافضل	الامام الناصر
الملك الظاهر	لدين الله امير
غازي	منين

Artuk 758 (20, 2.80, ill.; date missing, but this is the year of the alliance between al-Ẓāhir and al-Afḍal against al-ʿĀdil). Lowick (19, 2.82, ill.; 19, 2.42). *Cf.* the coins of Ḥamāh struck in 595 and 596 H.

596. *Type B—Overlord: al-ʿĀdil I*

As above, but the following obverse and reverse centre legends:

الملك	الامام
الظاهر غازي	الناصر احمد
ابن يوسف بن	الملك العادل
ايوب	ابو بكر

Berlin 610/1909. Paris (20, 2.86).

Al-Afḍal was defeated by al-ʿĀdil in Rabīʿ II 596 H, and al-Ẓāhir was obliged to recognize his uncle as his overlord. Hence al-ʿĀdil's name on the present coin.

597. *Aleppo—597 H*

No Overlord

As No. 587, but the following date:

سنة | سبع | وتسعين | وخمسمائة

ANS-Artūqid hoard (several specimens). Berlin-Mordtmann (20, 2.98, ill.). Leuthold-Ripostiglio (3 —, 2.93). Lowick (21, 2.88). Paris (19, 2.96, ill.).

Aleppo—598 H

Overlord: al-ʿĀdil I

598. *Type A*

As above, but the following date and centre legends:

سنة | ثمان و | تسعين | وخمسمائة

Centre:	Centre:
الملك	الامام
الظاهر غازي	الناصر لدين
ابن يوسف بن	الملك العادل بن
ايوب	ايوب

ANS-UM (20, 2.875). Berlin-Guthrie (20, 2.87). Lavoix 516 (20, 3.00). Lowick (20, 2.83; 20, 2.94). München 85152 (20, 2.689, ill.). Paris (20, 2.93).

599. *Type B*

As above, but the reverse centre:

الامام
الناصر احمد
الملك العادل
ابو بكر

Album. ANS (20, —, ill.).

600. *Type C*

As above, but the following obverse and reverse centre legends:

يوسف	صر
الملك الظاهر	الامام النا
غياث الدين غازي	الملك العا
بن	دل
[Segments *Kūfic*; centre *Naskh*]	[Segments and centre *Naskh*]

ANS-Artuqid hoard (20, —).

601. *Aleppo—599 H*

As No. 599, but the following date:

سنة | تسع | وتسعين | وخمسمائة

[*Kūfic* Script]

Album. ANS (21, 2.92; 20, 2.88, ill.). ANS-Newman (20.5, —). Balog (20, 2.95). Berlin 805/1904 (20, 2.72). BMC 302 (20, 2.93). da Cunha 1464 (21, 2.83). Lavoix 517 (20, 2.80, ill.). Lowick (20, 2.85; 20, 2.85; 20, 2.97; 20, 2.97). Østrup 1602 (—, 2.91). Paris (19, 2.94). Yapı-Kredi (20, 2.98; 20, 2.88; 20, 2.90; 21, 2.90).

Half Dirhem

602. *Aleppo—599 H*

Six-pointed star.

Border Segments:

ضر | ب | بحلب | سنة | تسع | تسعين

Centre:

الملك

الظاهر

Border Segments:

لا اله | الا ا | لله | محمد | رسول | الله

Centre:

الامام

الناصر

[*Kūfic* Script]

Paris (15, 1.45).

603. *Aleppo—600 H*

As No. 599, but the following date:

فى | سنة | ست | مائة

Album. ANS 56.125 (20, 3.00). ANS 72.75 (20, —). ANS-Wood (20, 2.54). Artuk 763 (20, 3.00). Berman 204 (20, 2.96). BMC 303 (20, 2.95). Lavoix 515 (20, 2.90, ill.). Lowick (20, 2.89). Paris (20, 2.95, ill.; 20, 2.84). Tewhid (19, —, ill.; 20, —; 20, —). Yapı-Kredi (21, 2.95; 20, 2.95; 20, 2.93).

Half Dirhem

604. *Aleppo—600 H*

As No. 602, but the following date and reverse segments:

فى | سنة | ست | مائة

لا | اله | الا | ا | لله | محمد | رسول

München 85018 (10, 1.409, ill.). Tewhid (11, —).

605. *Aleppo—601 H*

As No. 599, but the following date:

سنة | احدى | وست | مائة

Album. ANS (20, 2.77). ANS 56.125 (20, 2.973). Berlin 1145/1902 (21, 2.93). BMC 304 (19, 2.17, ill.). Glidden (20, —). Tewhid (20, —; 20, —). Yapı-Kredi (19, 2.95; 19, 2.93).

Half Dirhem

606. *Aleppo—601 H*

As No. 602, but the following date:

سنة | احدى | وست | مائة

Artuk 764 (15, 1.50). Lavoix 518 (15, 1.45, ill.). Prague 914 (14, 1.40).

607. *Aleppo—602 H*

As No. 599, but the following date:

سنة | اثني | ست | مائة

Album. ANS (20.5, 2.97). Berlin 139/1904 (21, 2.76; digit of the date: اثنين). Paris (19. 2.96, ill.). Yapı-Kredi (19, 2.90).

Half Dirhem

608. *Aleppo—602 H*

As No. 602, but the following date:

سنة | اثنين | ست | مائة

Paris (14, 1.45, ill.).

609. *Aleppo—603 H*

As No. 599, but the following date:

سنة | ثلث و | ست | مائة

Lavoix 523 (19, 2.90). Paris (19, 2.93).

610. *Aleppo—604 H*

As above, but the following date:

سنة | اربع | وست | مائة

Album. BMC 305 (19, 2.99). Çetinyalçın (23, —). Khediv. 1436. Paris (19, 2.95).

Half Dirhem

611. *Aleppo—604 H*

As No. 602, but the following date.

سنة | اربع | وست | مائة

ANS 72.75 (14.5, 1.497). BMC 306 (17, 1.45, ill.). Khediv. 1437. Lavoix 519 (14, 1.45). Paris (16, 1.48).

612. *Aleppo—605 H*

As No. 599, but the following date:

سنة | خمس | ست | مائة

Ashmolean-Thorburn (20, 2.89, ill.; the date is written: خمس | وست | مائة). Balog (20, 2.38, ill.). BMC 307 (22, 2.41). Çetinyalçın (24, —). Markov, p. 358, No. 1. Weyl 6537. Yapı-Kredi (20, 2.70). Ziya 1646 (20, —).

613. *Aleppo—606 H*

As above, but the following date:

سنة | ستة | ست | مائة

ANS (20, 2.40). Çetinyalçın (24, —; 24, —).

Half Dirhem

614. *Aleppo—606 H*

As No. 602, but the following date:

سنة | ستة | ست | مائة

Ashmolean-Thorburn (13, 1.48, ill.).

615. *Aleppo—607 H*

As No. 599. but the following date:

سنة | سبع | وست | مائة

BMC 308 (20, 2.80). Lavoix 520 (18, 2.91; misread for 606 H.)

616. *Aleppo—608 H*

As above, but the following date:

سنة | ثمانة (*sic*) | وست | مائة

ANS 56.125 (20, 2.979, ill.). ANS 72.25 (20, —). BMC 309 (19, 2.29). Yapı-Kredi (21, 2.95; 21, 2.90).

Half Dirhem

Aleppo—608 H

617. *Type A—Overlord: al-ʿĀdil I*

As above, but the following date and reverse segments:

سنة | ثمان | وست | مائة   لا اله | الا ا | لله | محمد | رسو | ل الله

ANS 72.75 (15, —). Berlin-Guthrie (15, 1.41). BM (15, 1.43).

618. *Type B—No Overlord*

As No. 602, but the following date:

سنة | ثمان | وست | مائة

ANS 72.75 (15, 1.48). Lavoix 521 (15, 1.41, ill.).

619. *Aleppo—609 H*

As No. 599, but the following date:

سنة | تسع | وست | مائة

Ashmolean-A. C. Kay (22, 2.86). Balog (20, 2.70, ill.; 20, 2.96). BM-Sir R. Burn (20, 2.74, ill.). Nicol (18.8, 2.67; date written [*sic*]: مئه | ست | تسع و; pellets inside top and bottom points of star on both sides; ornament above الناصر and ايوب with two pellets beneath).

620. *Aleppo—610 H*

As above, but the following date:

سنة | عشر | وست | مائة

ANS (20.5, 2.977). ANS 72.75 (20, —). Berlin (20, 2.80). Berlin-Guthrie (19, 2.49; 20, 2.81). Çetinyalçın (20, —). Lavoix 522 (19, 2.98). Leuthold-Ripostiglio 4 (—, 2.72). Paris (20, 2.94). Yapı-Kredi (19, 2.85; 20, 2.70).

Half Dirhem

621. *Aleppo—610 H*

Six-pointed star.

Border Segments:	Border Segments:
ضر | ب | بحلب | سنة | عشر | (ستمائة)	لا اله | الا ا | لله | محمد رسول | الله
Centre:	Centre:
الملك	الامام
الظاهر	الناصر

[*Kūfic* Script]

Album. ANS-Laties (several specimens).

622. *Aleppo—611 H*

As No. 599. but the following date:

سنة | احدى | عشر و | ستمائة

Album (2 specimens; one has date written: سنة ا | حد عشر | ستمائة). Markov, p. 358, No. 2. Yapı-Kredi (22, 2.85). Ziya 1647 (21, —).

Aleppo—612 H

623. *Type A*

As above, but the following obverse segments:

ماية ضرب | بحلب | سنة | اثنين و | عشر | وست

Note that the century ends in the upper right segment in which the mint and date formula begins: مائة ضرب.

Berlin-Guthrie (20, 2.60; 20, 2.79). Yapı-Kredi (19, 2.95; 19, 2.80). Ziya 1648 (20, —).

624. *Type B*

As above, but the following mint and date formula:

ضرب | بحلب | سنة ا | ثنين عشر | ست | مائة

ANS-Laties (20, —).

Half Dirhem

625. *Aleppo—612 H*

As No. 602, but the following date:

سنة | اثنين | عشر | ستمائة

Yapı-Kredi (15, 1.42).

Aleppo—613 H

626. *Type A*

As No. 599, but the following date:

سنة | ثلث | عشر و | ستمائة

ANS (20, 2.88). BMC 310 (19, 2.83). da Cunha 1466 (21, 3.16; attributed to Damascus, which must be an error). Lavoix 524 (20, 2.85). Lowick (20, —). Paris (20, 2.74).

627. *Type B*

As above, but the date is written:

سنة | ثلث عشر | ست | مائة

Album. ANS 72.75 (20, 2.94). ANS-Artūqid hoard; (several specimens). ANS-Newman (20.5, —, ill.).

Half Dirhem

628. *Aleppo—613 H*

As No. 602, but the following date:

سنة | ثلث | عشر و | ستمائة

Yapı-Kredi (15, 1.45).

AL-ẒĀHIR GHĀZĪ'S POSTHUMOUS SILVER COINAGE

al-Ẓāhir Ghāzī died in 613 H and the Council of Regency constituted to govern for his young son, al-ʿAzīz Muḥammad, started to strike silver in his name as early as 614 H. In fact, al-ʿAzīz Muḥammad's silver coinage was issued regularly throughout his reign until his death in 634 H. Although there are a few years for which no specimens are known, it is probable that they will turn up in the future. Therefore, it is surprising that there exist dirhems with al-Ẓāhir Ghāzī's protocol bearing dates after his death. Indeed, they range from 614 H to 629 H, with only the year 626 H missing from the series, and seem to have been struck concurrently with al-ʿAzīz Muḥammad's Aleppo dirhems.

These posthumous dirhems seem perfectly genuine, except for several anachronisms: the prince died in 613 H. Although Caliph al-Nāṣir died in 622 H, his name continues to appear on all the issues between 622 and 630 H. Moreover, Aleppo's overlord, al-ʿĀdil I, who died in 615 H, has his name displayed also on the dirhems to the end of the posthumous series. In other words, the type had become immobilised with only the date varying. Even the style of the *Kūfic* writing remains the same.

It is impossible to assume that the posthumous dirhems are genuine issues of the Aleppo mint, struck at the official mint, to circulate simultaneously with the ruling prince's (a-lʿAzīz Muḥammad) coins. There seems to be one likely explanation; namely, that the Crusader mint on the Syrian coast, which later issued the already-known imitations of al-Ṣāliḥ Ismāʿīl's Damascus dirhems, indulged, at this early period, in the imitation of the highly regarded silver coinage of the Aleppo mint. It is very improbable that the striking of the counterfeit coinage started earlier than 614 H when al-Ẓāhir Ghāzī was still on the throne. Once the imitations had begun to be issued, the political changes may have escaped the attention of the Crusader mint personnel.

Dr. Michael Bates has given his attention to this problem and has linked the end of the posthumous Aleppo coinage of al-Ẓāhir Ghāzī in 638 H with the appearance of huge quantities of Crusader imitation dirhems of al-Ṣāliḥ Ismāʿīl of Damascus (*Studies in Honor George C. Miles*, Beirut, 1974).

Note that the overlord is always al-ʿĀdil I, the caliph is always al-Nāṣir, and that all the coins are of the six-pointed star type.

629. *Aleppo—614 H*

Border Segments	Border Segments:
ضرب | بحلب | سنة ار | بع عشر | وست | مائة	لا اله | الا ا | لله | محمد | رسول | الله
Centre:	Centre:
الملك	الامام
الظاهر غازي	الناصر احمد
ابن يوسف بن	الملك العادل
ايوب	ابو بكر

[Ornate *Kūfic* on this and all following issues]

Album. ANS 72.75 (21, 2.90). ANS-Artuqid hoard, 310–317. Balog (20, 2.92; 20, 2.97; 20, 2.90; 20, 2.91). Damascus A. 2394 (and 3 other specimens). Lavoix 525 (25, 2.80). Paris (19, 2.67). Peus 1904. Prague 913a (20, 2.50). Tewhid (19, —). Yapı-Kredi (19, 2.78; 20, 2.75; 19, 2.55). Ziya 1649 (19, —).

Half Dirhem

630. *Aleppo—614 H*

Border Segments:	Border Segments:
ضرب | بحلب | سنة | اربع | عشر و | ستمائة	. . . | . . . | الا ا | لله | محمد | رسول
Centre:	Centre:
الملك	الامام
الظاهر	الناصر

ANS-Laties (16, —).

631. *Aleppo—615 H*

As No. 599. but the following date:

سنة \| خمس عشر \| ستمائة

Album. ANS-Artuqid hoard, 328–361. ANS-Newell (20, 2.78; 20, 2.91). Balog (20, 2.90, Ill.). Berman 207 (21, 2.97). BMC 310* (20, 2.61). Castiglioni, CLXXXV, Tav. XI, No. 8. Yapı-Kredi (18, 2.70). Ziya 1650 (20, —).

Half Dirhem

632. *Aleppo—615 H*

As No. 602. but the following date:

سنة \| خمس \| عشر \| ستمائة

ANS-Laties (15, —).

633. *Aleppo—616 H*

As No. 599, but the following date:

سنة | ستة | عشر | ستمائة

Album (digit of date: ست). ANS 72.75 (20, 2.893). ANS-Artuqid hoard, 362–393 (date: ست | عشر | ستاة). ANS-Laties (20, —). ANS-Newell (20.5, 2.88; 21, 2.815). ANS-Newman (20, —; digit of date: ست). Damascus 18154 (21, 2.90; 18155 (21, 2.75); 2399 (20, —); different small varieties. Ziya 1651 (19, —); 1652 (20, —).

634. *Aleppo—617 H*

As above, but the following date:

سنة | سبع | عشر | ستمائة

ANS-Artuqid hoard, 394–412. Damascus A. 2400 (20.5, —).

Half Dirhem

635. *Aleppo—617 H*

As No. 602, but the following date:

سنة | سبع | عشر | ستمائة

Yapı-Kredi (15, 1.35).

636. *Aleppo—618 H*

As No. 599, but the following date:

سنة | ثمان | عشر | ستمائة

ANS 56.125 (22.5, 2.86; 22.5, 2.91). ANS-Laties (21, —; date: سنة ثما | ن عشر | وست | مائة). BMC 310b (22, 2.82). Damascus A. 18156–18158 (23, 2.82; 22, 2.80; 22, 2.89). Ilisch 55 (listed as a dirhem, but no weight given: 14, —). Leuthold-Ripostiglio 5 (—, 2.87); 6 (—, 2.87). Zambaur, *N.C.*, 510 (20, 2.84). Ziya 1253 (21, —).

637. *Aleppo—619 H*

As above, but the following date:

سنة | تسع و | عشر | ستمائة

Album (date written: تسع | عشر و | . . .). ANS (21, 2.61, ill.). ANS 72.75 (19, 2.97). BM-Sir R. Burn (20, 2.78). Damascus A. 10043 (21, —). Yapı-Kredi (22, 2.65).

Half Dirhem

638. *Aleppo—619 H*

As No. 602, but the following date:

سنة | تسع | عشر | ستمائة

Çetinyalçın (14, —).

639. *Aleppo—620 H*

As No. 599, but the following date:

سنة | عشر | ين و | ستمائة

ANS (21.5, 2.865; 21, 2.79; 21, 2.77; 21.5, 2.37; date: عشرين). BMC 310c (21, 2.83). Damascus A. 18162 (5 specimens). Wien 665 (21, —). Ziya 1654 (20, —).

Half Dirhem

640. *Aleppo—620 H*

As No. 602, but the following date:

سنة|عشر|ين و|ستمائة

ANS-Laties (15, —). Ziya 1655 (14, —).

641. *Aleppo—621 H*

As No. 599, but the following date:

سنة احد|وعشرين|وست|مائة

ANS-Artuqid hoard, 582–584, 602, ANS-Newell (21, 2.925, ill.). ANS-Wright (20, 2.76). Yapı-Kredi (20, 2.73). Ziya 1656 (16, —).

642. *Aleppo—622 H*

As No. 599, but the following date:

سنة|اثنين و|عشرين|ستمائة

Album (date: سنة ا|ثنين). ANS 72.75 (20.5, 2.863; digit of the date: سنة ا|ثنين; 4 other specimens). ANS-Newell (19.5, 2.822). Damascus A. 2406, 13365 (20, 2.83); 2409 (date: ثنتي).

Half Dirhem

643. *Aleppo—622 H*

As No. 602, but the following date:

سنة |اثنين و|عشرين|ستمائة

Pellet above and beneath the obverse and reverse central legends:

●	●
الملك	الامام
الظاهر	الناصر
●	●

Album. ANS-Laties (15, —, ill.).

644. *Aleppo—623 H*

As No. 599, but the following date:

سنة|ثلاث|عشرين|ستمائة

ANS-Newell (21, 2.965; 2 other specimens). ANS-Wright (21, 2.81).

645. *Aleppo—624 H*

As above, but the following date:

سنة ار|بع عشر|ين ست|مائة

ANS (20, 2.87). ANS 72.75 (20.5, 2.85). ANS-Artuqid hoard, 722–793 (date divided in several ways). Balog (21, 2.97, ill.).

646. *Aleppo—625 H*

As above, but the following date:

سنة | خمس | عشرين | ستمائة

ANS-Artuqid hoard, 794–850 (date written in several ways). Yapı-Kredi (20, 2.75).

Half Dirhem

647. *Aleppo—625 H*

As No. 602, but the following date:

سنة | خمس | عشرين | ستمائة

ANS-Laties (15, —).

Aleppo—627 H

648. *Type A*

As No. 599, but the following date:

سنة | سبع | عشرين | ستمائة

ANS (20, 2.89). ANS-Artuqid hoard, 899–913. Damascus A. 2843.

649. *Type B*

As above, but the date is written:

سنة سبع | عشرين | ست | مائة

ANS 72.75 (20, 2.89, ill.). ANS-Artuqid hoard, 897–898. Damascus A. 13354 (20, 2.72).

Half Dirhem

650. *Aleppo—627 H*

As No. 602, but the following date:

سنة | سبع | عشرين | ستمائة

ANS-Laties (17, —).

651. *Aleppo—628 H*

As No. 599. but the following date:

سنة | ثمان | عشرين | ستمائة

Album (date written: سنة/ ثمانة/وعشرين). ANS-Artuqid hoard, 914–915 (date written: سنة / عمانة (*sic*) عشرين). Zambaur, *N.C.*, 511 (23, 2.78).

652. *Aleppo—629 H*

As above, but the following date:

سنة | تسع | عشرين | ستمائة

ANS 71.76 (63 specimens). Damascus A. 2407, 18160 (20, 3.02). Wien 664 (20, 2.63).

653. *Aleppo—630 H*

As above, but the following date:

Type A: سنة | ثلثين | ست | مائة

Type B: سنة | ثلاثين | ست | مائة

ANS 71.76 (hoard contains specimens with dates written two ways).

654. *Aleppo—638 H*

As above, but the following date:

سنة | ثمان | ثلثين | ستمائة

ANS 71.76 (21, —, ill.; 6 other specimens). Damascus 18164 (22, 2.68).

655. *Ḥamāh—595 H*

Overlord: al-Afḍal ʻAlī

Square-in-the-circle type.

Border Segments:

(ضرب بحماه) | سنة خمس | (تسعين و) | (خمسمائة)

Centre:

الملك الافضل
علي الملك ا
لظاهر غازي

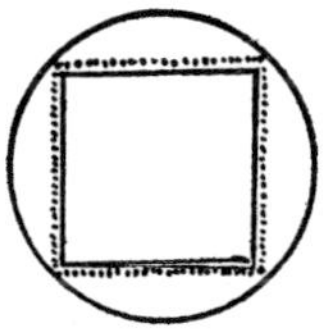

Border Segments:

لا اله | الا الله | وحده محمد | رسول الله

Centre:

الامام الناصر
لدين الله
امير المؤمنين

[*Naskh* Script]

Although the mint is missing on this, it should be attributed to Ḥamāh, being the only square-in-the-circle issue bearing the names of al-Afḍal and al-Ẓāhir.

Artuk 757 (21, 2.80, ill.).

656. *Ḥamāh—596 H*

As above, but the following obverse and reverse segments:

ضرب بحماه | سنة ست | تسعين و | ستمائة

لا اله الا | الله وحده | محمد رسو | ل الله

Leuthold-Ripostiglio 20 (20, 2.76, ill.).

By 592 H al-Afḍal had been stripped of all his possessions and, as compensation, received the unimportant town of Sarkhad. However, when al-ʻAzīz ʻUthmān died in Cairo in 595 H in a riding accident, al-Afḍal was elected to be the *atabek* of the young al-Manṣūr Muḥammad of Egypt. The Syrian princes were well-aware of their uncle al-ʻĀdil's ambition to become lord of all the Ayyūbid dominions, and regarded this as a direct threat to their own position. Therefore al-Ẓāhir Ghāzī of Aleppo supported his brother, al-Afḍal, in the struggle against al-ʻĀdil.

Although Ḥamāh was an independent principality within the empire, its ruler has a limited right of *sikkah*, which entitled him to issue copper only. A close ally of al-ʻĀdil, Ḥamāh's ruler al-Mansūr Muhammad I nevertheless produced an ephemeral silver coinage at his capital during the troubles of 595 to 596 H, of which nos. 655 and 656 above are examples. As al-Manṣūr Muḥammad was not entitled to put his name on the silver coins, they name only his temporary ally and protector, al-Ẓāhir Ghāzī, and his overlord, al Afḍal ʻAlī.

The appearance of al-Afḍal's name on the silver coins of Ḥamāh, dated 595 and 596 H, agrees with the inscriptions on the Aleppo dirhems of the same two years, as one would expect.

657. *Manbij—597 H*

Six-pointed star.

Border Segments:

ضرب | بمنبج | سنة | سبع | تسعين و | خمسمائة

Centre:

علي
الملك الافضل
الملك الظاهر
غازي

Border Segments:

لا | اله | الا ا | لله | محمد | رسو

Centre:

المؤ
الامام الناصر
لدين الله امير
منين

Broome (21, 2.88, ill.).

COPPER

Aleppo—589 H

658. *Type A*

Border on both sides: circle of dots between two plain circles.

Centre:

تسع ثمنين
الملك الظاهر
خمس مائة

Centre:

بحلب سنة
بن الملك الناصر
ضر ب

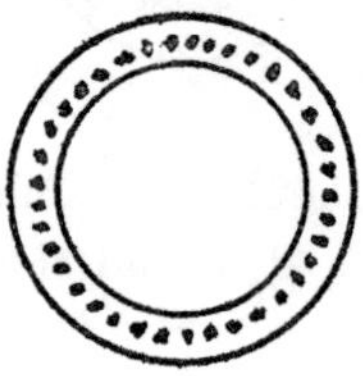

[Ornate *Kūfic* Script]

Lavoix 530 (23, 3.30); 531 (23, 2.45, ill.).

659. *Type B*

Border on both sides: circle of dots between two plain circles.

Centre:

تسع ثمنين
الملك الظاهر
خمس مائة

Centre:

ضر ب
بن الملك الناصر
بحلب سنة

[Ornate *Kūfic* script]

Album (2 specimens). BM-Amedroz (20, 4.47). BMC 311 (20, 4.48, ill.). München 86172 (20, 2.576). Paris (21, 3.94).

660. *Type C*

Border on both sides: circle of dots between two plain circles.

Centre:

ضر ب
الملك الظاهر
بحلب سنة

Centre:

تسع وثما
الامام الناصر
نين خمسمائة

[Ornate *Kūfic* script]

Ashmolean-Thorburn (24, 5.27). Berlin (21, 3.40; 21, 3.44). BM-Amedroz (21, —). BMC 311a (24, 4.30). Paris (22, 3.39, ill.).

661. *Type D*

Border on both sides: circle of dots between two plain circles.

Centre:

ضر ب

الملك الظاهر

بحلب سنة

Centre:

تسع ثما (نين)

الامام الناصر

وخمس مائة

[Ornate *Kūfic* script]

Album (2 specimens). ANS-Wright (23, 4.857, ill.).

662. *Type E*

Border on both sides: circle of dots between two plain circles.

Centre:

تسعين وخمس

الملك الظاهر

. . . .

Centre:

. . . .

بن الملك النا. .

بحلب سنة

Album.

663. *Aleppo—59x H*

Border on both sides: circle of dots between two plain circles.

Centre (Type C):

ضر ب

الملك الظاهر

بحلب سنة

Centre:

. . . . تسعين

الامام الناصر

وخمس مائة

[Ornate *Kūfic* script]

BMC 312 (23, 4.21).

664. *Aleppo—596 H*

Ornamented square in the circle. Border on both sides: plain circle. On both sides: dotted square, with a floweret in the centre of each side. Counterclockwise legends on both sides:

Obverse:

ضر ب|سـ نة|ـ تة|و تسـ

Centre:

الملك

الظاهر

غازي

Reverse:

بحـ لب|عين و|خمـ سـ|ما ئة

Centre:

الامام ا

لناصرامير

المؤمنين

[*Kūfic* in segments; *Naskh* in centres]

BMC 320 (22, 2.96, ill.).

665. *Aleppo—597 H*

As above, but the following date in the obverse and reverse segments:

ضرب|بحلب|سنة|سبع وتسعين|وخمس|مائة

Album. BM-Amedroz (21, —). Lavoix 532 (24, 3.54, ill.). München 85714 (22, 3.116; the *ālif* of al-Ẓāhir in the obverse centre has been transferred to the end of the first line: الملك ا.

لظاهر
غازي

Aleppo—598 H

666. *Type A*

As above, but the following date in the obverse and reverse segments:

ضرب|بحلب|سنة|ثمان وتسعين|وخمس|مائة

Album. Ashmolean-Corpus Christi (21, 3.10). Berlin-Guthrie (26, 3.04). Lagumina, p. 71, No. 17 (20, 3.04). Lavoix 533 (21, 3.27, ill.). Paris (22, 3.72; 22, 3.18).

667. *Type B*

As above, but the reverse centre inscription:

الامام
الناصر

Album.

Aleppo—599 H

668. *Type A*

As above, but the following border segments and centre legends:

ضرب|بحلب|سنة|تسع وتسعين|وخمس|مائة

Centre:

الملك
الظاهر

Centre:

الامام
الناصر

[All inscriptions in *Kūfic*]

ANS (23, 4.86). Ashmolean-A. C. Kay (23, 3.31, ill.). Paris (24, 3.78).

669. *Type B*

As above, but the following segments and centre legends:

ضرب|. . .|سنة|تسع ضرب|بحلب|سنة|تس . .

Centre:

الملك ا
لناصر
غازي

Centre:

الامام
الناصر امير
المؤمنين

[Note that segmented legends are *identical*]

Album.

670. *Aleppo—603 H*

Eight-pointed star type. Border of pellets on both sides, within which is an eight-pointed dotted star in a similar linear star. Counterclockwise legends in the segments:

ضر | ب | بحلا | ب | سنة | ثلث | وستة | مائة	لا | اله | الا | الله | محمد | رسو | ل | الله
Centre:	Centre:
الملك	الامام
الظاهر	الناصر

[Segments in *Kūfic*; centre in *Naskh*]

BMC 313 (23, 3.94); 313a (22, 4.16, ill.). Glidden. Lavoix 541 (20, 4.40, ill.). Weyl 6536 (21, —).

671. *Aleppo—604 H*

As above, but the following date:

سنة | اربع | وست | مائة

ANS (25, 4.04; 25, 4.04; 25, —). Yapı-Kredi (21, 3.90).

672. *Aleppo—605 H*

As above, but the following date:

سنة | خمس | وست | مائة

Album. BMC 314 (22, 4.26). Ilisch 47 (24, —). Lavoix 542 (20, 4.14). Paris (20, 2.63). Prague 61/66–3. Yapı-Kredi (22, 3.90; 24, 3.90).

673. *Aleppo—606 H*

As above, but the following date:

سنة | ست | وست | مائة

Album (2 specimens). ANS (24, 4.13; 23.5, 3.88). ANS-UM (23, 3.62). ANS-Wood (23, 4.14). ANS-Wright (22, 3.724). Lagumina, p. 73, No. 21 (21, 3.51). Østrup 1606.

674. *Aleppo—607 H*

As above, but the following date:

سنة | سبع | وست | مائة

Ashmolean-Christ Church 235. BMC 313a (22, —); 314a (23, 3.74). Miles-Antioch 159. Tewhid (24, —; 24, —).

675. *Aleppo—608 H*

As above, but the following date:

سنة | ثمان | وست | مائة

Album. ANS (23, 3.68). ANS-Wood (23.5, 3.97). Ashmolean-Thorburn (25, 3.10). BM-Clemenger (24, 3.93). Ilisch 48 (23, —). Lavoix 543 (23, 4.40); 544 (22, 3.95). Paris (23, 4.17; 23, 4.13, ill.; 23, 3.79). Østrup 1607. Soret à Dorn, 70.

676. *Aleppo—609 H*

As above, but the following date:

سنة | تسع | وست | مائة

Album. ANS (22, 3.72). BM (21, 3.87). Lavoix 545 (21, 3.75). Paris (24, 3.46; 20, 3.16). Prague 61/66–2.

677. *Aleppo—610 H*

As above, but the following date:

سنة | عشر | وست | مائة

Album. Ashmolean-A. C. Kay (22, —). Ilisch 49 (21, —); 50 (24, —); 54 (22, —; brockage). Lavoix 546 (23, 5.45); 547 (22, 4.20, ill.). Paris (24, —; 23, —; 23, —). München 85962 (23, 3.734). Østrup 1608 and 1609. Soret à Dorn, 71.

678. *Aleppo—611 H*

As above, but the following date:

ضر | ب | بحلب | سنة | احدى | عشر | وست | مائة

ANS (23, 4.05, ill.). Fraehn, *Nova Suppl.*, p. 91, No. 2a. München 85961 (23, 3.694). Paris (21, 6.38). Soret à Dorn, 72.

679. *Aleppo—612 H*

As above, but the following date:

سنة | اثني | عشر | وست | مائة

Album. Balog (23, 3.65, ill.; 24, 3.95). BMC 315 (23, 3.76; the date is written: سنة | اثنتاه | عشرة | ست | مائة); 316 (24, 4.32; the date is written: سنة | اثنتي | عشرة | ست | مائة). Paris (24, 4.30). Yapı-Kredi (22, 3.32).

680. *Aleppo—Date Missing*

As above, but the date is not present.

Balog (22, 3.34; 21, 3.06). BM-Amedroz (21, —). BMC 317 (23, 3.66); 318 (23, 2.80); 319 (22, 3.42); 320 (22, 2.96). Castiglioni, CLXXXIV. Khediv. 1444–1447. Lagumina, p. 70, Nos. 14–16. Lavoix 535, 538–540. Miles-Antioch 158. Østrup 1611 and 1612.

681. *Aleppo—Date Missing*

Six-pointed star type, similar to the dirhem. Star of dots between two plain lines.

Border Segments:

ضرب | (بحلب) | (سنة) | ... | ... | ...

Centre:

غا
الملك الظاهر غيا
ث الدنيا والدين
ز ي

Border Segments:

لا اله | الا ا | لله | (محمد) | (رسول) | (الله)

Centre:

المؤ
الامام الناصر
لدين الله امير
منين

Østrup 1605 (20, 2.52; it may be a dirhem encrusted with copper).

682. *Aleppo—603 H*

Six-pointed star.

Border Segments:

ضرب | . . . . | س | بحلب | سنة | ثلث

Centre:

الملك

الظاهر

Border Segments:

لا اله | الا | الله | محمد رسول | الله

Centre:

الامام

الناصر

Fraehn, *Nova Supp.*, p. 91, No. 2bb.

Fraehn's reading of the obverse segments is somewhat doubtful. It should be: ضرب | بحلب | سنة | ثلث | وست | مائة.

683. *Aleppo—605 H*

As above, but the following obverse border segments:

ضرب | . . | . . | خمس و | ست | مائة

Annulet above and beneath reverse centre.

Berman 206 (23, 4.67).

684. *[Aleppo]—xx5 H*

Six-pointed star.

Border Segments:

ضرب | بحلب | سنة | خمس | . . . | . . .

Centre:

الملك

الظاهر غازي

ابن يوسف بن

ايوب

Border Segments:

لا اله | الا ا | الله | محمد رسول | الله

Centre:

الامام

الناصر احمد

الملك العادل

ابو بكر

Fraehn, *Nova Suppl.*, p. 91, No. b–2.

Both coins Nos. 681 (described by Østrup), and 684 (published in Fraehn), may be silver dirhems encrusted with copper from their long stay in the soil. Østrup's coin has the weight of the dirhem rather than the usually heavier copper *fals*. Fraehn's coin (no weight given), with the digit five cannot be earlier than 615 H, because of al-ʿĀdil's name as overlord on the coin, and no posthumous copper of al-Ẓāhir is known. Furthermore, the legends are indentical with the silver issue of 615 H. (*Catalogue* No. 633).

685. *Ḥamāh 589 H*

Border on both sides: circle of dots between two plain circles.

Centre:

ضر ب

الملك الظاهر

بحما ه (سنة)

Centre:

تسع ثما

الامام الناصر

نين خمسمائة

[Ornate *Kūfic* script]

BM-Amedroz (21, 3.37, ill.).

This coin may confirm Bahā' al-Dīn's statement (Ed. Schultens, Leyde, 1755, in de Saulcy, 'Lettre à M. Reynaud,' *JA*, April 1842) that on the 1st of Rabīʿ II 588 H, Saladin deprived his great-nephew, al-Manṣūr Muḥammad I of Ḥamāh, of all his domains and instructed his two sons, al-Afḍal and al-Ẓāhir Ghāzī, to seize possessions of al-Manṣūr. Saladin's anger had been aroused by al-Manṣūr's ill-advised behaviour. In fact, the present *fals* struck in al-Ẓāhir's name, without that of al-Manṣūr, would be numismatic evidence of al-Ẓāhir Ghāzī's temporary occupation of Ḥamāh.

AL-ʿAZĪZ GHIYĀTH AL-DĪN ABŪ AL-MUẒAFFAR MUḤAMMAD IBN AL-GHĀZĪ

Prince of Aleppo [613–634 H = 1216–1236 AD]

All silver coins of this prince are of the *six-pointed star* type, and all were struck in Aleppo. The segments are always in *Kūfic*; the centres in *Naskh*.

686. *Aleppo—614 H*

Overlord: al-ʿĀdil I

Border Segments:
ضرب | بحلب | سنة | اربع | عشر و | ستمائة
Centre:
محمد
الملك العزيز
ابن غازي بن
يوسف

Border Segments:
لا اله | الا ا | لله | محمد | رسول | الله
Centre:
احمد
الامام الناصر
الملك العادل
ابو بكر

ANS-Newell (20. 5, 2.99, ill.). ANS-Wood (20.5, 2.889). Artuk 766 (20, 2.75). BMC 323 (20, 2.98). Khediv. 1450.

Aleppo—615 H

687. *Type A*

As above, but the following date:

سنة | خمسة | عشر | ستمائة

ANS-Laties (several specimens). Ashmolean-Thorburn (21, 2.91, ill.). Berman 207 (21, 2.97).

688. *Type B*

As above, but the digit of the date is written: خامس.

Album. ANS-Laties. Nicol (20.5, 2.85). Yapı-Kredi (21, 2.95).

Half Dirhem

689. *Aleppo—615 H*

No Overlord

Border Segments:
ضرب | بحلب | سنة | خامس (*sic*) | عشر و | ستمائة

Border Segments:
لا اله | الا ا | لله | محمد | رسول | الله

Centre:

الملك

العزيز

Centre:

الامام

الناصر

ANS-Laties (15, 1.43; 15, 1.44). BMC 324 (15, 1.49; date missing, but the same legends). New York trade (15, 1.42).

Aleppo—616 H

690. *Overlord: al-Kāmil I*

Border Segments:

ضرب | بحلب | سنة | ست | عشر و | ستمائة

Centre:

محمد

الملك العزيز

ابن غازي بن

يوسف

Border Segments:

لا اله | الا ا | لله | محمد | رسول | الله

Centre:

احمد

الامام الناصر

الملك الكامل

محمد

Khediv. 1451.

Aleppo—617 or 619 H

691. *Type A*

As above, but the following date and obverse centre legend:

ضرب | بحلب | سنة | سبع | عشر و | ستمائة

Centre:

محمد

الملك العزيز

ابن الملك الظاهر

غازي

Album. ANS 72.75 (19, 2.99). ANS-Laties. Artuk 767 (20, 2.95). Berlin-Gagarine 320/1885 (21, 2.96). Dorn, p. 71, No. 6. Tiesenhausen, *RNB* (1875), p. 370, No. 164.

692. *Type B*

As above, but the reverse segments and the obverse and reverse centre legends are:

محمد

الملك الكامل

الملك العزيز محمد

ابن الملك الظاهر

غازي

احمد

الامام الناصر

ولى عهده ابو نصر

محمد عدة الدنيا و

الدين

Balog (21, 3.00, ill.).

On both of the above types the digit of the date may be either سبع or تسع.

693. *Aleppo—619 H*

As No. 691, but the following date:

ضرب | بحلب | سنة | تسع | عشر و | ستمائة

ANS (19, 2.99, ill.). BMC 325 (20, 2.95). Miles-Antioch 161.

The digit of the date may be either سبع or تسع, since the teeth of the first two letters are uniform.

694. *Aleppo—623 H*

As above, but the following date and reverse centre:

سنة | ثلاث | عشرين | ستمائة

ابو جعفر
بالله
الامام المستنصر
الملك الكامل
محمد

Lavoix 553 (21, 3.00, ill.). Yapı-Kredi (21, 2.90; digit of date: ثلث).

695. *Aleppo—624 H*

As above, but the following date:

سنة | اربع | عشرين | ستمائة

Berman 208 (21, 2.96). Østrup 1613 (—, 2.90).

Aleppo—625 H

696. *Type A*

As above, but the following date:

سنة | خمس و | عشرين | وستمائة

ANS-Laties (21, —; 20, —).

697. *Type B*

Border Segments:

ضرب | بحلب | سنة | خمس | عشرين | ستمائة

Centre:

محمد
الملك الكامل
الملك الناصر
ايوب

Border Segments:

لا اله | الا ا | لله | محمد | (رسول | الله)

Centre:

الامام
المستنصر
بالله امير المؤ
منين

Nicol (20.8, 2.98).

Half Dirhem

698. *Aleppo—625 H*

As No. 694, but the following date and reverse centre:

ضرب | حلب | سنة خمس و | عشرين | ستمائة

○
الامام
المستنصر
○

[Annulets in place of ornaments on both obverse and reverse]

Album.

699. *Aleppo—626 H*

As No. 698, but the following date:

سنة | ستة | عشرين | ستمائة

ANS-Laties (several specimens; date written: سنة | ست | عشرين). Berlin 611/1909 (21, 2.94).

700. *Aleppo—627 H*

As above, but the following date:

سنة | سبع | عشرين | ستمائة

ANS-Laties (several specimens). Yapi-Kredi (20, 2.95).

701. *Aleppo—628 H*

As above, but the following date:

سنة | ثمان | عشرين | وستمائة

Album 26. München 85293 (19, 2.412).

702. *Aleppo—630 H*

As above, but the following date:

فى | سنة | ثلثين | وستمائة

ANS (21.5, 2.948, ill.). ANS 72.75 (21, 2.975, ill.). ANS-Laties.

Half Dirhem

703. *Aleppo—630 H*

As No. 698, but the following date:

ضرب | بحلب | سنة | (ثلثين) | ست | مائة

Lavoix 554 (16, 1.40, ill.). The decade has been rendered illegible by a hole, but in the segment between سنة and ستمائة, there is only space for one word, and this should be: ثلثين (30).

704. *Aleppo—631 H*

As No. 702, but the following date:

سنة | احدى | ثلثين | وستمائة

ANS-Laties. ANS-UM (21.5, 2.926).

705. *Aleppo—633 H*

As above, but the following date:

سنة | ثلث | ثلثين | وستمائة

Markov, p. 358, No. 7.

706. *Aleppo—634 H*

As above, but the following date.

سنة | اربع | ثلثين | ستمائة

Ashmolean-Thorburn (19, 2.74, ill.).

One-Fourth Dirhem

707. *Aleppo (?)—Date Missing*

The segments on both sides are missing.

Centre:	Centre:
○	○
الملك	الامام
العزيز	المستنصر
○	○

Since the Caliph is al-Mustanṣir, this coin must have been struck between 623 and 634 H.
Lavoix 555 (10, 0.60, ill.).

COPPER

708. *Aleppo—613 H*

On both sides: border of dots. Counterclockwise marginal legends on both sides:

ضرب بحلب سنة ثلث عشر وستمائة — لا اله الا الله محمد رسول الله

On both sides, an octalobe of dots in a linear octalobe.

Centre:	Centre:
الملك	الامام
العزيز	الناصر

On all the coins of this series the marginal legends are in *Kūfic*, and the centres in *Naskh* scripts.
ANS (22, 3.41).

709. *Aleppo—615 H*

As above, but only (س) خ سنة of the date in the obverse marginal legend is present; thus, it may be 625 H.
Erdmann, p. 237.

710. *Aleppo—618 H*

As above, but the following date:

سنة ثمان وعشر وستمائة

ANS (21, 3.405). Ashmolean-G. Stark (24, 4.10). Paris (20, —, ill.).

711. *Aleppo—620 H*

As above, but the following date:

سنة عشرين وستمائة

BM (23, 2.94). Lagumina, p. 74, No. 26 (19, 2.81; date uncertain; either 620 H, or the digit before عشرين is missing).

712. *Aleppo—621 H*

As above, but the following date:

سنة احد وعشرين وستمائة

Album. ANS (22, 3.316). Ashmolean-Christ Church (23, 3.14). Ashmolean-Christ Church 242 (22, 3.24). Ashmolean-Thorburn (22, 3.98). BMC 327 (24, 3.14); 328 (25, 3.19). Çetinyalçın (23, —). Lagumina, p. 74, No. 27 (23, 2.61); p. 75, No. 28 (23, 3.22). München (20, 3.126; 23, 3.299). Lavoix 556 (22, 3.20); 557 (22, 2.95, ill.); 559 (23, 2.94). Østrup 1694. Yapı-Kredi (21, 3.40).

713. *Aleppo—622 H*

As above, but the following date:

سنة اثنين عشرين وستمائة

Album. BMC 330a (21, 2.99, ill.). München (20, 3.305, ill.). Paris (22, —, ill.; the digit of the date is: ثاني). Yapı-Kredi (21, 2.95; the digit of the date is: ثاني).

714. *Aleppo—Date Missing*

As above, but the date is not present; name of Caliph al-Nāṣir.

Dorn, p. 71, No. 7; p. 72, Nos. 8 and 9. Ilisch 56 (21, —). Lagumina, p. 75, Nos. 29 (20, 3.24); 30 (21, 2.80); 31 (20, 2.29). Østrup 1615 and 1616. Pietraszewski 439.

715. *Aleppo—622 H*

As above, but the following date and centre legends:

سنة ثاني[*sic*]وعشرين ستمائة

Centre:	Centre:
الملك	O
العزيز	الامام
O	الظاهر

Balog (23, 3.04). Berlin (22, 2.97). BMC 329 (22, 2.99; the digit of the date is: اثنين). Paris (23, 3.76).

716. *Aleppo—623 H*

As above, but the following date:

سنة ثلث عشرين وستمائة

[No pellets over or under centre legends]

Balog (22, 3.16). BMC 330 (23, 3.00, ill.). Lavoix 562 (22, 2.87, ill.). Paris (22, 3.73). Prague 917 (20, —).

717. *Aleppo—Date Missing*

As above, but the date is not present; name of Caliph al-Ẓāhir.

Album (2 specimens). Fraehn, *Nova Suppl.*, p. 91, No. b-4. Ilisch 57 (21, —). Østrup 1617.

718. *Aleppo—623 H*

As above, but the following date and centre legends:

سنة ثلاث عشرين وستمائة

Centre:	Centre:
O	الامام
الملك	المستنصر
العزيز	

Ashmolean-Sir C. Warren (21, 3.34). BMC 330b (20, —). Østrup 1618 and 1619.

719. *Aleppo—629 H*

As above, but the following date:

سنة تسع وعشرين وستمائة

ANS (20, 3.257, ill.).

720. *Aleppo—Date Missing*

As above, but marginal legends missing on both sides.

Album. Ilisch 59 (25, —); 60 (24, —); 61 (25, —; the last two specimens are overstruck on older coins). Paris 20, —, ill.).

721. *No Mint—Undated*

With Caliph al-Nāṣir.

Border on both sides: circle of dots in plain circle. Six-pointed star of dots in linear star.

Centre:	Centre:
الملك	الامام
العزيز	الناصر

[*Naskh* script]

Glidden (19, —).

722. *No Mint—Undated*

With Caliph al-Mustanṣir.

Border on both sides: plain circle, within which are two waving intertwined trilobes consisting of a line of dots between two plain lines. The result is an intertwined ornamental six-foil. No legends except in the centre of the coin.

Centre:	Centre:
الملك	الامام
العزيز	المستنصر

[*Naskh* Script]

Album (2 specimens). ANS (23, —). ANS-Boyd (21, 3.888). ANS-UM (22, 3.09; 21, 3.03). ANS-Hisp. (23, 3.60; several other specimens). Ashmolean-Christ Church 246 (24, 3.33); 247 (22, 3.46); 249 (24, 3.69). Ashmolean-Christ Church (24, 3.34). Ashmolean-A. C. Kay (23, 3.62). Ashmolean-Thorburn (22, 3.29). Balog (23, 3.29; 23, 3.05; 19, 1.75). Berlin (24, 3.53). Berman 209 (22, 3.85). BMC 331 (24, —); 331a (24, —). Dorn, p. 72, Nos. 10, 11. Lagumina, p. 76, Nos. 32–38 (diameters 20–23; weights 2.25–3.38). Lavoix 565 (23, 3.70, ill.); 566 (24, 3.92, ill.); 567 (22, 3.20); 568 (21, 2.65); 569 (22, 2.46; several other specimens). Prague 917a (22, —). München 86008 (21, 3.649); 86009 (23, 2.899). Windisch-Graetz 170 (21, —); 171 (22, —); 172 (22, —). Yapı-Kredi (22, 3.60; 23, 3.52; 21, 2.85; 21, 2.82; 21, 2.95).

723. *No Mint—Undated*

Mule of the obverse; no caliph.

Border on both sides; plain circle.

Centre:	Centre:
الملك	الملك
العزيز محمد	العزيز محمد

[*Naskh* Script]

Balog (18, 2.60, ill.).

al-Nāṣir Ṣalāḥ al-Dīn Yūsuf II ibn al-ʿAzīz Muḥammad

Prince of Aleppo [634–658 H = 1236–1259 AD]

Sultan in Damascus [648–658 H = 1250–1259 AD]

SILVER

All of the Aleppo dirhems and half dirhems are of the *six-pointed star* type, except the unique Type B of 654 H, which is of the *square in the circle* type. On the six-pointed star issues the segments are in *Kūfic* and the centre in *Naskh*. However, the digit and decade of the date can, occasionally, be in *Naskh*. The 654 H, Type B dirhem of the square-in-the-circle is entirely in *Naskh*.

724. *Aleppo—634 H*

Overlord: al-Kāmil Muḥammad.

Border Segments:
(ضرب) | بحلب | سنة | اربع | (ثلا) ثين | ستمائة
Centre:
يوسف
الملك الناصر
صلاح الدين
بن الملك العزيز
محمد

Border Segments:
لا اله | الا ا | لله | محمد | (رسول) | الله
Centre:
ابو جعفر
بالله
الامام المستنصر
الملك الكامل
ناصر الدنيا والدين
محمد

Album 9.

725. *Aleppo—636 H*

Overlord: the Rūm Seljūq Kaykhusraw II; caliph: al-Mustanṣir.

Border Segments:
ضرب | بحلب | سنة | ست | ثلثين | ستمائة
Centre:
يوسف
الملك الناصر
صلاح الدين
ابن الملك العزيز
محمد

Border Segments:
لا اله | الا ا | لله | محمد | رسول | الله
Centre:
ابو جعفر
بالله
الامام المستنصر
السلطان
الاعظم كيخسر
وا (*sic*)

Album 29. ANS (22.5, 2.95; 21.5, 2.91, ill.). ANS 56.125 (22, 3.02; 22.5, —; 23, 3.11; 22, 2.95; on the last two specimens the date is slightly miswritten). Ashmolean-Thorburn (22, 2.95). BM-Whitehead (21, 2.91).

The names of this issue reflect the alliance of al-Nāṣir Yūsuf with the Rūm Seljūq Sulṭān Kaykhusraw II against the incursions of Khwārizmian bands who were encouraged to attack their lands by the ruler of Egypt. Other Ayyūbid princes, menaced by these devastating *razzias*, also joined the temporary pact. Kaykhusraw II is the nominal overlord on the coins.

726. *Aleppo—637 H*

Type A

Overlord: Kaykhusraw II

Caliph: al-Mustanṣir

As above, but the following date:

سنة | سبع | وثلثين | ستمائة

Album. ANS-UM (23, 2.954). ANS 56.125 (23, 2.96; 22, 2.98; 23, 2.95; 22, 2.96; 22, 2.99). Awad (22, 3.00). Balog (21, 2.95). Berlin-Jerusalem II (22, 2.90). BM-Spink (23, 2.90, ill.). Lowick (22, 2.92, ill.). Paris (23, 2.92; 23, 2.93). Tewhid (20, —). Yapı-Kredi (22, 3.05).

727. *Type B*

Overlord: Kaykhusraw II

Caliph: al-Mustaʿṣim

As above, but the reverse centre legend:

ابو احمد
بالله
الامام المستعصم
السلطان ٧●
الاعظم كيخسر
و

Album 30 (Kaykhusraw without the *ālif* in the last line of the reverse). ANS 72.95 (21, 2.955, ill.). Balog (22, 2.98, ill.). Ilisch 62 (either 637 or 639 H).

This is a mule. There is no doubt about the date, which is clearly 637 H. The reverse has the name of Caliph al-Mustaʿṣim, who started to reign in 640 H when the alliance with Kaykhusraw was still valid. Thus, an old, out-of-date obverse (637 H) was inadvertently used with a new, up-to-date reverse.

728. *Aleppo—638 H*

Overlord: Kaykhusraw II

Caliph: al-Mustanṣir

As No. 726, but the following date:

سنة | ثمان | ثلثين | ستمائة

ANS (23, 2.95). Lavoix 570 (ill.). Zambaur, N.C. 522 (22, 2.97).

729. *Aleppo—639 H*

Overlord: al-Ṣāliḥ Ayyūb

Caliph: al-Mustaʿṣim

Border Segments:

ضرب | بحلب | . . . | تسع | وثلثين | ستمائة

Border Segments:

لا اله | الا ا | الله | محمد | رسول | الله

Centre:
يوسف
الملك الناصر
صلاح الدين
ابن الملك العزيز
محمد

Centre:
ابو احمد
بالله
الامام المستعصم
الملك الصالح
نجم الدين ايوب
بن محمد

Album 8 (digit of date is probably تسع; decade is definitely ثلثين).

730. *Half Dirhem*
Aleppo—639 H

Border Segments:
ضرب | بحلب | سنة | تسع | ثلثين | (ستمائة)
Centre:
O
الملك
الناصر
O

Border Segments:
لا اله | الا ا | لله | محمد | رسول | الله
Centre:
O
الامام
المستنصر
O

ANS (17, 1.477).

731. *Half Dirhem*
Aleppo—640 H

As above, but the following date:

سنة | اربعين | وست | مائة

Lavoix 572 (11, 1.46, ill.; the date is not certain; characters are too small and indistinct).

732. *Aleppo—640 H*

As No. 719, but the obverse and reverse border segments:

ضرب | بحلب | سنة | اربعين | وست | مائة

لا ا | له ا | الا ا | لله | محمد ر | سول الله

ANS 56.125 (22, 2.969). Istanbul (20, —).

733. *Half Dirhem*
No Overlord; Caliph: al-Mustaʿṣim

Border Segments:
ضر | ب | بحلب | سنة | اربعين | وستمائة
Centre:
O
الملك
الناصر
O

Border Segments:
لا اله | الا ا | لله | محمد | رسول | الله
Centre:
O
الامام
المستعصم
O

Ashmolean-A. C. Kay (16, 1.36, ill.; date is not certain; the writing in the segments is minute and indistinct).

734. *Aleppo—642 H*
No Overlord
Caliph: al-Musta'ṣim

Border Segments:	Border Segments:
ضرب | بحلب | سنة | اثنين | اربعين | ستمائة	لا اله | الا ا | الله | محمد | رسول | الله
Centre:	Centre:
يوسف	بالله
الملك الناصر	الامام المستعصم
ابن الملك العزيز	امير المؤ
محمد	منين

ANS (22.5, 2.75). ANS 71.76 (22, 2.91). Izzet 293. Zambaur, *Contrib.* I, p. 38, No. 73.

735. *Aleppo—643 H*

Border Segments:	Border Segments:
	(*sic*)
ضرب | بحلب | سنة | ثلث | اربعين | ستمائة	لا اله | الا ا | الله | محمد | رسول | الله
Centre:	Centre:
يوسف	
الملك الناصر	الامام المستعصم
صلاح الدين	بالله ابو احمد
ابن الملك العزيز	عبد الله امير المؤمنين
محمد	

ANS (20, —). ANS 71.76 (20, 2.831, ill.). Yapı-Kredi (21, 2.60).

736. *Half Dirhem*

As No. 733, but the following date:

ضرب | بحلب | سنة | ثلث | اربعين | ستمائة

ANS 71.76 (17, —, ill.). Leuthold-Ripostiglio 8 (16, 1.42).

737. *Aleppo—644 H*
Overlord: al-Ṣāliḥ Ayyūb

As No. 732, but the obverse and reverse border segments:

ضرب | بحلب | سنة | اربع | اربعين | ستمائة	لا اله | الا ا | الله | محمد | رسول | الله
or	
اربعة	

ANS (20.5, 2.89, ill.). ANS 71.76 (20.5, 2.89; 20, —). Yapı-Kredi (21, 2.88).

738. *Aleppo—645 H*
No Overlord

Border Segments:	Border Segments:
ضرب | بحلب | سنة | خمس | واربعين | ستمائة	لا اله | الا ا | الله | محمد | رسول | الله

Centre:	Centre:
يوسف	ابو
الملك الناصر	بالله
بن الملك العزيز	الامام المستعصم
محمد	امير المومنين
	احمد

ANS (22, 2.19; 20, 2.83, ill.; other specimens from the ANS 71.76 hoard [digit is sometimes written: خمسه; on other coins in *Naskh*: خمس]). Leuthold-Ripostiglio 9 (21, 2.73); 10 (21, 2.85, ill.).

Aleppo—646 H

739. *Type A*

No Overlord

As above, but the following date and centre legends:

سنة|ستة|اربعين|ستمائة

Centre:	Centre:
يوسف	ابو
الملك الناصر	بالله
بن الملك العزيز	الامام المستعصم
محمد	امير المؤمنين
	احمد

Album 11 (2 specimens; century is written: ستـا). ANS 71.76 (20.5, —, ill.; 20, —; 23, —; 20, —).

740. *Type B*

Overlord: al-Ṣāliḥ Ayyūb

As above, but the obverse and reverse centre legends:

يوسف	ابو احمد
الملك الناصر	بالله
ابن الملك العزيز	الامام المستعصم
محمد	الملك الصالح ايوب
	محمد
	بن

ANS 71.76 (20.5, —).

Half Dirhem

741. *Aleppo—646 H*

As No. 733, but the following date:

سنة|ست|اربعين|ستمائة

ANS-Newell (15, 1.254). ANS 71.76 (15, —).

Aleppo—647 H

742. *Type A*

No Overlord

As No. 739, but the following date:

سنة|سبع|اربعين|ستمائة

ANS 71.76 (29 specimens, ill.) Izzet 297. Leuthold-Ripostiglio 12 (22, 2.80); 13 (21, 2.82); 14 (22, 2.86).

743. *Type B*

Overlord: al-Ṣāliḥ Ayyūb

As No. 740, but the following date:

سنة | سبع | اربعين | ستمائة

[Obverse exergue has either a ● or ɔc or no ornaments]

Album 12. ANS (21, 3.04; 21.5, 2.91; 20.5, 2.77; 20, 2.82; many other specimens). Ashmolean-Thorburn (21, 2.76, ill.). Yapı-Kredi (22, 2.80; 22, 2.80; 20, 2.80; 20, 2.75). Ziya 1703 (20, —).

744. *Type C*

As above, but the reverse centre:

ابو
بالله
الامام المستعصم
الملك الصالح ايوب
احمد

Album (point benaeth the ب of سبع shows this is 647, not 649 H).

According to Dr. Michael Bates, reverse die-links with the previous and the following years demonstrate that in 647 H dirhems were struck in Aleppo (Ḥalab) in the following order: first, in the name of al-Nāṣir Yūsuf alone; second, with al-Ṣāliḥ Ayyūb as overlord; and finally, after al-Ṣāliḥ's death in Sha'bān 647 H, with no overlord.

745. *Aleppo—648 H*

As above, but the following date and centre legends:

سنة | ثمنية | اربعين | ستمائة

Centre:	Centre:
يوسف	ابو
الملك الناصر	بالله
بن الملك العزيز	الامام المستعصم
محمد	امير المؤمنين
ɔc	احمد

ANS (21, 2.739). ANS 71.76 (21, 2.84; 22, 2.93; 21, 2.68; 95 other specimens). ANS-Newell (21.5, 2.746). Istanbul (23, 2.80). Ziya 1704 (21, —).

On 17 Rabi' II, al-Nāṣir Yūsuf became the head of the Ayyūbid empire. Egypt was a Mamlūk sultanate, but Syria and Mesopotamia acknowledged al-Nāṣir Yūsuf as their overlord. Note how difficult it is to distinguish between the cursively written digit خمس of 645 H and ثمنية of the 648 H issues.

Half Dirhem

746. *Aleppo—648 H*

Reported by Dr. Michael Bates, ANS (12, 1.48).

747. *Aleppo—649 H*

As No. 739, but the following date:

سنة | تسع | اربعين | ستمائة

ANS (21, 2.91, ill.). ANS 71.76 (133 specimens). ANS-Newell (20, 2.82). ANS-Wood (20, 2.51). ANS-Wright (20, 3.04; 20, 2.91; 20, 2.77). Leuthold-Ripostiglio 15 (20, 2.84).

There is some doubt as to whether the digit is seven or nine. Generally the reading is clear: for seven there is a dip before the tooth of the *bā*ʾ; in the nine there is no dip. It is سبع for seven; تسع for nine.

748. *Aleppo—650 H*

As above, but the following date:

سنة | خمسين | وست | مائة

ANS (20, 2.86, ill.).

749. *Aleppo—651 H*

As above, but the following date:

سنة | احدى | وخمسين | ستمائة

ANS (20, 2.78, ill.). ANS 71.76 (79 specimens, ill.). Istanbul (20, —; 20, —). Yapı-Kredi (21, 2.70).

750. *Aleppo—652 H*

As above, but the following date:

سنة | اثنين | خمسين | ستمائة

ANS (20, 2.77, ill.). ANS 71.76 (92 specimens). Yapı-Kredi (22, 2.70; digit of the date: اثنى).

751. *Aleppo—653 H*

As above, but the following date:

سنة | ثلاث و | خمسين | وستمائة

ANS (22, 2.677, ill.; 20, 2.89, ill.).

Aleppo—654 H

752. *Type A*

Six-pointed star type. As above, but the following date and centre legends:

سنة | اربع | خمسين | ستمائة

Centre:

يوسف
الملك الناصر
بن الملك العزيز
محمد

Centre:

ابو
بالله
الامام المستعصم
امير المؤمنين
احمد

Album. ANS (20.5, 2.80, ill.). Paris-R.N. 1935 (20, 2.83). Lagumina, p. 77, No. 39 (19, 2.39; date missing, but it has the ornament characteristic for this year's issue). Ziya 1705 (20, —).

753. *Type B*

Variety 1

Square-in-the-circle.

Border Segments:

ضرب بحلب | سنة اربعة | وخمسين | وستمائة

Centre:

الملك الناصر

صلاح الدين

يوسف ابن محمد

Border Segments:

لا اله ا | لا الله | محمد رسو | ل الله

Centre:

الامام

المستعصم

بالله ابو احمد

امير المؤمنين

Album. ANS 72.75 (20.5, 2.797). BM-Sir R. Burn (21, 2.59, ill.). Yapı-Kredi (20, 2.75; 20, 2.70).

In this year the Aleppo mint adopted the *square-in-the-circle* dirhem type of Damascus, but in the following issues it reverted to the traditional *six-pointed star* type.

754. *Variety 2*

Border Segments:

بسم الله | ضرب بحلب(؟) | سنة اربع | وخمسين

Centre:

○

الملك الناصر

صلاح الدين

ϒ

يوسف بن محمد

Border Segments:

(لا اله ا) | لا الله | محمد رسو(ل) | (الله)

Centre:

الامام

ϒ

المستعصم

●

بالله ابو احمد

ϒ

امير المؤمنين

The date is without the century. Only the base of the mint name is on the flan, but it seems to be Ḥalab.

Berlin-Dahlem J. 23/71 (21, 2.75).

755. *Aleppo—655 H*

As No. 752, but the following date and centre legends:

سنة | خمس | خمسين | ستمائة

Centre:

يوسف

الملك الناصر

♡

بن الملك العزيز

محمد

Centre:

ابو

بالله

الامام المستعصم

////////// (*sic*)

امير المؤمنين

Album. ANS (20.5, 2.94, ill.). Yapı-Kredi (21, 2.90; 19. 2.65).

756. *Aleppo—656 H*

As above, but the following date and reverse centre:

سنة | ست | وخمسين | وستمائة

ابو
بالله
المستعصم
امير المؤمنين
احمد

ANS (20, 2.92, ill.).

757. *Aleppo—658 H*

Caliph's name not included. As above, but the following date and centre legends:

سنة | ثمان | خمسين | وستمائة

Centre:	Centre:
يوسف	
الملك الناصر	لا اله الا الله
بن الملك العزيز	محمد رسول الله
محمد	

BMC 334 (19, 2.82; The date is missing, but the caliph's protocol on the reverse is replaced by a religious legend. Therefore, this coin must have been struck in 657 or 658 H, after al-Musta'ṣim's execution by the Ilkhān Hulagu). Zambaur, *Contrib.* I, p. 38, No. 74.

COPPER

758. *Aleppo—643 H*

Square-in-the-circle type. Border on both sides: plain circle in circle of dots, within which is a square in a square of pellets.

Border Segments:	Border Segments:
ضرب بحلب | سنة . . . | . . . | وستمائة	(ضرب) بحلب | سنة ثلاث | وار . . . | . . .
Centre:	Centre:
الملك	الامام
الناصر	المستنصر

Album 27.

759. *Aleppo—6x3 H*

Border on both sides: plain square within a beaded square, all within a circle.

Border Segments:	Border Segments:
ضرب بحلب | . . . | . . . | وستمائة	ضرب بحلب | سنة ثلاث | . . . | . . .
Centre:	Centre:
الملك	الامام
الناصر	المستعصم

Traces of the decade suggest this reading of date as most probable.

Album.

760. *Aleppo—655 H*

Border on both sides: plain circle in circle of pellets, within which is a thin dotted square in a square of pellets.

<table>
<tr><td>Border Segments:
O|O يوسف O|O الدين O|O صلاح O
بن محمد O
Centre:
الملك
الناصر</td><td>Border Segments:
ضرب بحلب|سنة خمس|وخمسين|وستمائة
Centre:
الامام
المستعصم</td></tr>
</table>

Ashmolean-Thorburn (21, 1.69, ill.). Balog (20, 1.48). Lagumina, p. 80, No. 45 (19, 1.25; date missing, but the coin belongs to this series).

761. *Aleppo—Undated*

Border on both sides: circle of pellets between two plain circles.

<table>
<tr><td>Centre:
O يوسف O
الملك الناصر
ابن محمد</td><td>Centre:
O امير المؤمنين O
بالله
الامام المستعصم
ضرب بحلب</td></tr>
</table>

[Naskh script; second line in tall characters]

Tewhid (18, —; 19, —, ill.). Wien 676 (18, —). Yapı-Kredi (19, 2.22).

SILVER

Damascus—648 H

This and the subsequent issues have the name of Caliph al-Musta'ṣim and are all of the *square-in-the-circle* type.

762. *Type A*

Mint and date in the obverse segments.

<table>
<tr><td>Border Segments:
ضرب بدمشق|سنة ثمان|واربعين|وستمائة
Centre:
٢
الملك الناصر
صلاح الدنيا وا
سف
لدين يو بن محمد</td><td>Border Segments:
لا اله الا ا|لله وحده|لا شريك له|محمد رسول الله
Centre:
الامام
٢
المستعصم
بالله ابو احمد
امير المؤمنين</td></tr>
</table>

Album 28. ANS (21.5, 2.86). Balog (22, 2.92; 20, 2.88, ill.). BMC 332 (21.5, 3.02, ill.).

763. *Type B*

Mint and date in the reverse segments.

<table>
<tr><td>Border Segments:
(لا اله الا)|الله محمد|(رسول)|(الله)</td><td>Border Segments:
(ضرب بدمشق)|سنة ثمان|(واربعين)|(وستمائة)</td></tr>
</table>

Centre:
الملك الناصر
سف
صلاح الدين يو
الملك العزيز محمد
[No *ibn* between *Yūsuf* and *al-Malik al-ʻAzīz*]

Centre:
الامام المستعصم
بالله ابو احمد
امير المؤمنين

Balog (21, 2.82).

Half Dirhem

764. *Damascus—648 H*

Square-in-the-circle type.

Border Segments:
(ضرب بدمشق) | سنة ثمان | واربعين | (وستمائة)
Centre:
الملك
٢
الناصر

Border Segments:
لا اله | الا ا | لله وحده | لا شريك له
Centre:
الامام
٢
المستعصم

Album. Balog (15, 1.47, ill.; 14, 1.35, ill.).

765. *Damascus—649 H*

Mint and date in the obverse segments; reverse segments missing.
ضرب بدمشق | سنة تسع | (واربعين) | (وستمائة)
[Centre legends, both sides, as No. 763]

Balog (20, 2.70, ill.). Nicol (22, 2.73).

Half Dirhem

766. *Damascus—649 H*

As above. Although only the digit of the date is on the flan, it can be neither 639 nor 659 H. Struck from dirhem dies.

Balog (16, 1.61).

767. *Damascus—651 H*

As No. 762, but the following date:
سنة احد | وخمسين | وستمائة

Album. Balog (21, 2.93, ill.; 21, 2.98).

768. *Damascus—653 H*

As above, but the obverse segments:
ضرب بدمشق | سنة ثلث | وخمسين | وستمائة

Balog (21, 2.98, ill.).

769. *Half Dirhem*

Border Segments:

. . .|سنة ثلاث|. . .|. . .

Centre:

. . .ك الناصر

. . .ح الدين يوسف

. . . . محمد

Border Segments:

لا اله|. . .|. . .|. . .

Centre:

الامام المستعصم

بالله احمد

امير المؤمنين

[Struck from dirhem dies]

Album.

770. *[Damascus]—654 H*

As No. 765, but the following obverse and reverse border segments:

. . .|.اربعة|وخمس . . . .|. . .

لا اله الا|. . .|. . .|. . .

Album.

771. *Damascus—656 H*

Border Segments beginning at bottom:

ضرب بد|مشق سنة|ست وخمسين|وستمائة

Centre:

الملك الناصر

صلاح الدين يوسف

الملك العزيز محمد

[Border Segments Missing]

Centre:

الامام المستعصم

بالله ابو احمد

امير المؤمنين

[No *ibn* between *Yūsuf* and *al-Malik al-ʿAzīz*]

Leuthold 41 (21, 2.71); 42 (21, 2.95, ill.).

Half Dirhem

Damascus—Date Missing

772. *Type A*

Special half dirhem dies. As the 648 H half dirhems, but the date is missing, as is most of the mint. However, the Damascus mint is most probable, since the only square-in-the-circle dirhem issued in Aleppo is of a late date (654 H).

Balog (14, 1.44; 14, 1.50, ill.).

773. *Type B*

Normal dirhem die on the obverse; special die on the reverse.

[Segments Missing]

Centre:

الملك الناصر

صلاح الدين يوسف

الملك العزيز محمد

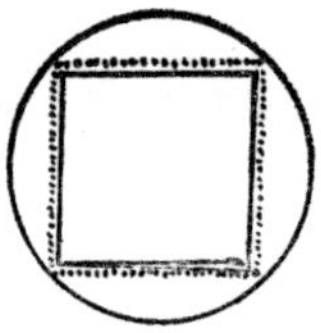

Segments [Reconstructed]

لا اله|الا ا|الله وحده|لا شريك له

Centre:

الامام

المستعصم

Balog (16, 1.27, ill.).

774. *Type C*

Normal dirhem dies on both sides. Segments missing on both sides.

Obverse Centre:

as above

Reverse Centre:

٢

الامام المستعصم

بالله ابو احمد

امير المؤمنين

Balog (13, 1.12).

One-Fourth Dirhem

775. *Damascus—Date Missing*

As No. 773, but the weight indicates that the denomination is a one-fourth dirhem.

Balog (16, 0.65, ill.).

776. *Ḥamāh—648 H*

Square-in-the-circle type.

Border Segments:

ضرب بحماه | سنة ثمان | واربعين | وستمائة

Centre:

٢

الملك الناصر

صلاح الدنيا وا

لدين يوسف بن محمد

Border Segments:

لا اله الا | الله وحده | لا شريك له | محمد رسول الله

Centre:

الامام

المستعصم

٢

بالله ابو احمد

٢

امير المؤمنين

[*Naskh* script]

Balog (21, 2.78). Leuthold-Ripostiglio 24 (23, 2.84); 25 (23, 2.85); 26 (22, 2.86).

777. *Ḥamāh—651 H*

As above, but the following date:

سنة احد | وخمسين | وستمائة

Balog, *BIE* XXXIV (1952) (22, 2.69). Balog (22, 2.65; 23, 2.72; 24, 2.76, ill.).

778. *Ḥamāh—655 H*

As above, but the following date:

سنة خمس | وخمسين | وستمائة

Balog, *BIE* XXXIV (1952) (23, 2.70, ill.).

779. *Ḥamāh—657 H*

As above, but the following date:

سنة سبع | وخمسين | وستمائة

Balog (23, 2.88, ill.).

COPPER

(see also nos. 758–761)

No Mint—Undated

780.

Type A

No Caliph

Six-pointed star, similar to that on the dirhem, but larger and wider. All the legends are in *Naskh*. The segments are blank or contain minute illegible scrawls. No date can be read.

Centre:

○
الملك
الناصر
○

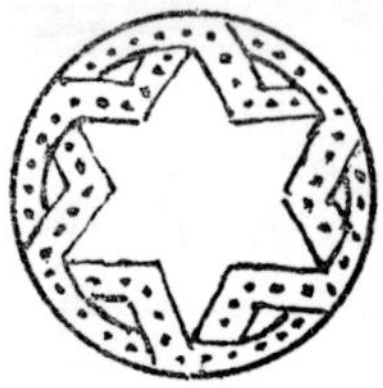

Centre:

بن
الملك
العزيز
○

Album. ANS (23.5, 3.96; 23, 3.65; 24, 3.59; and many other specimens). Artuk 773 (22, 3.10). Ashmolean-Bodleian (20, 3.42; 24, —). Ashmolean-Christ Church 251 (22, 3.58). Ashmolean-Thorburn (17, 1.69). BMC 335 (23, 3.28, ill.); 336 (24, 3.50). Fraehn, *Nova Suppl.*, p. 91, No. 5a. Ilisch 65 (21, —); 66 (23, —). Lagumina, p. 78, Nos. 41 (22, 3.58); 42 (24, 3.40). Lavoix 577 (22, 3.26, ill.). München 86368 (24, 3.68); 86369 (22, 2.662); 86982 (22, 3.117). Paris (21, 3.29; 22, 2.75). Webdale (20, 2.96).

781.

Type B

Caliph al-Musta'ṣim

Centre:

○
الملك
الناصر
○

Centre:

○
الامام
المستعصم
○

Album (2 specimens). BMC 337 (20, 2.46, ill.); 338 (20, —). Ilisch 67 (16, —); 68 (18, —).

782.

No Caliph

Border on both sides: plain circle in circle of dots, within which is a linear square, with central arch on each side. Ringlet in the arches.

Centre:

الملك
الناصر

Centre:

بن الملك
العزيز

Album (2 specimens). Lagumina, p. 78, No. 40 (16, 1.82). Lavoix 578 (18, 2.18, ill.). Paris (20, 2.50).

783.

Caliph al-Musta'ṣim

On both sides: sixfoil with annulet outside each cusp.

Centre:

○
الملك
الناصر
○

Centre:

○
الامام
المستعصم
○

Album (2 specimens; no annulets above or beneath centre legends). Berlin (17, 1.20). BMC 338 (22, —, ill.). BMC 340 (is not Ayyūbid, but was minted by the Baḥrī Mamlūk al-Nāṣir Muḥammad). Yapı-Kredi (18, 1.75).

784. *Caliph al-Musta'ṣim*

Border on both sides: plain circle, in which a linear *dodekalobe*.

Centre:	Centre:
الملك	الامام
الناصر	المستعصم

Ashmolean (18, 1.31, ill.). Ashmolean-Thorburn (18, 1.45, ill.). Ashmolean-P. J. Parr. München 91856 (18, —).

785. *Mint and Date Missing*

Caliph al-Musta'ṣim

Border on both sides: plain circle. Counterclockwise marginal legend on both sides:

(صلاح) الدين يوسف	[Reverse missing]

Plain circle on both sides:

Centre:	Centre:
○	○
الملك	الامام
الناصر	المستعصم
○	○

[Large *Naskh* Script]

ANS-Newell (23, 3.22). Lagumina, p. 79, No. 43 (17, 1.00). Paris 18, —, ill.; 21, —, ill.).

786. *Mint and Date Missing*

No Caliph

Religious legend on the reverse. Marginal legends missing.

Centre:	Centre:
يوسف	لا اله الا
الملك الناصر	الله محمد
بن الملك العزيز	رسول الله
محمد	

Ziya 206.

787. *Aleppo—Undated*

Border on both sides: plain circle in circle of dots.

Centre:	Centre:
○ يوسف ○	○ امير المؤمنين ○
الملك الناصر	الامام المستعصم
○ بن محمد ○	○ ضرب بحلب ○

Album (3 specimens; mint present). Ilisch 64 (19, —; mint present). Paris (20, —, ill.; mint is missing, but same type).

788. *[Aleppo]—Undated*

Mule of two obverses of No. 787.

Album.

789. *Aleppo(?)—Undated*

Obverse in plain hexalobe within plain circle:

Reverse:

. . . . ب
الملك
الناصر
ضرب

[Final ب of mint very clear]

Album.

PRINCIPALITY OF DAMASCUS

AL-AFḌAL NŪR AL-DĪN ABŪ AL-ḤASAN ʿALĪ IBN ṢALĀḤ AL-DĪN

[582–592 H = 1186–1196 AD]

Although endowed with Damascus by Saladin in 582 H, al-Afḍal started to issue coins only after his father's death in 589 H. He inherited the *sultanate* and was recognized as head of the dynasty; and while the territories assigned him were impressive, his real power was very limited. For example, he only struck coins in Damascus and Ḥimṣ between 589 and 592 H, although, in theory, he held the right of *sikkah,* which would have suggested coinage in his name in other parts of the empire too. In addition, the prince of Egypt, al-ʿAzīz ʿUthmān, issued silver in Damascus in 590 and 591 H simultaneously with al-Afḍal ʿAlī.

SILVER

790. *Damascus* (?)—*589 H*

Border on both sides: plain circle in a circle of dots. Counterclockwise marginal legends on both sides:

بسم الله ضرب درهم (*sic*) سنة تسع وثمنين وخمسمائة

لا اله الا الله محمد رسول الله صلى الله عليه

On both sides: linear octalobe in an octalobe of dots.

Centre:
الملك الافضل
علي بن الملك الناصر
يوسف بن ايوب

Centre:
الامام الناصر
امير المؤمنين عدة
الدنيا والدين

[Marginal legends in *Kūfic*; central legends in elegant *Naskh*]

Berlin 628/1896 (20, 2.80). Tewhid (21, —). Yapı-Kredi (21, 2.65; 21, 2.87).

791. *Damascus—589 H*

As above, but the obverse marginal legend:

بسم الله ضرب بدمشق سنة تسع وثمنين وخمس مائة

Seen at the ANS (21, 2.76). ANS (21, 2.99). Balog (20, 2.91, ill.). BM (20, 2.98, ill.). Lavoix 496 (21, 2.78, ill.); 497 (21, 2.98); 498 (21, 2.97).

Half Dirhem

792. *Damascus—589 H*

Border missing on both sides. Counterclockwise marginal legends on both sides:

[Reconstructed] ضرب بدمشق سنة تسع (وثمنين و خمسا (*sic*)

[Reconstructed] لا اله الا الله محمد رسول الله

Octalobe of dots on both sides.

Centre:
الملك الافضل
بن الملك الناصر

Centre:
الامام الناصر
امير المؤمنين

[Marginal legends in *Kūfic*; central legends in elegant *Naskh*]

Ahmed Tewhid 1 (15, —, ill.); 2 (14, —).

793. *Damascus—590 H*

No details.

Busso Peus 1899.

794. *Damascus—591 H*

As No. 791, but the obverse marginal legend:

ضرب بدمشق سنة اجدى وتسعين وخمس مائة

Album 37. Lavoix 499 (21, 2.00, ill.).

795. *Damascus—592 H*

As above, but the obverse marginal legend:

بسم الله ضرب بدمشق سنة اثنين وتسعين وخمس مائة

Artuk 755 (21, 2.80). Berman 179 (21, 2.70). BMC 285 (20, 3.02, ill.; floweret over al-Afḍal).

796. *Ḥimṣ—589 H*

Border on both sides: plain circle in circle of dots. Counterclockwise marginal legend on both sides:

بسم الله ضرب بحمص سنة تسع وثمنين وخمسمائة

لا اله الا الله محمد رسول الله صلى الله عليه

Linear octalobe in octalobe of dots on both sides.

Centre:
الملك الافضل
علي بن الملك الناصر
يوسف بن ايوب

Centre:
الامام الناصر
امير المؤمنين عدة
الدنيا والدين

Album. Artuk 756 (20, 2.75). Lowick (20, 2.86, ill.). Şerafettin Erel III, 15 (21, 2.80; obverse second line: علي (ابن الملك الناصر).

797. *Ḥimṣ—591/592 H*

As above, but the obverse marginal legend:

بسم الله ضرب بحمص سنة ا . . . وتسعين وخمسمائة

Paris (21, 2.95; digit is missing; date can be 591 or 592 H).

AL-ʿĀDIL I

Lord of Damascus [592–596 H = 1195–1199 AD]

During his rule as local prince al-ʿĀdil did not issue coins in Damascus. The right of *sikka* belonged to the Egyptian overlord, al-ʿAzīz ʿUthmān, whose silver, struck in the Syrian capital up to 595 H, is well-known. Only after al-ʿĀdil was recognized as head of the dynasty, did he issue dirhems in Damascus.

al-Muʿaẓẓam ʿĪsa and al-Ashraf Mūsā, though they possessed Damascus and large parts of Syria and the Jazīrah, never issued coinage in Damascus. They meticulously respected the Egyptian ruler al-Kāmil Muḥammad's right of *sikka,* which extended over Damascus, Ḥimṣ and Ḥamāh.

AL-ṢĀLIḤ ʿIMĀD AL-DĪN ISMĀʿĪL IBN AL-ʿĀDIL I

First Reign: Muḥarram to Jumādā I [635 H = 1237 AD]

Second Reign: [637–643 H = 1239–1245 AD]

According to Zambaur, *Manuel* (p. 79, f. n. 9), al-Ṣāliḥ Ismāʿīl's first reign started before the end of 634 H and, by implication, al-Kāmil must have died in 634 H. For proof, he refers to dirhem No. 437e of the BMC, the date which Lane-Poole read as 634 H. Mr. N. M. Lowick of the British Museum and I have examined this coin carefully and agree that the date is 637 H. Therefore, the numismatic evidence for al-Ṣāliḥ Ismāʿīl's investiture as lord of Damascus remains 635 H, which agrees with Arab chronicles.

SILVER

798. *Damascus—635 H*

Border Segments:

بسم الله|ضرب بدمشق|سنة خمس|ثلثين وستمائة

Centre:

الملك الصالح
عماد الدنيا والدين
اسمعيل بن ابي بكر

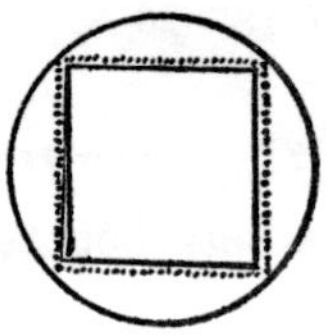

Border Segments:

لا اله الا ا|لله وحده|لا شريك له|محمد رسول الله

Centre:

الامام
المستنصر
بالله ابو جعفر
المنصور امير المؤمنين

BMC 434 (20, 2.99). Lavoix 665 (20, 2.98). Weyl 6545 (21, 8.00(?); digit of the date with query).

799. *Damascus—637 H*

As above, but the following date:

سنة سبع و|ثلاثين وستمائة

ANS (22, 2.66). ANS 71.76 (22, 2.94; 21, 2.90). Balog (22, 2.90, ill.; 21, 2.87). BMC 437e (23, 2.92; Lane-Poole read the date on this coin as 634 H). Yapı-Kredi (21, 2.85; 20, 2.98).

Half Dirhem

800. *Damascus—637 H*

Border Segments:

ضرب | بدمشق سنة | سبع ثلاثين | وستمائة

Centre:

الملك

الصالح

Border Segments:

لا اله الا | الله وحده | محمد رسو | ل الله

Centre:

الامام

المستنصر

Leuthold (12 × 15, 1.61).

Although this half dirhem has only the prince's *laqab* on it, there can be no doubt about the attribution to al-Ṣāliḥ Ismāʿīl because of the date.

Damascus—638 H

801. *Type A*

As No. 798, but the following date:

سنة ثمان و | ثلاثين وستمائة

ANS (22, 2.71, ill.; 22. 2.88; 22.5, 2.92). ANS 71.76 (22, —, ill.; 22.5, 2.98). Balog (21. 2.91; 21, 2.92, ill.). BMC 435 (20, 2.93). München 92455 (20, 2.50); 92456 (21, 2.628); 92457 (23, 2.943); 92458 (22, 2.932); 91856 (20, 2.211). Yapı-Kredi (22, 2.95); 21, 2.98).

802. *Type B*

As above, but the obverse segments:

ضرب بدمشق | سنة ثمانة (*sic*) | وثلثين | وستمائة

Album 19.

Half Dirhem

Damascus—638 H

803. *Type A*

Border Segments:

بسم الله | ضرب بدمشق | سنة ثمان و | ثلاثين وستمائة

Centre:

الملك الصالح

عماد الدنيا والدين

اسمعيل بن ابى بكر

Border Segments:

لا اله الا ا | لله وحده | لا شريك له | محمد رسول الله

Centre:

الامام

المستنصر

بالله ابو جعفر

المنصور امير المؤمنين

Balog (15, 1.43, ill.). Prague 912 (18, 1.29). Yapı-Kredi (15, 1.30; 14, 1.45).

804. *Type B*

Border Segments:

لا اله | الا الله | محمد رسو | ل الله

Centre:

الملك

الصالح

Border Segments:

ضرب بد | مشق سنة | ثمان وثلا . . | . . ستمائة

Centre:

الامام

المنصر [*sic*]

Nicol (17, 1.24).

805. *Damascus—639 H*

As No. 799, but the following date:

سنة تسع | ثلاثين وستمائة

ANS (23.5, 2.76, ill.).

Half Dirhem

806. *Damascus—639 H*

As No. 800, but the following date:

سنة | تسع ثلاثين | وستمائة

Leuthold-Ripostiglio (14, 1.62, ill.; the date, written in minute characters, is difficult to read and 639 H is given here with reservation).

Damascus—640 H

807. *Type A*

No Overlord

Caliph: al-Mustanṣir

As No. 799, but the border segments on both sides:

●لا اله الا ا● | ●لله وحده● | ●لا شريك له● | ●محمد رسول الله●

بسم الله | ضرب بدمشق | سنة اربعين | وستمائة

Berman 202 (21, 2.73). Zambaur, *Contrib.* I, p. 38, No. 76.

808. *Type B*

Overlord: Kaykhusraw II

Caliph: al-Mustanṣir

As above, but the border segments, both sides, and the reverse centre legend:

●لا اله الا● | ●الله وحده● | ●لا شريك له● | ●محمد سول الله●

●الملك لله● | ●ضرب بدمشق● | ●سنة اربعين● | ●وستمائة●

Centre:

بالله

الامام المستنصر

السلطان

الاعظم كيخسر وا [*sic*]

Artuk 760 (21, 2.82, ill.). Balog (22, 2.82).

809. *Type C*

Overlord: Kaykhusraw II

Caliph: al-Mustaʿṣim

As above, but the reverse centre:

الامام

المستعصم

بالله السلطان

الاعظم كيخسر و

ANS 71.76 (21, 2.94; 20, —).

810. *Type D*

No Overlord

Caliph: al-Musta'ṣim

As above, but the border segments, both sides, and the reverse centre legend:

الملك لله | ضرب بدمشق | سنة اربعين | وستمائة

الامام | لا اله لا | الله وحده | محمد رسول الله

Centre:

بالله

المستعصم

ابو احمد عبد

الله امير المؤمنين

ANS 56.125 (21.5, —). ANS (19, —; it is not certain that the reverse segments of the two ANS specimens are exactly as read here). Balog (21, 2.82, ill.). Berlin-Guthrie (21, 2.89).

Damascus—641 H

811. *Type A*

Overlord: Kaykhusraw II

As above, but the border segments, both sides, and the reverse centre legend:

بسم الله | ضرب بدمشق | سنة احد و | اربعين وستمائة

لا اله الا | الله وحده | لا شريك له محمد | رسول الله

Centre:

الامام

المستعصم

بالله امير المؤمنين

السلطان الاعظم

The last line of the reverse centre contains the title of Kaykhusraw, al-Sulṭān al-A'ẓam, without his name. There is, however, no doubt that the title is his and not that of al-Ṣāliḥ Ismā'īl.

Balog (21, 2.78). BMC 437 (21, 2.97, ill.).

Type B

812. *Variety 1*

No Overlord

As above, but the border segments, both sides, and the reverse centre legend:

بسم الله | ضرب بدمشق | سنة احد | اربعين وستمائة

لا اله الا | الله وحده | لا شريك له | محمد رسول الله

Centre:

الامام

المستعصم

بالله ابو احمد

امير المؤمنين

ANS (22, —). ANS 71.76 (20.5, —). ANS-Hisp. (20, 2.80). ANS-Newell (21, —; 21, —). Balog (20, 2.78; 20, 2.75; 20, 2.76, ill.). Ziya 1692 (20, —).

Type B

813. *Variety 2*

As above, but the following obverse segments:

ضرب بدمشق|سنة احد|واربعين|ستمائة

ANS 71.76 (21, 2.94; 20, 2.90).

Type C

814. Overlord: al-Ṣāliḥ Ayyūb

[al-Ṣāliḥ Ismāʿīl's Name Omitted]

As above, but the obverse border segments:

بسم الله|ضرب بدمشق|سنة احد ا|ربعين ستمائة

Centre:

الملك الصالح
نجم الدنيا والدين
ايوب ابن محمد

ANS (20, 2.928).

Dr. Michael Bates identifies this coin as the very first issue on which al-Ṣāliḥ Ismāʿīl recognized al-Ṣāliḥ Ayyūb as his overlord in the treaty of 641 H. The present dirhem shows only the name of al-Ṣāliḥ Ayyūb, not that of al-Ṣāliḥ Ismāʿīl, although the latter was the recognized ruler of Damascus. It may represent al-Ṣāliḥ Ayyūb's initial position. However, on the next issue al-Ṣāliḥ Ismāʿīl's name appears again; but the place of honour, the entire obverse centre, is reserved for al-Ṣāliḥ Ayyūb; while the protocol of the prince of Damascus, al-Ṣāliḥ Ismāʿīl, is relegated to the bottom of the reverse centre, after that of the Caliph. This is the only case where a ruling prince's name takes second place on a coin.

815. *Type D*

Overlord: al-Ṣāliḥ Ayyūb

As above, but the obverse border segments:

الملك لله|ضرب بدمشق|سنة احد و|اربعين ستمائة

Centre:	Centre:
الملك الصالح	الامام
نجم الدين	المستعصم بالله
ايوب بن محمد	امير المؤمنين الملك
	الصالح اسمعيل

Album (2 specimens). ANS (19, 2.92). ANS 56.125 (21, —). ANS-Newell (20, 2.93; 20.5, 2.94). ANS-Newman (20, 2.88). ANS-Starosselsky (20.5, 2.95). Artuk 749 (23, 2.90). Balog, *BIE* XXXIV (1952) 1 (22, 2.76, ill.); 2 (20, 2.79); 3 (22, 2.85); 4 (21, 2.90, ill.); 5 (20, 2.96); 6 (20, 2.89); 7 (22, 2.87); 8 (20, 2.65). Berlin-Guthrie (20, 2.89). Paris (20, 2.81). Yapı-Kredi (20, 2.98; 21, 2.86).

816. *Damascus—641 H*

As No. 813, but muled with al-Mustanṣir reverse die.

Reverse Centre:
الامام
المستنصر
بالله ابو جعفر
المنصور امير المؤمنين

Album.

Damascus—642 H

817. *Type A*

As No. 812, but the following obverse segments:

بسم الله|ضرب بد|مشق سنة اثنين|اربعين ستمائة

Album 10 (bottom and right reverse segments: محمد رسو|ل الله). BM-Amedroz, *N.C.*, 3rd series, XIII (1893), p. 77 (20, 2.84, ill.).

818. *Type B*

As above, but the following obverse segments:

بسم الله|ضرب بدمشق|سنة اثني|اربعين وستمائة

ANS 71.76 (20, 2.84). Artuk 759 (21, 2.60). Balog (19, 2.85).

819. *Half Dirhem*

Border Segments:
ضرب بد|مشق سنة اثنين|اربعين|وستمائة
Centre:
الملك
الصالح

Border Segments:
لا اله الا|الله وحده|محمد رسو|ل الله
Centre:
الامام
المستعصم

Leuthold-Ripostiglio 38 (15, 1.42). Yapı-Kredi (12, 1.48).

Damascus—643 H

820. *Type A*

As No. 818, but the following date:

سنة ثلاث و|اربعين وستمائة

ANS (20, 2.846). Balog (20, 2.86, ill.).

821. *Type B*

As above, but parts of obverse and reverse border segments are written:

سنة ثلث|واربعين وستمائة

لا اله الا ا|لله وحده

Tewhid (22, —).

Half Dirhem

822. *Damascus—Date Missing*

As above, but the obverse and reverse border segments:

ضرب بد|مشق سنة|. . . . اربعين|وستمائة

لا اله|الا الله|محمد رسو|ل الله

Balog (15, 1.40, ill.). Lavoix 672 (15, 1.36). Østrup 1594 (—, 1.42). Paris (15, 1.35).

These half dirhems may have been issued by al-Ṣāliḥ Ismāʿīl (640–643 H), as well as al-Ṣāliḥ Ayyūb (644–647 H). However, after his conquest of Damascus in 644 H, al-Ṣāliḥ Ayyūb issued new dirhems and half dirhems with the multilobe design. Therefore, it seems more likely that the square-in-the circle type half dirhems belong to al-Ṣāliḥ Ismāʿīl. Dr. Michael Bates of the ANS considers that they are probably Crusader imitations of the original Damascus half dirḥemṣ of al-Ṣāliḥ Ismāʿīl.

823. *Damascus—Date Missing*

Border Segments:

. . .|ضرب بدمشق|. . .|. . .

Centre:

الملك الصالح
عماد الدنيا والدين
اسمعيل بن ابي بكر

Border Segments:

(لا اله الا الله)|الملك الموحد|محمد رسول الله ا|نساب الأشرف

Centre:

(الامام)
ا(لمستنصر)
بالله ابو جعفر
المنصور امير المؤمنين

ANS (21, —, ill.). The legends in the reverse segments are unusual.

The coins on which the Rūm Seljūqid, Kaykhusrāw II, is represented as the nominal overlord, dated 640 and 641 H, show clearly how hard al-Ṣāliḥ Ismāʿīl tried to form some alliance against his nephew, al-Ṣāliḥ Ayyūb of Egypt. Later, in 641 H, he was obliged to recognize the Egyptian sultan's supremacy, a submission that is reflected by the prominent display of al-Ṣāliḥ Ayyūb's name and protocol on the Damascus coins as the overlord, and the simple mention of the name of the prince of Damascus after the caliphal protocol on the obverse (*Catalogue* No. 815).

Crusader Imitations of the Damascus Dirhem of al-Ṣāliḥ Ismāʿīl

In 1952 I described silver dirhems which seemed to belong to al-Ṣāliḥ Ismāʿīl of Damascus, bearing his protocol and that of Caliph al-Mustanṣir. The dates, so far as they can be read with any certainty, are 641 and 644 H, but they are often garbled and faulty. Since the caliph died before 641 H and al-Ṣāliḥ Ismāʿīl was evicted from Damascus in 643 H, the coins are blatant anachronisms which could never have been produced by the Damascus mint. That they must be the product of Crusader mints is further evidenced by numerous dirhems which show the same two protocols, but a Christian date.

As these issues could be the source of perplexity to the reader who is not sufficiently acquainted with the appropriate literature, it is thought useful to mention them here and also to refer to a few existing articles where their descriptions can be found:

—Paul Balog, *BIE* XXXIV (1952);
—Balog and Yvon, *RN* (1958); and
— Michael L. Bates, *Studies in Honor of George C. Miles*, Beirut, 1974.

PRINCIPALITY OF ḤAMĀH

Saladin's favorite nephew, al-Muẓaffar Taqī al-Dīn ʿUmar, received Ḥamāh as his principal fief from his uncle, together with numerous other possessions. His principality was, however, to remain in a dependent position vis-à-vis Saladin. Taqī al-Dīn's son, al-Manṣūr Muḥammad I, inherited all his possessions in 587 H and was the first prince of Ḥamāh to issue copper coinage in his own name. The first issue has al-ʿAzīz ʿUthmān of Egypt as his overlord (589 H). The second issue, on which his name is engraved, recognizes the Ayyūbid prince al-Ẓāhir Ghāzī of Aleppo as his overlord.

AL-MANṢŪR NĀṢIR AL-DĪN MUḤAMMAD I IBN AL-MUẒAFFAR TAQĪ AL-DĪN ʿUMAR
[587–617 H = 1191–1220 AD]

COPPER

Ḥamāh—Undated

824. *Type A*

Overlord: al-ʿAzīz ʿUthmān of Egypt

Border on both sides: plain circle in circle of pellets.

ضرب
عثمان
الملك العزيز
الملك المنصور محمد
بحماه

∴ المؤ ∴
الامام الناصر
لدين الله امير
✳ منين ✳

[*Naskh* script]

Album. ANS (19, 2.93; 20, —). Berlin-Guthrie (21, 2.24). BMC 467 (19, 2.36, ill.); 468 (22, 2.40); 468a (23, 3.10). Lavoix 508 (21, 3.19, ill.); 509 (20, 3.20). Lane-Poole, *Coins of the Urtuqi Turcomans*, p. 39, No. 77 (attributed to al-Manṣūr Nāṣir al-Dīn Artūq Arslān).

825. *Type B*

Overlord: al-Ẓāhir Ghāzī of Aleppo

Border on both sides: plain circle in circle of pellets.

الملك الظاهر
الملك المنصور

ضر ب
الامام الناصر
بح ماه

[Ornate *Kūfic* script]

Album (ornaments vary slightly). ANS (20, 2.92). ANS-Charles Panish (21, 4.59, ill.). ANS-Wood (21, 3.38). BMC 464 (22, 1.20, ill.); 465 (24, 3.45, ill.); 467 (19, —). Ilisch 45 (21, —; shows traces of ضرب and the mint may be Manbij on the reverse). Paris (20, 4.90, ill.). Wien 682 (22, —, ill.). Zambaur, *NC*, Nos, 513 515 (average diameter 20; average weight 3.30).

826. *Ḥamāh 589 H*

Border on both sides: plain circle.

ضر ب
الملك المنصور
بحم . . سنة

تسع ثم(نين)
الامام النا ([illegible])
وخمس (ماية)

Album 13.

Manbij—Undated

827. *Type A*

Border of pellets between two plain lines.

الملك العزيز	الامام الناصر
الملك المنصور	منبج

[*Kūfic* script]

BM-Ilisch (21, 3.77, ill.). Castiglioni, p. 218, No. CXCII; Pl. IV, No. 5 (ill.; Castiglioni erroneously attributed it to al-Nāṣir Qilij Arslān).

828. *Type B*

As above, but the reverse centre:

ضر ب
الامام الناصر
بمنبج

Album 14.

829. *Type C*

Border on both sides: plain circle.

عثمان	المؤ
الملك العزيز	الامام الناصر
الملك المنصور محمد	لدين الله امير
منبج	منين

[*Naskh* script]

ANS (20, —, ill.). Balog (19, 1.45, ill.).

830. *Type D*

Border on both sides: circle of pellets between two plain circles.

	ضر ب
الملك العزيز	الامام الناصر
الملك المنصور	للدين امير المؤمنين
	بمنـ بج

[*Kūfic* script]

Ashmolean-Corrigan (22, 5.05, ill.). Ilisch 44 (20, —; incomplete specimen). Paris (24, —, ill.).

831. *No Mint—Undated*

Border missing on both sides.

عثمان	المؤ
الملك العزيز	الامام الناصر
الملك المنصور	لدين الله امير
محمد	منين

[*Naskh* Script]

Album (2 specimens, 1 with *Kūfic* script). Paris (19, —, ill.).

832. *Ḥarrān—587 H*

Border of dots. Counterclockwise marginal legend:

الملك المنصور بن عمر . . . .

Circle of small pellets, in which sultan (?) sits crosslegged, facing, holding up a large crescent. A star is under each elbow.

Border of dots in which is a square of dots. Segments:

ضرب بحر(ان)|سنة سبع|(وثمانين|(وخمسمائة

Centre:

الملك الناصر
صلاح الدين
يوسف بن ايوب

Berlin (25, 6.03, ill.). BM (25, —); [الملك ال(منصور ؟) is legible in the obverse margin. Similar to the Berlin coin; therefore probably an issue of al-Manṣūr Muḥammad—Saladin is only the overlord.] Zambaur, *Contrib. I*, p. 36, No. 72.

833. *Ḥarrān—589 H* (?)

Border not distinguishable.
Counterclockwise marginal legend:

الملك المنصو (*sic*) محمد

Sultan (?) sits cross-legged, facing, holding large crescent.

As above, but date in segments:

ضرب بحران|سنة تس. . . .|. . . . .|. . . . .

de Saulcy à Reynaud, *JA* (April 1842), pp. 315–326.

834. *Ḥarrān—Date Missing*

As 587 H, but most of the marginal legends and segments are missing. Lagumina attributed his specimens to Saladin, as did Ghalib Edhem.
Ghalib 190. Lagumina, p. 67, Nos. 7 (25, 5.90); 8 (26, 4.75); p. 68, Nos. 9 (26, 8.85); 10 (28, 6.63).

Another interesting copper issue should be mentioned. When Saladin deprived Kökbörī of Ḥarrān, he struck a Zengid-type copper coin there in 586 H. On this coin the obverse centre contains Saladin's protocol in large characters and on the reverse he is represented by a sitting, cross-legged, turbaned figure holding up a large crescent. When he presented his grand-nephew, al-Manṣūr Muḥammad I of Ḥamāh, with the city as a fief in 587 H, al-Manṣūr maintained the coin-type and continued to put his great-uncle's protocol in the place of honour. However, he had his own protocol engraved around the crescent.

I now believe that the incomplete or badly preserved specimens of Lagumina, which he attributed to Saladin, may belong to al-Manṣur Muḥammad I, as on all these coins both the obverse and reverse marginal legends are missing. They also are absent on Ghalib Edhem's Coin No. 190 (*Monnaies Turcomanes*, Catalogue of the Imperial Museum, Constantinople). De Saulcy, in his letter to Reynaud (*JA*, April 1842), does not even mention the marginal legends.

This last scholar dated his coin to 589 H. Only the two first letters of the digit of the date are on the flan. The letters تسـ and تسـ in *Kūfic* are often difficult to differentiate. In addition, Saladin died in Ṣafar 589 H; that is, during the second month of the new year; and after Saladin's death it is hardly likely that coins with his name as overlord would have continued to be issued. Therefore, 587 H is the more likely date, but I have listed the Lagumina and Ghalib specimens below.

There are no coins of al-Manṣūr Muḥammad I from Ḥarrān for 588 H. This is due to his being in disgrace with Saladin. After his father's death in 587 H, al-Manṣūr wrote to Saladin and asked him to promise, on written oath, that he would not deprive al-Manṣūr of his heritage. Saladin fell into a rage at this insult of his good faith and promptly stripped al-Manṣūr Muḥammad of all his properties. It cost al-ʿĀdil and other influential personalities protracted negotiations and great diplomatic skill, lasting well into 588 H, to induce Saladin to forgive his great-nephew for the tactless letter and restore his domains to him.

AL-MANṢŪR SAYF AL-DĪN MUḤAMMAD II IBN AL-MUẒAFFAR MAḤMŪD II [642–683 H = 1244–1284 AD]

COPPER

[Lavoix 698 is not an Ayyūbid dirhem, but belongs most probably to Qalāʿun.]

835. *[Ḥamāh?]—Undated*

Overlord: al-Ṣāliḥ Ayyūb

On both sides: six-pointed star interlaced with the margin. Both composed of a line of dots between two plain lines.

Centre:		Centre:
الملك المنصور		الملك الصالح

Album. BM (18, 2.07).

836. *[Ḥamāh]—Undated*

As above, but on both sides: six-pointed star of pellets in a circle of pellets:

Album.

837. *[Ḥamāh]—Undated*

As above, but on both sides: square of pellets within circle of pellets. In segments of obverse, one pellet in each segment.

Album (2 specimens; the second one has 2 pellets in each obverse segment).

838. *[Ḥamāh]—Undated*

Overlord: al-Nāṣir Yūsuf

On both sides: six-pointed star of pellets in a circle of pellets.

Centre:
الملك
المنصور

Centre:
الملك
الناصر

[*Naskh* Script]
BM (20, —, ill.).

839. [*Ḥamāh*]—*Undated*

As No. 837, but the reverse centre:

الملك
الناصر

Album.

840. *Ḥamāh—Undated*
Overlord: al-Nāṣir Yūsuf

Border on both sides: plain circle in circle of dots.

Centre:
الملك المن(صور)
ضرب بحماة

Centre:
يوسف
الملك الناصر

[*Naskh* script]
BM (20, , ill.).

PRINCIPALITY OF THE JAZĪRAH

AL-AWḤAD NAJM AL-DĪN AYYŪB IBN AL-ʿĀDIL I

Mayāfāriqīn and Sinjār [596–607 H = 1199–1210 AD]
Southern Armenia (Khilāṭ) [604–607 H = 1207–1210 AD]

COPPER

841. *Mayāfāriqīn: 599 H*

Border on both sides: plain circle in a circle of pellets.

Counterclockwise Marginal Legend:
سنة تسع وتسعين وخمستمائة هاجرية ضرب بميافرقين

Plain circle in which is a facing bust of the prince, covered by a bonnet. Hair hangs from temples. He wears a mantle, held together in front by a clasp, from which a pendant hangs down. The bust is set at the edge of the flan. Counterclockwise legend to the right and left of the head:
Left: نجم الدين : Right: الملك الاوحد :

Counterclockwise Marginal Legend
[Beginning at the right]:
|سيف الدين|ابو بكو بن ايوب الملك العادل

Centre:
لا اله الا الله
محمد رسول
الله الامام
الناصر لدين
الله امير
المؤمنين

Berlin-Guthrie (27, 8.79). BMC 440 (26, 6.48, ill.). Lavoix 674 (26, 7.18, ill.). München 85667 (26, 7.667). Østrup 1625 and 1626. Peus 1913. Soret à Sawélieff 71 (erroneously attributed to Mārdīn). Yapı-Kredi (26, 7.10; 26, 6.75).

842. *Mayāfāriqīn—600 H*

As above, but the following date:

ضرب هذا الدرهم بمافرقين سنة ستمائة

And the short legends right and left of the head:

Left: الاوحد Right: الملك

Album. ANS-Orlowsky (26.5, 7.44, ill.). ANS-Wood (26, 7.52). Artuk 775 (26, 9.70). BMC 441 (27, —; the date ends ؟(بال(هجرة)). Castiglioni, CLXXX, Pl. XI, No. 7 (new number of the Castello Sforzesco Museum in Milan: 350; 25, —, ill.). Lavoix 674 *bis*, *RN* 1935 (27, 11.68); 675 (27, 5.00). München 11789 (26, 4.737, ill.). Yapı-Kredi (27, 6.65; 25, 6.25). On Nos. 842–844 and 862–864, *Mayāfāriqīn* is written: Māfāriqīn.

843. *Mayāfāriqīn—601 H*

As above, but the following date:

ضرب هذا الدرهم بمافرقين سنة احد وستمائة

Album. ANS (33.5, 12.00). ANS-Newell (26, 8.74). ANS-Subhy Pasha (27, 7.51, ill.). Berlin-Guthrie (26, 9.73). BMC 442 (26, —). Castiglioni, CLXXXI (28, —). Lavoix 675 (26, 9.20. ill.). Prague 38/68 (26, —).

844. *Mayāfāriqīn: 602 H*

As above, but the following date:

ضرب هذا الدرهم بمافرقين سنة اثنين وستمائة قمرية

ANS (27, 7.96). Ashmolean-Christ Church 257 (27, 9.51, ill.). Lavoix 677 (27, 9.48, ill.). Lane-Poole, *Fasti Arabici* V (may be the coin now in the Ashmolean). Paris (26, —).

845. *Mayāfāriqīn(?)—605 H*
Overlord: al-ʿĀdil I

No mint, but the Mayāfāriqīn type.

Border of pellets. Counterclockwise marginal legend:

الملك الاوحد نجم الدنيا والدين شاه ارمن ابو الفتح بن الملك العادل

Facing bust of turbaned prince, earrings or pendants hanging. Cloak around shoulders, gathered in the centre with left hand. Head is flanked by a short, counterclockwise legend:

Left: وستمائة Right: سنة خمس

Border: plain circle in circle of pellets, within which is a linear six-pointed star formed by two triangles.

In the external segments:

الدين | ابو بكر | بن ايوب الملك | العادل | سيف |

In the small triangles:

الله | امير | المؤ[*sic*]الامام | الناصر | لدين |

Centre:

لا اله ا
لا الله محمد
رسول
الله

Album. ANS-Newell (28.5, 10.31). ANS-Newman (30, 10.53). ANS-Proskey (29, 8.19). ANS-Torrey (30, 10.47; 32, 12.45; 29.5, 13.85, ill.; digit: خمسة). ANS-Wright (30, —; digit: خمسة). Artuk 776 (30, 12.65). Berlin-Guthrie (30, 11.16). Berman 213 (28, 13.10). BMC 444 (29, 8.86; clasps robe with his right hand; [reverse segments: العادل | سيف الد | ين ابو بكر الملك]; 445 (30, 11.89); [reverse segments: الملك العاد[*sic*] | سف[*sic*]ا | لد ين]; 446 (30, 11.54); [reverse centre: ل‌الله | محمد رسو | الا الله | لا اله]; 447 (30, 14.60); 448 (30, 12.30). Butak I, p. 109, No. 123 (30, —). Castiglioni, CLXXXII (28, —). Ghalib 194 [obverse marginal legend: . . . . شاه ارمن ايوب ابن الملك العا(دل); reverse small triangles: الا ما | امير المؤ | الله | لد | النا; reverse centre: لا اله | الا الله | محمد رسو | ل الله]. Izzet 340 and 341. Lavoix 678 (29, 11.45, ill.; clasp in left hand); 679 (30, 12.72, ill.; clasp in right hand); 680 (28, 9.92; clasp in right hand); 681 (29, 12.82; clasp in right hand); 682 (30, 10.85; clasp in left hand). München 97750 (29, 12.483; reverse segments: الملك | العاد[*sic*] | سيف ا | لدين | ابو بكر | بن ايوب; inner triangles: امير المؤ | الله | لدين | الناصر | الامام; centre: لا الله محمد | لا اله اا | [*sic*] الله | رسول). Private collection, Izmir, Turkey (28, —; clasp in left hand). Tewhid (29, —).

Armenia

SILVER

846. *Khilāṭ or Akhlāṭ—Date Missing*

Border on both sides: double intertwined trilobes, composed of a line of pellets between two plain lines.

Border Segments:	Border Segments:
. . . | خلاط سنة | . . . | . . . | . . .	لا | اله | الا | الله | محمد | رسو ل الله
Centre:	Centre:
شاه	احمد
الملك الاوحد	٢
ابو الفتح ايوب	الامام الناصر
ارمن	الملك العادل
	ابو بكر

[*Naskh* script]

al-Awḥad's title is Shāh Armān. Artuk 774 (20, 2.75, ill.). BMC 439 (19, 2.62, ill.). Ziya 1659 (19, —).

AL-ASHRAF MUẒAFFAR AL-DĪN ABŪ AL-FATḤ MŪSĀ IBN AL-ʿĀDIL I

Mayāfāriqīn, Sinjār and Ḥarrān [607–617 H = 1210–1220 AD]

Southern Armenia (Khilāṭ) [607–617 H = 1210–1220 AD]

Damascus (No Coinage) [626–634 H = 1229–1237 AD]

SILVER

847. *Mayāfāriqīn—615 H*

Six-pointed star type.

Border Segments:	Border Segments:
ضرب | بميه | فرقين | خمس | عشرو | . . .	. . . | الا ا | لله | محمد | رسول | الله
Centre:	Centre:
ابو بكر	الامام
الملك العادل	الناصر الدين
الملك الاشرف	الله امير المؤ
موسى	منين

Album.

COPPER

848. *[Mayāfāriqīn]—608 H*

With Title: Shāh Armān; Overlord: al-ʿĀdil I

Border on both sides: plain circle in a circle of pellets.

Counterclockwise marginal legend:

الملك الاشرف مظفر الدين شاه ارمن ابو الفتح موسى

The turbaned prince, seated facing, right leg drawn up; orb in right hand, with left hand on hip.

Counterclockwise legend at both sides of the head:

Left: وستمائة Right: سنة ثمان

Triangular shield with convex side-centres, composed of a plain line in a line of dots, the shield touching the border.

Counterclockwise marginal legend in the segments between border and shield, beginning at right:

الملك العاد|ل سيف الدين|ابو بكر بن ايوب

In the shield:

منين
الامام الناصر
لدين الله
امير المؤ

Ziya 1680 (31, —).

[Mayāfāriqīn]—612 H

849. *Type A*

As above, but the date to the right and left of the head:

Left: وستمائة Right: سنة ثنا عشر

Album. ANS-Newell (31, 10.57). ANS-Newman (30.5, 10.57; 30, 11.34; 31.5, 11.50). ANS-Wood (29, 10.82; 30, 9.57; 28, 8.44; 29, 9.56; 31, 12.57; 31, 10.57; 29, 11.08). ANS-UM (31, 12.40; 31, 10.65; 31, 11.57; 29, 11.81; many other specimens). ANS-Wright (28.5, 11.35; 30, 11.95). Ashmolean-St. John's College and Covernton Collection (30, 12.71). Ashmolean-Thorburn (30, —). Balog (31, 11.30, ill.). Berlin-Guthrie (30, 10.25, ill. [obverse marginal legend ends: ابو الفتح مو; 30, 13.26; 29, 12.628 [obverse marginal legend ends: موسى; on the body of the prince, downward: سى]; 32, 15.00). Ghalib 196 (29, —). Lagumina, p. 92, No. 74 (27, 13.55). Lavoix 683 (31, 11.97); 684 (30, 13.20); 685 (29, 11.70); 686 (27, 12.60); 687 (30, 13.45); 688 (27, 8.50); 689 (28, 12.20). Mitchell-Brown (30, 10.45). Nicol (31.8, 11.81). Paris 87 (25, 8.82). Prague 38/68 (22, —). Vatican (30, —; 29, —). Wien 684 (27, —); 685 (26, —). Ziya 1681 (29, —); 1682 (28, —).

850. *Type B*

As above, but the reverse marginal legend and centre:

الملك العادل|سيف الدين|ابو بكر

Reverse Centre:

الامام الناصر
لدين الله
امير المؤمنين
ايوب

BMC 452 (29, 12.90, ill.). München 97749 (28, 11.426); 85663 (30, 11.608); 85792 (30, 11.411); 85666 (30, 11.551); Unnumbered (30, 12.76).

Mayāfāriqīn—612 H

851. *Type A*

With Title: Shāh Armān; Overlord: al:'Ādil I

As above, but the following marginal legends on both sides:

الملك الاشرف مظفر الدين شاه ارمن ابو الفتح موسى ضرب بميافرقين   الملك العاد|ل سيف الدين|ابو بكر بن ايوب

The mint is either complete: بميافرقين, or only partially written: بما.

ANS (32, 13.42; 30, 12.06; 30, 11.09). ANS-UM (31, 12.57; 30, 13.41; 31, 10.67). Artuk 777 (30, 13.40). Berlin (31, 11.47; mint: بما). Berlin 33/1878 (30, 10.70; mint بمافرقين), Berlin Mordtmann (30, 10.66; mint: بما). BMC 453 (30, —, ill.; reverse segments: العادل; reverse overstruck on al-Awḥad's 605 H coin); 454 (30, —, ill.; countermark: GG). Butak I, p. 110, No. 124. Castiglioni, CLXXXIII, Pl. IV, No. 4. Izzet 327. Krehl 1. Lagumina, p. 91 No. 73 (31, 10.60), Ziya 1 (29, —), 2 (28, —).

852. *Type B*

Without Title: Shāh Armān

As above, but the following obverse marginal legend:

الملك الاشرف مظفر الدين ابو الفتح موسى ضرب بما

Berman 214 (30, 11.55). BMC 450 (28, —, ill.); 451 (28, —, ill.). Ghalib 195 (30, —). Lagumina, p. 91, No. 73 (21, 10.60).

853. *Sinjār—615 H*

With title: Shāh Armān; Overlord: al-Kāmil I

Border on both sides: plain circle with counterclockwise marginal legends:

الملك الاشرف شاه ارمن موسى بن ابى بكر

Centre:

Plain circle. Prince sits facing, with legs drawn in, oriental fashion. Turbaned head and halo of minute dots around head. Right hand holds orb; the left rests on his lap. Small figure.

Counterclockwise legend to right and left of the head:

Left: خمسعشر ستمائة   Right: سنجار سنة

لا اله|الا الله|محمد رسو|ل الله

Centre:

الامام الناصر
لدين الله
امير المؤمنين
الملك الكامل
محمد

In bottom segments, clockwise: رسو; counterclockwise: محمد.

Album (2 specimens). Balog (25, 9.65). Berlin-Guthrie (23, 6.80). BM-Pietraszewski (24, —). BMC 456 (24, 9.64, ill.). Butak I, p. 111, No. 125. Ghalib 198 (24, —); 199 (25, —). Lavoix 690 (24, 10.40, ill.). Yapı-Kredi (25, 11.00; 26, 8.90).

Sinjār—617 H

854. *Type A*

As above, but the following date:

Left: عشر وستمائة   Right: سنجار سبع

and the orb is in the *left* hand.

Album. ANS (24.5, 7.33; 24, 7.15; 26, 9.35; 25.5, 9.38; 27.5, 10.84; 24, 6.67; 25, 8.12). Ashmolean-Christ Church 259 (25, —). Ashmolean-A. C. Kay (29, —; 29, —). Berlin-Guthrie (24, 9.30). Berman 215 (25, 9.45). BMC 457 (24, 7.05, ill); 458 (23, 7.06); 459 (24, 7.84); 460 (29, 14.52). da Cunha 1467 (28, —). Fraehn, *Nova Suppl.*, p. 93, No. 7a. Ghalib 200 (26, —). Lavoix 691 (24, 9.40, ill.); 692 (24, 8.80). Miles—*Sinjār*, 37 (24, —). Paris (24, 9.92; 25, 11.28; 26, 9.66, ill.). Peus 1916. Yapı-Kredi (24, 9.25; 25, 8.15; 25, 11.68). Ziya 1 (24, —); 2 (25, —).

855. *Type B*

As above, but the orb is in the *right* hand.

ANS (26, —; 24, —; 25, —; 23, —, ill.; 24, —). BMC 456 (24, 7.05). Krehl 2. Miles-*Sinjār*, 38 (24, —); 39 (25, —).

856. *Mint and Date Missing*

Type not stated.

Marginal Legend:
.... وستماية
Centre:
الملك
الاشرف موسى بن
الملك .....

[Marginal legend missing]

Centre:
الامام
بالله
المستنصر
الملك العادل

Izzet 328.

SILVER

857. *Ḥarrān—617 H*

Overlord: al-Kāmil I

Square-in-the-circle type.

Border Segments:
بسم الله|ضرب بحران|سنة سبع|عشر وستمائة
Centre:
الملك الكامل محمد
الملك الاشرف
موسى بن ابي بكر

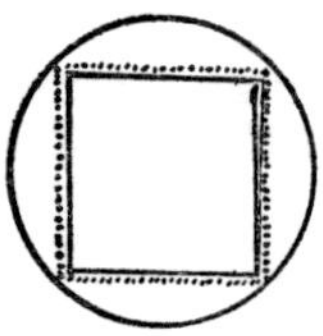

Border Segments:
لا اله الا ا|لله وحده|لا شريك له|محمد رسول الله
Centre:
الامام الناصر
لدين الله امير
المؤمنين احمد

[*Naskh* script]

ANS 72.162 (21, —, ill.).

Ḥarrān—618 H

Overlord: al-Kāmil I

858. *Type A*

As above, but the obverse segments and both centre legends:

بسم الله|ضرب بحران|سنة ثمان|عشر وستمائة

Centre:
الملك الكامل
محمد الملك الاشر
ف موسى بن ابي بكر
∴

Centre:
الامام الناصر
لدين الله امير
المؤمنين احمد

ANS (22, —). BM (22, 3.02, ill.).

859. *Type B*

As No. 858, but the obverse border segments and centre legend:

ناصر الدين محمد |ضرب بحران|سنة ثمانية|عشر وستمائة

Centre:
الملك الكامل
الملك الأشرف
موسى بن ابى بكر

Album 51. ANS-Laties (21, 2.959, ill.). BM.

Half Dirhem

860. *Ḥarrān—618 H*

Border Segments:
ضرب| . . . . سنة|ثمان عشر|وستمائة
Centre:
الملك
الاشرف

[Border Segments missing]

Centre:
الامام الناصر
لدين الله امير
المؤمنين احمد

ANS-Laties (15, 1.13).

861. *Akhlāṭ—617 H*

Ovorlord: al Kāmil I

Six-pointed star type.

Border Segments:
ضرب|اخلط|سنة|سبع|عشر و|ستمائة

Border Segments:
لا اله|الا ا|لله|محمد|رسول|الله

Centre:
موسى
الملك الاشرف
بن بو (*sic*) بكر ابن
ايوب

Centre:
احمد
الامام الناصر
الملك الكامل
محمد

[*Kūfic* script]

Abū of *Abū Bakr* without an *alif*: بو.

ANS (20, 2.97, ill.). ANS-Laties (20, 2.625). München 85013 (19, 2.76, ill.; date missing).

AL-MUẒAFFAR SHIHĀB AL-DĪN GHĀZĪ IBN AL-ʿĀDIL ABŪ BAKR I

Mayāfāriqīn [617–642 H = 1220–1242 AD]

Khilāṭ [617–621 H = 1220–1224 AD]

COPPER

862. *Mayāfāriqīn—617 H*
With Title: al-Malik
Overlords: al-Kāmil I; al-Ashraf Mūsā
Caliph: al-Nāṣir

Square-in-the-circle type. Transliteration from Weyl; the hypothetic arrangement of the individual letters is based on the 618 H coins.

Border Segments:
ضرب بمافار|قين سنة|سبع عشر|وستمائة
Centre:
الملك الاشرف
موسى الملك ا
لمظفر غازي

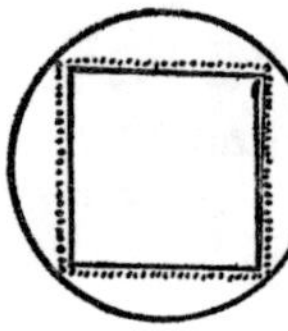

Border Segments:
لا اله الا|الله وحده لا|شريك له محمد|رسول الله
Centre:
الامام الناصر
احمد الملك ا
لكامل محمد

[*Naskh* script]

Weyl 6550 (24, —).

863. *Mayāfāriqīn—618 H*

As above, but the obverse border segments:

ضرب بميافار|قين سنة|ثمان وعشرة|وستمائة

[Above الناصر in reverse centre: ٢]

Album. ANS (31.5, 10.23; 31.5, 11.01; 30.5, 12.00; 22.5, 7.26; 24.5, 7.61; mint missing on last 2, but there is no doubt that it is Mayāfāriqīn). Artuk 778 (20, 8.85). Ashmolean-Thorburn (25, 8.47, ill.). Balog (24, 6.88, ill.). BMC 462 (32, 13.68). Butak I, p. 112, No. 126 (31, —; Butak read the date as 628 H, but it is 618 H). da Cunha 1468 (26, —). Ghalib 201 (31, —); 202 (28, —); 203 (25, —); 204 (24, —). Izzet 332 to 339 (only 332 is fully described. As the caliph is al-Nāṣir, it must be 618 H and not 628 H). Lavoix 693 (25, 7.52, ill.; date was read as 627 H, but it *is* 618 H). Yapı-Kredi (25, 8.25; 20, 5.72; 23, 5.40; the date was read as 628, but it *is* 618 H). Zambaur, *NC*, 517 to 519 (average diameter and weight: 25, 6.25; obverse segments: ضرب بميا|فارقين سنة|ثمان عشرة|وستمائة).

864. *Mayāfāriqīn—[617–622 H]*
Caliph: al-Nāṣir

As above, but the digit or the digit and the decade of the date missing.

Album (3 specimens). BMC 461 (25, 8.94); 463 (25, 10.99). Lavoix 694 (29, 10.06). Pietraszewski 451. Prague 922 (27, —).

865. *Mayāfāriqīn—627 H*

As above, but with Caliph al-Mustanṣir and the following date:

(ضرب بميا فا|رقين) سنة|سبع عشرين|وستمائة

Reverse Centre:

الامام
المستنصر
بالله امير المؤ
منين

Çetinyalçın (22, —; mint missing, but it most likely is *Mayāfāriqīn*). Lavoix 695 (21, 4.25, ill.; date missing).

866. *Mayāfāriqīn—628 H*

As above, but the following date:

(ضرب بميافا|رقين) سنة|ثمان وعشرين|وستمائة

Wien 7804 (22, —; mint missing, but it is mostly likely *Mayāfāriqīn*.

867. *Mayāfāriqīn—624 or 634 H*
Overlord: al-Kāmil I; al-Ashraf Mūsā

Six-pointed linear star in six-pointed dotted star.

Border Segments:

. . .|بميافار|قين سنة|اربعة|. . .|. . .

Centre:

الملك
الاشرف موسى
الملك المظفر
غازي

Border Segments:

لا اله|الا|الله|(محمد|رسول|الله)

Centre:

الامام
بالله
المستنصر
الملك الكامل
محمد

Album.

868. *Mayāfāriqīn—Date Missing*

As above, but the following obverse border segments and reverse centre:

ضرب|بميا|فرقين سنة|. . . . .|وثلاثين

Centre:

الامام
بالله
المستنصر
الملك الكامل
محمد

Album (2 specimens). Balog (21, 1.42, ill.). BMC 466 (20, 2.79); 466a (20, 2.82, ill.; date: 63x H). Lavoix 696 (20, 3.10). Paris (20, 4.16; 20, —). Pietraszewski 453. Prague 923 (20, —).

869. *Mayāfāriqīn—634 H*

Overlord: al-Kāmil I

As above, but the following date and centre legends:

اربع | وثلاثين | وستمائة

Centre:

الملك

الكامل محمد

الملك المظفر

غازي

Centre:

الامام

المستنصر

بالله امير المؤ

منين

Album 15 (3 specimens, one with digit: اربعة ; others incomplete). Nicol (19.6, 3.263; date incomplete). Paris (19, 3.42; 18, 2.74; 20, 2.63, ill.).

870. *Mayāfāriqīn—641 H or Later*

Overlord: al-Ṣāliḥ Ayyūb; Caliph: al-Mustaʿṣim

Linear hexalobe type. Border on both sides: plain circle in circle of dots. Counterclockwise marginal legend on both sides:

ضرب بميافارقين سنة احد واربعين وستمائة

لا اله الا الله وحده لا شريك له محمد رسول الله

Linear hexalobe on both sides.

Centre:

الملك

الصالح ايوب

الملك المظفر

غازى

Centre:

الامام

المستعصم

بالله امير المؤ

منين

Album (date missing). ANS (20, 2.17, ill.; date missing). Ashmolean-Thorburn (22, 3.76; date missing). Berlin-Guthrie (21, 4.34; date missing). Butak I, p. 112, No. 127 (20, —; Butak read a date, although it is actually off the flan. He also mistakenly read فى before سنة). Lavoix 697 (21, 4.80, ill.; date missing). Yapı-Kredi (20, 5.00; 20, 4.45).

871. *Mayāfāriqīn—647 H*

Border on both sides: linear circle in circle of pellets, within which is a linear square in a square of pellets.

Border Segments:

(ضرب بميافر) | قين سنة | سبع و | (اربعين وستمائة

Centre:

الملك الصالح ا

يوب الملك الكا

مل محمد غازي

Border Segments:

لا اله ا | لا الله | محمد ر | سول الله

Centre:

الامام

المستعصم

بالله امير المؤ

منين

Yapı-Kredi (27, —, ill.).

With Title: al-Sulṭān al-Malik

Careful examination of the coins shows that the caliph is al-Mustanṣir and not al-Mustaʿṣim. The date is missing, but on one of the Paris *fulūs* the beginning of the digit: ار = اربع can be deciphered.

The title *sulṭān* and the absence of an overlord seem to indicate that the coins were struck after the death of al-Ashraf Mūsā in 634 H, when al-Muẓaffar Ghāzī became virtually independent. The digit of the date (four) would indicate 634 H. The other coins were probably issued between 634 and 640 H; that is, before the advent of al-Musta ʿṣim. The title of *sulṭān* is, of course, self-bestowed.

872. *Mayāfāriqīn—634 H*

Border on both sides: plain circle in a circle of pellets.

Border Legend:	Border Legend [Beginning at left]:
ضرب بمافر|قين سنة|ار . . . .|. . . .	لا اله|الا الله|محمد|رسول الله
Centre:	Centre:
السلطان ا	الامام
الملك المظفر	المستنصر
غازي بن ايوب	بالله امير
	المؤمنين

[*Kūfic* script]

Album (2 specimens). ANS (20, 2.17, ill.; 18, 1.86, ill.). Ashmolean-Thorburn (21, 3.52, ill.). Paris (23, 3.55. ill.; 18, —, ill.).

873. *Mayāfāriqīn: Date Missing*

As above, but border legends begin at the right on both sides.

Border Legend:	Border Legend:
ضرب (بما) فار|قين|. . .|. . .	
Centre:	Centre:
السلطان	الامام
الملك المظفر	المستنصر
غازي بن ايوب	بالله امير ا
	(لمؤ) منين

Album 16.

874. *Khilāṭ—618 H*

Overlords: al-Kāmil Muḥammad I; al-Ashraf Mūsā I

Square-in-the-circle type.

Border Segments:	Border Segments:
ضرب بخلاط|سنة ثمان|(عشرو)|ستمائة	لا اله الا|الله وحده|لا شردك له محمد|رسول الله
Centre:	Centre:
الملك الاشرف	الامام الناصر
موسى الملك ا	احمد الملك ا
لمظفر غازي	لكامل محمد

Album 52. ANS (24, —, ill.). Ziya 1685 (30, —).

AL-KĀMIL ABŪ AL-MAʿĀLĪ NĀṢIR AL-DĪN MUḤAMMAD II IBN AL-MUẒAFFAR GHĀZĪ
Mayāfāriqīn and Āmid [642–658 H = 1244–1259 AD]

SILVER

875. *Mayāfāriqīn—Date Missing*

Title: al-Sulṭān al-Malik; Caliph: al-Mustaʿṣim

No Overlord

Linear square in a square of small pellets.

Border Segments:

ضرب. . .؟|معا . . .؟|. . .|. . .

Centre:

السلطان الملك ا

لكامل ناصر الدنيا وا

لدين ابو المعالي محمد

بن غازي بن ابـي بكر بن ايوب

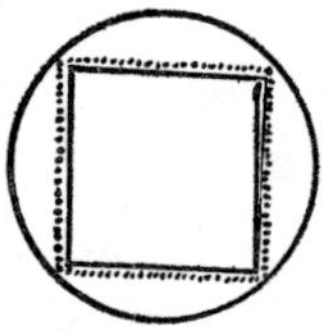

Border Segments:

الملك|. . .|. . .|. . .

Centre:

لا اله الا الله

وحده لا شريك له

محمد رسول الله

؟الامام المستعصم لله؟

[*Naskh* script]

Zambaur, *NC*, 520 (23, 3.44).

Zambaur's reading of the segments is not confirmed by his illustration. Taking into consideration existing similar coins, I believe that his specimen is a copper *fals* silvered at a later stage. I doubt his reading of the last line of the reverse centre, as rendered above, and believe that it should be: ارسله بالهدى ودين الحق. I also believe that the present coin belongs to Type D of the copper series, with the following legends in the reverse segments: ضرب هذا|الدرهم بما|فارقين|المحروسة.

I am tempted to date this coin between the death of the ʿAbbāsid caliph in 656 H and the Mongol occupation of Mayāfāriqīn in 658 H.

876. *Mayāfāriqīn—65x H*

No Overlord; No Caliph

Ornamented double trefoil consisting of a line of dots between two plain lines.

Border Segments:

ضرب|بما|فار|قين|سنة|. . .|خمسين|ستمائة

Centre:

خير

الصحابه ابو بكر

عمر وعثمان وعلي

محمد ابن غازي ابن ابـي

بكر

Border Segments:

لا|اله|ا|لله|محمد|رسول|الله

Centre:

لا

اله الا الله و

حده لا شريك له

محمد رسول الله

[*Naskh* script]

Artuk 779 (22, 3.15, ill.). Tewhid (22, —).

The religious legend, with its invocation to the four orthodox caliphs, and the absence of the caliph's name, indicate a date between 656 and 658 H.

COPPER

Mayāfāriqīn—642 to 644 H

[Kaykāwus died in 644 H]

Overlord: Kaykāwus II; Caliph: al-Musta'ṣim

877. *Type A*

Variety 1

Border on both sides: circle of pellets.

Centre:
ضرب بما فرقين
السلطان الاعظم عز
الدنيا والدين كيكاوس
والملك الكامل
ناصر الدين محمد
بن غازي

Centre:
لا اله الا الله
محمد رسول الله
المستعصم

Istanbul (21, —).

878. *Type A*

Variety 2

As above, but the obverse inscription:
السلطان
الاعظم عز الد
نيا والدين كيكاوس
بن كيخسرو الملك الكامل
بن غازي

Istanbul (20, —).

Mayāfāriqīn—647 H

Title: al-Malik; Overlord: al-Ṣāliḥ Ayyūb; Caliph: al-Musta'ṣim

879. *Type B*

Linear square in a square of dots or small pellets

Border Segments:
ضرب بميافر|قين سنة|سبع اربعين|وستمائة
Centre:
الملك الصالح
ايوب الملك الكا
مل محمد بن غازي

Border Segments:
لا اله ا|لا الله|محمد|رسول الله
Centre:
الامام
المستعصم
بالله امير المؤ
مين

Album (mint and date missing, but this coin). Yapı-Kredi (24, 6.00; 23, 2.95).

880.

Type C

Mayāfāriqīn—651(?) H

Title: al-Sulṭān al-Malik; No Overlord; No Caliph

Linear square in a square of small pellets.

Border Segments:	Border Segments:
(سنة) | (احـ)دى ؟ | وخمسين | وستمائة	ضرب | (هذا الدر | هم) بميا | فارقين
Centre:	Centre:
السلطان الملك ا	لا اله الا الله
لكامل ناصر الدنيا وا	وحده لا شريك له محمد
لدين ابو المعالي محمد	رسول الله ارسله
بن غازي بن ابـي بكر ابن ايوب	بالهدى ودين الحق

Album. Ashmolean-Thorburn (25, 2.58, ill.; 24, 3.21, ill.; 24, 2.08; date missing, but probably the same issue). Paris (22, 3.49, ill.; on this specimen: محمد is at the beginning of the reverse third line instead of at the end of the second).

881.

Mayāfāriqīn—656 H

As above, but the following date:

. . نة | ستة | خمـ . . | . . .

Album.

882.

Type D

Mayāfāriqīn al-Maḥrūsah—655 H

Title: al-Sulṭān al-Malik; No Overlord; No Caliph

As above, but the following border segments and reverse centre legend:

سنة | خمس | وخمسين | (وستمائة)	ضرب هذا | الدرهم | بميافرقين | المحروسة
	Centre:
	لا اله الا الله
	وحده لا شريك له
	محمد رسول الله ار
	سله بالهدى ودين الحق

Artuk 780 (21, 4.90, ill.). Tewhid (26, —, ill.).

883.

Āmid—65x H

Title: al-Malik; No Overlord; Caliph: al-Mustaʿṣim

Linear square in a square of small pellets or dots.

Border Segments:	Border Segments:
ضرب بامد | . . . . . | وخمسين | وستمائة	لا اله الا | الله وحده | محمد | رسول الله
Centre:	Centre:
الملك الكامل ناصر	* الامام *
الدنيا والدين ابو	المستعصم بالله
المعالي محمد بن غا	ابو احمد عبد
زي بن ابـي بكر بن ايوب	الله امير المؤمنين

Album. ANS (20, —, ill.; 20, —). Tewhid (22, —, ill.).

The two small six-pointed stars flanking the word الامام on the reverse are characteristic for this issue of *Āmid*. Therefore, I believe that Zambaur, *Nouvelles Contrib.* 521 (21, 2.93) and ANS (21, 2.43), on both of which the mint missing, but the two small stars are plainly visible on the reverse, are from Āmid.

884. *Ḥiṣn (?)—(6) × 6 H*

No Overlord; Caliph: al-Musta'ṣim

Linear square in a square of pellets.

Border Segments:

ضرب بحصن؟|سنة ست . . .|. . .|. . .

Centre:

الملك الكامل

محمد ابي بكر

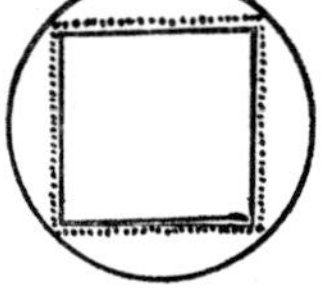

Border Segments:

لا اله|الا الله|محمد|رسول الله

Centre:

الامام

المستعصم

بالله امير المؤمنين

Tewhid (22, —).

The filiation is curious. al-Kāmil II was a son of al-Muẓaffar Ghāzī ibn al-'Ādil Abū Bakr. Therefore it is possible that the protocol is only a simplified or abbreviated form, as the name of the prince is followed directly by that of his grandfather. The mint, i.e., 'castle': حصن is yet to be identified. It cannot be Ḥiṣn-Kayfā, which was in the possession of al-Mu'aẓẓam Tūrānshāh or his son, al-Muwaḥḥid 'Abd Allāh, when al-Kāmil Muḥammad II reigned.

885. *[Mayāfāriqīn?]—(64)7 H*

Overlord: al-Ṣāliḥ Ayyūb

Border on both sides: plain circle in a circle of dots, in which a linear square in a square of dots. Mint name is missing.

Border Segments:

. . . .|. . .|سنة|سبع و(اربعين)|(ستمائة)

Centre:

الملك الصالح ا

يوب الملك الكامل

محمد بن غازي

Border Segments:

. . . .|. . . .|. . . .|رسول الله

Centre:

الامام

المستعصم

بالله امير المؤ

منين

Ashmolean (21, —, ill.). Paris (21, —, ill.).

The specimen in the Ashmolean is overstruck, probably on a copper coin of Āmid of the *six-pointed, convex-sided star* type of al-Ṣāliḥ Ayyūb. Three arches are still visible and in the top arch there are traces of a word which may be *Āmid*.

PRINCIPALITY OF ḤIṢN-KAYFĀ

Ḥiṣn-Kayfā is the only Ayyūbid principality that survived the Īlkhānid onslaught of 658 H (1260 AD) and lasted until 930 H (1523 AD). In 629 H (1231 AD) al-Kāmil Muḥammad I took Ḥiṣn-Kayfā from its last Artuqid prince and gave it to his son, al-Ṣāliḥ Ayyūb, who, in 635 H (1237 AD), entrusted it to his own son, al-Mu'aẓẓam Tūrānshāh. Henceforth, Ḥiṣn-Kayfā remained in the hands of Tūrānshāh's branch. Two foreign occupations interrupted their rule: first was that of the Mongols in 658 H, which may not have lasted long; and second, in 866 H—that of the Aq Qoyunlu.

All the Ḥiṣn-Kayfā Ayyūbid issues are *silver*, except one of al-Muwaḥḥid ʿAbd Allāh and two of al-Kāmil Khalīl ibn Aḥmad, which are copper *fulus*. The first Ḥiṣn-Kayfā Ayyūbid to strike coins was:

AL-MUWAḤḤID TAQĪ AL-DĪN ʿABD ALLĀH IBN AL-MŪʿAẒẒAM TŪRĀNSHĀH
[647–659 H = 1249–1260 AD]

SILVER

886. *Ḥiṣn—654 H*

Overlord: al-Nāṣir Yūsuf

Border of pellets on both sides. Counterclockwise marginal legend on both sides:

ضرب هذا الدرهم بحصن سنة اربع خمسين وستمائة

لا اله الا الله وحده محمد رسول الله

Circle of pellets on both sides

Centre:
الله
سف
الملك الناصر يو
الملك الموحد
عبد

Centre:
الله
لا اله الا الله
وحده لا شريك له
محمد رسول

[*Kūfic* script]

Tewhid-Bruxelles 1 (20, 1.70).

887. *Ḥiṣn—656 H*

Six-pointed star type.

Border Segments:
ضرب هذا|الدرهم|حصن|سنة ستة|خمسين و
Centre:
الله
الملك الناصر يوسف
الملك الموحد
عبد

Border Segments:
لا|اله|الا|الله|محمدر|سول الله
Centre:
الله
لا اله الا الله
وحده لا شريك له
محمد رسول

[*Kūfic* script]

Şerafettin Erel III, No. 14 (21, 1.70).

888. *Ḥiṣn—657 H*

As No. 886, but the following mint and date legend:

حصن|سنة سبع|وخمسين وستمائة

Plain circle on both sides.

Tewhid (20, 1.50, ill.; 20, 1.70).

889. *Ḥiṣn—658 H*

Overlords: Mangū Qān and Hūlāgū Īlkhān

Date missing, but must be 658 H because the Īlkhānid conquest came in 658 H and Mangū died in the same year. Six-pointed star type.

Border Segments:
لا | اله | الله | الا | الله | محمد ر | سول الله
Centre:
الله
الملك الموحد
تقي الدين
عبد

Border Segments:
ضرب | حصن | سنة | ثمان | خمسين | وستمائة
Centre:
منكو
قا ان العادل
هولاكو ايلخان
المع
[i.e.: المعظم]

[*Kūfic* script]

ANS-Nilsson (21, 2.027, ill.). Artuk 782 (20, 1.75, ill.). Tewhid-Bruxelles 2 (21, 2.45, ill.; reverse centre, last two words probably misread). Yapı-Kredi (19, 2.08).

890. *Ḥiṣn—658 H*

Overlord: Hūlāgū alone

Six-pointed star type.

Border Segments:
لا اله | الا | الله | محمد | رسول | الله
Centre:
الله
الملك الموحد
تقي الدين
عبد

Border segments:
ضرب | حصن | سنة | ثمان | خمسين | وستمائة
Centre:
خان
هولاكو
المعظم
ايل

[*Kūfic* script]

Yapı-Kredi (21, 1.55).

COPPER

890A. *Mint and Date Missing*

Border missing:
الله الملك
الموحد
تقي الدين

Plain circle:
دل هولا
ايلخان كو
المعظم
Left segment: قا

The legend دل الله is divided, دل appearing on the reverse and الله on the obverse.

Private collection, Geneva (21, —).

AL-KĀMIL ABU BAKR MUḤAMMAD IBN AL-MUWAḤḤID ʿABD ALLĀH

[682 H—(?) H = 1283 AD—(?) AD]

COPPER

891. *Mint and Date Missing*

Obverse: single beaded circle. Reverse: one plain circle within another plain circle.

Obverse	Reverse
Margin:	Margin:
قل الله مالك الملك تؤتي الملك من تشاء	. . . . ضرب هذا ا . . . .
[*sic*]	[Very crude calligraphy]
Centre:	Centre:
قا ان	لا اله الا الله
الاعظم	محمد رسول الله
هولاكو خان	الملك الكامل
المعظم	بن الملك . . .

[Late *Kūfic* script]

Album.

The last line of the reverse centre legend is somewhat obscure. The style is similar to specimens of al-Ḥiṣn and Akhlāṭ, issued in the name of Hūlāgū's successor, Abaqa. Also, Hūlāgū died in 663 H, but his name is retained on coins of Mardīn and elsewhere at least as late as 675 H.

AL-ʿĀDIL MUJĪR AL-DĪN MUḤAMMAD IBN AL-KĀMIL

[Dates Not Known; No Coins Issued]

AL-ʿĀDIL SHIHĀB AL-DĪN GHĀZĪ IBN AL-ʿĀDIL MUḤAMMAD

[Dates Not Known; No Coins Issued]

AL-ṢĀLIḤ ABŪ BAKR IBN AL-GHĀZĪ

[?–780 H = ?–1378 AD]

[No Coins Issued]

AL-ʿĀDIL FAKHR AL-DĪN [or ʿIZZ AL-DĪN] SULAYMĀN IBN GHĀZĪ

[780–828 H (?) = 1378–1424 AD (?)]

SILVER

892. *Ḥiṣn—Undated*

Title: al-Sulṭān al-Malik

Border on both sides: plain circle in circle of pellets,

within which is a double linear hexagon standing on one point. Ringlets at points of hexagon. Between border and hexagon ornaments are ornaments composed of three overlapping arches on each side of the hexagon.

within which is a border of tendrils enclosing double linear pentalobe. Hidden among the tendrils are names of the four orthodox caliphs. But only fragments are to be seen at one point: ابو|بكر|عمر|عثمان|علي.

Centre:
ضرب
السلطان الملك العادل
سليمان ابن غازي الايوبي
عز الله بقاه وملكه
حسن

Centre:
صلى الله عليه
لا اله الا
الله محمد
رسول الله

[Obverse in *Naskh;* reverse in *Kūfic* script]
Note the spelling of Ḥiṣn: حسن.
Artuk 784 (25, 4.25, ill.). Tewhid-Bruxelles 3 (25, 4.20, ill.).

893. *Ḥiṣn—Date Uncertain*

Title: al-Sulṭān al-Malik

Plain border in a border of pellets, within which is a thick linear square.

Border Segments:
ضرب|ستة؟ خمس؟|. . . .|. . . .
Centre:
السلطان الملك
ضرب
سليمان الايوبي
حصن
(خلد الله ملكه)

Similar border, within which is a double linear and dotted pentafoil.

Border Segments:
ابو بكر عمر عثمان علي
Centre:
الله
لا اله الا
محمد

[Obverse in *Naskh*; reverse in *Kūfic* script]
Note the spelling of Ḥiṣn is correct: حصن.
Tewhid-Bruxelles 4 (25, 4.35).

894. *Ḥisn—813 H*

Title: al-Sulṭān al-Malik

Border on both sides; plain circle in a circle of pellets, within which is a dotted square in a linear square. In the segments, counterclockwise:

ضرب|
حصن|سنة ثلثة|عشر|ثمانمائة
Centre:
السلطان الملك العادل
سليمان غازى الايوبي
خلد الله بقاه وملكه

within which is a dotted pentafoil in a linear pentafoil. In the segments, counterclockwise, beginning at the bottom:

حصن ابوبكو عمر عثمان على
Centre:
الله
صلى لا اله الا عليه
الله محمد
رسول الله

ضرب in upper cartouche, حسن in lower cartouche.

[Obverse in *Naskh:* reverse in *Kūfic* script]

Note the spelling of Ḥiṣn in obverse centre: حسن; and in obverse and reverse segments: حصن.

Album, *NC* (1976, p. 147, No. 49 (—, 4.35; reverse variety). Artuk 785 (26, 4.20, ill.). Balog (29, 4.27, ill.; 27, 4.25; 27, 3.72; date missing), Şerafettin Erel II, No. 5 (25, 4.20). Tewhid (25, 4.35, ill.; 25, 4.20). Tewhid-Bruxelles 5 (26, 4.40; date missing). Yapı-Kredi (27, 3.80; 28, 4.32; 22, 3.88; 25, 3.55; 25, 3.15; 24, 3.85).

895. *Ḥiṣn—826 H*

Title: al-Sultān

Border on both sides: plain circle in a circle of pellets,

within which is a dotted square in a linear square. Counterclockwise legend in the segments:

ضرب
حصن | سنة ست | عشرين | وثمانمائة

Centre:

السلطان العال د
ضرب
سليما الايوبي
حصن
خلد الله ملكه

within which is a double linear pentafoil, external line thick, inner line thin. Ringlets between the top of the arches and border. Counterclockwise legend in the segments:

ابو بكر عمر عثمان علي

Centre:

الله
لا اله الا
محمد
رسول الله

[Obverse in *Naskh*; reverse in *Kūfic* script]

Note the spelling of Ḥiṣn: حصن.

Album, *NC* (1976), p. 147, No. 50 (—, 4.29; date obscure: في before سنة). ANS (25, 4.30, ill.; 24, 4.26, ill.). Artuk 783 (25, 4.30, ill.; date missing). Şerafettin Erel II, No. 1 (26, 4.20).

896. *Ḥiṣn—828 H*

As above, but the following date:

ضرب |
حصن | سنة ثمان | عشرين | وثمانمائة

Şerafettin Erel II, No. 2 (25, 4.30).

897. *Ḥiṣn—8x7 H*

Title: al-Sulṭān

Border missing, but within a double linear square with segments:

ضرب حصن | سنة سبعة | . . . | . . .ائة

Centre:

السلطان العادل
سليمان الايوبي
خلد الله ملكه

Border: a plain thick circle, within which is a thick linear pentafoil with segments:

ابو بكر عمر عثمان علي

Centre:

الله
لا اله الا
الله محمد
رسول الله

[Obverse in *Naskh*; reverse in *Kūfic* script]

Album 54.

898. *[Ḥiṣn]—8xx H*

As above, but the following obverse segments and reverse centre:

....|وثمانمائة

Centre:

الله
لا اله الا
الله محمد
رسول الله
صلى الله عليه

Ilisch 71 (26, —; date is 8x8 H; Ilisch believes probably 818 H). Şerafettin Erel II, No. 7 (25, 4.20). Yapı-Kredi (27, 3.71).

899. *[Ḥiṣn]—82x H*

Title: al-Sulṭān

Border: double circle of pellets, within which is a double linear square. Counterclockwise legend in the segments:

.....|عشرين|وثما|نمائة

Centre:

في زمن السلطان
العادل سليمان
الايوبى خلد
الله ملكه

Border: plain circle in a circle of pellets, within which is a double linear pentafoil.

ابو بكر عمر عثمان علي

Centre:

الله
لا اله الا
محمد
رسول الله

[Obverse in *Naskh*; reverse in *Kūfic* script]

Şerafettin Erel II, No. 3 (26, 4.20).

900. *Ḥiṣn—8x6 H*

Title: al-Sulṭān

Border missing, but within a linear square. Segments:

حصن|سنة ست|....|....

Centre:

السلطان العال د
ضرب ❖
سليمان الايو بي
❦ حصن ❦
خلد الله ملكه

Border: plain circle, within which is a double linear tetrafoil. Segments, beginning at top right:

ابو بكر|عمر|عثمان|علي

Centre:

الله
❖
لا اله الا
محمد
رسول الله

[Obverse in *Naskh*; reverse in *Kūfic* script]

ANS-UM (24.5, 4.30; as above, but the reverse segments: عمر|عثمان|علي|ابو بكر ANS-Wood (24, 4.262).

901. *Ḥiṣn—Date Missing*
Title: al-Sulṭān

Border missing on both sides

	Counterclockwise legend in segments:
	ابو بكر|عمر|عثمان|علي
Double linear pentafoil.	Double linear square.
Centre:	Centre:
ضرب	لا اله الا ا
حصن	لله محمد
السلطان العادل	رسول الله
سليمان بن غازي	
خلد الله ملكه	

[Obverse in *Naskh*; reverse in square *Kūfic* script]

Şerafettin Erel II, No. 6 (25, 4.35).

902. *Ḥīzān—Undated*
Title: al-Sulṭān al-Malik

Border on both sides: plain circle in a circle of dots. Double linear central fusiform medallion with arabesque at both ends.

Counterclockwise marginal legend:	[Border missing; marginal legend, if any, missing.]
Top:	Linear pentalobe (?), but only the upper lobes are visible.
السلطان الملك العادل	
Bottom:	Reverse Centre:
سليمان ابن غازي الايوبي	الله
In the medallion:	لا اله ان
ضرب	الله محمد
حيزان	رسول الله

[*Naskh* script on obverse; Īlkhānid *Kūfic* on reverse]

Şerafettin Erel II, No. 4 (20, 3.30). Yapı-Kredi (23, 3.32, ill.). Ḥīzān was a dependency of Ḥiṣn-Kayfā. According to Yāqūt, the small town of Ḥīzān stood near Saʿirt (or Isʿirt) north of Tall Fāfān, which itself is about 50 miles east of Ḥiṣn-Kayfā (cf. Le Strange, *Lands of the Eastern Caliphate*, p. 114).

AL-ʿĀDIL ASHRAF SHARAF AL-DĪN AḤMAD IBN SULAYMĀN
[?–836 H = ?–1432 AD]

SILVER

Ḥiṣn—Undated
Title: al-Sulṭān
903. *Type A*

Border of pellets. Double linear octalobe.	Border: plain circle in a circle of pellets.

Centre:
ضرب
السلطان العادل
اشرف احمد بن سليمان
خلد الله ملكه
حصن

Segments:
ابو بكر | عمر | عثمان | علي
Linear square.
Centre:
الله
لا اله الا
محمد
رسول الله

[Obverse in *Naskh*; reverse in angular *Kufic* script]

Artuk 786 (23, 4.30, ill.). Şerafettin Erel II, No. 9 (26, 4.25). Tewhid (28, 3.80, ill.).

904. *Type B*

Border: linear multilobe.
[Centre as above]

Double circle of small pellets. Segments:
عثمان | علي | ابو بكر | عمر
Linear square.
Reverse Centre:
الله
لا اله الا
محمد رسول الله
صلى الله عليه

[Obverse and reverse in angular *Kūfic* script]

Tewhid-Bruxelles 8 (27, 4.35, ill.). Ziya 1710 (25, —); 1711 (26, —); digit missing in date: 83x).

905. *No Mint—Undated*

Title: al-Sulṭān al-Malik

Border: plain circle.
Centre:
السلطان
الملك الاشرف
احمد بن سليمان
الايوبى

Plain circle in a circle of pellets.
Segments:
ابو بكر | عمر | عثمان | علي
Linear square.
Centre:
الله
لا اله الا
ضرب
محمد
حصن
رسول الله

[Obverse in *Naskh:* reverse in *Kufic* script]

Artuk 787 (23, 3.50, ill.). Ilisch 69 (25, ; with small arabesque on the reverse second line). Tewhid Bruxelles 7 (26, 4.50, ill.; reverse variety: لا الـه الا | ضرب | الله محمد | حصن | رسول الله square on the reverse).

906. *Ḥiṣn—Undated*

Title: al-Sulṭān al-Malik

Border: circle of beads in which is a plain double cinquefoil containing a cinquefoil of pearls.

Centre:

ضر

ب

السلطان العادل الكامل

اشرف احمد سليمان

خلد الله ملكه

حصن

Border: plain circle in a circle of pearls, in which is a plain square. Floral arabesque in the segments:

ابو بكر | على | عثمان | علي

Centre:

الله

لا اله الا

محمد

رسول الله

Ilisch 70 (24, —). Tewhid-Bruxelles 6 (27, 4.35).

907. *Ḥiṣn—8xx H*

Title: al-Sulṭān

Linear square in plain circle.

Segments:

. . . . | . . . . | . . . . | وثمانمائة

Centre:

السلطان الاشرف

ضرب

احمد بن سليمان

حصن

خلد الله ملكه

[Border missing]. Linear pentalobe. [Marginal legends, if any, missing]

Centre:

الله

لا اله الا

الله محمد

رسول الله

[Obverse in *Naskh*; reverse in *Kūfic* script]

Artuk 788 (23, 4.50, ill.). Şerafettin Erel II, No. 8 (25, 4.30).

AL-KĀMIL ṢALĀḤ AL-DĪN KHALĪL I IBN AL-ASHRAF AḤMAD
[836–856 H = 1249–1259 AD]

SILVER

908. *Ḥiṣn—Undated*

Title: al-Sulṭān

Border: plain circle in a circle of dots.

Centre:

ضرب حصن

السلطان الكامل

خليل بن احمد بن سليمان

الايوبي جلد الله

ملكه

[Border missing]. In the segments: probably the four orthodox caliphs. In double linear square:

Centre:

الله

لا اله الا

محمد

رسول الله

[Obverse in *Naskh*; reverse in *Kūfic* script]

Artuk 790 (22, 3.85, ill.). Tewhid-Bruxelles 9 (27, 3.80); 10 (24, 3.90). Ziya 1712 (24, —).

909. *Ḥiṣn—Undated*

Title: al-Sulṭān

Border on both sides: plain circle in a circle of pellets, within which is a double linear square (inner line thin; external line thick). Semicircular arch in the centre of each side.

Centre:
ضرب
السلطان الكامل
العزة خليل بن احمد بن سليمان لله
الايوبي خلد الله
ملكه

Segments:
ابو بكر | عمر | عثمان | علي
Centre:
الله
لا اله الا
ضرب
محمد
حصن
رسول الله

In the lower left quarter of the reverse is a round countermark (diameter: ca. 8 mm.): حسبي الله.
Artuk 789 (32 × 24, 2.60, ill.). Tewhid (25, —).

910. *Ḥiṣn—Undated*

Title:al-Sulṭān

[Border missing]. Linear hexagon; small annulets at the corners, open inside.

Centre:
ضرب
السلطان الكامل
خليل بن احمد بن
سليمان خلد الله
ملكه
حصن

Circle of pellets.

Centre:
الله
لا اله الا
محمد
رسو ل ا
لله

[Obverse in *Naskh*; reverse in *Kūfic* script]
Şerafettin Erel II, No. 10 (23, 2.65).

911. *No Mint—Undated*

Title: al-Sulṭān

Border: double circle in a circle of pellets.

Centre:
ضرب
السلطان الكامل
خليل عبد الله ابن عبد الله
رحمه الله خلد
الله ملكه

Border: plain circle in a circle of pellets.

Segments:
ابو بكر | عثمان | علي | عمر
Centre in linear square:
الله
لا اله الا
محمد
رسول الله

[Obverse in *Naskh;* reverse in *Kūfic* script]
İbrahim Artuk reads the first word of the fourth obverse line as plural: رحمهم. I am more inclined to believe it is singular: رحمه. This blessing is normally invoked for the dead only.
Istanbul (26, —).

912. *Ḥiṣn—Date Missing*

Title: al-Sulṭān

Border: plain circle.
Segments:
سنة | . . . . | ؟ | . . . .
Centre in thick linear square:
السلطان الكامل
خليم بن احمد
الايوبي خلد الله

[Border missing]. Double linear pentalobe (external line thick; inner line thin). Segments, beginning at top right:
على | ابو | بكر | . . . | . . .
Centre:
لله
لا اله الا ا
محمد
رسول الله
حصن

ANS-Wright (27, 4.163, ill.). Ilisch 22 (14, —). Tewhid-Bruxelles 11 (24, 4.35, ill.).

913. *Ḥiṣn—Undated*

Title: al-Sulṭān al-Mālik

In hexalobe:
خلد
ن
السلطا الملك
الكامل احمد (بن)
خليل الا (يوبي)
ملكه

[Border missing]. External linear square.
Segments:
. . . | ابو بكر | . . . | . . .
Inner linear square.
Centre in linear square:
ضرب
حصن

Ilisch 73 (24, —).

914. *Mint and Date Missing*

Title Missing

[Marginal legend, if any, missing]
In hexalobe:
(الكا) مل احمد (بن)
خليل الايوبي
خلد ملكه

[Border missing]. [External square legend missing]. Second square legend:
(الا الله) | محمد ر | سول | (لا الله)
Centre in small circle:
الله

Ilisch 74 (22, —).

915. *Ḥiṣn—8xx H*

Title: al-Sulṭān

[Border missing]
Centre:
(السلطا)ن الكامل
بن
خليل احمد بن
(سليمان) خلد ملكه

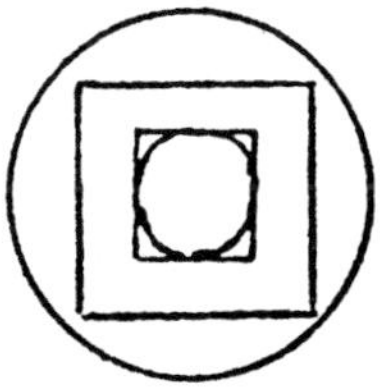

Border: plain circle in circle of pellets. Counterclockwise marginal legend between border and external linear square:

ثمانمائة| . . . .| . . . .| . . . .

Second linear square. In the space between the two linear squares, counterclockwise legend:

لا اله الا الله| . . . .| . . . .|صلى الله عليه

Central linear circle in inner square, in which:

ضرب
بحصن

[Obverse in *Naskh*]
[All reverse legends in *Kūfic*; central legend in *Naskh*]

ANS-Wright (20, 1.986, ill.).

916. *Ḥiṣn—Undated*

Title: al-Sulṭān

Border on both sides: plain circle in a circle of pellets.

Counterclockwise marginal legend:
السلطان الكامل خليل بن احمد بن سليماية

Circle of dots. Centre:
ضرب
حصن

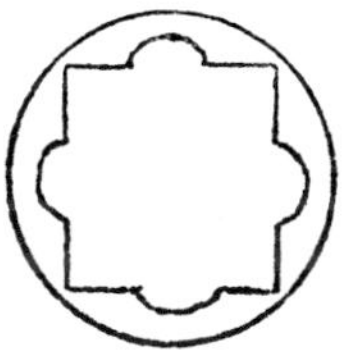

[No marginal legend on reverse] Linear square, with a semicircular arch in the centre of each side.

Centre:
الله
لا اله الا
محمد
رسول الله

Album (2 specimens). Yapı-Kredi (20, 1.55; 20, 1.45; 20, 1.42; 20, 1.27).

COPPER

917. *Ḥiṣn—Undated*

Title: al-Sulṭān

Border: probably circle of dots. Counterclockwise marginal legend:
السلطان الكامل خليل
Inner circle of dots.
Centre:
ضرب
حصن

Border: circle of dots. Counterclockwise marginal legend:
بن احمد بن سليمان
Inner circle of dots.
Centre:
[Religious legend?]

[*Naskh* on both sides]

Şerafettin Erel II, No. 11 (18, 1.50; his illustration is a drawing, not a photograph).

918. *Mint and Date Missing*

Border missing on both sides.

Centre:

. . . . . .

. . . . خليل بن احمد

. . . . سليمان خلد الله . .

Centre:

(الله)

لا اله الا

محمد

رسول الله

Şerafettin Erel II, No. 12 (10, 2.00; illustration is a drawing).

AL-ʿĀDIL NĀṢIR AL-DĪN AḤMAD IBN KHALĪL

[856 H–(?) H = 1452 H–(?) AD]

Probably identical with: al-Kāmil Aḥmad ibn Khalīl (856–? H = 1452–? AD).

SILVER

919. *Ḥiṣn—Undated*

Title: al-Sulṭān al-Malik

Traces of multilobe.

Centre:

(السلطا)ن الملك العادل

ناصر الدين الايوبي

خلد الله ملكه

Description in text summary: religious legend and the four orthodox caliphs. On the drawing, centre in plain square:

ضرب

حصن

Şerafettin Erel II, No. 13 (25, 2.65).

AL-ʿĀDIL KHALAF IBN AḤMAD IBN SULAYMĀN

[?–866 H = ?–1461 AD]

SILVER

920. *Ḥiṣn—Undated*

Title: al-Sulṭān al-Malik

Border: plain circle (?), within which is a double linear hexagon, placed on edge. The hexagon is surrounded by scrolls.

Centre:

ضرب

السلطان الملك

العادل خلف بن

محمد (؟) بن سليمان

حصن

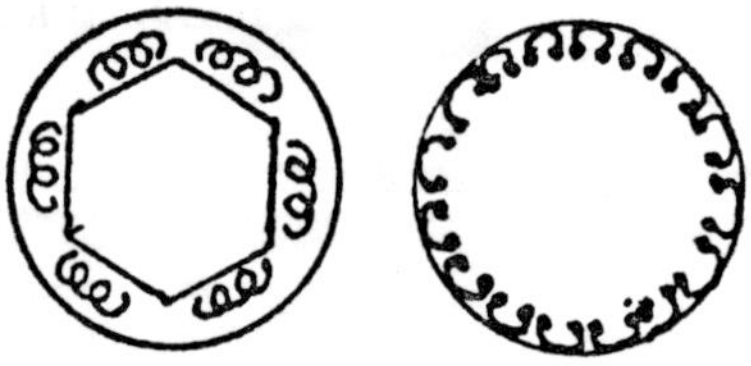

Border of pellets, linked with small arches.

Centre:

الله

لا اله الا

ضرب

محمد

حصن

رسول الله

[Obverse in *Naskh*; reverse in *Kūfic* script]

Şerafettin Erel II, No. 14 (20, 2.00).

921. *Ḥiṣn—Undated*

As above, but the following centre legends:

ن
السلطا الملك
العادل خلف بن
محمد (؟) بن سليمان
خلد

لا اله الا
ضرب
الله محمد
حصن
رسول الله
عثمان

Album.

This design was probably first introduced by Qarā Yūsuf Qarā-Qoyūnlū in 814 H at Bidlis and other mints in his realm.

922. *Ḥiṣn—Undated*

Title: al-Sulṭān al-Malik

In hexalobe:

ملكه

ن
السلطا الملك
العادل خلف

ن
بن محمد بن سليما
خلد

[Border not mentioned]. Clockwise square legend, beginning at right:

ابو بكر علي عثمان عمر

Linear square, in which counterclockwise legend:

لا اله الا الله محمد رسول الله

Inner square, in which linear circle.

Centre:

ضرب
حصن

Ilisch 77 (18, —); 78 (19, —); 79 (20, —); 80 (21, —); 81.B (21, —).

AL-KĀMIL KHALĪL II IBN SULAYMĀN IBN AḤMAD

[866–? H = 1461–? AD]

SILVER

923 *Ḥiṣn-Kayfā—Date Missing*

Title: al-Sulṭān

Border on both sides: plain circle in a circle of pellets.

Double linear pentafoil, with ringlet at the top of each arch; pellet in the ringlets.

Linear square.

On both sides, counterclockwise marginal legend in the segments:

ضرب | حصن | كيفا | سنة | . . . . .

ابو | بكر | عمر | عثمان | علي

Centre:
السلطان
الكامل خليل
الايوبى

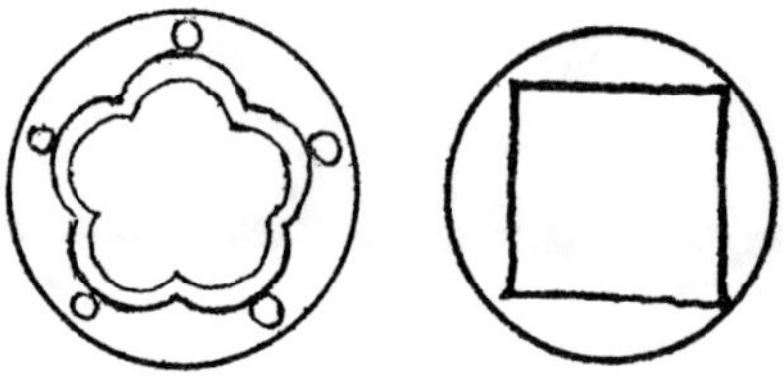

Centre:
لا
اله الا الله
محمد
رسول الله
حصن

Istanbul (29, —). Tewhid (24, —, ill.).

924.

Ḥiṣn—Date Missing

Title: al-Sulṭān

Obverse border: plain circle, within which is a linear pentalobe with ringlet at the top of each arch. Counterclockwise legend between border and pentalobe, beginning at upper left:

ضرب | حصن | . . . . . | . . . . . | . . . . .

Centre:
السلطان
الكامل خليل
الايوبي

[Border missing]. Ornate, curved-sided linear *miḥrāb*. Counterclockwise marginal legend around the *miḥrāb*, beginning at right:

Left: *Right:*
ابو بكر عمر | عثمان علي

In the *miḥrāb:*
لا
اله الا الله
محمد رسول
الله

[All legends in *Naskh* script]

Istanbul (23, —, ill.).

The attribution of the last two issues to al-Kāmil Khalīl II ibn Sulaymān ibn Aḥmad is posited by Şerafettin Erel.

925.

Ḥiṣn—Date Missing

Title: al-Sulṭān

On both sides: border consisting of a plain circle in a circle of pellets, within which is a linear pentafoil with loops at the top of the arches, and a pellet in the loops. Both obverse and reverse are identical in arrangement and the obverse is like the obverse of the two preceding coins.

Border Segments:
. . . | حصن | . . . | . . . | . . . | . . .

Centre:
السلطان
الكامل خليل
الايوبي

Border Segments:
ابو | بكر | عمر | عثمان | علي

Centre:
لا
اله الا الله
محمد
رسول الله

Artuk 791 (23, 4.05, ill.).

926. *Ḥiṣn—Date Missing*
Title: al-Sulṭān

Border: plain circle in a circle of beads.
Marginal Legend:
ضرب حصن . . . .
Centre:
السلطان الكامل
خليل بن احمد
بن سليمان . . .
. . . .

[Border missing]
Border Segments:
. . . . | . . . . |عثمان|علي
Double linear square.
Centre:
الله
لا اله الا
محمد
رسول الله

Tewhid (24, 3.90, ill.).

PRINCIPALITY OF THE YEMEN

AL-MUʿAẒẒAM SHAMS AL-DĪN TŪRĀNSHĀH IBN AYYŪB

[569–575 H = 1173–1179 AD]

GOLD

927. *ʿAdan—573 H*

Border on both sides: plain circle. Counterclockwise marginal legends on both sides:
محمد رسول الله ارسله بالهدى ودين
بسم الله ضرب هذا الدينار بعدن سنة ثلث وسبعين وخمسمائة
Double circle on both sides.

Centre:
الملك المعظم
ملك اليمن
شمس الدين
تورانشاه بن
ايوب

Centre:
الامام
لا اله الا الله
محمد رسول الله
المستضي بامر
الله امير المؤ
منين

[*Kūfic* script]

Artuk 792 (24, 2.45; date missing, but must be this date). Balog, *ANSMN* 9 (1960), (24, 2.28, ill.).

This and the subsequent gold issues are of base alloy. They were struck in Tūrānshāh's name, although he was not in the Yemen at the time, and moreover did not have the right to place his own name on gold.

928. *ʿAdan—576 H*

Although Tūrānshāh left the Yemen in 572 H, he was not replaced by his brother Tughtegīn until 577 H. Therefore, this issue also must be considered as belonging to Tūrānshāh. However, now only Saladin's protocol is on the coin. Border on both sides: double circle. Counterclockwise marginal legend on both sides:
محمد رسول الله ارسله بالهدى ودين الحق ليظهره على
بسم الله ضرب هذا الدينار بعدن سنة ست وسبعين [*sic*]
Double circle on both sides.

Centre:
الملك الناصر
صلاح الدنيا والدين
يوسف بن ايوب

Centre:
الامام
لا اله الا الله
محمد رسول الله
الناصر لدين الله
امير المؤمنين

[Poorly drawn *Kūfic* on this and following issues]
Balog, *ANSMN* 9 (1960) (22, 2.31, ill.).

AL-'AZĪZ SAYF AL-ISLĀM ABŪ AL-FAWĀRIS ṬUGHTEGĪN IBN AYYŪB
[577–593 H = 1181–1196 AD]

GOLD

929. *'Adan—580 H*

As above, but the following date:

بعدن سنة ثمانين [*sic*]

Balog, *ANSMN* 9 (1960) (22, 2.35, ill.).

930. *'Adan—583 H*

As above, but the following date:

بعدن سنة ثلث وثمانين [*sic*]

The obverse margin ends: على ال
ANS-Newell (21, —). Balog, *ANSMN* 9 (1960) (21, 2.16, ill.).

AL-MU'IZZ NAṢĪR AL-DĪN ISMĀ'ĪL IBN ṬUGHTEGĪN
[593–598 H = 1196–1201 AD]

SILVER
[All Inscriptions in *Kūfic*]

931. *Ta'izz—594 H*

Border on both sides: plain circle in a circle of pellets. Counterclockwise marginal legend on both sides:

الملك المعز نصير الدنيا والدين سلطان المسلمين اسمعيل بن طغتكين

بسم الله الرحمن الرحيم ضرب هذا الدرهم بتعز سنة اربع وتسعين وخم [*sic*]

Plain circle interlaced with an inner linear square, with a triangular projection from each side. The resulting pattern is a sort of eight-pointed star:

Centre:
صر
الامام النا
لدين الله احمد
امير المؤ
منين

Centre:
لا اله الا الله
محمد رسول
الله صلى الله
عليه

Balog, *BIE* XXXVI (1954) (22, 1.88, ill.). Istanbul (23, 1.90). Mingana. [Note the title *Sulṭān al-Muslimīn* adopted by Ismā'īl].

932. *Ta'izz—595 H*

As above, but the following date:

سنة خمس وتسعين [*sic*]

Awad (22, —). Mingana.

933. *Ta'izz—596 H*

As above, but the following date and obverse centre legend:

سنة ستة تسعين وستمائة

Obverse Centre:

الامام النا
صر لدين الله
امير المؤ
منين

Mingana. Şerafettin Erel I, No. 4 (22, 2.00).

934. *Ta'izz—597 H*

As above, but obverse marginal legend ends:

اسمعيل بن طغه [*sic*]

As above, but the following date:

سنة سبع وتسعين وخم [*sic*]

Balog, *BIE* XXXVI (1954) (23, 1.88, ill.).

935. *Zabīd—594 H*

As above, but obverse marginal legend ends:

اسمعيل بن طغتك [*sic*]

As above, but the following mint and date:

ضرب هذ (*sic*) الدرهم بزبيد سنة
اربع وتسعين وخمسماة (*sic*)

Balog, *BIE* XXXVI (1954) (21, 1.88, ill.). Mingana (7 specimens).

936. *Zabīd—595 H*

As above, but the following date:

سنة خمس وتسعين [*sic*]

Mingana (2 specimens).

937. *Zabīd—596 H*

As above, but the following date:

سنة ست وتسين [*sic*]

Balog (22, 2.00). Mingana.

938. *Ṣan'ā—595 H*

As above, but the following mint and date:

نصنعا سنة خمس تسين وخمسمائة

'Adan Museum (courtesy of Mrs. Helen Mitchell-Brown). Mingana (5 specimens).

939. *ʿAdan—594 H*

As above, but the following mint and date:

بعدن سنة اربع وتسعين وخم [*sic*]

Balog, *BIE* XXXIV (1954) (23, 2.05, ill.). Mingana (2 specimens).

940. *ʿAdan—595 H*

As above, but the following date:

سنة خمس وتسعين وخم [*sic*]

Mingana (3 specimens).

941. *ʿAdan—596 H*

As above, but the following date:

سنة ست وتسعين وخم [*sic*]

Balog, *BIE* XXXVI (1954) (23, 2.10, ill.). Mingana (1 specimen).

COPPER

942. *Mint Missing—595 H*

The two specimens are in a poor state of preservation, but they seem to be similar to the dirhems, only larger. Traces of a linear border are visible. Counterclockwise marginal legends on both sides (reconstructed):

. . . سنة خمس وتسعين وخمسمائة

الملك المعز نصير الدنيا والدين اسمعيل بن طغتكين

Interlaced with the inner circle on both sides is an eight-pointed star formed by a linear square with a central edge on each side.

Centre [Reconstructed]:	Centre [Reconstructed]:
لا اله الا الله محمد رسول الله صلى الله عليه	صر الامام النا لدين الله احمد امير المؤ منين

ʿAdan Museum (29, 7.92, ill.; 28, 9.87; courtesy of Mrs. Helen Mitchell-Brown).

AL-NĀṢIR ABŪ AL-MUẒAFFAR AYYŪB IBN ṬUGHTEGĪN

[598–611 H = 1201–1214 AD]

[All the following coins are in *Kūfic* script]

[Overlord on all is al-ʿĀdil I]

SILVER

943. *Taʿizz—601 H*

Border on both sides: plain circle in a circle of dots. On both sides, counterclockwise marginal legend:

بسم الله الرحمن الرحيم ضرب هذا الدرهم بتعز سنة احدى وستمائة

الملك العادل ابو بكر الناصر ابو المظفر ايوب ابن ظغتكين

Plain circle, in which eight-pointed star is formed by a linear square with triangular projection from each side interlaced with the circle.

Centre:

صر
الامام النا
لدين الله احمد
امير المؤ
منين

Centre:

○
لا اله الا الله
محمد رسول
الله صلى الله
عليه
[Pellet over centre]

Yapı-Kredi (23, 2.05).

944. *Ta'izz—602 H*

As above, but the following date:

سنة اثنين وستمائة

Mingana. Yapı-Kredi (23, 2.05).

945. *Ta'izz—603 H*

As above, but the following date:

سنة ثلث وستمائة

Yapı-Kredi (23, 1.95).

946. *Ta'izz—604 H*

As above, but the following date:

سنة اربع وستمائة

Webdale (21, 1.70). Yapı-Kredi (24, 1.95).

947. *Ta'izz—605 H*

Border on both sides: plain circle in a circle of dots. Counterclockwise marginal legend on both sides:

بسم الله الرحمن الرحيم ضرب هذا الدرهم بتعز سنة خمس وستمائة

الملك العادل ابو بكر والملك الناصر ابو الظغر ايوب بن طغتكين

Plain circle on both sides, in which two interlaced cordons ,with four points jutting out at the four sides, form a sort of rounded, eight-pointed star:

Centre:

صر
الامام النا
لدين الله احمد
امير المؤ
منين

Centre:

○
لا اله الا الله
محمد رسول
الله صلى الله
عليه

[Pellet above centre of reverse]

[Ornamented *Kufic* script]

Miles-*Yaman* 1 (22, 2.05).

948. *Ta'izz—606 H*

Border on both sides: plain circle in a circle of dots. Counterclockwise marginal legend on both sides:

بسم الله الرحمن الرحيم ضرب هذا الدرهم بتعز سنة ستمائة وستة الملك العادل ابو بكر والملك الناصر ابو المظفر ايوب بن طغتكين

On both sides: inner circle, in which is a thin linear octalobe within an octalobe of pellets.

Centre:	Centre:
صر	●
الامام النا	لا اله الا الله
لدين الله احمد	محمد رسول
امير المؤ	الله صلى الله
منين	عليه

[Pellet above centre of reverse]

Artuk 793 (21, 2.00). Balog, *BIE* XXXVI (1954) (20, 2.12, ill.). Mingana (3 specimens).

949. *Ta'izz—608 H*

Border on both sides: plain circle in a circle of dots. Counterclockwise marginal legend on both sides:

بسم الله الرحمن الرحيم ضرب هذا الدرهم بتعز سنة ثمان وستمائة

The inner circle is broken into four equal segments that intertwine at the four cardinal points and produce a sharp, outward thrusting edge at each point.

Centre:	Centre:
صر	لا اله الا الله
الامام النا	محمد رسول
لدين الله احمد	الله صلى الله
امير المؤ	عليه
منين	

[Pellet above centre of reverse]

BMC 468 p (23, 2.16, ill.; Lane-Poole could not decide whether to read ثمان or خمس; also, the coin was listed under 'Adan). Lavoix 699 (22, 2.23).

950. *Ta'izz—609 H*

As above, but the following date:

سنة تسع وستماية

In the obverse margin طغتكين is abbreviated to طغتكه. No floweret over امير.

Miles-*Yaman* 2 (22, 2.00).

951. *Ta'izz—610 H*

As above, but the following date:

سنة عشرة ستمائة

Miles-*Yaman* 3 (22, 2.10).

952. *Ta'izz—611 H*

As above, but the following date:

سنة احد عشرة سا [*sic*]

Miles-*Yaman* 4 (22, 2.10).

953. *Zabīd—601 H*

Border on both sides: plain circle in a circle of dots. Counterclockwise marginal legend on both sides:

بسم الله الرحمن الرحيم ضرب هذا الدرهم بزبيد سنة احدى و ستماية   الملك العادل ابو بكر والملك الناصر ايوب ابن طغتكين (*sic*)

On both sides a plain circle, within which is a thin linear octalobe in an octalobe of dots.

Centre:
صر
الامام النا
لدين الله احمد
امير المؤ
منين

Centre:
O
لا اله الا الله
محمد رسول
الله صلى الله
عليه

[Pellet above the reverse centre]

Berlin 989/1928 (22, 2.18). Mingana. Yapı-Kredi (22, 2.25).

954. *Zabīd—602 H*

As above, but the following date:

سنة اثنين وستمائة

Berlin 991/1928 (22, 2.06); 990/1928 (22, 2.04). Mingana. Yapı-Kredi (22, 2.05).

955. *Zabīd—603 H*

As above, but the following date:

سنة ثلث وستمائة

Berlin 992/1928 (21, 2.14). Yapı-Kredi (22, 2.00).

956. *Zabīd—604 H*

As above, but the following date:

سنة اربع وستمائة

Yapı-Kredi (22, 2.00).

957. *Zabīd—605 H*

As above, but the following date:

سنة خمس وستمائة

Yapı-Kredi (22, 2.10).

958. *Zabīd—606 H*

As above, but the following date:

سنة ستمئةوستة

Note: ستمائة وستة written as one word.

Berlin 987/1928 (20, 2.03); 988/1928 (22, 2.17). Mingana.

959. *Zabīd—607 H*

As above, but the following date:

سنة سبع وستمائة

Mingana.

960. *Zabīd—608 H*

As above, but the following date:

سنة ثمان وستمائة

Miles-*Yaman* 5 (22, 2.20; the digit of the date is put with a query). Webdale (23, 2.17).

961. *Zabīd—609 H*

As above, but the following date:

سنة تسع وستمائة

Miles-*Yaman* 6 (22, 2.10).

962. *Zabīd—610 H*

Border on both sides: plain circle in a circle of dots. Counterclockwise marginal legend on both sides: Two interlaced, broken circular lines forming a medallion on both sides.

الملك العادل ابو بكر والملك الناصر ابو المظفر ايوب بن طغتكين	بسم الله الرحمن الرحيم ضرب هذا الدرهم بزبيد سنة عشرة ستمائة
Centre:	Centre:
صر الامام النا لدين الله احمد امير المؤ منين	● لا اله الا الله محمد رسول الله صلى الله عليه

[Pellet above reverse centre]

Miles-*Yaman* 7 (22, 2.15, ill.).

963. *al-Dumlūwah—600 H*

Border on both sides: plain circle in a circle of dots. Counterclockwise marginal legend on both sides:

الملك العادل ابو بكر والملك الناصر ابو المظفر ايوب بن طغتكين	بسم الله الرحمن الرحيم ضرب هذا الدرهم بالدملوة سنة ستمائة

On both sides: plain circle, in which is a thin linear octalobe within an octalobe of dots.

Centre:	Centre:
صر الامام النا لدين الله احمد امير المؤ منين	● لا اله الا الله محمد رسول الله صلى الله عليه

[Pellet above reverse centre]

Istanbul (22, —, ill.). Mingana. Şerafettin Erel I, No. 3 (22, 2.10; now in the Yapı- ve Kredi Bankası, Istanbul).

964. *Ṣanʿā—605 H*

As above, but the following mint and date:

بصنعا سنة خمس وستماة [*sic*]

Pellet above the reverse centre.

Balog, *BIE* XXXVI (1954) (21, 2.09, ill.). Yapı-Kredi (23, 2.10).

965. *ʿAdan—601 H*

As above, but the following mint and date:

بعدن سنة احد وستمائة

Pellet above the reverse centre:.

Yapı-Kredi (22, 2.00).

966. *ʿAdan—604 H*

As above, but the following date:

سنة اربع وستمائة

Pellet above the reverse centre.

Webdale (20, 2.07).

967. *ʿAdan—606 H* (?)

As above, but the following date:

سنة ستميه ستم [*sic*]

Mingana.

968. *ʿAdan—608 H*

Border on both sides: plain circle in a circle of dots. Counterclockwise marginal legend on both sides:

بسم الله الرحمن الرحيم ضرب هذا الدرهم بعدن سنة ثمان وستمائة | الملك العادل ابو بكر والملك الناصر ابو المظفر ايوب بن طغتكين

Circle formed by two intertwined broken circles, in which is a medallion with four sharp points and four rounded corners, on both sides.

Centre:	Centre:
	○
صر	لا اله الا الله
الامام النا	محمد رسول
لدين الله احمد	الله صلى الله
امير المؤ	عليه
منين	

BMC 468m (23, 2.16, ill.; ثمان is written امن). Mingana.

AL-MASʿŪD ṢALĀḤ AL-DĪN YŪSUF IBN AL-KĀMIL I

[612–626 H = 1215–1228 AD]

The royal protocol starts with the name of the Egyptian overlord: first, al-ʿĀdil I, and later al-Kāmil I. However, a certain lag in the changeover from al-ʿĀdil to al-Kāmil occurs after the former's death in 615 H. In Ṣanʿā, the capital, al-Kāmil is recorded as overlord on al-Masʿūd Yūsuf's first issue in 617 H, but in Taʿizz the 620 H dirhem still has al-ʿĀdil's protocol. As the next Taʿizz coin is dated 625 H, it is not possible to ascertain the year in which the change was effected. In Zabīd there seems to be a first issue in 622 H (Miles, No. 28) with al-ʿĀdil, but in the same year another dirhem was struck with al-Kāmil as overlord (Miles, No. 29). In ʿAdan the 622 H dirhem still has al-ʿĀdil's name and only the next issue of 625 H bears al-Kāmil's protocol as overlord. The posthumous mention of Caliph al-Nāṣir occurs on some coins of ʿAdan, dated 626 H. In Zabīd, too, al-Nāṣir is still on the coins in 623 H, although al-Ẓāhir appears on later coins of the same year.

al-Masʿūd Yūsuf's dirhems present a completely new arrangement. The marginal legend has disappeared and the border has become a plain circle in a circle of pellets. The inscriptions are on several horizontal lines in *Naskh*, and at the beginning of the reign, quite handsomely engraved, but later increasingly degenerate and difficult to read.

al-ʻĀdil's name as overlord is always followed by that of his son and heir, al-Kāmil. al-Masʻūd Yūsuf's title is *walī ʻahd* (ولي عهد) which in this context must mean simply 'lieutenant' (of al-Kāmil).

SILVER

969. *Taʻizz—612 H*

Overlord: al-ʻĀdil I

الله
بسم
و
الملك العادل ابو بكر
لي عهده الملك الكامل محمد و
لي عهده الملك المسعود
يوسف

الله
ل
لا اله الا الله محمد سو
الامام الناصر لدين الله احمد
ب
امير المؤمنين ضر بتعز سنة
اثنيى عشر ستماية

[Pellet above obverse]

Miles-*Yaman* 9 (23, 2.05); 10 (23, 2.10, ill.; diverse scrolls and floral sprigs, on the obverse and reverse). Webdale (21, 2.11).

970. *Taʻizz—620 H*

Overlord: al-ʻĀdil I [Posthumous]

As above, but the following date:

عشرين ستمائة

Ornaments: obverse, first line: ○ الله; reverse, fourth line: المؤمنين. Miles-*Yaman* 11a (23, 2.10); 11b (23, 2.05); 12 (23, 2.20; various points and scrolls).

971. *Taʻizz—625 H*

Overlord: al-Kāmil I; Caliph: al-Mustanṣir

الله
بسم
الملك الكامل ابو
المعالى محمد ولي عهد
الملك المسعود
يوسف

ل
الله الامام ابو سو
ر
لا اله الا الله محمد
بالله
جعفر المنصور المستنصر
ب
امير المؤمنين ضر بتعز سنة
خمس عشرين ستمائة

[عهده without the final *hā*]

Miles-*Yaman* 13 (24, 2.05; numerous points and scrolls).

972. *Zabīd—612 H*

○
الله
بسم
الملك العادل ابو بكر
لي عهد الملك الكامل محمد
لي عهد الملك المسعود
يوسف

وستمائة
لا اله الا الله محمد
رسول الله الامام النا
ب
صر احمد ضر بزبيد سنة
اثنيى عشر

Miles-*Yaman* 15a (22, 2.00); 15b (22, 2.15; obverse third and fourth line: و omitted from ولى in both cases, and the final ه omitted from عهده in both cases); 16 (22, 2.15; as above, but the date is entirely on the last line: اثنيى عشر ستمائة). Webdale (21, 2.11).

973. *Zabīd—613 H*

As above, but the following date entirely on the last line:

ثلث عشرة ستمائة

Miles-*Yaman* 17 (22, 1.95).

974. *Zabīd—614 H*

As above, but the following date:

اربع عشر ستمائة

Floral sprigs over: الله and محمد on the reverse.

Miles-*Yaman* 18 (22, 2.10); 19 (22, 2.20; the letter و of both words ولى remains at the end of the third and fourth lines of the obverse).

975. *Zabīd—617 H*

Overlord: al-ʿĀdil I [Posthumous]

الله
بسم
الملك العادل ابو بكر و
لي عهده الملك الكامل ابو ا
لمعالى محمد ولي عهده
الملك المسعود
يوسف

ل
الله سو
ر
لا اله الا الله محمد
ا
الامام الناصر لدين الله حمد
ب
امير المؤمنين ضرب بزبيد سنة
سبع عشرة ستمائة

Miles-*Yaman* 20 (22, 2.10, ill.).

976. *Zabīd—618 H*

As above, but the first line is:

○
○ الله

As above, but the following date:

ثمان عشرة ستمائة

Miles-*Yaman* 21 (22, 2.00).

977. *Zabīd—620 H*

Obverse	Reverse
الله	ل
بسم	الله سو
الملك العادم ابو بكر و	ر
لي عهد الملك الكامل محمد	لا اله الا الله محمد
لي عهد الملك المسعود	الامام الناصر لدين الله احمد
يوسف	ب
	امير المؤمنين ضرب زبيد سنة
	عشرين ستمائة

Miles-*Yaman* 22 (21, 2.10, ill.; obverse: و of the second ولي is omitted, as well as the final *hā* of both عهده: عهد); 23 (22, —; obverse as No. 22, but رسول is transferred from the second line of the reverse to its first line: رسول الله).

978. *Zabīd—621 H*

●

As above, but the first line: pellet over الله; fourth line: و at the end omitted; fifth line: scroll over المسعود.

As above, but the following date:
احد عشرين ستمائة

Miles-*Yaman* 24 (22, 2.25); 25 (22, 2.10; end of the third line of the reverse: احمد has shrunk to: حـ); 26 (22, 2.15; digit of the date: احدى); 27 (22, 2.25; obverse: و of ولي omitted twice).

Zabīd—622 H

979. *Type A*

As above, but the following date:

اثنيى عشرين ستمائة

and the first line: الله ل سو
ر

Album. Miles-*Yaman* 28 (24, —).

980. *Type B*

Overlord: al-Kāmil I; Caliph: al-Nāṣir

Obverse	Reverse
الله	ل
بسم	الله سو
الملك الكامل ابو ا	ر
لمعالي محمد ولي عهده	لا اله الا الله محمد
الملك المسعود	الامام الناصر لدين الله احمد
يوسف	ب
	امير المؤمنين ضرب زبيد سنة
	اثنيى عشرين ستمائة

Miles-*Yaman* 29 (22, 2.10); 30 (22, 2.10; no ornaments); 31 (23, 2.20; ornaments; date erroneously written: اثنيى عشرة).

981. *Type C*

Overlord: al-Kāmil I; Caliph: al-Nāṣir

الله
بسم
الملك الكامل ابو ا
لمعالى محمد ولي عهده
الملك المسعود
يوسف

وستمائة
لا اله الا الله محمد
رسول الله الامام النا
صر احمد ضرب بزبيد سنة
اثنيى عشرة

Miles-*Yaman* 32 (23, 2.00; the date is erroneously written as 612 H).

982. *Type D*

Overlord: al-Kāmil I; Caliph: al-Nāṣir

الله
بسم
الملك الكامل ابو ا
لمعالي محمد ولي عهده
الملك المسعود
يوسف

وستمائة
لا اله الا الله محمد
رسول الله الامام النا
ب
صر احمد ضر بزبيد سنة
اثني عشرة

[Numerous scrolls and dashes]

Miles-*Yaman* 33 (23, 2.05; date erroneously 612 H instead of 622 H).

Zabīd—623 H

983. *Type A*

Overlord: al-Kāmil I; Caliph: al-Nāṣir [Posthumous]

الله
بسم
الملك الكامل ابو ا
لمعالي محمد ولي عهده
الملك المسعود
يوسف

ل
الله سو
ر
لا اله الا الله محمد
الامام الناصر لدين الله ا
ب حمد
امير المؤمنين ضر بزبيد سنة
ثلث عشرين ستمائة

Miles-*Yaman* 34 (22, 2.10).

984. *Type B*

Overlord: al-Kāmil I; Caliph: al-Ẓāhir

الله
بسم
الملك الكامل ابو ا
لمعالى محمد ولي عهده
الملك المسعود
يوسف

ل
الله سو
ر
لا اله الا الله محمد
الامام الظاهر ابو نصر محمد
امير المؤمنين ضرب بزبيد سنة
ثلاث عشرين ستمائة

[Various points and scrolls]

Miles-*Yaman* 35 (23, 2.05).

985. *Zabīd—624 H*

Overlord: al-Kāmil I; Caliph: al-Mustanṣir

[Obverse as above]

الله الامام
ل
لا اله الا الله محمد سو
ر
ابو جعفر المنصور المستنصر
بالله امير المؤمنين ضرب بزبيد سية
اربع عشرين ستمائة

Miles-*Yaman* 36 (23, 2.10).

986. *Zabīd—625 H*

Overlord: al-Kāmil I; Caliph: al-Mustanṣir

[Obverse as above]

ل
الله الامام ابو سو
ر
لا اله الا الله محمد
جعفر المنصور المستنصر بالله
امير المؤمنين ضرب بزبيد سنة
خمس عشرين ستمائة

Miles-*Yaman* 37 (23, 2.15, ill.); 38 (23, —; 39 (23, 2.05; the first two lines of the reverse are: ل الله الامام رسو/لا اله الا الله محمد); 40a (23, 2.15); 40b (22, 2.05); 40c (22, —).

987. *Zabīd—626 H*

Overlord: al-Kāmil I; Caliph: al-Mustanṣir

الله
بسم
الملك الكامل ابو المعا
لي محمد ولي عهد . . .
الملك المسعود يو
سف

[Numerous scrolls and dashes]

لله الامام ابو جعفر
لا اله الا الله محمد رسول
ا
المنصور المستنصر بالله مير
ب
المؤمنين ضر بزبيد سنة
ست عشرين ستمائة

Miles-*Yaman* 41a (23, 2.10, ill.); 41b (22, 2.15).

988. *Zabīd—627 H*

Overlord: al-Kāmil I; Caliph: al-Mustanṣir

الله
بسم
الملك الكامل محمد ابو ا
لمعالي محمد ولي عهده ا
لملك المسعود
يوسف

ل الله الامام ابو
لا اله الا الله محمد سو
ر
جعفر المنصور المستنصر بالله
ب
امير المؤمنين ضر بزبيد سنة
سبع عشرين ستمائة

[Numerous ornaments]

Miles-*Yaman* 42 (23, 2.05).

989. *Ṣanʿā—617 H*

Overlord: al-ʿĀdil I [Posthumous]

الله
بسم
الملك العادل ابو بكر و
لي عهده الملك الكامل محمد و
لي عهده الملك المسعود
يوسف

الله ل
سو
لا اله الا الله محمد ر
الامام الناصر لدين الله احمد
امير المؤمنين ضرب بصنعا سنة
سبع عشرة ستمائة

Miles-*Yaman* 43 (20, 2.00).

Ṣanʿā—621 H

Overlord: al-Kāmil I; Caliph: al-Nāṣir

990. *Type A*

○الله
بسم
الملك الكامل ابو ا
لمعالي محمد ولي عهده
الملك المسعود
يوسف

الله ل
سو
د
لا اله الا الله محمد
ا
الامام الناصر لدين الله حمد
ب
امير المؤمنين ضر بصنعا سنة
احدى عشرين ستمائة

Miles-*Yaman* 44 (22, 1.95).

991. *Type B*

Obverse	Reverse
الله	الله ل
بسم	سو
الملك الكامل ابو ا	لا اله الا الله محمد ر
لمعالي محمد ولي عهده	الامام الناصر لدين الله احمد
الملك المسعود يو	امير المؤمنين ضرب بصنعا سنة
سف	احدى عشرين ستمائة

[Various points and scrolls]

Miles-*Yaman* 45 (23, 2.00).

Ṣanʿā—623 H

Overlord: al-Kāmil I; Caliph: al-Ẓāhir

992. *Type A*

Obverse	Reverse
الله	الله ل
بسم	سو
الملك الكامل ابو ا	لا اله الا الله محمد ر
لمعالي محمد ولي عهده	الامام الظاهر ابو نصر محمد
الملك المسعود يو	ب
سف	امير المؤمنين ضر بصنعا سنة
	ثلاث عشرين ستمائة

[Various points and scrolls]

Miles-*Yaman* 46 (23, 2.05).

993. *Type B*

Obverse	Reverse
الله	[Reverse as above]
بسم	
الملك الكامل ابو ا	
لمعالي محمد ولي عهده	
الملك المسعود	
يوسف	

Miles-*Yaman* 47a (23, 2.05); 47b (23, 1.90).

994. *Ṣanʿā—625 H*

Overlord: al-Kāmil I; Caliph: al-Mustanṣir

Obverse	Reverse
الله	الله الامام ل
بسم	سو
الملك الكامل ابو ا	لا اله الا الله محمد ر
لمعالي محمد ولي عهده	ابو جعفر المنصور المستنصر
الملك المسعود	بالله
يوسف	امير المؤمنين ضرب بصنعا سنة
	خمس عشرين ستمائة

[Various scrolls and dashes]

Miles-*Yaman* 48 (24, 2.10, ill.).

995. *Ṣanʻā—626 H*

Overlord: al-Kāmil I; Caliph: al-Mustanṣir

[Obverse as above]

ل
الله الامام ابو سو
ر
لا اله الا الله محمد
جعفر المنصور المستنصر بالله
سنة
امير المؤمنين ضرب بصنعا
ست عشرين ستمائة

Miles-*Yaman* 49 (24, 2.10, ill.).

996. *ʻAdan—613 H*

Overlord: al-ʻĀdil I; Caliph: al-Nāṣir

Border on both sides: plain circle in a circle of dots.

الله
بسم
الملك العادل ابو بكر و
لي عهده الملك الكامل محمد و
لي عهده الملك المسعود
يوسف

∴
اللـــه
ل
لا اله الا الله محمد رسو
الامام الناصر لدين الله احمد
امير المؤمنين ضرب بعدن سنة
ثلاث عشر وستمائة

Webdale (22, 2.18).

997. *ʻAdan—616 H*

Overlord: al-ʻĀdil I [Posthumous]; Caliph: al-Nāṣir

الله
بسم
الملك العادل ابو بكر و
لي عهده الملك الكامل محمد و
لي عهده الملك المسعود
يوسف

ل
الله سو
ر
لا اله الا الله محمد
الامام الناصر لدين الله احمد
ب
امير المؤمنين ضر بعدن سنة
ست عشر ستمائة

[Various points]

Miles-*Yaman* 50 (19, 2.20).

998. *'Adan—618 H*

Overlord: al-'Ādil I [Posthumous]; Caliph: al-Nāṣir

الله	الله
بسم	ل
الملك العادل ابو بكر	سو
ولي عهده الملك الكامل محمد و	لا اله الا الله محمد ر
ولي عهد الملك المسعود	الامام الناصر لدين الله (احمد)
يوسف	ب
	امير المؤمنين ضرب بعدن سنة
	ثمان وستمائة

Although the date is ostensibly 608 H [ثمان وستمائة], there is no doubt that the decade has been erroneously omitted by the engraver. al-Nāṣir Ayyūb was still ruler of the Yemen in 611 H, and al-Mas'ūd Yūsuf did not not occupy the throne until 612 H. If my notes are correct, there is a superfluous و at the end of the fourth obverse line.

Berlin 907/1912 (22, 2.14). Webdale (22, 2.18).

'Adan—621 H

Overlord: al-'Ādil I [Posthumous]; Caliph: al-Nāṣir

999. *Type A*

الله	الله
بسم	ل
الملك العادل ابو بكر	سو
لي عهد الملك الكامل محمد	لا اله الا الله محمد ر
لي عهد الملك المسعود	الامام الناصر لدين الله احمد
يوسف	ب
	امير المؤمنين ضرب بعدن سنة
	احدى ستمائة
	عشرين

[No ornaments]

Miles-*Yaman* 51 (23, 2.20; obverse ولي without the *wāw*, and عهده without the final *hā* in the fourth and fifth lines).

1000. *Type B*

[Obverse as above] — As above, but the date is entirely on the last line: احدى عشرين ستمائة

Miles-*Yaman* 52 (22, 2.20; obverse: ولي without the *wāw*, and عهده without the final *hā* on the fourth and fifth lines).

1001. *'Adan—622 H (?)*

Overlord: al-'Ādil I [Posthumous]; Caliph: al-Nāṣir

[Obverse as above] — As above, but the date on the last line: ثنتين عشرين ستمائة

Miles-*Yaman* 53 (22, 2.00; ثنتين with a query).

ʿAdan—625 H

Overlord: al-Kāmil I; Caliph: al-Mustanṣir

1002. *Type A*

الله
بسم
الملك الكامل ابو ا
لمعالى محمد ولي عهد [*sic*]
الملك المسعود
يوسف

ستمائة
ل الله الامام ابو
بالله
جعفر المنصور المستنصر
ب سنة
امير المؤمنين ضر بعدن
خمس عشرين

[Various scrolls and points]

Miles-*Yaman* 54a (22, 2.15); 54b (122, 1.95).

1003. *Type B*

As above, but a loop ornament over the س of بسم.

ل الامام سو
ر
لا اله الا الله محمد
بالله
ابو جعفر المنصور المستنصر
امير المؤمنين ضرب بعدن سنة
خمس عشرين ستمائة

Miles-*Yaman* 55 (23, 2.10).

ʿAdan—626 H

Overlord: al-Kāmil I; Caliph: al-Mustanṣir

1004. *Type A*

○
الله
بسم
الملك الكامل ابو ا
لمعالي محمد ولي عهد [*sic*]
الملك المسعود
يوسف

الله الامام ابو سو . . .
لا اله الا الله محمد . . .
بالله
جعفر المنصور المستنصر
ب
امير المؤمنين ضر بعدن سنة
ست عشرين ستمائة

Miles-*Yaman* 56a (24, 2.15); 56b (24, 2.09); 57 (24, 2.15); 60 (23, 2.10; as above, but the digit of the date is missing).

1005. *Type B*

[Obverse as above]

الله ل سو
ر
لا اله الا الله محمد
الامام الناصر لدين الله احمد
ب
امير المؤمنين ضر بعدن سنة
ست ستمائة
وعشرين

[Various points and scrolls]

Miles-*Yaman* 58a (24, 2.15); 58b (23, 2.20); 59 (23, 2.05; the digit of the date is missing).

1006. *'Adan—627 H*

Overlord: al-Kāmil I; Caliph: al-Mustanṣir

○
الله
بسم
الملك الكامل ابو ا
لمعالي محمد ولي عهد [*sic*]
الملك المسعود
يوسف

ستمائة
ل الله الامام ابو سو
ر
لا اله الا الله محمد
بالله
جعفر المنعصور المستنصر
ب سنة
امير المؤمنين ضر بعدن
خمس عشرين

Miles-*Yaman* 61 (24, 2.05).

According to the historians, the Rasūlids took possession of the Yemen in 626 H, but the evidence of the coins seems to contradict this. Either al-Mas'ūd Yūsuf was still alive in 627 H, or, as it so often happened in the Ayyūbid coinage of the Yemen, there is some anachronism; for example, posthumous coins are by no means exceptional. However, there is good reason to believe that Ayyūbid rule was maintained by the Rasūlid governors, even if only nominally to allow them enough time to consolidate their position, at least during the year 628 H. It will be seen that there are coins of this year issued in the name of yet another Ayyūbid prince, al-'Ādil Sayf al-Dīn Abū Bakr ibn al-Mas'ūd Yūsuf.

1007. *Raydah—612 H*

الله
بسم
الملك العادل ابو بكر و
لي عهده الملك الكامل محمد و
لي عهد [*sic*] الملك المسعود
يوسف

[Numerous scrolls and ornaments]

الله
ل
سو
ر
لا اله الا الله محمد
الامام الناصر لدين الله احمد
ب
امير المؤمنين ضر بريدح
ثنتين [؟] عشر ستمائة

Miles-*Yaman* 14 (22, 2.15, ill.; the digit of the date ثنتين is questionable).

1008. *Raydah—617 H*

[Obverse as above]

As above, but the following date:

سبع ستمائة
عشرة

Webdale (21, 1.90).

COPPER

1009. *Mint and Date Missing*

Beaded square-in-the-circle type; margin illegible.

Centre:

. . . د الملك
المسعود
يوسف

Centre:

حورال
المستنصر
. . امير الم. . . .

Album (the top line of the reverse is uncertain; rest is clear).

AL-ʿĀDIL SAYF AL-DĪN ABŪ BAKR IBN AL-MASʿŪD YŪSUF
[628 H = 1230 AD]

SILVER

ʿAdan—628 H

Overlord: al-Kāmil I; Caliph: al-Mustanṣir

1010. *Type A*

∴
اللــه
بسم
الملك الكامل ابو المعالى
محمد الملك العادل سيف
الدين ابو بكر ابن يو
سف

ل الله الامام ابو
سو
ر
لا اله الا الله محمد
بالله
جعفر المنصور المستنصر
ب
امير المؤمنين ضر بعدن سنة
ثمان عشرين وستمائة

Balog (24, 2.04, ill.; ringed).

1011. *Type B*

الله
بسم
الملك الكامل ابو المعالى
محمد الملك العادل سف
الدين (ابو) بكر بن
يوسف

[Numerous points and scrolls]

ل
سو
ر
الله الامام ابو
لا اله الا الله محمد
بالله
جعفر المنصور المستنصر
ب
امير المؤمنين ضر بعدن سنة
ثمان عشرين ستمائة

Miles-*Yaman* 65 (23, 2.10, ill.).

1012. *Unidentified Mint—628 H*

الله

بسم

الملك الكامل ابو المعا

لي محمد الملك العادل

سيف الدين ابو بكر (بن)

يوسف

ابو

ل

سو

ر

الله الامام

لا اله الا الله محمد

بالله

جعفر المنصور المستنصر ا

ب

مير المؤمنين ضر [illegible] ؟

سنة

ثمان عشرين ستمائة

[Numerous points and scrolls; also annulets]

Miles-*Yaman* 66 (22, 1.95); 67 (24, 2.05, ill.; last two lines of the obverse: ا سيف الدين ابى بكر|بن يوسف).

1013. *Unidentified Mint—62x H*

[Obverse as above]

ل الله الامام ابو

سو

لا اله الا الله محمد ر

بالله

جعفر المنصور المستنصر

امير المؤمنين ضر (*sic*) [illegible] سنة (؟)

. . . . عشرين ستمائة

Miles-*Yaman* 68 (24, 2.10, ill.).

This prince seems to be ignored by the historians and his name occurs only on the coins. In *The Ayyūbid Dynasty of the Yaman and Their Coinage*, George Miles deals with the historical problems extensively and entertains the possibility that al-ʿĀdil Sayf al-Dīn Abū Bakr was one of the sons of al-Masʿūd Yūsuf and succeeded him after Yūsuf's death in 625 or 626 H. From the evidence of the coins, it would seem that Miles' assumption is a probability rather than a mere possibility.

AL-KĀMIL MUḤAMMAD I OF EGYPT
[As Overlord, without name of local ruler]

SILVER

1014. *'Adan—627 H*

الله
بسم
الملك الكامل
ابو المعالي محمد
بن ابى بكر بن
ايوب

ابو
ل
سو
الله الامام ر
لا اله الا الله محمد
بالله
جعفر المنصور المستنصر
امير المؤمنين ضرب بعدن سنة
سبع عشرين ستمائة

[Numerous points and scrolls]

Miles-*Yaman* 62 (24, 2.10); 63 (24, 2.15); 64 (24, 2.05; obverse fifth line begins with ابن and the reverse first and second lines read : ابو / ل / الله الامام سو without a *rā* for رسول).

It is somewhat unusual for a Yemeni issue, outside of the rare early gold in the sole name of Saladin, to show an overlord's name on the coins without that of the local prince. In his excellent article, 'The Ayyūbid Dynasty of the Yaman and Their Coinage,' Miles described the above coins and advanced the theory that they were minted by an Ayyūbid official of al-Kāmil and not by the Rasūlids. But the preceding *dirham* (No. 1013)—also in al-Kāmil's name without the local ruler—bears the date 620 H, the year during which al-Mas'ūd Yūsuf, al-Kāmil's son and ruler of Yemen, was absent from the Yemen and when there were several rebellions as well.

As Miles observed, the Rasūlid takeover of the Yemen was not an abrupt move, but rather a laborious conquest of the fortified centres that resisted them, either out of loyalty to the Ayyūbids or because they hoped for independence. Nevertheless, the first Rasūlid, al-Manṣūr 'Umar continued to issue coin in the name of al-Kāmil Muḥammad, putting his own protocol on the copper and silver only after al-Kāmil's death in 635 H.

COPPER

1015. *Zabīd—620 H*

Border on both sides of plain circle. Counterclockwise marginal legends on both sides:

بسم الله ضر ب هذا الفلس بزبيد سنة عشرين و ستمائة

بسم الله ضر ب هذا الفلس بزبيد سنة عشرين وستمائة

Broken circle in which is an intertwined eight-pointed star

Centre:
الملك ا
———
لكامل محمد

Centre:
لا اله ا
———
لا الله

[*Kūfic* script]

Ashmolean-Thorburn (23, 3.66, ill.).

INDEX OF MINTS

AH Date	Metal	Ruler	Catalogue No.
Missing	CU	al-ʻAzīz ʻUthmān	224
589	AR	al-Ẓāhir Ghāzī	581–582
590	,,	,,	583
591	,,	,,	584–585
593	,,	,,	586–589
594	,,	,,	590–591
595	,,	,,	592–594
596	,,	,,	595–596
597	,,	,,	597
598	,,	,,	598–600
599	,,	,,	601–602
600	,,	,,	603–604
601	,,	,,	605–606
602	,,	,,	607–608
603	,,	,,	609
604	,,	,,	610–611
605	,,	,,	612
606	,,	,,	613–614
607	,,	,,	615
608	,,	,,	616–618
609	,,	,,	619
610	,,	,,	620–621
611	,,	,,	622
612	,,	Saladin	623–625
613	,,	,,	626–628
614	,,	,,	629–630
615	,,	,,	631–632
616	,,	al-Ẓāhir Ghāzī	633
617	,,	,,	634–635
618	,,	,,	636
619	,,	,,	637–638
620	,,	,,	639–640
621	,,	,,	641
622	,,	,,	642–643
623	,,	,,	644
624	,,	,,	645
625	,,	,,	646–647
627	,,	,,	648–650
628	,,	,,	651
629	,,	,,	652
630	,,	,,	653
638	,,	,,	654
589	CU	,,	658–662
59x	,,	,,	663
596	,,	,,	664
597	,,	,,	665
598	,,	,,	666–667
599	,,	,,	668–669
603	,,	,,	670, 682

AH Date	Metal	Ruler	Catalogue No.
604	CU	al-Ẓāhir Ghāzī	671
605	,,	,,	672, 683
606	,,	,,	673
607	,,	,,	674
608	,,	,,	675
609	,,	,,	676
610	,,	,,	677
611	,,	,,	678
612	,,	,,	679
Missing	,,	,,	680
,,	,,	,,	681
xx5	,,	,,	684
614	AR	al-ʿAzīz Muḥammad	686
615	,,	,,	687–689
616	,,	,,	690
617	,,	,,	691–692
619	,,	,,	693
623	,,	,,	694
624	,,	,,	695
625	,,	,,	696–698
626	,,	,,	699
627	,,	,,	700
628	,,	,,	701
630	,,	,,	702–703
631	,,	,,	704
633	,,	,,	705
634	,,	,,	706
Missing	,,	,,	707
613	CU	,,	708
615	,,	,,	709
618	,,	,,	710
620	,,	,,	711
621	,,	,,	712
622	,,	,,	713, 715
Missing	,,	,,	714
623	,,	,,	716, 718
Missing	,,	,,	717
629	,,	,,	719
Missing	,,	,,	720
634	AR	al-Nāṣir Yūsuf	724
636	,,	,,	725
637	,,	,,	726–727
638	,,	,,	728
639	,,	,,	629–630
640	,,	,,	731–733
642	,,	,,	734
643	,,	,,	735–736
643	CU	,,	758
644	AR	,,	737

AH Date	Metal	Ruler	Catalogue No.
645	AR	al-Nāṣir Yūsuf	738
646	,,	,,	739–741
647	,,	,,	742–744
648	,,	,,	745–746
649	,,	,,	747
650	,,	,,	748
651	,,	,,	749
652	,,	,,	750
653	,,	,,	751
654	,,	,,	752–754
655	,,	,,	755
656	,,	,,	756
658	,,	,,	757
655	CU	,,	760
Undated	,,	,,	761, 787–789
6x3	,,	,,	759

ALEXANDRIA [الاسكندرية]

AH Date	Metal	Ruler	Catalogue No.
567	AU	Saladin	4
568	,,	,,	5
569	,,	,,	6
Missing	AR	Saladin (Alexandria ?)	7
570	AU	Saladin	19
571	,,	,,	20
572	,,	,,	21
573	,,	,,	22
574	,,	,,	23
575	,,	,,	24
Missing	AR	Saladin (Alexandria ?)	25
576	AU	Saladin	50
578	,,	,,	51
579	,,	,,	52
580	,,	,,	53
581	,,	,,	54
582	,,	,,	55
583	,,	,,	56
584	,,	,,	57
585	,,	,,	58
586	,,	,,	59
588	,,	,,	60
589	,,	,,	61
Undated	,,	,,	62
589	,,	al-'Azīz 'Uthmān	191
590	,,	,,	192
593	,,	,,	193
Missing	AR	,,	196–200
595	AU	al-Manṣūr Muḥammad	228
596	,,	,,	229
Missing	AR	,,	230–232

AH Date	Metal	Ruler	Catalogue No.
596	AU	al-ʿĀdil I	252
597	,,	,,	253–254
598	,,	,,	255
599	,,	,,	256
600	,,	,,	257
601	,,	,,	258
602	,,	,,	259
603	,,	,,	260
604	,,	,,	261
605	,,	,,	262
606	,,	,,	263–264
607	,,	,,	265
608	,,	,,	266
609	,,	,,	267
610	,,	,,	268
611	,,	,,	269
613	,,	,,	270
614	,,	,,	271
615	,,	,,	272
Missing	AR	,,	273–274
617	AU	al-Kāmil Muḥammad I	386
618	,,	,,	387
619	,,	,,	388
623	,,	,,	389–390
624	,,	,,	391
625	,,	,,	392
626	,,	,,	393
627	,,	,,	394
628	,,	,,	395
629	,,	,,	396
630	,,	,,	397
632	,,	,,	398
634	,,	,,	399
635	,,	,,	400
Missing	AR	,,	402
636	AU	,,	507
637	,,	,,	508
Missing	,,	al-Ṣāliḥ Ayyūb	533

ĀMID [آمد]

AH Date	Metal	Ruler	Catalogue No.
636	CU	al-Ṣāliḥ Ayyūb	568
637	,,	,,	569
638	,,	,,	570
Missing	,,	,,	571
65x	,,	al-Kāmil Muḥammad II	883

CAIRO [القاهرة]

AH Date	Metal	Ruler	Catalogue No.
567	AU	Saladin	1
568	,,	,,	2

AH Date	Metal	Ruler	Catalogue No.
569	AU	Saladin	3
Missing	AR	,,	7
570	AU	,,	12
571	,,	,,	13
572	,,	,,	14
573	,,	,,	15
574	,,	,,	16
575	,,	,,	17
576	,,	,,	36
577	,,	,,	37
578	,,	,,	38
579	,,	,,	39
580	,,	,,	40
581	,,	,,	41
582	,,	,,	42
583	,,	,,	43
584	,,	,,	44
585	,,	,,	45
586	,,	,,	46
587	,,	,,	47
588	,,	,,	48
589	,,	,,	49
576	AR	,,	63
Missing	,,	,,	64–65
585	,,	,,	66
586	,,	,,	67
Missing	CU	,,	68
Undated	Glass/Paste	Saladin (No ruler; caliph only)	26
,,	,,	,,	27
,,	,,	,,	28
589	AU	al-ʿAzīz ʿUthmān	184
590	,,	,,	185
591	,,	,,	186
592	,,	,,	187
593	,,	,,	188
594	,,	,,	189
595	,,	,,	190
Missing	AR	,,	196–200
595	AU	,,	226
596	,,	,,	227
Missing	AR	,,	230–232
596	AU	al-ʿĀdil I	233
597	,,	,,	234–235
599	,,	,,	236
600	,,	,,	237
601	,,	,,	238
602	,,	,,	239
603	,,	,,	240
606	,,	,,	241

AH Date	Metal	Ruler	Catalogue No.
607	AU	al-ʿĀdil I	242
608	,,	,,	243
609	,,	,,	244
610	,,	,,	245–246
612	,,	,,	247
613	,,	,,	248
614	,,	,,	249
615	,,	,,	250–251
Missing	AR	,,	273–274
598	,,	,,	275
600	,,	,,	276
601	,,	,,	277
605	,,	,,	278
616	AU	al-Kāmil Muḥammad I	364
618	,,	,,	365
619	,,	,,	366
621	,,	,,	367
622	,,	,,	368
623	,,	,,	369–370
624	,,	,,	371
625	,,	,,	372
626	,,	,,	373
627	,,	,,	374
628	,,	,,	375
629	,,	,,	376
630	,,	,,	377
631	,,	,,	378
632	,,	,,	379
633	,,	,,	380
634	,,	,,	381
635	,,	,,	382
Missing	AR	,,	402
622	,,	,,	403
622/623	,,	,,	404
625	,,	,,	405
626	,,	,,	406
632	,,	,,	407
623/623	,,	,,	408
635	,,	,,	409
Missing	,,	,,	410
635	AU	al-ʿĀdil II	504
636	,,	,,	505
637	,,	,,	506
637	,,	al-Ṣāliḥ Ayyūb	516
638	,,	,,	517
639	,,	,,	518–519
640	,,	,,	520
641	,,	,,	521
642	,,	,,	522

AH Date	Metal	Ruler	Catalogue No.
643	AU	al-Ṣāliḥ Ayyūb	523–524
644	,,	,,	525–526
645	,,	,,	527–528
646	,,	,,	529–530
647	,,	,,	531–532
Missing	AR	,,	534
641	,,	,,	535
645	,,	,,	536
Missing	,,	,,	537
645	,,	,,	538–539
646	,,	,,	540
640	CU	,,	541
Missing	,,	,,	542
647	AR	al-Mu'aẓẓam Tūrānshāh IV	576

AH Date	Metal	Ruler	Catalogue No.
		DAMASCUS [دمشق]	
570	CU	Saladin	8, 9, 10
571	,,	,,	11
571	AR	,,	29
573	,,	,,	30
575	,,	,,	31
Undated	,,	,,	32, 33, 34
575	,,	,,	80–81
576	,,	,,	82
577	,,	,,	83
578	,,	,,	84–55
579	,,	,,	86–87
580	,,	,,	88
581	,,	,,	89
582	,,	,,	90–91
(583)	AU	,,	79
583	AR	,,	92–93
584	,,	,,	94
585	,,	,,	95–96
586	,,	,,	97–98
587	,,	,,	99–100
588	,,	,,	101–102
Undated	,,	,,	104–106
583	CU	,,	143
584	,,	,,	144, 149
585	,,	,,	145
586	,,	,,	146
587	,,	,,	147
589	,,	,,	149
Missing	,,	,,	150 151
590	AR	al-'Azīz 'Uthmān	202
591	,,	,,	203–204
593	,,	,,	205–208
594	,,	,,	209–211

AH Date	Metal	Ruler	Catalogue No.
595	AR	al-ʿAzīz ʿUthmān	212–213
Undated	,,	,,	214–216
594	CU	,,	222
595	,,	,,	223
598	AR	al-ʿĀdil I	280
599	,,	,,	281
600	,,	,,	282–284
601	,,	,,	285
602	,,	,,	286–287
603	,,	,,	288–290
604	,,	,,	291
605	,,	,,	292
606	,,	,,	293–295
608	,,	,,	296
609	,,	,,	297
610	,,	,,	298–300
611	,,	,,	301
612	,,	,,	302–304
613	,,	,,	305–307
614	,,	,,	308
615	,,	,,	309
59x	,,	,,	310–312
596	CU	,,	317
598	,,	,,	318–319, 321
599	,,	,,	320–321
608	,,	,,	322
609	,,	,,	323
610	,,	,,	324
Missing	,,	,,	325–326
615	AR	al-Kāmil Muḥammad I	422–424
616	,,	,,	425–426
617	,,	,,	427–429
618	,,	,,	430–431
619	,,	,,	432–434
620	,,	,,	435
621	,,	,,	436–437
622	,,	,,	438–439
Missing	,,	,,	440
623	,,	,,	441–442, 444
Missing	,,	,,	443
624	,,	,,	445–446
626	,,	,,	447
627	,,	,,	448
628	,,	,,	449
629	,,	,,	450
Missing	,,	,,	451–452
630	,,	,,	453–454
631	,,	,,	455–456
632	,,	,,	457–458

AH Date	Metal	Ruler	Catalogue No.
633	AR	al-Kāmil Muḥammad I	459–460
634	,,	,,	461–462
63x	,,	,,	463
631	CU	,,	464
62x	,,	,,	466–467
633	,,	,,	465, 468
635	AR	al-ʿĀdil II	509–510
636	,,	,,	511
637	,,	,,	512–514
Missing	,,	,,	515
636	,,	al-Ṣāliḥ Ayyūb	543–546
644	,,	,,	547–549
645	,,	,,	550–553
646	,,	,,	554–556
647	,,	,,	557–558
Missing	,,	,,	559–561
64x	CU	,,	564
Missing	,,	,,	565
647	AR	al-Muʿaẓẓam Tūrānshāh IV	577–578
648	,,	,,	579
648	,,	al-Nāṣir Yūsuf	762–764
649	,,	,,	765–766
651	,,	,,	767
653	,,	,,	768–769
654	,,	,,	770
656	,,	,,	771–774
Missing	,,	,,	775
589	,,	al-Afḍal ʿAlī	790
590	,,	,,	793
591	,,	,,	794
592	,,	,,	795
635	,,	al-Ṣāliḥ Ismāʿīl	798
637	,,	,,	799–800
638	,,	,,	801–804
639	,,	,,	805–806
640	,,	,,	807–810
641	,,	,,	811–816
642	,,	,,	817–819
643	,,	,,	820–821
Missing	,,	,,	822–823
		AL-DUMLŪWAH [الدملوّة]	
600	AR	al-Nāṣir Ayyūb	963
		FILASṬĪN [فلسطين]	
592	AU	al-ʿAzīz ʿUthmān	201
		GHAZZAH [غزة]	
624	AR	al-Kāmil Muḥammad I	469–471
625	,,	,,	472
634	,,	,,	473

AH Date	Metal	Ruler	Catalogue No.
		ḤAMĀH [حماة]	
Undated	AR	Saladin	35
57x	,,	,,	107
580	,,	,,	108–109
582	,,	,,	112–113
583	,,	,,	114–115
583	CU	,,	152
584	AR	,,	116
585	,,	,,	117–119
587	,,	,,	120–121
Undated	,,	,,	122
585	CU	,,	153
Undated	,,	,,	154
594	AR	al-ʿAzīz ʿUthmān	217
595	,,	,,	218–219
597	,,	al-ʿĀdil I	313
Missing	CU	,,	327–328
645	AR	al-Ṣāliḥ Ayyūb	562
646	,,	,,	563
641	CU	,,	566
647	AR	al-Muʿaẓẓam Tūrānshāh IV	580
595	,,	al-Ẓāhir Ghāzī	655
596	,,	,,	656
589	CU	,,	685
648	AR	al-Nāṣir Yūsuf	776
651	,,	,,	777
655	,,	,,	778
657	,,	,,	779
Undated	CU	al-Manṣūr Muḥammad I	824–825
589	,,	,,	826
Undated	,,	al-Manṣūr Muḥammad II	835–840

AH Date	Metal	Ruler	Catalogue No.
		ḤARRĀN [حرّان]	
586	CU	Saladin	175
589	,,	al-ʿĀdil I	358
590	,,	,,	359
591	,,	,,	360
596	,,	,,	361–362
598	,,	,,	363
623	AR	al-Kāmil Muḥammad I	476–478
624	,,	,,	479
622/623	CU	,,	480
623	,,	,,	481
624	,,	,,	482
625	,,	,,	483
627	,,	,,	484
628	,,	,,	485–486
632	,,	,,	487
634	,,	,,	488

AH Date	Metal	Ruler	Catalogue No.
Missing	CU	al-Kāmil Muḥammad I	489
634	AR	al-Ṣāliḥ Ayyūb	567
587	CU	al-Manṣūr Muḥammad I of Ḥamāh	832
589	,,	,,	833
Missing	,,	,,	834
617	AR	al-Ashraf Mūsā I	857
618	,,	,,	858–860
		ḤIMṢ [حمص]	
577	AR	Saladin	123
Undated	,,	,,	124
578(?)	,,	,,	125
592	,,	al-ʿAzīz ʿUthmān	220
598	,,	al-ʿĀdil I	314
599	,,	,,	315
589	,,	al-Afḍal ʿAlī	796
591	,,	,,	797
		ḤIṢN (?) [حصن]	
632	CU	al-Kāmil Muḥammad I	502
Missing	,,	,,	503
6x6	,,	al-Kāmil Muḥammad II	884
		ḤIṢN-KAYFĀ [حصن كيفا]	
654	AR	al-Muwaḥḥid ʿAbd Allāh	886
656	,,	,,	887
657	,,	,,	888
658	,,	,,	889–890
Undated	,,	al-ʿAdīl Sulaymān	892
?	,,	,,	893
813	,,	,,	894
826	,,	,,	895
828	,,	,,	896
8x7	,,	,,	897
8xx	,,	,,	898
82x	,,	,,	899
8x6	,,	,,	900
Missing	,,	,,	901
Undated	,,	al-Ashraf Aḥmad ibn Sulaymān	903–904
,,	,,	,,	900–907
,,	,,	al-Kāmil Khalīl	908–910
Missing	,,	,,	912
Undated	,,	,,	911, 913–916
,,	CU	,,	917
,,	AR	al-ʿĀdil Aḥmad ibn Khalīl	919
,,	,,	Khalaf	920
Missing	,,	Khalīl II	923–926
		ḤĪZĀN [حيزان]	
Undated	AR	al-ʿAdil Sulaymān	902

AH Date	Metal	Ruler	Catalogue No.
		KHILĀṬ [خلاط]	
Missing	AR	al-Awḥad Najm al-Dīn Ayyūb	846
617	,,	al-Ashraf Mūsā I	861
618	CU	al-Muẓaffar Ghāzī	874
		MANBIJ [منبج]	
597	AR	al-Ẓāhir Ghāzī	657
Undated	CU	al-Manṣūr Muḥammad I of Ḥamāh	827–830
		MĀRDĪN [ماردين]	
581	AR	Saladin	165
		MAYĀFĀRIQĪN [ميافارقين]	
589	AR	Saladin	166
581	CU	,,	167–169
587	,,	,,	170–171
591	,,	al-ʿĀdil I	337–340
592	,,	,,	341
595	,,	,,	342
596	,,	,,	343
601	,,	,,	344
608	,,	,,	345
617	AR	al-Kāmil Muḥammad I	474
Missing	,,	,,	475
599	CU	al-Awḥad Najm al-Dīn Ayyūb	841
600	,,	,,	842
601	,,	,,	843
602	,,	,,	844
605	,,	,,	845
612	,,	al-Ashraf Mūsā I	851–852
615	AR	,,	847
617	CU	al-Muẓaffar Ghāzī	862
618	,,	,,	863
Missing	,,	,,	864
627	,,	,,	865
628	,,	,,	866
Missing	,,	,,	867–868
634	,,	,,	869, 872
641	,,	,,	870
647	,,	,,	871
Missing	,,	,,	873
,,	AR	al-Kāmil Muḥammad II	895
65x	,,	,,	876
Missing	CU	,,	877–878
647	,,	,,	879
651	,,	,,	880
655	,,	,,	882
656	,,	,,	881

AH Date	Metal	Ruler	Catalogue No.
		MAKKAH (Mecca) [مكة]	
594	AU	al-ʻAzīz ʻUthmān	225
		MINT MISSING	
Missing	CU	Saladin	162–163
,,	AU	al-ʻAzīz ʻUthmān	195
,,	AR	al-ʻĀdil I	316
,,	CU	,,	329–330
607	AR	,,	335
635	CU	al-Kāmil Muḥammad I	501
640	,,	al-Ṣāliḥ Ayyūb	572
64x	,,	,,	573
Missing	,,	,,	574–575
,,	,,	al-Nāṣir Yūsuf	785–786
,,	,,	al-Ashraf Mūsā I	856
,,	,,	al-Kāmil Muḥammad II	885
,,	,,	Ismāʻīl ibn Tughtegīn	942
,,	,,	al-Kāmil Muḥammad	891
,,	,,	al-Kāmil Khalīl	918
,,	,,	al-Masʻūd Yūsuf	1009
		MIṢR [مصر]	
573	AU	Saladin	18
590	,,	al-ʻAzīz ʻUthmān	194
623	,,	al-Kāmil Muḥammad I	383
624	,,	,,	384
62x	,,	,,	385
		NIṢIBĪN [نصيبين]	
578	CU	Saladin	172–174
631	,,	al-Kāmil Muḥammad I	492
632	,,	,,	493
634	,,	,,	494
Missing	,,	,,	495
		NO MINT	
582	CU	Saladin	176
583	,,	,,	177
584	,,	,,	178
586	,,	,,	170, 182–183
587	,,	,,	180
589	,,	,,	181
Undated	Glass/Paste	,,	69–78
Missing	CU	al-ʻĀdil I	329–330
Undated	AR	,,	336
635	AU	al Kāmil Muḥammad I	401
Undated	Glass/Paste	,,	411–415
,,	CU	,,	416–421
,,	,,	al-ʻAzīz Muḥammad	721–723
,,	,,	al-Nāṣir Yūsuf	780–784

AH Date	Metal	Ruler	Catalogue No.
595	AR	Ismā'īl ibn Tughtegīn	932
596	,,	,,	933
597	,,	,,	934
601	,,	al-Nāṣir Ayyūb	943
602	,,	,,	944
603	,,	,,	945
604	,,	,,	946
605	,,	,,	947
606	,,	,,	948
608	,,	,,	949
609	,,	,,	950
610	,,	,,	951
611	,,	,,	952
612	,,	al-Mas'ūd Yūsuf	969
620	,,	,,	970
625	,,	,,	971
		UNIDENTIFIED MINT	
628	AR	al-'Ādil Abū Bakr	1012
62x	,,	,,	1013
		ZABĪD [زبيد]	
594	AR	Ismā'īl ibn Tughtegīn	935
595	,,	,,	936
596	,,	,,	937
601	,,	al-Nāṣir Ayyūb	953
602	,,	,,	954
603	,,	,,	955
604	,,	,,	956
605	,,	,,	957
606	,,	,,	958
607	,,	,,	959
608	,,	,,	960
609	,,	,,	961
610	,,	,,	962
612	,,	al-Mas'ūd Yūsuf	972
613	,,	,,	973
614	,,	,,	974
617	,,	,,	975
618	,,	,,	976
620	,,	,,	977
621	,,	,,	978
622	,,	,,	979–982
623	,,	,,	983–984
624	,,	,,	985
625	,,	,,	986
626	,,	,,	987
627	,,	,,	988
620	CU	al-Kāmil Muḥammad I of Egypt	1015

INDEX OF YEARS

AH Date	Mint	Metal	Ruler	Catalogue No.
567	Cairo	AU	Saladin	1
,,	Alexandria	,,	,,	4
568	Cairo	,,	,,	2
,,	Alexandria	,,	,,	5
569	Cairo	,,	,,	3
,,	Alexandria	,,	,,	6
570	Damascus	CU	,,	8–10
,,	Cairo	AU	,,	12
,,	Alexandria	,,	,,	19
571	Damascus	CU	,,	11
,,	Cairo	AU	,,	13
,,	Alexandria	,,	,,	20
,,	Damascus	AR	,,	29
572	Cairo	AU	,,	14
,,	Alexandria	,,	,,	21
573	Cairo	,,	,,	15
,,	Miṣr	,,	,,	18
,,	Alexandria	,,	,,	22
,,	Damascus	AR	,,	30
,,	ʿAdan	AU	al-Muʿaẓẓam Tūrānshāh I	927
574	Cairo	,,	Saladin	16
,,	Alexandria	,,	,,	23
575	Cairo	,,	,,	17
,,	Alexandria	,,	,,	24
,,	Damascus	AR	,,	31
,,	,,	,,	,,	80–81
576	Cairo	AU	,,	36
,,	Alexandria	,,	,,	50
,,	Cairo	AR	,,	63
,,	Damascus	,,	,,	82
,,	ʿAdan	AU	,,	928
577	Cairo	,,	,,	37
,,	Damascus	AR	,,	83
,,	Ḥimṣ	,,	,,	123
578	Cairo	AU	,,	38
,,	Alexandria	,,	,,	51
,,	Damascus	AR	,,	84–85
578?	Ḥimṣ	,,	,,	125
578	Niṣibīn	CU	,,	172–174
579	Cairo	AU	,,	39
,,	Alexandria	,,	,,	52

AH Date	Mint	Metal	Ruler	Catalogue No.
579	Damascus	AR	Saladin	86–87
,,	Aleppo	,,	,,	127
580	Cairo	AU	,,	40
,,	Alexandria	,,	,,	53
,,	Damascus	AR	,,	88
,,	Ḥamāh	,,	,,	108–109
,,	Aleppo	,,	,,	128–129
,,	Ramlah	CU	,,	164
,,	ʿAdan	AU	,,	929
581	Cairo	,,	,,	41
,,	Alexandria	,,	,,	54
,,	Damascus	AR	,,	89
,,	Aleppo	,,	,,	130–131
,,	Mārdīn	,,	,,	165
,,	Mayāfāriqīn	CU	,,	167–169
582	Cairo	AU	,,	42
,,	Alexandria	,,	,,	55
,,	Damascus	AR	,,	90–91
,,	Ḥamāh	,,	,,	112–113
,,	Aleppo	,,	,,	132
,,	None (the Jazīrah)	CU	,,	176
583	Cairo	AU	,,	43
,,	Alexandria	,,	,,	56
,,	Damascus	,,	,,	79
,,	ʿAdan	,,	,,	930
,,	Damascus	AR	,,	92–93
,,	Ḥamāh	,,	,,	114–115
,,	,,	CU	,,	152
,,	Aleppo	AR	,,	133
,,	Damascus	CU	,,	143
,,	None (the Jazīrah)	,,	,,	177
584	Cairo	AU	,,	44
,,	Alexandria	,,	,,	57
,,	Damascus	AR	,,	94
,,	Ḥamāh	,,	,,	116
,,	Aleppo	,,	,,	134
,,	,,	CU	,,	155
,,	Damascus	,,	,,	144, 149
,,	None (the Jazīrah)	,,	,,	178
585	Cairo	AU	,,	45
,,	Alexandria	,,	,,	58
,,	Cairo	AR	,,	66
,,	Damascus	,,	,,	95–96
,,	Ḥamāh	,,	,,	117–119
,,	Aleppo	,,	,,	135
,,	Damascus	CU	,,	145
,,	Ḥamāh	,,	,,	153
,,	Aleppo	,,	,,	156–157
586	Cairo	AU	,,	46

AH Date	Mint	Metal	Ruler	Catalogue No.
586	Alexandria	AU	Saladin	59
,,	Cairo	AR	,,	67
,,	Damascus	,,	,,	97–98
,,	Aleppo	,,	,,	136–137
,,	Damascus	CU	,,	146
,,	Ḥarrān	,,	,,	175
,,	None (the Jazīrah)	,,	,,	179
,,	,,	,,	,,	182–183
587	Cairo	AU	,,	47
,,	Damascus	AR	,,	99–100
,,	Ḥamāh	,,	,,	120–121
,,	Aleppo	,,	,,	138
,,	,,	CU	,,	159
,,	Damascus	,,	,,	147
,,	Mayāfāriqīn	,,	,,	170–171
,,	None (the Jazīrah)	,,	,,	180
,,	Ḥarrān	,,	al-Manṣūr Muḥammad I (Ḥamāh)	832
588	Cairo	AU	Saladin	48
,,	Alexandria	,,	,,	60
,,	Damascus	AR	,,	101–102
,,	Aleppo	,,	,,	139
,,	,,	CU	,,	160
589	Cairo	AU	,,	49
,,	Alexandria	,,	,,	61
,,	Damascus	AR	,,	103
,,	Aleppo	,,	,,	140–142
,,	,,	CU	,,	161
,,	Mayāfāriqīn	AR	,,	166
,,	None (the Jazīrah)	CU	,,	181
,,	None (Damascus)	AR	al-Afḍal ʿAlī	791–792
,,	Damascus	,,	,,	790
,,	,,	CU	,,	148
,,	Ḥarrān	,,	al-Manṣūr Muḥammad I (Ḥamāh)	833
,,	Ḥamāh	,,	al-Manṣūr Muḥammad I	826
,,	Cairo	AU	al-ʿAzīz ʿUthmān	184
,,	Alexandria	,,	,,	191
,,	Ḥimṣ	AR	al-Afḍal ʿAlī	796
,,	Aleppo	,,	al-Ẓāhir Ghāzī	581–582
,,	,,	CU	,,	658–662
,,	Ḥamāh	,,	,,	685
,,	Ḥarrān	,,	al-ʿĀdil I	358
590	Cairo	AU	al-ʿAzīz ʿUthmān	185
,,	Alexandria	,,	,,	192
,,	Miṣr	,,	,,	194
,,	Damascus	AR	,,	202
,,	,,	,,	al-Afḍal ʿAlī	793
,,	Aleppo	,,	al-Ẓāhir Ghāzī	583
,,	Ḥarrān	CU	al-ʿĀdil I	359
591	Cairo	AU	al-ʿAzīz ʿUthmān	186

AH Date	Mint	Metal	Ruler	Catalogue No.
591	Damascus	AR	al-ʻAzīz ʻUthmān	203–204
,,	,,	,,	al-Afḍal ʻAlī	794
,,	Ḥimṣ	,,	,,	797
,,	Aleppo	,,	al-Ẓāhir Ghāzī	584–585
,,	Mayāfāriqīn	CU	al-ʻĀdil I	337–340
,,	Ḥarrān	,,	,,	360
592	Cairo	AU	al-ʻAzīz ʻUthmān	187
,,	Filasṭīn	,,	,,	201
,,	Ḥimṣ	AR	,,	220
,,	Damascus	,,	al-Afḍal ʻAlī	795
,,	Mayāfāriqīn	CU	al-ʻĀdil I	341
593	Cairo	AU	al-ʻAzīz ʻUthmān	188
,,	Alexandria	,,	,,	193
,,	Damascus	AR	,,	205–208
,,	Aleppo	,,	al-Ẓāhir Ghāzī	586–589
594	Cairo	AU	al-ʻAzīz ʻUthmān	189
,,	Damascus	AR	,,	209–211
,,	Ḥamāh	,,	,,	217
,,	Damascus	CU	,,	222
,,	Mekkah (Mecca)	AU	,,	225
,,	Aleppo	AR	al-Ẓāhir Ghāzī	590–591
,,	Taʻizz	,,	Ismāʻīl ibn Tughtegīn	931
,,	Zabīd	,,	,,	935
,,	ʻAdan	,,	,,	939
595	Cairo	AU	al-ʻAzīz ʻUthmān	190
,,	Damascus	AR	,,	212–213
,,	Ḥamāh	,,	,,	218–219
,,	Damascus	CU	,,	223
,,	Cairo	AU	al-Manṣūr Muḥammad	226
,,	Alexandria	,,	,,	228
,,	Mayāfāriqīn	CU	al-ʻĀdil I	342
,,	Taʻizz	AR	Ismāʻīl ibn Tughtegīn	932
,,	Zabīd	,,	,,	936
,,	Ṣanʻā	,,	,,	938
,,	ʻAdan	,,	,,	940
,,	Mint Missing	CU	,,	942
,,	Aleppo	AR	al-Ẓāhir Ghāzī	592–594
,,	Ḥamāh	,,	,,	655
596	Cairo	AU	al-Manṣūr Muḥammad	227
,,	Alexandria	,,	,,	229
,,	Cairo	,,	al-ʻĀdil I	233
,,	Alexandria	,,	,,	252
,,	Damascus	CU	,,	317
,,	Mayāfāriqīn	,,	,,	343
,,	Ḥarrān	,,	,,	301–302
,,	Aleppo	AR	al-Ẓāhir Ghāzī	595–596
,,	Ḥamāh	,,	,,	656
,,	Aleppo	CU	,,	664

AH Date	Mint	Metal	Ruler	Catalogue No.
596	Ta'izz	AR	Ismā'īl ibn Tughtegīn	933
,,	Zabīd	,,	,,	937
,,	'Adan	,,	,,	941
597	Cairo	AU	al-'Ādil I	234–235
,,	Alexandria	AU	,,	253–254
,,	Ḥamāh	AR	,,	313
,,	Aleppo	,,	al-Ẓāhir Ghāzī	597
,,	,,	CU	,,	665
,,	Manbij	AR	,,	657
,,	Ta'izz	,,	Ismā'īl ibn Tughtegīn	934
598	Cairo	,,	al-'Ādil I	275
,,	Alexandria	AU	,,	255
,,	Damascus	AR	,,	280
,,	Ḥimṣ	,,	,,	314
,,	Damascus	CU	,,	318–319, 321
,,	Ḥarrān	,,	,,	363
,,	Aleppo	AR	al-Ẓāhir Ghāzī	598–600
,,	,,	CU	,,	666–667
599	Cairo	AU	al-'Ādil I	236
,,	Alexandria	,,	,,	256
,,	Damascus	AR	,,	281
,,	Ḥimṣ	,,	,,	315
,,	Damascus	CU	,,	320–321
,,	Aleppo	,,	al-Ẓāhir Ghāzī	668–669
,,	,,	AR	,,	601–602
,,	Mayāfāriqīn	CU	al-Awḥad Najm al-Dīn Ayyūb	841
600	Cairo	AU	al-'Ādil I	237
,,	Alexandria	,,	,,	257
,,	Cairo	AR	,,	276
,,	Damascus	,,	,,	282–284
,,	Aleppo	,,	al-Ẓāhir Ghāzī	603–604
,,	Mayāfāriqīn	CU	al-Awḥad Najm al-Dīn Ayyūb	842
,,	al-Dumlūwah	AR	al-Nāṣir Ayyūb	963
601	Cairo	AU	al-'Ādil I	238
,,	Alexandria	,,	,,	258
,,	Cairo	AR	,,	277
,,	Damascus	,,	,,	285
,,	Mayāfāriqīn	CU	,,	344
,,	Qal'at Ja'bar	,,	,,	346–347
,,	Ta'izz	AR	al-Nāṣir Ayyūb	943
,,	Zabīd	,,	,,	953
,,	'Adan	,,	,,	965
,,	Aleppo	AR	al-Ẓāhir Ghāzī	605–606
,,	Mayāfāriqīn	,,	al-Awḥad Najm al-Dīn Ayyūb	843
602	Cairo	AU	al-'Ādil I	239
,,	Alexandria	,,	,,	259
,,	Damascus	AR	,,	286–287
,,	al-Ruhā	CU	,,	349
,,	Qal'at Ja'bar	,,	,,	348

AH Date	Mint	Metal	Ruler	Catalogue No.
602	Aleppo	AR	al-Ẓāhir Ghāzī	607–608
,,	Mayāfāriqīn	CU	al-Awḥad Ayyūb	844
,,	Ta'izz	AR	al-Nāṣir Ayyūb	944
,,	Zabīd	,,	,,	954
603	Cairo	AU	al-'Ādil I	240
,,	Alexandria	AU	,,	260
,,	Damascus	AR	,,	288–290
,,	al-Ruhā	CU	,,	350
,,	Aleppo	AR	al-Ẓāhir Ghāzī	609
,,	,,	CU	,,	670, 682
,,	Ta'izz	,,	al-Nāṣir Ayyūb	945
,,	Zabīd	,,	,,	955
604	Alexandria	AU	al-'Ādil I	261
,,	Damascus	AR	,,	291
,,	al-Ruhā	CU	,,	351
,,	Aleppo	AR	al-Ẓāhir Ghāzī	610–611
,,	,,	CU	,,	671
,,	Ta'izz	AR	al-Nāṣir Ayyūb	946
,,	Zabīd	,,	,,	956
,,	'Adan	,,	,,	966
605	Alexandria	AU	al-'Ādil I	262
,,	Cairo	AR	,,	278
,,	Damascus	,,	,,	292
,,	al-Ruhā	,,	,,	331
,,	,,	CU	,,	352
,,	Aleppo	AR	al-Ẓāhir Ghāzī	612
,,	,,	CU	,,	672
,,	Mayāfāriqīn	,,	al-Awḥad Najm al-Dīn Ayyūb	845
,,	Ta'izz	AR	al-Nāṣir Ayyūb	947
,,	Zabīd	,,	,,	957
,,	Ṣan'ā	,,	,,	964
606	Cairo	AU	al-'Ādil I	241
,,	Alexandria	,,	,,	263–264
,,	Damascus	AR	,,	293–295
,,	Aleppo	,,	al-Ẓāhir Ghāzī	613–614
,,	,,	CU	,,	673
,,	Ta'izz	AR	al-Nāṣir Ayyūb	948
,,	Zabīd	,,	,,	958
,,	'Adan	,,	,,	967
607	Cairo	AU	al-'Ādil I	242
,,	Alexandria	AU	,,	265
,,	Aleppo	AR	al-Ẓāhir Ghāzī	615
,,	,,	CU	,,	674
,,	Zabīd	AR	al-Nāṣir Ayyūb	959
608	Cairo	AU	al-'Ādil I	243
,,	Alexandria	AU	,,	266
,,	Damascus	AR	,,	296
,,	,,	CU	,,	322
,,	Mayāfāriqīn	,,	,,	345

AH Date	Mint	Metal	Ruler	Catalogue No.
608	Aleppo	AR	al-Ẓāhir Ghāzī	616–618
,,	,,	CU	,,	675
,,	None (Mayāfāriqīn)	,,	al-Ashraf Mūsā I	848
,,	Ta'izz	AR	al-Nāṣir Ayyūb	949
,,	Zabīd	,,	,,	960
,,	'Adan	,,	,,	968
609	Aleppo	,,	al-Ẓāhir Ghāzī	619
,,	,,	CU	,,	676
,,	Ta'izz	AR	al-Nāṣir Ayyūb	950
,,	Zabīd	,,	,,	961
,,	Cairo	AU	al-'Ādil I	244
,,	Alexandria	,,	,,	267
,,	Damascus	AR	,,	297
,,	,,	CU	,,	323
610	Cairo	AU	,,	245–246
,,	Alexandria	,,	,,	268
,,	Damascus	AR	,,	298–300
,,	,,	CU	,,	324
,,	Aleppo	AR	al-Ẓāhir Ghāzī	620–621
,,	,,	CU	,,	677
,,	Ta'izz	AR	al-Nāṣir Ayyūb	951
,,	Zabīd	,,	,,	962
611	Alexandria	AU	al-'Ādil I	269
,,	Damascus	AR	,,	301
,,	al-Ruhā	,,	,,	332
,,	,,	CU	,,	353–355
,,	Aleppo	AR	al-Ẓāhir Ghāzī	622
,,	,,	CU	,,	678
,,	Ta'izz	AR	al-Nāṣir Ayyūb	952
612	Cairo	AU	al-'Ādil I	247
,,	Damascus	AR	,,	302–304
,,	al-Ruhā	CU	,,	356
,,	Aleppo	AR	al-Ẓāhir Ghāzī	623–625
,,	,,	CU	,,	679
,,	None (Mayāfāriqīn)	,,	al-Ashraf Mūsā I	849–850
,,	Mayāfāriqīn	,,	,,	851–852
,,	Zabīd	AR	al-Mas'ūd Yūsuf	972
,,	Raydah	,,	,,	1007
,,	Ta'izz	,,	,,	969
613	Cairo	AU	al-'Ādil I	248
,,	Alexandria	,,	,,	270
,,	Damascus	AR	,,	305–307
,,	Zabīd	,,	al-Mas'ūd Yūsuf	973
,,	'Adan	,,	,,	996
,,	Aleppo	,,	al-Ẓāhir Ghāzī	626–628
,,	,,	CU	al-'Azīz Muḥammad	708
614	Cairo	AU	al-'Ādil I	249
,,	Alexandria	,,	,,	271
,,	Damascus	AR	,,	308

AH Date	Mint	Metal	Ruler	Catalogue No.
614	al-Ruhā	CU	al-ʿĀdil I	357
,,	Aleppo	AR	al-Ẓāhir Ghāzī [Posthumous]	629–630
,,	,,	,,	al-ʿAzīz Muḥammad	686
,,	Zabīd	,,	al-Masʿūd Yūsuf	974
615	Cairo	AU	al-ʿĀdil I	250–251
,,	Alexandria	,,	,,	272
,,	Damascus	AR	,,	309
,,	al-Ruhā	,,	,,	333–334
,,	Sinjār	CU	al-Ashraf Mūsā I	853
,,	Mayāfāriqīn	AR	,,	847
,,	Damascus	,,	al-Kāmil Muḥammad I	422–424
,,	Aleppo	,,	al-Ẓāhir Ghāzī [Posthumous]	631–632
,,	,,	,,	al-ʿAzīz Muḥammad	687–689
,,	,,	CU	,,	709
616	Cairo	AU	al-Kāmil Muḥammad I	364
,,	Damascus	AR	,,	425–426
,,	al-Ruhā	,,	,,	490
,,	Aleppo	,,	al-Ẓāhir Ghāzī [Posthumous]	633
,,	,,	,,	al-ʿAzīz Muḥammad	690
,,	ʿAdan	,,	al-Masʿūd Yūsuf	997
617	Alexandria	AU	al-Kāmil Muḥammad I	386
,,	Damascus	AR	,,	427–429
,,	Mayāfāriqīn	,,	,,	474
,,	al-Ruhā	,,	,,	491
,,	Aleppo	,,	al-Ẓāhir Ghāzī [Posthumous]	634–635
,,	,,	,,	al-ʿAzīz Muḥammad	691–692
,,	Sinjār	CU	al-Ashraf Mūsā I	854–855
,,	Ḥarrān	AR	,,	857
,,	Khilāṭ	,,	,,	861
,,	Mayāfāriqīn	CU	al-Muẓaffar Ghāzī	862
,,	Zabīd	AR	al-Masʿūd Yūsuf	975
,,	Ṣanʿā	,,	,,	989
,,	Raydah	,,	,,	1008
618	Cairo	AU	al-Kāmil Muḥammad I	365
,,	Alexandria	,,	,,	387
,,	Damascus	AR	,,	430–431
,,	Aleppo	,,	al-Ẓāhir Ghāzī [Posthumous]	636
,,	,,	CU	al-ʿAzīz Muḥammad	710
,,	Ḥarrān	AR	al-Ashraf Mūsā I	858–860
,,	Mayāfāriqīn	CU	al-Muẓaffar Ghāzī	863
,,	Khilāṭ	,,	,,	874
,,	Zabīd	AR	al-Masʿūd Yūsuf	976
,,	ʿAdan	,,	,,	998
619	Cairo	AU	al-Kāmil Muḥammad I	366
,,	Alexandria	,,	,,	388
,,	Damascus	AR	,,	432–434
,,	Aleppo	,,	al-Ẓāhir Ghāzī [Posthumous]	637–638
,,	,,	,,	al-ʿAzīz Muḥammad	693
620	Damascus	,,	al-Kāmil Muḥammad I	435

AH Date	Mint	Metal	Ruler	Catalogue No.
620	Aleppo	AR	al-Ẓāhir Ghāzī [Posthumous]	639–640
,,	,,	CU	al-ʿAzīz Muḥammad	711
,,	Zabīd	AR	al-Masʿūd Yūsuf	977
,,	,,	CU	al-Kāmil Muḥammad	1015
,,	Taʿizz	AR	al-Masʿūd Yūsuf	970
621	Cairo	AU	al-Kāmil Muḥammad	367
,,	Damascus	AR	,,	436–437
,,	Aleppo	,,	al-Ẓāhir Ghāzī [Posthumous]	641
,,	,,	CU	al-ʿAzīz Muḥammad	712
,,	Zabīd	AR	al-Masʿūd Yūsuf	978
,,	Ṣanʿā	,,	,,	990–991
,,	ʿAdan	,,	,,	999–1000
622	Cairo	AU	al-Kāmil Muḥammad I	368
,,	,,	AR	,,	403–404
,,	Damascus	,,	,,	438–439
,,	Aleppo	,,	al-Ẓāhir Ghāzī [Posthumous]	642–643
,,	,,	CU	al-ʿAzīz Muḥammad	713, 715
,,	Zabīd	AR	al-Masʿūd Yūsuf	979–982
,,	ʿAdan	,,	,,	1001
623	Cairo	AU	al-Kāmil Muḥammad I	369–370
,,	Miṣr	,,	,,	383
,,	Alexandria	,,	,,	389–390
,,	Cairo	AR	,,	404, 408
,,	Damascus	,,	,,	441–442, 444
,,	Ḥarrān	,,	,,	476–478
,,	,,	CU	,,	480–481
,,	Aleppo	AR	al-Ẓāhir Ghāzī [Posthumous]	644
,,	,,	,,	al-ʿAzīz Muḥammad	694
,,	,,	CU	,,	716, 718
,,	Zabīd	AR	al-Masʿūd Yūsuf	983–984
,,	Ṣanʿā	,,	,,	992–993
624	Cairo	AU	al-Kāmil Muḥammad I	371
,,	Miṣr	,,	,,	384
,,	Alexandria	,,	,,	391
,,	Damascus	AR	,,	445–446
,,	Ghazzah	,,	,,	469–471
,,	Ḥarrān	,,	,,	479
,,	,,	CU	,,	482
,,	Aleppo	AR	al-Ẓāhir Ghāzī [Posthumous]	645
,,	,,	,,	al-ʿAzīz Muḥammad	695
,,	Zabīd	,,	al-Masʿūd Yūsuf	985
625	Cairo	AU	al-Kāmil Muḥammad I	372
,,	Alexandria	,,	,,	392
,,	Cairo	AR	,,	405
,,	Ghazzah	,,	,,	472
,,	Ḥarrān	CU	,,	483
,,	Aleppo	AR	al-Ẓāhir Ghāzī [Posthumous]	646–647
,,	,,	,,	al-ʿAzīz Muḥammad	696–698
,,	Taʿizz	,,	al-Masʿūd Yūsuf	971

AH Date	Mint	Metal	Ruler	Catalogue No.
625	Zabīd	AR	al-Mas'ūd Yūsuf	986
,,	Ṣan'ā	,,	,,	994
,,	'Adan	,,	,,	1002–1003
626	Cairo	AU	al-Kāmil Muḥammad I	373
,,	Alexandria	,,	,,	393
,,	Cairo	AR	,,	406
,,	Damascus	,,	,,	447
,,	Aleppo	,,	al-'Azīz Muḥammad	699
,,	Zabīd	,,	al-Mas'ūd Yūsuf	987
,,	Ṣan'ā	,,	,,	995
,,	'Adan	,,	,,	1004–1005
627	Cairo	AU	al-Kāmil Muḥammad I	374
,,	Alexandria	,,	,,	394
,,	Damascus	AR	,,	448
,,	Ḥarrān	CU	,,	484
,,	Aleppo	AR	al-'Azīz Muḥammad	700
,,	Mayāfāriqīn	CU	al-Muẓaffar Ghāzī	865
,,	Aleppo	AR	al-Ẓāhir Ghāzī [Posthumous]	648–650
,,	Zabīd	,,	al-Mas'ūd Yūsuf	988
,,	,,	,,	,,	916
,,	'Adan	,,	,,	1006
,,	,,	,,	al-'Ādil Abū Bakr	1014
628	Cairo	AU	al-Kāmil Muḥammad I	375
,,	Alexandria	,,	,,	395
,,	Damascus	AR	,,	449
,,	Ḥarrān	CU	,,	485–486
,,	Aleppo	AR	al-Ẓāhir Ghāzī [Posthumous]	651
,,	,,	,,	al-'Azīz Muḥammad	701
,,	Mayāfāriqīn	CU	al-Muẓaffar Ghāzī	866
629	Cairo	AU	al-Kāmil Muḥammad I	376
,,	Alexandria	,,	,,	396
,,	Damascus	AR	,,	450
,,	Qal'at Ja'bar	CU	,,	498
,,	Aleppo	AR	al-Ẓāhir Ghāzī [Posthumous]	652
,,	,,	CU	al-'Azīz Muḥammad	719
630	Cairo	AU	al-Kāmil Muḥammad I	377
,,	Alexandria	,,	,,	397
,,	Damascus	AR	,,	453–454
,,	Aleppo	,,	al-Ẓāhir Ghāzī [Posthumous]	653
,,	,,	,,	al-'Azīz Muḥammad	702–703
631	Cairo	AU	al-Kāmil Muḥammad I	378
,,	Damascus	AR	,,	455–456
,,	,,	CU	,,	464
,,	Nisibīn	,,	,,	492
,,	Qal'at Ja'bar	,,	,,	499
,,	Aleppo	AR	al-'Azīz Muḥammad	704
632	Cairo	AU	,,	379
,,	Alexandria	,,	,,	398
,,	Cairo	AR	,,	407

AH Date	Mint	Metal	Ruler	Catalogue No.
632	Damascus	AR	al-Azīz Muḥammad	457–458
,,	Ḥarrān	CU	,,	487
,,	Niṣibīn	,,	,,	493
,,	Ḥiṣn	,,	,,	502
633	Cairo	AU	,,	380
,,	Damascus	AR	,,	459–460
,,	,,	CU	,,	465, 468
,,	Aleppo	AR	,,	705
634	Cairo	AU	al-Kāmil Muḥammad I	381
,,	Alexandria	,,	,,	399
,,	Damascus	AR	,,	461–462
,,	Ghazzah	,,	,,	473
,,	Ḥarrān	CU	,,	488
,,	Niṣibīn	,,	,,	494
,,	Qal'at Ja'bar	,,	,,	500
,,	Aleppo	AR	al-'Azīz Muḥammad	706
,,	,,	,,	al-Nāṣir Yūsuf	724
,,	Mayāfāriqīn	CU	al-Muẓaffar Ghāzī	869, 872
,,	Ḥarrān	AR	al-Ṣāliḥ Ayyūb	567
635	Cairo	AU	al-Kāmil Muḥammad I	382
,,	Alexandria	,,	,,	400
,,	Cairo	AR	,,	409
,,	Mint Missing	CU	,,	501
,,	Cairo	AU	al-'Ādil II	504
,,	Damascus	AR	,,	509–510
,,	,,	,,	,,	798
636	Cairo	AU	,,	505
,,	Alexandria	,,	,,	507
,,	Damascus	AR	,,	511
,,	,,	,,	al-Ṣāliḥ Ayyūb	543–546
,,	Āmid	CU	,,	568
,,	Aleppo	AR	al-Nāṣir Yūsuf	725
637	Cairo	AU	al-'Ādil II	506
,,	Alexandria	,,	,,	508
,,	Damascus	AR	,,	512–514
,,	Cairo	AU	al-Ṣāliḥ Ayyūb	516
,,	Āmid	CU	,,	569
,,	Aleppo	AR	al-Nāṣir Yūsuf	726–727
,,	Damascus	,,	al-Ṣāliḥ Ismā'īl	799–800
638	Cairo	AU	al-Ṣāliḥ Ayyūb	517
,,	Aleppo	AR	al-Ẓāhir Ghāzī [Posthumous]	654
,,	,,	,,	al-Nāṣir Yūsuf	728
,,	Damascus	,,	al-Ṣāliḥ Ismā'īl	801–804
,,	Āmid	CU	al-Ṣāliḥ Ayyūb	570
639	Cairo	AU	,,	518–519
,,	Aleppo	AR	al-Nāṣir Yūsuf	729–730
,,	Damascus	,,	al-Ṣāliḥ Ismā'īl	805–806
640	Cairo	AU	al-Ṣāliḥ Ayyūb	520
,,	,,	CU	,,	541

AH Date	Mint	Metal	Ruler	Catalogue No.
640	Mint Missing	CU	al-Ṣāliḥ Ayyūb	572
,,	Aleppo	AR	al-Nāṣir Yūsuf	731–733
,,	Damascus	,,	al-Ṣāliḥ Ismā'īl	807–810
641	Cairo	AU	al-Ṣāliḥ Ayyūb	521
,,	,,	AR	,,	535
,,	Ḥamāh	CU	,,	566
,,	Damascus	AR	al-Ṣāliḥ Ismā'īl	811–816
,,	Mayāfāriqīn	CU	al-Muẓaffar Ghāzī	870
642	Cairo	AU	al-Ṣāliḥ Ayyūb	522
,,	Aleppo	AR	al-Nāṣir Yūsuf	734
,,	Damascus	,,	al-Ṣāliḥ Ismā'īl	817–819
643	Cairo	AU	al-Ṣāliḥ Ayyūb	523–524
,,	Aleppo	AR	al-Nāṣir Yūsuf	735–736
,,	,,	CU	,,	758
,,	Damascus	AR	al-Ṣāliḥ Ismā'īl	820–821
644	Cairo	AR	al-Ṣāliḥ Ayyūb	525–526
,,	Damascus	,,	,,	547–549
,,	Aleppo	,,	al-Nāṣir Yūsuf	737
645	Cairo	AU	al-Ṣāliḥ Ayyūb	527–528
,,	,,	AR	,,	536, 538–539
,,	Damascus	,,	,,	550–553
,,	Ḥamāh	,,	,,	562
,,	Aleppo	,,	al-Nāṣir Yūsuf	738
646	Cairo	AU	al-Ṣāliḥ Ayyūb	529–530
,,	,,	AR	,,	540
,,	Damascus	,,	,,	554–556
,,	Ḥamāh	,,	,,	563
,,	Aleppo	,,	al-Nāṣir Yūsuf	739–741
647	,,	,,	,,	742
,,	Cairo	AU	al-Ṣāliḥ Ayyūb	531–532
,,	Damascus	AR	,,	557–558
,,	Aleppo	,,	,,	743–744
,,	Mayāfāriqīn	CU	al-Muẓaffar Ghāzī	871
,,	,,	,,	,,	879
,,	Cairo	AR	al-Kāmil Muḥammad II	576
,,	Damascus	,,	al-Mu'aẓẓam Tūrānshāh IV	577–578
,,	Ḥamāh	,,	,,	580
648	Damascus	,,	,,	579
,,	Aleppo	,,	al-Nāṣir Yūsuf	745–746
,,	Damascus	,,	,,	762–764
,,	Ḥamāh	,,	,,	776
649	Aleppo	,,	,,	747
,,	Damascus	,,	,,	765–766
650	Aleppo	,,	,,	748
651	,,	,,	,,	749
,,	Damascus	,,	,,	767
,,	Ḥamāh	,,	,,	777
,,	Mayāfāriqīn	CU	al-Kāmil Muḥammad II	880
652	Aleppo	AR	al-Nāṣir Yūsuf	750

AH Date	Mint	Metal	Ruler	Catalogue No.
653	Aleppo	AR	al-Nāṣir Yūsuf	751
,,	Damascus	,,	,,	768–769
654	,,	,,	,,	770
,,	Aleppo	,,	,,	752–754
,,	Ḥiṣn	,,	al-Muwaḥḥid ʿAbd Allāh	886
655	Aleppo	,,	al-Nāṣir Yūsuf	755
,,	,,	CU	,,	760
,,	Ḥamāh	AR	,,	778
,,	Mayāfāriqīn	CU	al-Kāmil Muḥammad II	882
656	Aleppo	AR	al-Nāṣir Yūsuf	756
,,	Damascus	,,	,,	771–774
,,	Mayāfāriqīn	CU	al-Kāmil Muḥammad II	881
,,	Ḥiṣn-Kayfā	AR	al-Muwaḥḥid ʿAbd Allāh	887
657	Ḥamāh	,,	al-Nāṣir Yūsuf	779
,,	Ḥiṣn-Kayfā	,,	al-Muwaḥḥid ʿAbd Allāh	888
658	,,	,,	,,	889–890
,,	Aleppo	,,	al-Nāṣir Yūsuf	757
813	Ḥiṣn-Kayfā	,,	al-ʿĀdil Sulaymān	894
826	,,	,,	,,	895
828	,,	,,	,,	896

PLATES

PLATE I

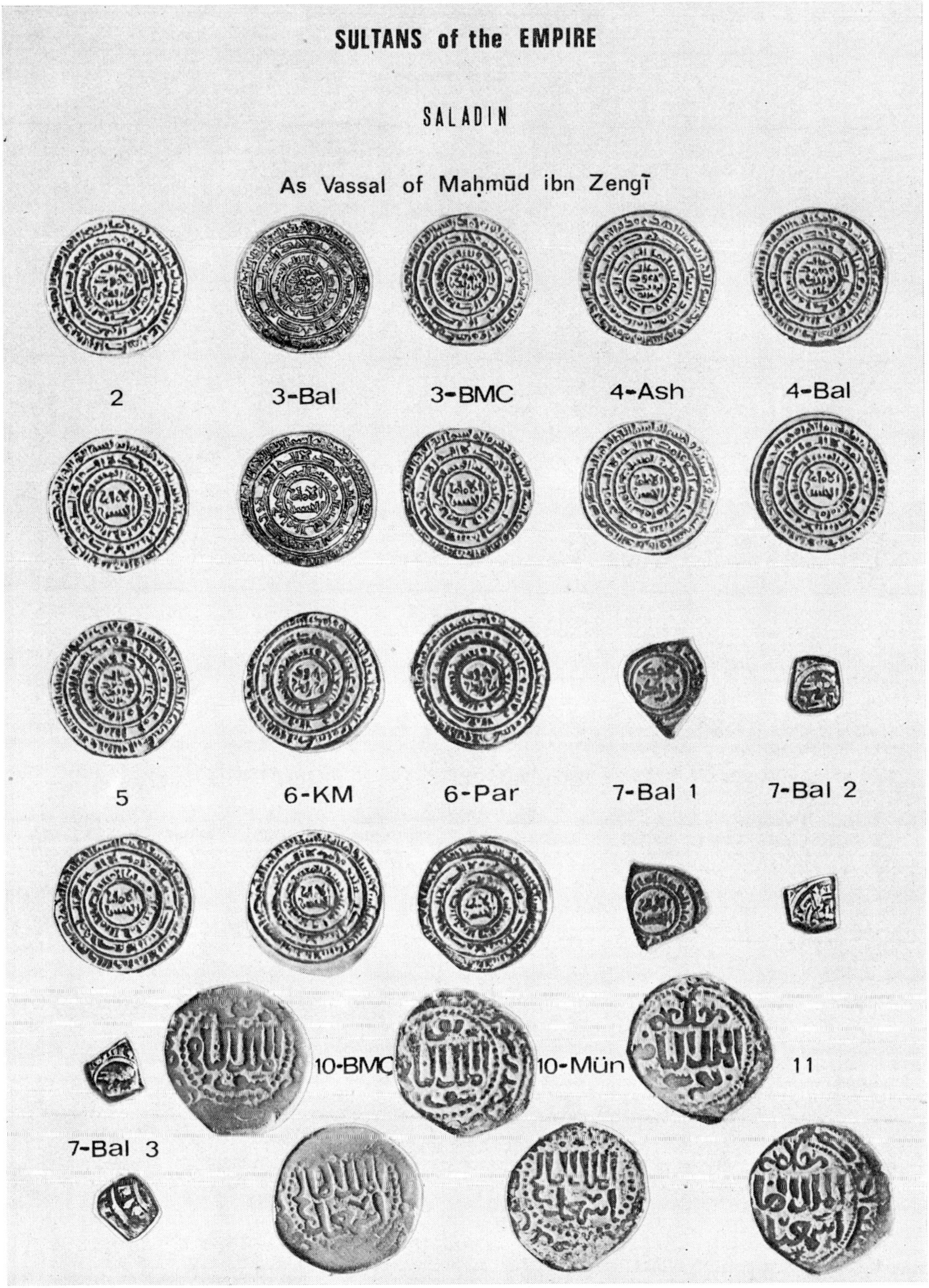

SULTANS of the EMPIRE
SALADIN
As Vassal of Maḥmūd ibn Zengī
2
3-Bal
3-BMC
4-Ash
4-Bal
5
6-KM
6-Par
7-Bal 1
7-Bal 2
10-BMC
10-Mün
11
7-Bal 3

PLATE II

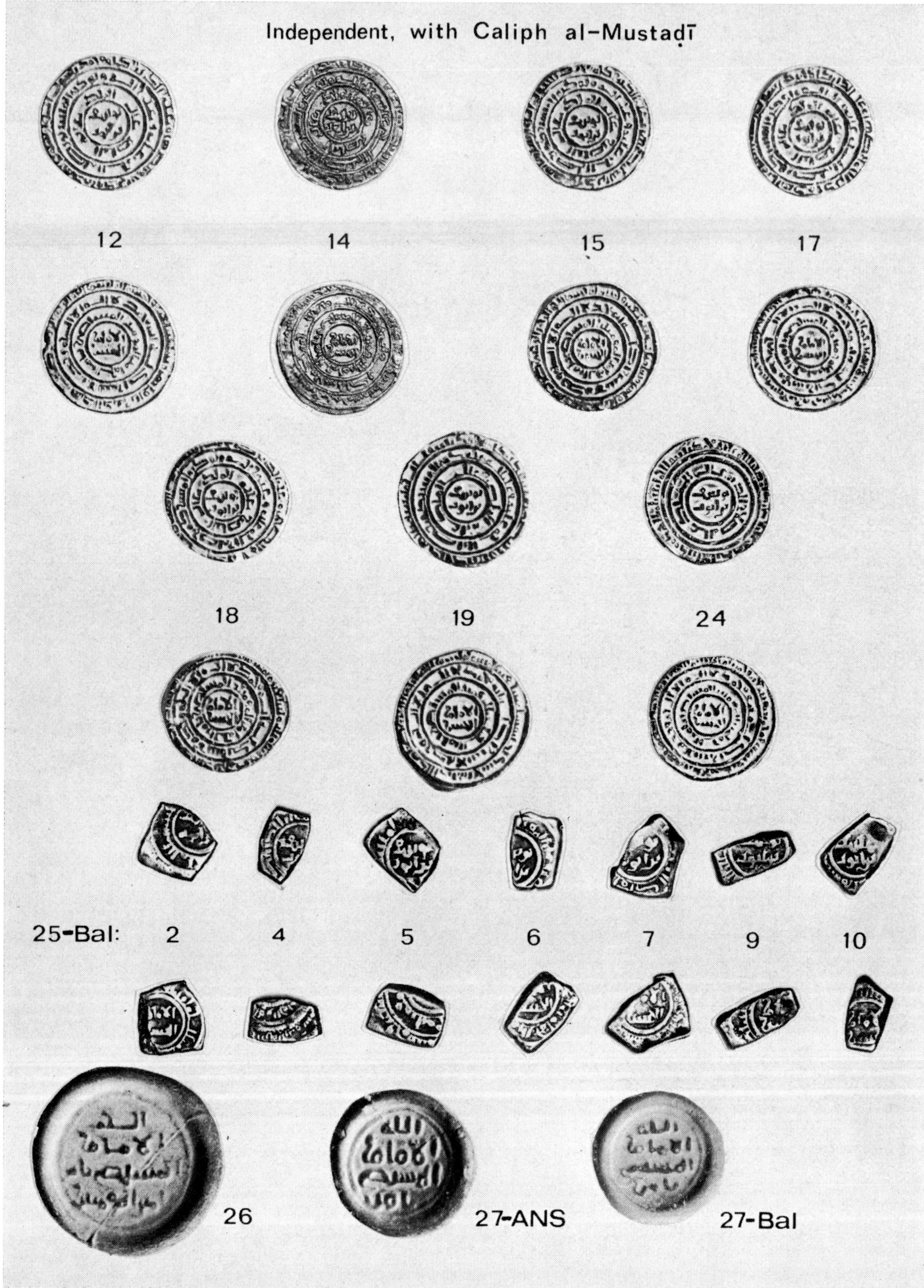
Independent, with Caliph al-Mustaḍī
12
14
15
17
18
19
24
25-Bal: 2
4
5
6
7
9
10
26
27-ANS
27-Bal

PLATE III

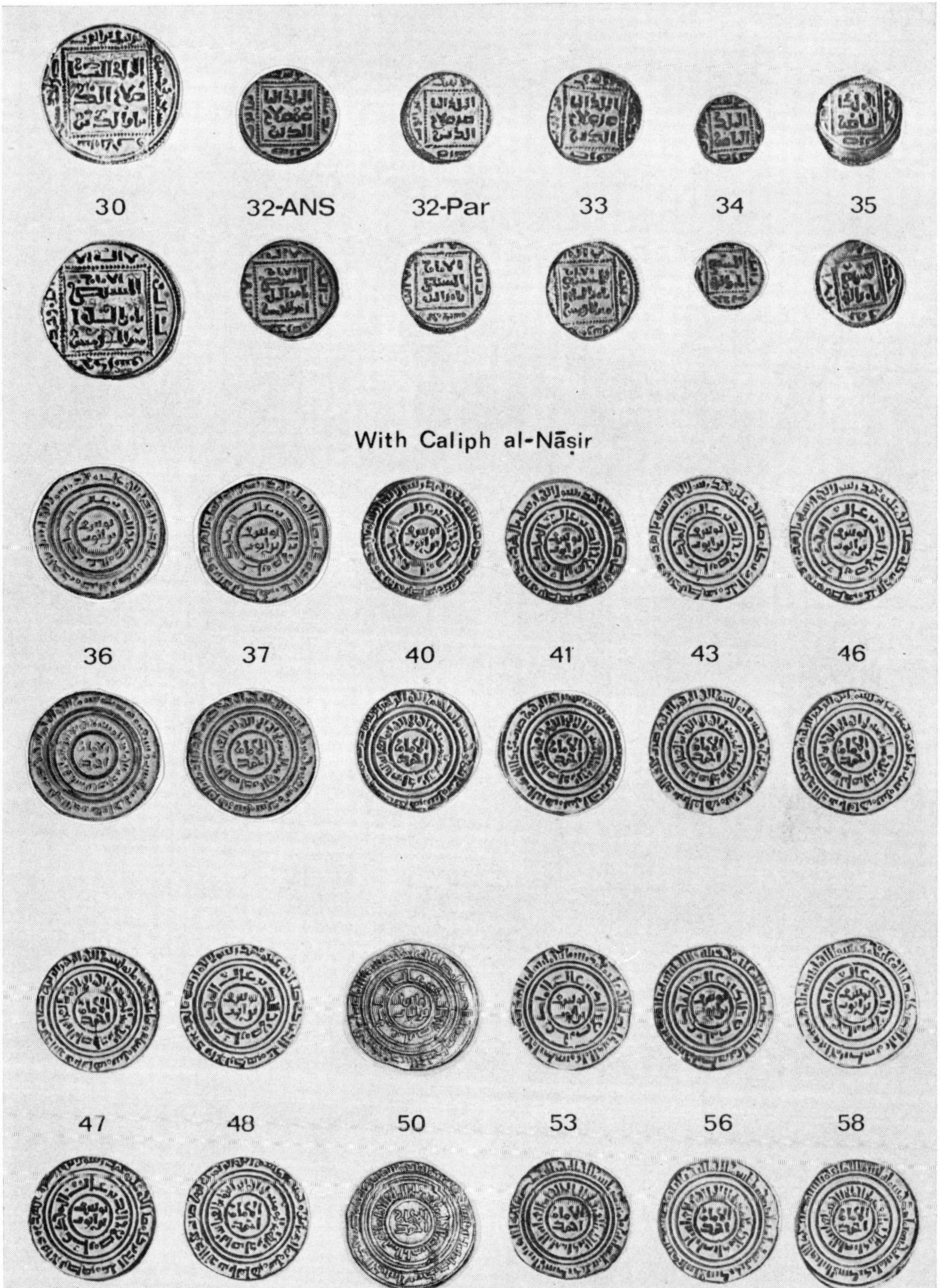
30
32-ANS
32-Par
33
34
35
With Caliph al-Nāṣir
36
37
40
41
43
46
47
48
50
53
56
58

PLATE IV

62
63
64-Bal: 9
10
11
13
64-Bal: 21
23
24
64-BMC
65-Bal: 12
3
15
67-ANS
67-Bal
67-BM
68
69-Bal 16
69-Bal 17
71-Bal 15
71-Bal 23
72

PLATE V

73 76-Bal 32 76-Bal 33a 79-Ash 79-Bal

80 82 83 87-Lav 87-Par 89

90 92 95-Bal 1 95-Bal 2 96 97

PLATE VI

99
102
104
105
108
110
111
115
117
118
119-Par
119-YK
120
122
124
126
127
128

PLATE VII

129 131 133 145-ANS 145-Ash 146
148-Par 1 148-Par 2 148-BMC 149-ANS 149-Ash
150 151 153 156-BMC1 156-BMC2 158

PLATE VIII

160-Mün 160-Par 161-Ash 161-Mün 163-Ash

163-Mün 165 166-Ber 166-BM 167

168-BMC 168-Leut

PLATE IX

Artūqid
Prototype

172

173

174-ANS 1

174-ANS 2

174-BM 1

174-BM 2

177-Ash

PLATE X

177-Lav 182-Ash 182-Par

AL-ᶜAZĪZ ᶜUTHMĀN

184 186 187 189 190 192

195 196-Bal 196-Bal 1 196-Bal 3

197-Bal 7 197-Bal 10 197-Bal 11 197-Bal 12

PLATE XI

198-Bal 5
198-Bal 12
199
200
201
204
205
206
207
208
209
211
215
216
217
222
223-Bal
223-Par
224
225-Bal
225-Par

PLATE XII

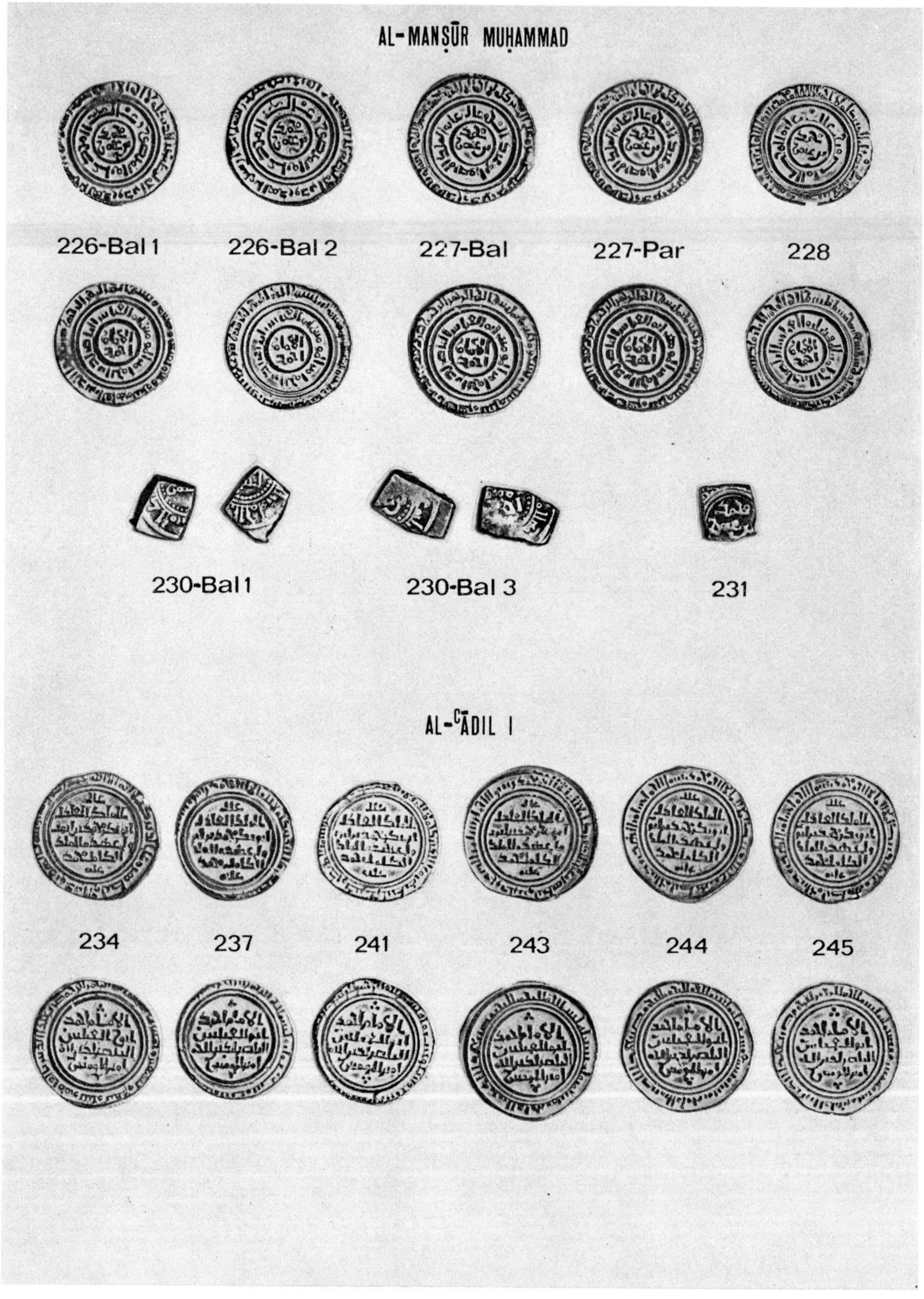
AL-MANṢŪR MUḤAMMAD
226-Bal 1
226-Bal 2
227-Bal
227-Par
228
230-Bal 1
230-Bal 3
231
AL-ᶜĀDIL I
234
237
241
243
244
245

PLATE XIII

246
248
251
252
253
260
267
270
271
273-Bal: 1
2
3
274
275-ANS
275-Bal
276
277
280
281

PLATE XIV

284
285
286
288
290
293-Ash
293-Bal
296-Ash
296-Lav
296-Par
298-Gl
298-Lav
299
303-BM
303-Mün
305
308-Ber
308-ANS
309-BMC
309-Par
310-Ash

PLATE XV

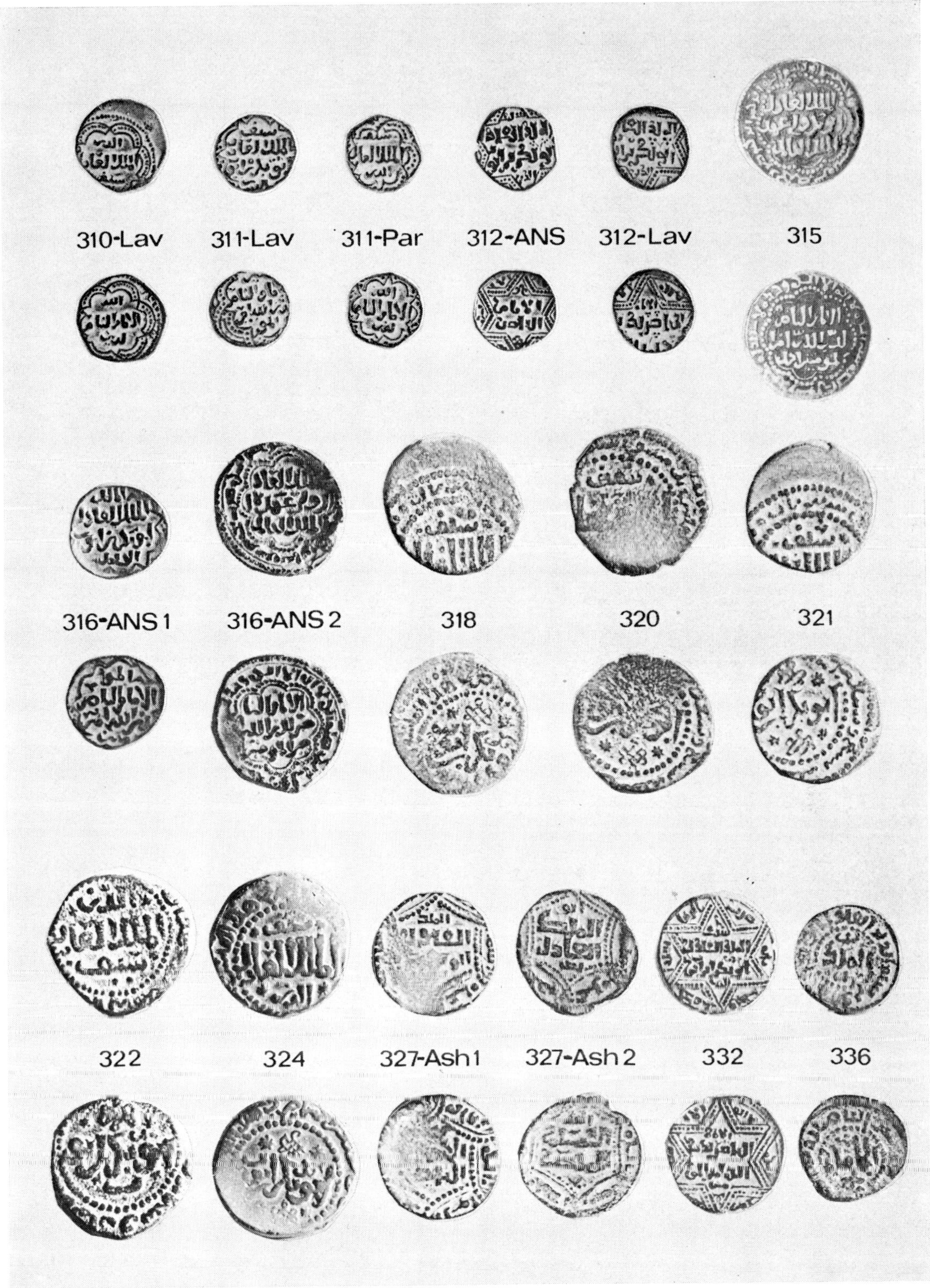

310-Lav
311-Lav
311-Par
312-ANS
312-Lav
315
316-ANS 1
316-ANS 2
318
320
321
322
324
327-Ash 1
327-Ash 2
332
336

PLATE XVI

337-ANS

337-ANS·UM

337-BMC

338-Ber

338-Cas

338

340-ANS

340-Iz

343

PLATE XVII

346
347-Ar
347-Lav
347-Mün
349
350
351-Mün
351-W
352
353-Ber
353-Ist
358-Ash
358-Ber
358-Lav
360-BMC
360-BM
361-Bal
361-W
363-BMC
363-BM

PLATE XVIII

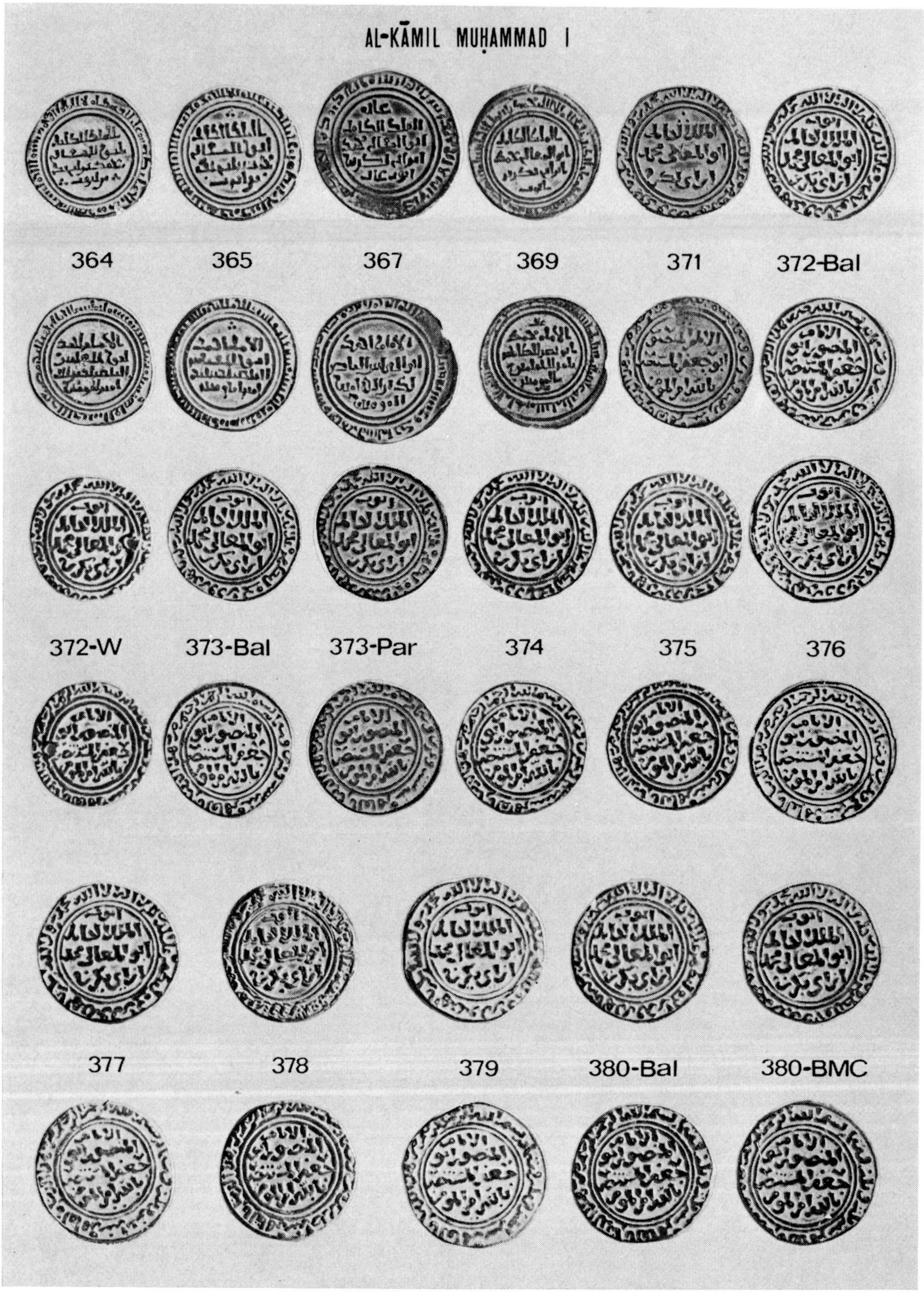
AL-KĀMIL MUḤAMMAD I
364
365
367
369
371
372-Bal
372-W
373-Bal
373-Par
374
375
376
377
378
379
380-Bal
380-BMC

PLATE XIX

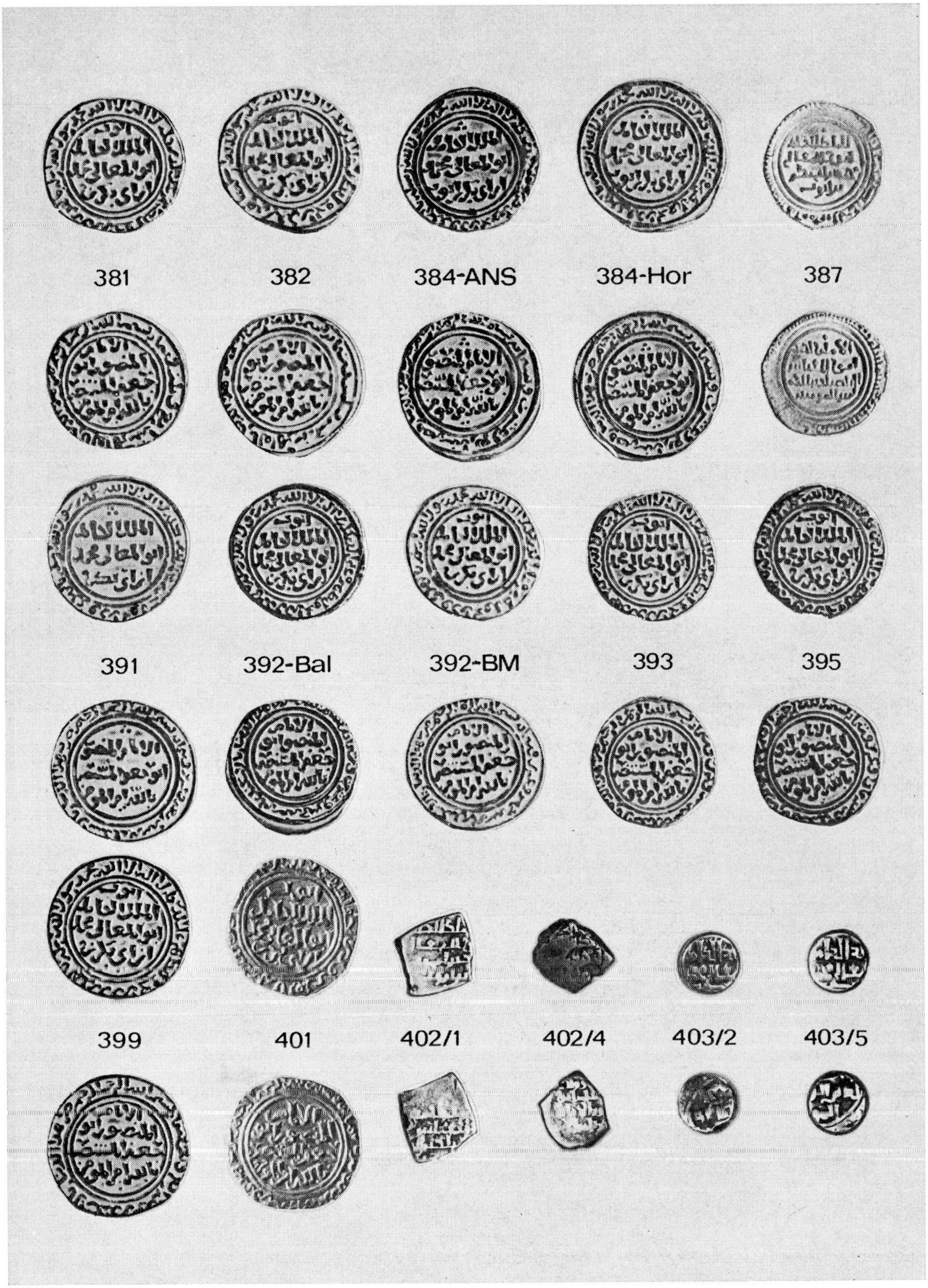

381 382 384-ANS 384-Hor 387

391 392-Bal 392-BM 393 395

399 401 402/1 402/4 403/2 403/5

PLATE XX

403/7
403/8
403/9
403/10
403/14
404/3
404/8
404/9
404/10
407
410/1
410/3
410/9
410/16
411
412
413
414
415
417-Bal
417-Par1
417-Par2
417-Par3
419/1
419/2

PLATE XXI

420-Bal 3
420-Bal 4
423
424-BMC
424-Hor
425-Bal
425-BMC
425-BM
426
427-Bal 1
427-Bal 2
428
430-Ash
430-Bal
432
433
438-ANS
438-Ash

PLATE XXII

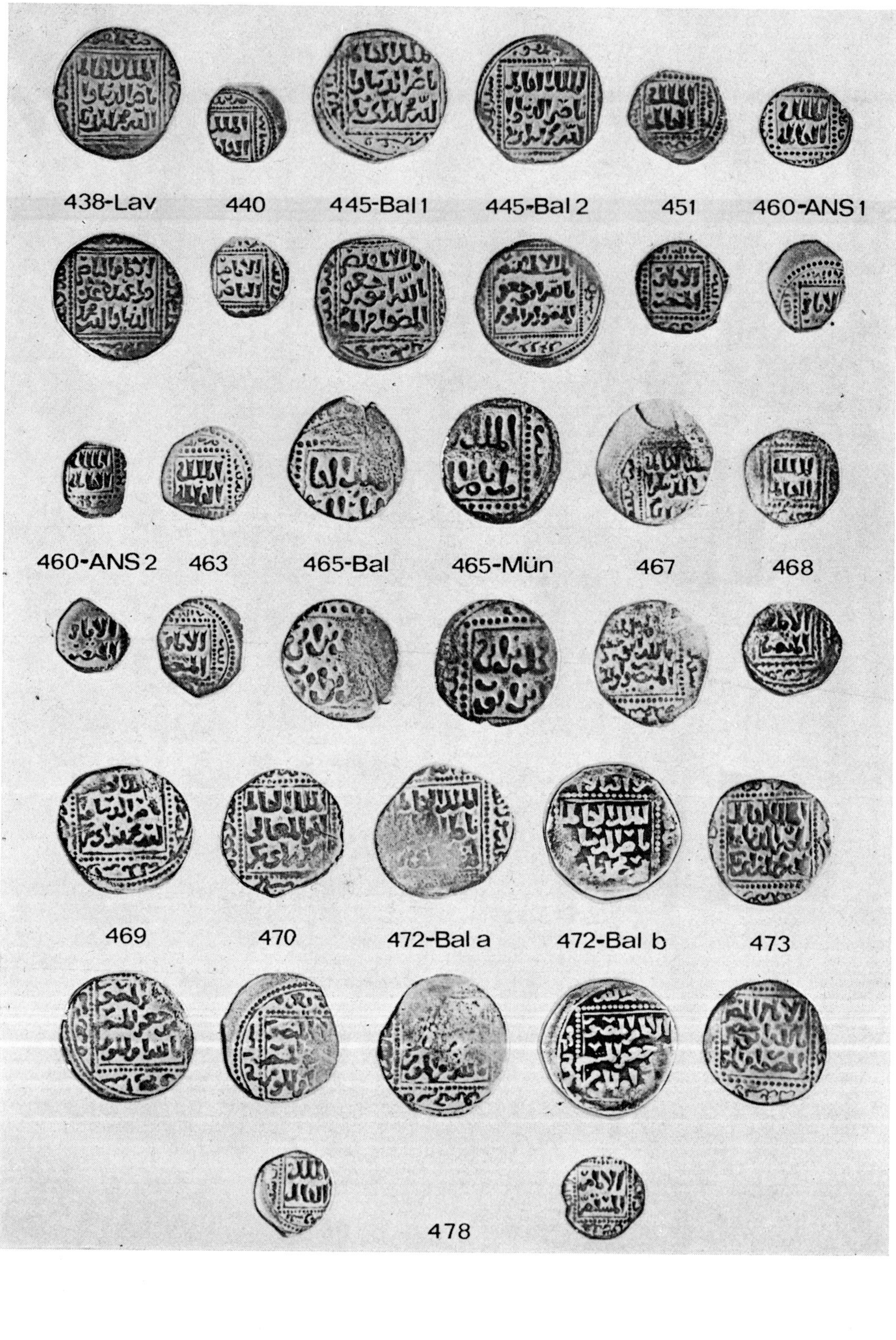

438-Lav 440 445-Bal 1 445-Bal 2 451 460-ANS 1

460-ANS 2 463 465-Bal 465-Mün 467 468

469 470 472-Bal a 472-Bal b 473

478

PLATE XXIII

479-ANS
479-Sea
481-Lav
481-Par
482
486
489-Bal
489-Lav
490-ANS
490-BM
491
493-Lav
493•Pa
494
497

PLATE XXIV

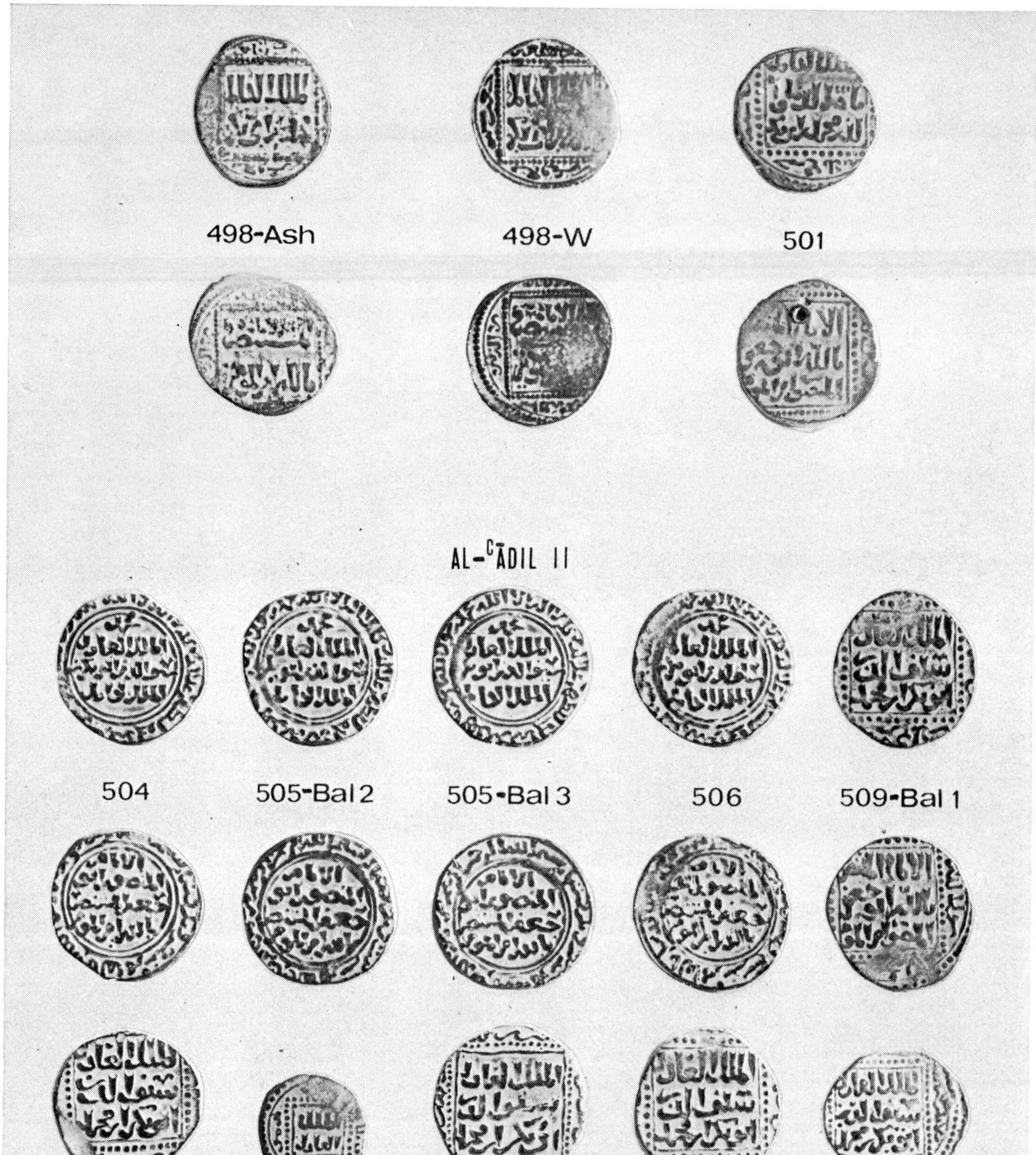
498-Ash
498-W
501
AL-ᶜĀDIL II
504
505-Bal 2
505-Bal 3
506
509-Bal 1
509-Bal 2
510
511
512
513

PLATE XXV

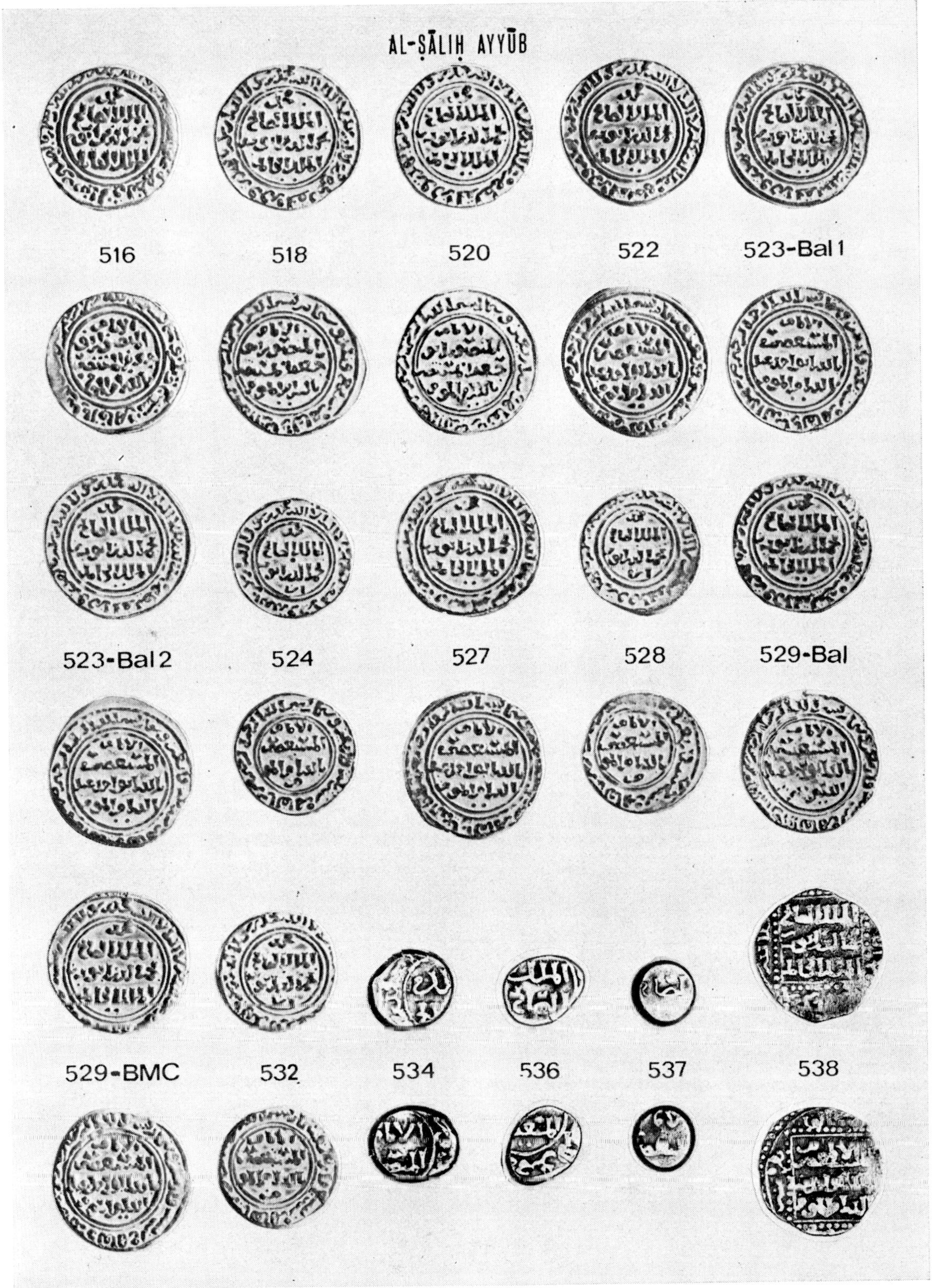
AL-ṢALIḤ AYYŪB
516
518
520
522
523-Bal 1
523-Bal 2
524
527
528
529-Bal
529-BMC
532
534
536
537
538

PLATE XXVI

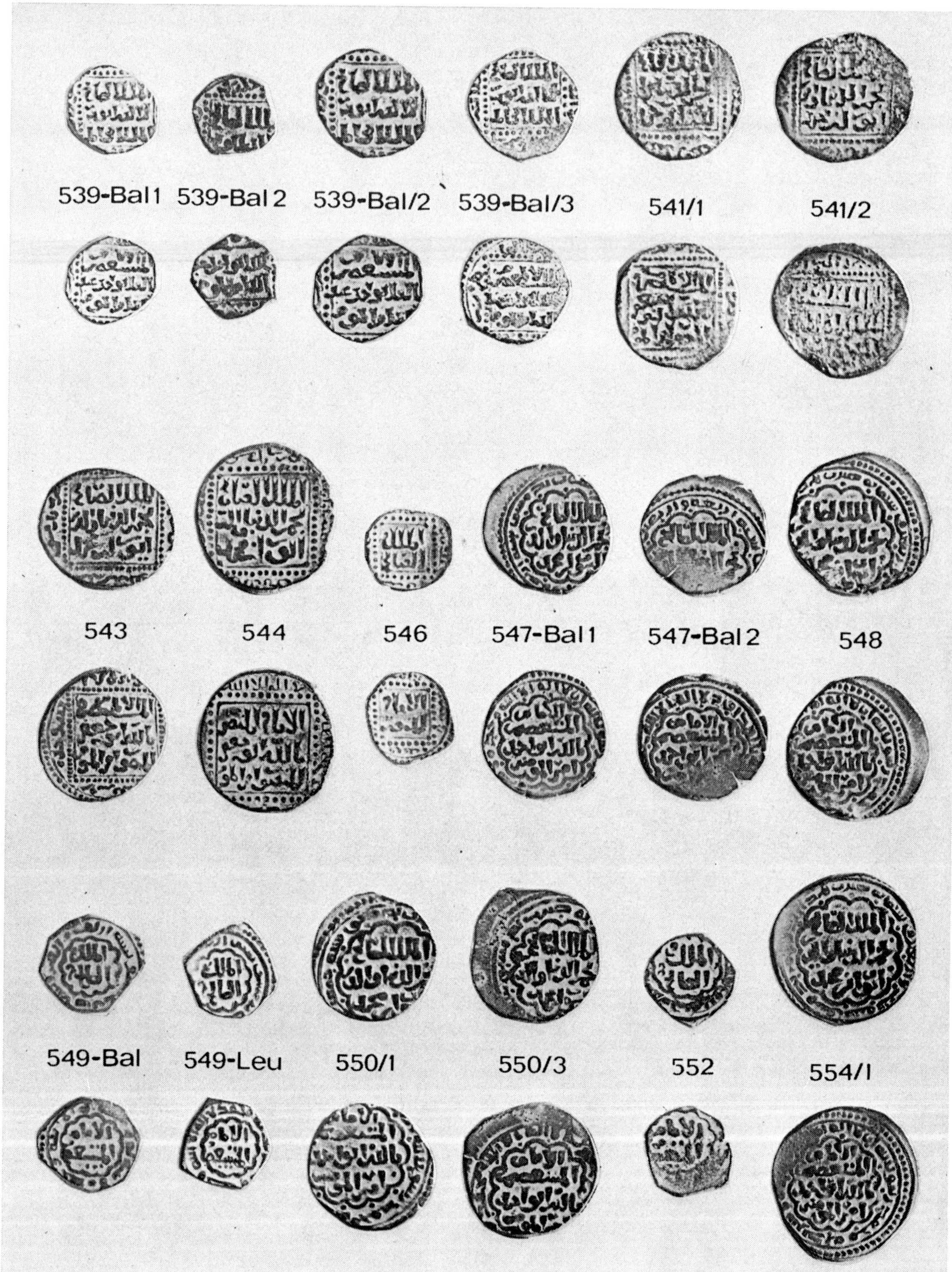

539-Bal 1 539-Bal 2 539-Bal/2 539-Bal/3 541/1 541/2

543 544 546 547-Bal 1 547-Bal 2 548

549-Bal 549-Leu 550/1 550/3 552 554/1

PLATE XXVII

554/3
554/5
557/1
557/2
557/6
557/9
561
562/1
562/3
562/6
562/9
563
564
565
566-ANS
566-Ash
566-Bal

PLATE XXVIII

PLATE XXIX

PRINCIPALITIES IN SYRIA

ALEPPO

AL-ẒĀHIR GHĀZĪ

581 583 584 586 587-Lav

587-Mün 588 590-Art 590-Ash 591

592 594 595-Low

PLATE XXX

595-Art
597-Ber
597-Par
598
599
601-ANS
601-Lav
603-Lav
603-Par
603-Tew
604
605
606
607
608
611

PLATE XXXI

612-Ash

612-Bal

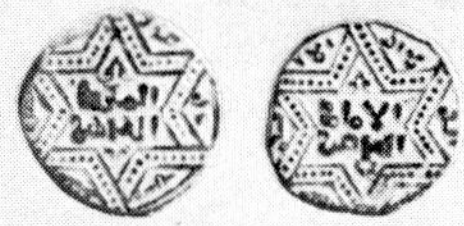

614

616

618

619-Bal

619-BM

627 Obverse Only

Posthumous Silver: 614 – 638 H

631 637 641 643 645

649

654

PLATE XXXII

655
656
657
658
659
660
661
664
665
666
668
670-BMC
670 - Lav
675
677

PLATE XXXIII

678 679 685

AL-ᶜAZĪZ MUḤAMMAD

686 687 692 693 694

702-ANS1 702-ANS2 703 706 707

PLATE XXXIV

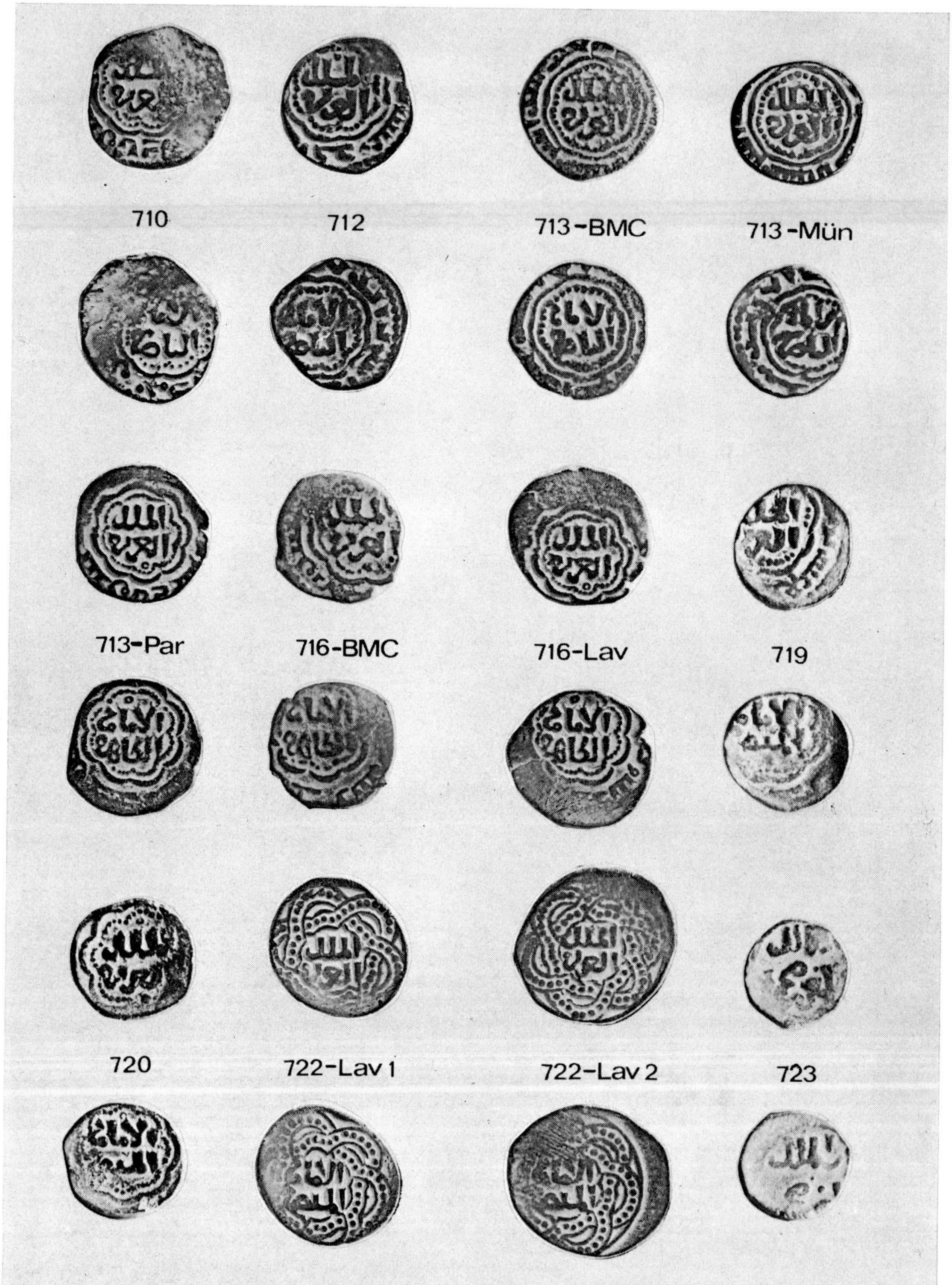
710
712
713-BMC
713-Mün
713-Par
716-BMC
716-Lav
719
720
722-Lav 1
722-Lav 2
723

PLATE XXXV

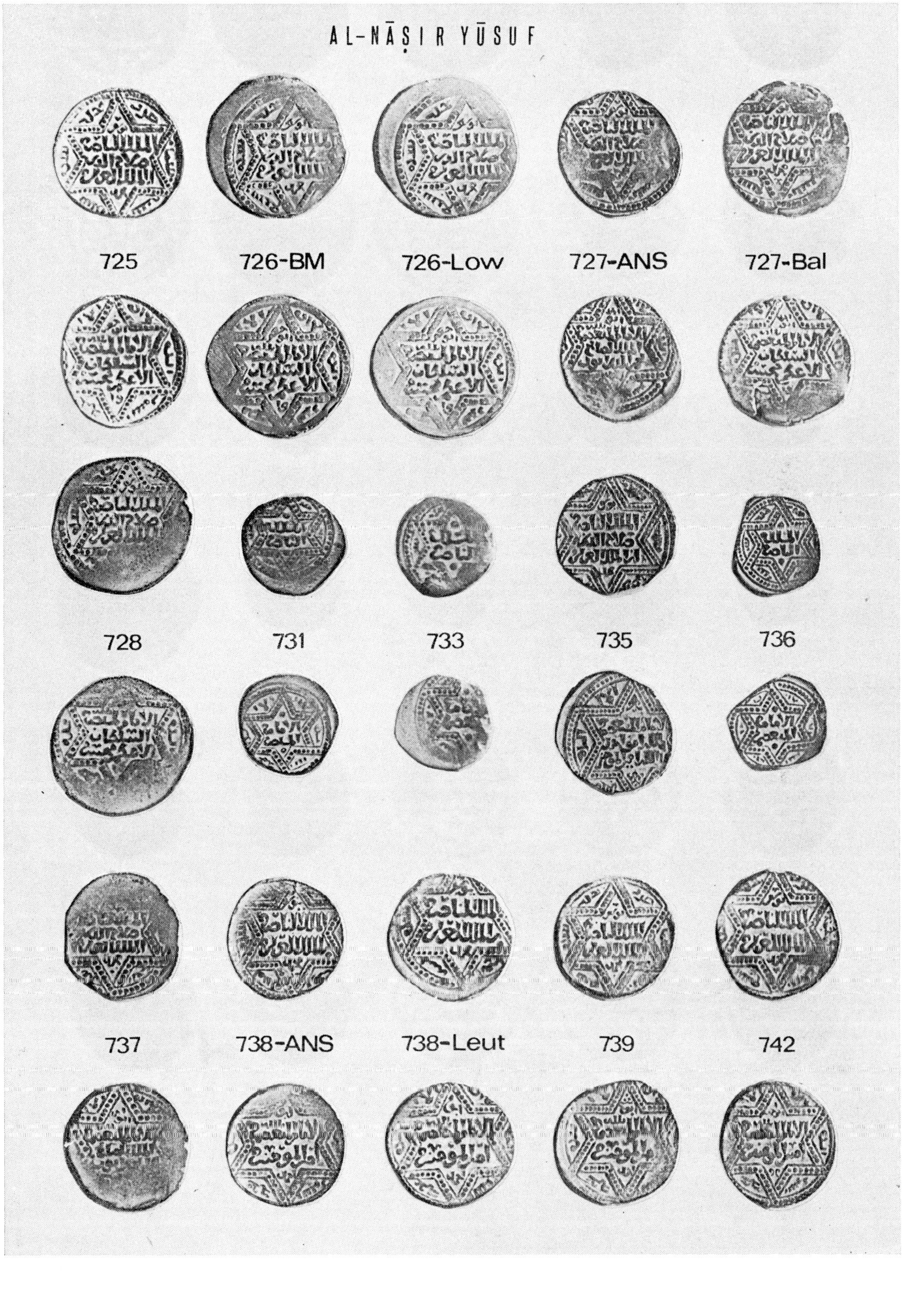
AL-NĀṢIR YŪSUF
725
726-BM
726-Low
727-ANS
727-Bal
728
731
733
735
736
737
738-ANS
738-Leut
739
742

PLATE XXXVI

743
747
748
749-ANS 1
749-ANS 2
750
751-ANS1
751-ANS2
752
753
755
756
760
761
762-Bal1

PLATE XXXVII

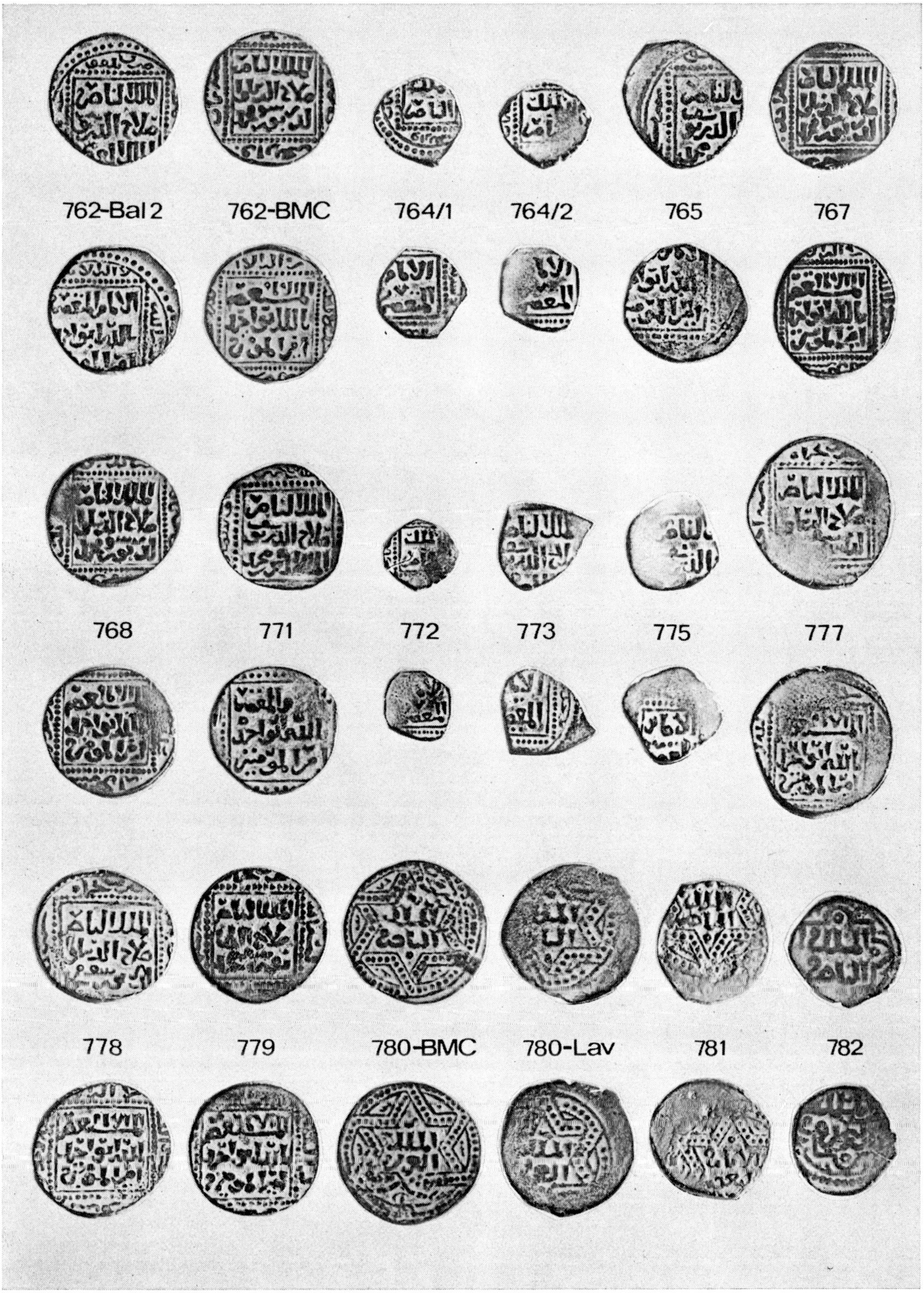

PLATE XXXVIII

PLATE XXXIX

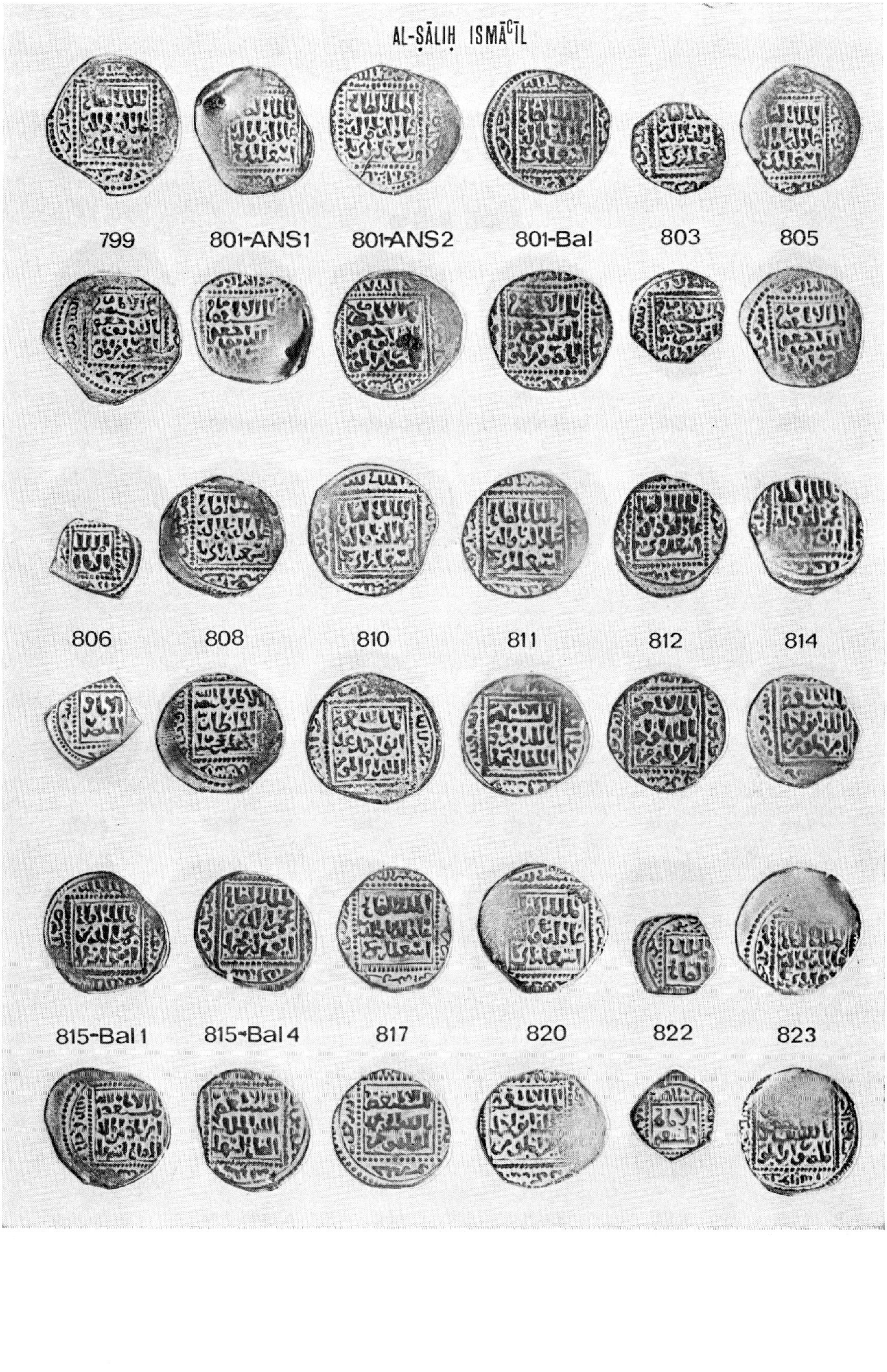
AL-ṢĀLIḤ ISMĀᶜĪL
799
801-ANS1
801-ANS2
801-Bal
803
805
806
808
810
811
812
814
815-Bal1
815-Bal4
817
820
822
823

PRINCIPALITY OF ḤAMĀH
AL-MANṢŪR MUḤAMMAD I
824-BMC
824-Lav
825-ANS
825-BMC1
825-BMC2
825-Par
825-W
827-BM
827-Cas
829-ANS
829-Bal
830-Ash
830-Par
831
832-Ber
832-BM

AL-MANṢŪR MUḤAMMAD II

838 840

PRINCIPALITIES IN THE JAZĪRAH

AL-AWḤAD NAJM AL-DĪN AYYŪB

841-BMC 841-Lav 842-ANS 842-Cas

842-Mün 843-ANS 843-Lav 844-Ash

844-Lav 845-ANS 845-Lav1 845-Lav2

846-Art 846-BMC

AL-ASHRAF MŪSĀ I

849-Bal 849-Ber 850 851-BMC1

851-BMC 2
852-BMC 1
852-BMC 2
853-BMC
853-Lav
854-BMC
854-Lav
854-Par
855
857
858
859
861-ANS
861-Mün

PLATE XLIV

AL-MUẒAFFAR GHĀZĪ
863-Ash
863-Bal
863-Lav
865
868-Bal
868-BMC
869
870-ANS
870-Lav
871
872-ANS1
872-ANS2
872-Ash
872-Par1
872-Par2
874

PLATE XLV

AL-KĀMIL MUḤAMMAD II

876 880-Ash1 880-Ash2 880-Par 882-Art

882-Tew 883-ANS 883-Tew 885-Ash 885-Par

PRINCIPALITY OF ḤIṢN-KAYFĀ

AL-MUWAḤḤID ᶜABD ALLĀH

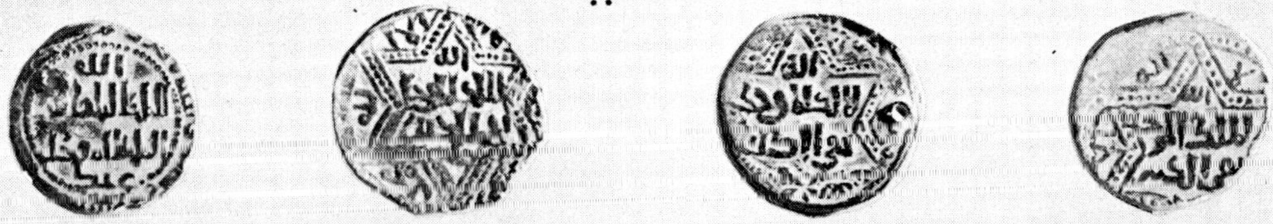

888 889-ANS 889-Art 889-Tew

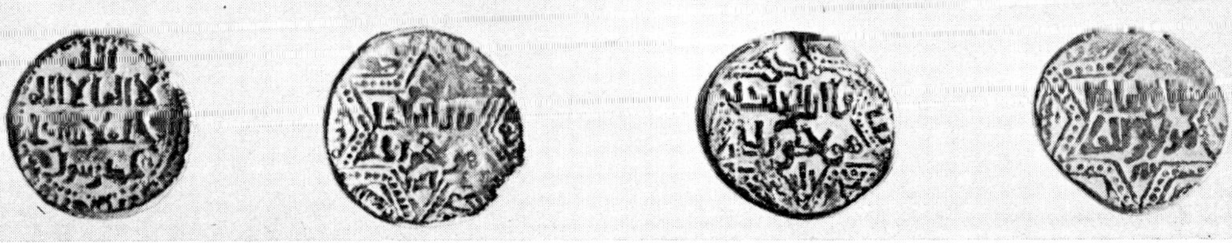

PLATE XLVI

SULAYMĀN IBN GHĀZĪ
892-Art
892-Tew
894-Art
894-Bal
894-Tew
895-ANS1
895-ANS2
895-Art
902
AL-ASHRAF AḤMAD
903-Art
903-Tew

PLATE XLVII

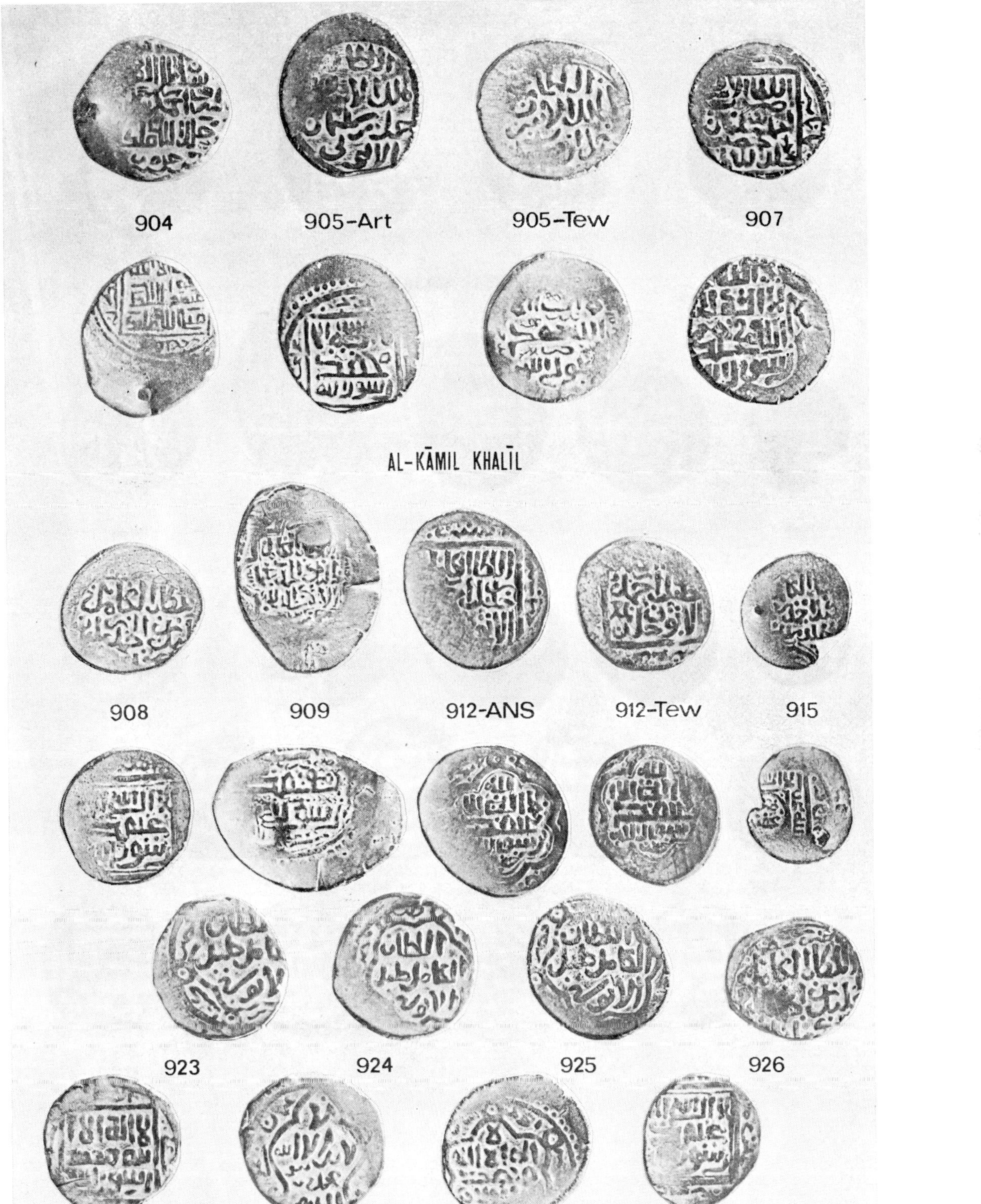
904
905-Art
905-Tew
907
AL-KĀMIL KHALĪL
908
909
912-ANS
912-Tew
915
923
924
925
926

AYYŪBIDS OF THE YEMEN

AL-MUʿAẒẒAM TŪRĀNSHĀH

927

928

AL-ʿĀZĪZ TUGHTEGĪN

929

930

ISMĀʿĪL IBN TUGHTEGĪN

931

934

935

939

941

942

PLATE XLIX

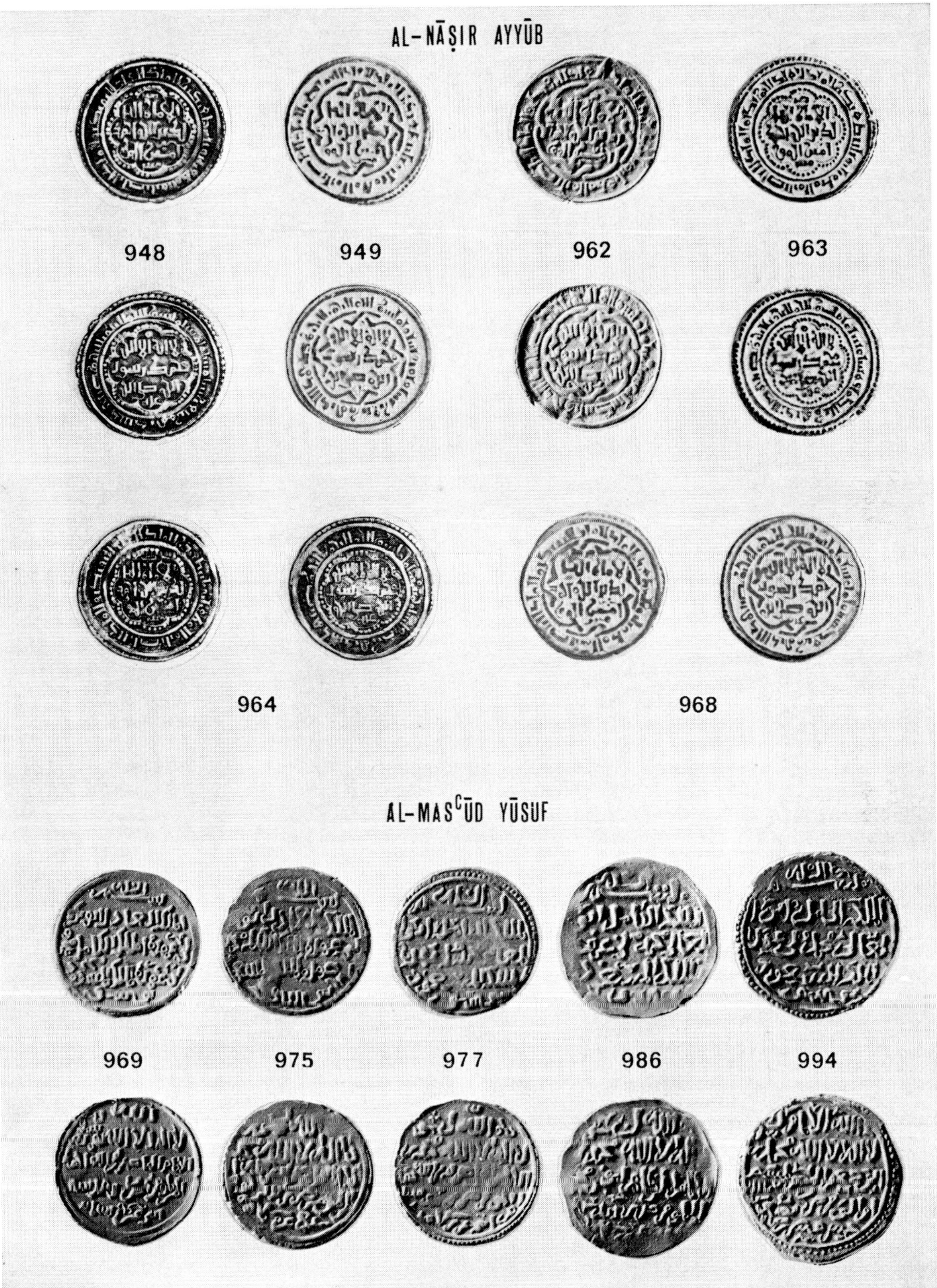
AL-NĀṢIR AYYŪB
948
949
962
963
964
968
AL-MAS^CŪD YŪSUF
969
975
977
986
994

PLATE L

995

1007

AL-[c]ĀDIL ABŪ BAKR

1010 1011 101 1013

AL-KĀMIL MUḤAMMAD I of EGYPT

1014 1014

1015